POLITICS AND SOCIETY IN WALES

Making Sense of Wales

POLITICS AND SOCIETY IN WALES SERIES
Series editor: Ralph Fevre

The Politics and Society in Wales Series examines issues of politics and government, and particularly the effects of devolution on policy-making and implementation, and the way in which Wales is governed as the National Assembly gains in maturity. It will also increase our knowledge and understanding of Welsh society and analyse the most important aspects of social and economic change in Wales. Where necessary, studies in the series will incorporate strong comparative elements which will allow a more fully informed appraisal of the condition of Wales.

POLITICS AND SOCIETY IN WALES

Making Sense of Wales

A SOCIOLOGICAL PERSPECTIVE

By

GRAHAM DAY

Published on behalf of the Social Science Committee
of the Board of Celtic Studies of the University of Wales

UNIVERSITY OF WALES PRESS
CARDIFF
2002

© Graham Day, 2002

British Library Cataloguing-in-Publication Data.
A catalogue record for this book is available from the British Library.

ISBN 0–7083–1771–5

The right of Graham Day to be identified as author of this work has been asserted by him in accordance with the Copyright, Designs and Patents Act 1988.

Typeset by Mark Heslington, Scarborough, North Yorkshire
Printed in Great Britain by Henry Ling Limited, The Dorset Press, Dorchester

Series Editor's Foreword

The Politics and Society in Wales Series provides an opportunity for the publication of social-scientific descriptions and analyses of Welsh society. Graham Day's book reminds us that such work was undertaken long before the series was conceived. Social scientists have been making sense of Wales for half a century or more. They have even, from time to time, put on courses for undergraduates and postgraduates to help them do the same thing. Day thinks, quite rightly, that it is time to take stock and appraise all of this effort. The result is a marvellous work which shows us how far we have come and how we must approach our social science, and particularly our sociology, in the future.

Sociology is the main discipline represented here but other disciplines like geography, regional planning and anthropology have clearly made very important contributions. Many of the concepts and theories that have been used to make sense of Wales were developed elsewhere, and an appraisal of social-scientific studies of Welsh society cannot help but discuss some of the more important intellectual influences on social science in the second half of the twentieth century. Yet Day points out that the application of these concepts and theories has not always been a straightforward matter since it is not self-evident that there is a Welsh society for social scientists to analyse and describe. He reminds us that we can learn much about sociology by thinking about the way a Welsh society can be constructed for analysis and description.

A great deal of *Making Sense of Wales* is concerned with social and economic change. Day is interested in all the conscious efforts that have been made to bring about change through planning, policy and constitutional innovation but he is particularly concerned with problems of economic development and the practical steps that have been taken to solve them. There is inevitably plenty of discussion here of coal and steel, but Day is somewhat unusual in combining an interest in industrial change with a lifelong interest in rural sociology. He tells us how change in the countryside has been discussed and analysed in the same authoritative way he approaches the discussion of social and economic change in industrial Wales. Of course economic development and planning are never far from view in the countryside either but the discussion of rural Wales also allows Day to introduce the themes of migration and language which figure so strongly in the second half of the book.

Day discusses in some detail all of the more contentious issues that have been debated in Wales in the last fifty years. He does this with some authority and with a very cool head. He gives us an informed but dispassionate discussion of debates about how far, and how well, the Welsh economy has been transformed at the end of the twentieth century. He also provides similarly dispassionate discussions of studies of language, culture and nationalism. By the end of the book these disparate strands have been woven together in a most helpful way. Day shows us that it makes little sense for us to treat issues such as nationalism and economic development as separate subjects. What *Making Sense of Wales* shows is that none of the things that interest us – questions of identity, political change, the fate of class, gender and ethnicity, the disappearance of community, prospects for prosperity – can be profitably studied in isolation. Of course it is easier to pursue these questions separately but the simple findings we come up with when we try to make sense of complex reality in this way may be thoroughly misleading.

What Day prescribes instead is a classical sociological approach – as practised by Max Weber for example – in which we must be prepared to use all of the available conceptual resources from sociology and, where necessary, other social sciences, together with the evidence, and especially the statistics, compiled by government and researchers. *Making Sense of Wales* provides a benchmark in two senses. Firstly, since it appraises the work done by those who dedicated their time and ingenuity to the study of Wales in the past fifty years or so it provides a summary of our current knowledge. Secondly, it shows us what sociology now has to do if it is to provide useful accounts of complex and difficult topics. For both of these reasons *Making Sense of Wales* will be the benchmark for studies of Welsh society for many, many years. Graham Day was the only person who could have written this work and he brings to it all the authority and insight born of twenty-five years of careful thinking and research on the subject. On behalf of everyone else who has ever tried to make sense of Wales, I express our gratitude to him for giving us this splendid book.

Ralph Fevre
Cardiff, June 2002

Contents

Acknowledgements

The contribution made by the University of Wales Centre at Gregynog to the developments described in this book has been invaluable; over the years it has provided a relaxed venue for networking and debate. I would also like to take this opportunity to acknowledge my thanks to John Williams and the staff and students of the Department of Economic and Social History and Sociology at the University of Wales, Aberystwyth for the stimulation they provided during the department's too brief period of existence. I have particular debts to Gareth Rees, Dennis Thomas, Jon Murdoch and Andy Thompson. While their influence may be discernible at various points in what follows, they cannot be held responsible for what I have made of it. I am especially grateful to Pam and Dai Michael, Neil Evans and Andrew Thompson for their encouragement. They have helped me avoid some of the more egregious errors. Much as I would like to pass responsibility to them for the mistakes which remain, in accordance with the conventions, I fully accept that they are entirely my own. This book is dedicated to Daphne, with love, and the deepest appreciation for all her patience.

Introduction

The opening of a new millennium seems to have thrown British intellectuals into a turmoil of introspection. Hardly a day passes without the publication of some new book, television series or newspaper article in which the nature and direction of British society, the state of the United Kingdom, and what it means to be British or to belong to one of the constituent nationalities of these islands, is put under scrutiny (Paxman, 1999; Marr, 1999; Nairn, 2000; Chen and Wright, 2000). These discussions mingle millennial angst with anxieties about place in the world, and more local concerns to do with the impact of political devolution, and European integration. Radically different views, each capable of gathering supportive evidence, are put forward: for example, on the one hand Britain is viewed as a tolerant society, open to new sentiments of multiculturalism, prepared to cede sovereignty to gain the rewards of closer harmony with Europe, and eager to embrace the gifts of globalization – a standpoint endorsed strongly by Prime Minister Tony Blair. On the other hand, in the light of events surrounding the murders of Stephen Lawrence and other victims of racial violence, and its responses to migration pressures, Britain is castigated for being riddled with institutional racism, and latent xenophobia. As a state, its boundaries seem to be becoming simultaneously more porous – vulnerable, if alarmists are to be believed, to floods of refugees, asylum seekers, economic migrants and tourists – and more compartmentalized, as formerly united nations prepare to go their separate ways. Either possibility throws existing ideas about Britishness and collective identity into disarray. These diverse accounts are echoed and built upon by politicians and others, who take from them competing conclusions about how policy should be shaped to deal with the problems they pose. Much of this excitement may be mere froth, but still it makes this a propitious time to consider the situation as it appears from within one of the fissile parts of the 'kingdom', Wales.

Like Britain as a whole, during recent decades Wales has undergone a series of profound, and often traumatic, alterations, leading to it being described as 'a laboratory of social change' (Lovering, 1996: 16). Economically, socially, culturally and politically, it is barely recognizable as the same place it was before; and this has precipitated a considerable industry of stock-taking analysis, as well as numerous attempts to project new and exciting directions for its future development. During its first few months of existence, the new National Assembly for Wales produced a flood of consultation papers, policy documents, and programme proposals intended to stake out a specifically Welsh conception of the style and aims of government, and of the problems which need to be tackled. Among those labouring hard to make sense of these changes has been a small number of social scientists and policy analysts who have made use of a range of sociological frameworks and approaches to try to bring order to the confusion. As well as reacting to the flow of events occurring around them, the interpretations they have proposed have also reflected inevitably some of the developments taking place within sociology as a discipline, its shifting priorities and intellectual frameworks. Often they have felt themselves to be marginalized by a concern with questions which others have tended to regard as peripheral to the main business; and yet what has happened in Wales could be said to be highly instructive and illuminating about some general patterns and influences of much wider interest. In many ways, indeed, the questions which have been pursued among social scientists with an interest in Wales have pre-empted some of the developments and topics that are now at the forefront of sociological debate.

The everyday themes of social life in Wales can be shown to be intimately related to a far more fundamental set of social processes and changes taking place across western society. There can be little doubt that these have necessitated a rethinking of some of sociology's basic tenets. Classically, western sociology has organized itself around an analysis of 'societies', conceptualized as bounded units with relatively well defined and internally coherent structures. Whether explicitly, or more often implicitly, it has been assumed that these principal units for investigation correspond more or less closely with the framework of independent states, and that such societies normally have a publicly recognized national existence. Such a convergence of society, state, nation and people has been so readily presumed (Albrow, 1999) that it has come to appear natural, and very often this has meant that, in the absence of any serious reflection upon it, dominant common-sense conceptions have been allowed to take the place of more carefully thought out analytical models. Sociologists have been comfortable working with 'ready-made' entities like the USA, France, Japan and so on, treating them as convenient containers for the relationships and structures which they seek to explore. A particular preoccupation has been with the hierarchical arrangements of social classes and inequalities within such units. Relationships between states, and across international borders have been handed over to experts in international relations, while subdisciplines of regional studies and human geography have dealt with issues relating to subnational social formations.

All this has changed quite markedly. Many of these assumptions have dissolved in the face of increasing globalization, and the recognition of the complexity and multiplicity of contemporary social distinctions, especially those of gender, sexuality, 'race' and ethnicity. There has also been an important 'turn' towards a greater emphasis upon the cultural processes through which members of societies create a sense of order and construct their own social arrangements. Consequently, at every level, the sociological map is being redrawn (Albrow, 1999; Urry, 2000). We have seen the emergence of new ways of thinking about society, and societies, which leave the old theoretical agenda behind. They include accounts of society as an ongoing process of 'structuration' (Giddens, 1984); as a set of flows and fluidities (Lash and Urry, 1994); as a constellation of networks and groupings (Castells, 1996). These shifts in the conceptual universe are matched by the frequency with which old social forms are claimed to have been transcended by the appearance of new, or 'post', forms: modernity by postmodernity, industrialism by post-industrialism, nationalism by postnationalism, and so on. With these transformations, attention moves towards new issues: identity, belonging, 'difference', locality, territoriality, hybridity, 'complexity'.

However these are themes which are familiar to anyone who has worked upon or in 'marginal' contexts and 'esoteric' locations and tried to understand their social worlds. The 'old' topics resonate with the viewpoint of the centre: the classic sociologists, such as Durkheim, Weber and Parsons all spoke (although not necessarily uncritically) on behalf of the dominant national-state-society and its social order. To varying degrees, they blanked out the concerns, issues and experiences of the margins. More recently, partly related to the greater mobility and cross-national fertilization of the discipline, sociologists have been more eager to voice the views of the mobile, the residual and those who are in some way 'different' or outside the norm. Sometimes they have taken their inspiration from earlier figures who themselves held a more marginal social position, such as Marx and Simmel. It should be no surprise that sociologists, anthropologists and others with an interest in (so-called) peripheral places and distinctive cultures should be among those pushing for the reformulation or critique of the old ideas. In his work on Scotland, and nationalism, for example, McCrone has to consider the questions, what do we mean by a 'society', and is Scotland one? While Scotland plainly exists at a common-sense level, McCrone concedes that its status as 'a meaningful sociological category is highly problematic' (1992: 16) – is it a country, a place, a nation, a set of 'overlapping networks of social interaction', or what? Precisely because these questions arise, however, in a way which cannot be ignored or side-lined, McCrone can assert that 'Scotland stands at the forefront of sociological concerns in the late twentieth century. Rather than being an awkward, ill-fitting case, it is at the centre of the discipline's post-modern dilemma' (1992: 1).

Ignoring the rhetorical hubris which goes along with the attempt to grab people's attention for a neglected field, McCrone is surely justified in his claim that any serious examination of the Scottish case opens up enormous rifts in the conventional model of society as a self-contained and bounded totality, coterminous with the nation-state; in any case, he would contend that this conception is losing its *raison d'être* in the contemporary world. Exactly the same questions arise about Wales, as indeed they would about any other 'society' once we begin to think properly about its nature. It is a fact, for example, that virtually all existing nation-states have within them groups of people who deviate in quite radical ways, culturally, ethnically, linguistically or on some other vital criterion, from the supposed 'national' norm; few 'societies' are composed of anything like homogeneous member-ships. Just as people in outlying parts of Britain will be continually irritated by metropolitan broadcasters' assumptions that everyone has the same weather, so they will be reminded again and again that what seems natural and uncomplicated in social life elsewhere is strange or irrelevant to their own immediate experience and concerns. It is one of the pre-eminent tasks of social science to document and explain such differences.

So far as Wales is concerned, there is no shortage of commentators of various kinds prepared to rise to this challenge. But until recently, there was not enough, or enough sufficiently integrated work, upon these issues to warrant discussion as a distinctive contribution to social scientific under-standing. One reason for this, it has been suggested, is because 'to focus upon the analysis of Welsh issues and problems has been to run the risk of accusations of "parochialism" from the wider British social science commu-nity' (Day and Rees, 1987: 1) among whom the theorization of 'things Welsh' has not been highly rewarded (Rees and Rees, 1980b: 31). However, it may be that the developments in sociological perspective just described have moderated the tendency to denigrate a concern with the 'local' and specific in favour of the general and abstract. Certainly there have been many who have argued that contemporary social developments compel us to pay much closer attention to questions of differentiation, diversity and particularity, and this in turn may have encouraged sociologists to be a little more self-critical with regard to their own social, geographical and national attachments.

Meanwhile, the pace of change in Wales, together with the delayed maturation of the social sciences in Welsh institutions of higher education, has served to stimulate a greater weight of attention from researchers, located both within and outside Wales, and this has encouraged some definite progress. An earlier contribution to the sociology of Wales lamented the 'poverty of knowledge' which afflicted analysis at that time: surprisingly little was known about the structure and composition of Welsh society (Rees and Rees, 1980b: 32) and there were large and important topics which were virtually unexplored. Hopefully, twenty years or so later, we are now better placed to make sense of Wales and its situation. It is true that sociologists with an interest in Wales remain thin on the ground, and even those who are interested also have other matters to which to attend. The sociology of Wales as such therefore lacks critical mass. It certainly does not bear comparison with the institutional strength and coherence achieved by Welsh history. Nevertheless, there has been sufficient impetus to enable the emergence of a reasonably coherent body of knowledge, which provides a more critically informed appreciation of conditions and developments in Welsh society.

Academically, there have been two especially important moments facilitating this. The stream of work in community studies which emanated from the Geography department of the University College of Wales Aberystwyth during the 1940s and 1950s generated a distinguished intellectual lineage with significant implications for the early development of British sociology (Day, 1998a), which continues to provide an essential point of reference for some current concerns. The activity of the British Sociological Association's Sociology of Wales Study Group between 1978 and 1985 provided an invaluable forum within which a new generation of researchers were able to cut their teeth on questions about Wales, and formulate what amounted to a new research agenda (Day, 1979). Neither of these could be said to adhere to a narrow professional or disciplinary definition of sociology, and indeed this openness around disciplinary frontiers has been one of the strengths of the work that has ensued, and one on which the discussion that follows will trade. More latterly, the journal *Contemporary Wales* has played its part, providing a setting in which work by economists, geographers, political scientists, sociolinguists and others could be brought together to stimulate debate and ideas. One of the hopes expressed at its launch in 1987 was that the accumulation of knowledge and research would allow understanding to move beyond the level of stereotypes and images to get closer to the realities of the sea change taking place in Welsh economic and social structure. Social research and analysis, it was felt, should help temper some of the wilder excesses of prevailing selective and simplified accounts (Day and Rees, 1987). From the point of view of the development of a sociology of Wales, there has been a long enough period of exploration and discussion by now to merit an examination as to how far and in what ways this has been achieved. Having had the privilege and pleasure of participating in some of these developments, it is my aim in the chapters which follow to provide an overview and assessment of some of the main ways in which the social science community has dealt with the changing nature of contemporary Wales and Welsh society. Even with regard to the contribution of the social sciences, it does not purport to be an exhaustive account. There are many specific areas of work about which it has little or nothing to say – these include the nature and role of the family in Wales, relationships of age and generation, religion, education and popular culture. Either these are areas with which I am personally less familiar, and/or in which there is a less substantial body of sociological work to consider. A recent edited collection (Dunkerley and Thompson, 1999) provides a useful indication of the current state of sociological knowledge, and shows that there are still some significant gaps to be filled. Of course, there are also other ways of looking at Wales. Reference has been made already to the particularly strong contribution made by historians of modern Wales, and there are also important approaches from the perspective of literature and poetry (Humphreys, 1983; G. Jones, 1968; Curtis, 1988) which afford a different slant on questions of language, culture, identity and society. However, in addressing the main themes and strengths of actual sociological work on Wales, the discussion which follows may help identify some of the remaining areas of weakness and ignorance in our understanding of the issues facing Wales today.

1

Visions of Wales

In 1981 the annual conference of the British Sociological Association (BSA) was held at the University College of Wales, Aberystwyth. Around 300 members of the sociological profession met to discuss the topic of inequality. The conference organizers were taken aback somewhat when certain delegates asked if they could be given a tour of the local collieries. The nearest coal mines to Aberystwyth were some 80 miles away, a considerable journey by country roads, and would not normally have been thought part of the itinerary for any visitor to the locality. Despite their expertise in British society, and critical engagement with information and ideas about it, these visitors were responding to an image of Wales in which the mental landscape was dominated by winding gear, the blackened faces of miners and doubtless some associated scenery of rugby football and male voice choirs. None of these were at all significant in the daily life of most of the people who lived in this small Welsh rural seaside town; whereas to the sociologically alert, knowledge of some other aspects of life in Aberystwyth could have been highly informative.

For example, back in 1969, Aberystwyth had played host to the then Duke of Cornwall, who was learning the Welsh language at the university prior to his investiture as the Prince of Wales. The everyday use of Welsh was very much a feature of the town, and one which might be thought to be of interest to these social observers, though in fact most seemed to be unaware of its existence. Charles's induction into the Welsh language was a way of trying to make him more 'Welsh', and so more acceptable to the people of Wales. However, the presence of a member of the British Royal Family in Aberystwyth had aroused intensely contradictory feelings among locals, angering nationalists but giving royalists something in which to delight. Doubtless both factions included some of those whose disapproval just a few years earlier had helped blacken the reputation of a Principal of the University College, Goronwy Rees, whose readiness to offer undergraduates sherry on a Sunday morning had affronted the lingering remnants of Nonconformist sabbatarianism. Rees got his own back by describing the town, with its twenty-two chapels, as a 'sluggish backwater' isolated from the mainstream of contemporary life; he depicted the University College as beset with difficulties arising from primitive and atavistic 'Welsh tribal feeling' (Rees, 1972: 248). Aberystwyth was still throwing up interesting questions about its social nature some years after the BSA conference, when the visit of the Queen to open an extension to the National Library of Wales occasioned a massive police presence, and the threat of student demonstrations forced the abandonment of plans for a celebratory lunch on campus.

Already we have the threads of a number of issues to do with Wales and Welshness, and what is special about it, taken from this particular local context. Aberystwyth is a thoroughly Welsh place, and contains clues to much that makes Wales distinctive; but it is not identical with every other Welsh place, nor can we learn all there is to know about contemporary Wales from its limited vantage point. In fact, a well-known Welsh political commentator who studied there some forty years ago remarked recently that in Aberystwyth, which seemed to him little changed, perhaps it was always 1959. So both time and place seem to be relevant considerations when deciding what lessons can be taken from this particular example.

The sociological question posed by these opening remarks is a familiar, but important one: how are we to move between the sorts of generality and theoretical proposition that lie at the core of sociology as a discipline, and the concrete specificity of a given instance, which in the end is what we might want to understand? How can we draw general conclusions without losing sight of the particular and unique? This is what I mean by the problem of 'making sense'. The same question arises at a broader level of generalization when one thinks about Wales, as an entity, and what sociology can usefully say about it, or learn from it. Wales (like Aberystwyth) is a specific place, and signifies a very particular social formation. What kind of reality does it represent for the sociologist, and how is it usefully to be compared and contrasted with other such entities? What indeed is the appropriate sort of comparison to make? In the case of Wales, the answer is complicated because sometimes it is treated as a region, at others as a nation, and sometimes as part of a strange amalgam called 'England-and-Wales'. The points of reference which are used to bring out its particular characteristics vary widely, and change over time. There are times when, in the course of examination, its very existence seems to be in question, and frequently there is extreme puzzlement and dissension about its nature and trajectory. Book such as *When was Wales?* (Williams, 1985), the curiously titled *Wales! Wales?* (Smith, 1984) and *Wales: The Imagined Nation* (Curtis, 1986) convey something of this puzzlement. In fact, it has become almost obligatory in recent years to note how variously Wales is imagined, represented and packaged, and to acknowledge the confusion that exists about which of these accounts, if any, is closest to reality.

These questions are not peculiar to Wales, by any means, and yet they arise in a pressing way for anyone who wishes to understand it, presenting a challenge which until recently was not felt universally for all such particular societies. Many wide-ranging discussions of themes and topics in sociology such as class, race, gender, industrial structure and so on, have been produced, drawing exclusively upon information and relationships which refer to Britain, or even to England, without anyone finding this remarkable. It is as if the Englishness, or Britishness, of the example can be allowed simply to fade into the background, as an irrelevancy, a merely contingent feature, without in any way contaminating what is being learned. For example, during the 1960s and 1970s, entire theories of affluence and the remaking of the working class were built upon the narrow base of a sample survey of workers in four Luton factories; Luton was treated as 'prototypical' of British experience (Goldthorpe et al., 1969) and British experience was regarded as self-evidently instructive for more or less anyone with an interest in social change. However, when a group of sociologists chose to turn the spotlight onto Wales, in the context of the BSA Sociology of Wales Group, they were faced immediately with the objection that there could not possibly be anything interesting or significant enough about Wales to warrant such attention – you might as well, said one critic, do the sociology of Norfolk!

Yet, why not? Unless they are to be understood as purely geographical expressions, places on the map, as indeed Wales was once notoriously described, both Norfolk and Wales seem to signify much more to people than this dismissive suggestion would warrant: in their different ways, they enter into people's understanding of the world they inhabit, as having their own unique properties, and as representing various quite complex phenomena, with a historical presence and ongoing existence which makes them, in a variety of respects, real and effective forces in their lives. They are, Durkheimians might conclude, social facts, external and constraining. Arguably Wales is just as much a part of the 'real' world as Britain, or Europe, or indeed, Luton and Norfolk: so why should it be any less worthy of study? Need a special case be made for its consideration? The same question is raised by the editors of a recent volume about regional and local planning, when they draw attention to the over-reliance among British planners on evidence and examples from England, and the failure to appreciate developments in Wales and Scotland 'as Scottish or Welsh phenomena, rooted in their national context' (Macdonald and Thomas, 1997: 1). Generalizations are drawn from English experience which become misleading when extended beyond England's boundaries, even if they are valid within them.

This implies that there is indeed something distinctive about Welsh planning, or at least planning in Wales, because it can be understood fully only from within the particular setting of a Welsh 'nation'. Certainly once one moves from planning to the world of social policy and administration, Wales figures quite prolifically in the literature, legislation and ruminations of decision-makers, so that it would seem almost laughably absurd to question its existence or importance – it is simply there, manifest, for all to see, in the dense body of administrative acts, organizations and structures. There are whole libraries of material relating to Wales; and by now there is also a multiplicity of Welsh websites providing a different sort of confirmation of its existence. The 'real' Wales has its 'virtual' presence in cyberspace, as well as being represented in the thoughts and imaginations of social observers. If anything, the volume of discussion about Wales, and the range of forms which register its existence, has been increasing – because through the fact of devolution, Wales has assumed a new political as well as social significance, and gained new foci of attention. A salient example is the decision of the Economic and Social Research Council (ESRC) to commission a Welsh extension to its Household Panel Study from 1999 onwards in order to improve the quality of its dedicated information about Wales. This is a direct expression of the view that greater independence in decision-making needs to be backed up by more effective research and data collection.

Not everyone would agree with this conclusion. According to one deliberately provocative comment, 'most of the Welsh never talk about Wales. For most of us, Wales is a team and a nice place from which to get a letter. It exists for the purpose of sport and sentiment' (T. Williams, 1996). In its denial of any major significance to the issue, this is a minority view and, paradoxically of course, itself forms part of the very attempt to interpret and make sense of what Wales is all about with which we are concerned. Apart from anything else, it immediately poses some pertinent questions – who is this 'us' which is being referred to, and how accurate are the writer's assumptions about 'our' views? While it is true that, for much of the time, most people wherever they are do not reflect consciously upon the nature of the society to which they belong, but simply go about the business of daily life, nevertheless occasions arise on which they do have to give thought to such matters. Arguably, such occasions have grown more frequent in recent years. Contrary to the view expressed, there are others who might riposte that, far from never talking about Wales, there are quite a number of Welsh people (and a few non-Welsh individuals) who seem to talk about little else. Indeed, Williams himself makes the point that there are now many who are able to earn quite a decent living out of doing so; and in the process they are very argumentative, producing a multitude of different impressions of the country. Perhaps the particular perspective of sociology can contribute something towards cutting through the resulting cacophony of voices.

MORE THAN ONE WALES

There are many efforts to make sense of Wales, and these produce many definitions and understandings of what Wales is about. This is not surprising, since it has become quite acceptable among sociologists now to recognize that there is rarely, if ever, one definitive version or story to be told. Rather, there are multiple realities, intelligible from differing stand-points and anchored in different sets of social experiences and social positions.

Among the positions that are likely to be relevant in their formation, we could include: place or territorial location; class, or position within a struc-tured system of inequalities; gender; ethnicity or 'race'; and generation. Each of these provides a vantage point from which people can and do see the world differently. Since people, individually and collectively, occupy all of these positions simultaneously, they are liable to create highly complex sets of understandings of their social worlds. A wide range of raw materials can be worked upon to produce these selective accounts, within which some-times the same elements are capable of assuming very different meanings. They might consist, among other things, of a mixture of fragments of personal knowledge and direct experience, collective memories, cultural assumptions and lessons absorbed from education or the media. Often these can be encapsulated in quite specific images, such as are provided by artists and writers (Humphreys, 1995). However, the interpretation of these images usually requires the application of a considerably larger body of information and experience which enables access to their social meaning: to grasp what they are about, we have to be able to enter into the appropriate social world. The implication that a particular social world offers a preferable, or indeed, the only convincing angle of vision is often an inherent aspect of the way in which reality is construed: as well as a descriptive content, there is usually a persuasive element to images and analyses which tends to coincide with the furthering of particular interests or sets of purposes.

Since the significance of the various positions people occupy can change over time and in the light of circumstances, the resulting perspectives are not hard and fast, nor are they always totally distinct and separate from one another. Rather they are produced and reproduced in an endless process of conversation and negotiation, at times mingling quite promiscuously, at others becoming more sharply defined and distanced. Participation in this conversation does much to sustain the sense there is something worth discussing. As a discipline, sociology makes its own important contribution to this process, lending qualified support to some positions, helping to undermine others, often putting itself forward as an especially 'authorita-tive' version of reality. This claim is made on the grounds that sociology is more explicitly informed by theory, more closely tied to evidence, and more consciously self-critical, than many of the competing perspectives. It is not always a claim that is justifiable because, like everyone else, sociologists have their own axes to grind.

The sociologists who came to Aberystwyth with their ready-made images of Wales were simply responding to one very strong vision of Wales, maybe the one that at the time was most resonant and widespread outside Wales. Its appeal to them probably also owed quite a lot to their own political and ideological preconceptions as sociologists: it was perhaps their preferred image, best fitted to how they felt Wales *ought* to be. It is a vision that projects a powerful conception of a proletarian Wales, dominated by a strong and well-established industrial working class, symbolized above all by the mining industry. The figure of the 'coal smudged, cloth-capped Welsh miner' has served as a 'universal icon of working-class radicalism' (Adamson, 1998). As we will see, at best this is a gross oversimplification of any actual state of Wales, but it is the Wales that most people believe they know something about, represented most obviously, in its often clichéd version, in books and films like Richard Llewellyn's *How Green is my Valley* and A. J. Cronin's *The Citadel*, and by a wealth of other artistic representations. It forms the backdrop, conscious or implicit, to a great deal of the work which has been done on Wales over the past few decades, a considerable amount of which is concerned to gain some distance from, and perspective upon, the underlying set of experiences and relationships that are implicated within it.

Like other visions, it is circumscribed both historically and geographically, and it is capable of taking on somewhat mythic proportions. There have been times when it was propagated assiduously, because it served a particular purpose. It is a version of Wales dating from the industrial revolution, which was the decisive moment in the formation of modern Wales. It crystallized in the first half of the twentieth century, and by now it has faded almost entirely into history. It is also a conception which never applied to the whole of Wales, but which had its strongest realization in the valleys of south Wales. It was the experience of the South Wales Coalfield in particular that generated much of the social fabric, and the associated political and cultural traits, upon which it draws. Between 1750 and 1911 the population of the coalfield area grew at a phenomenal rate, expanding by about a million and a half, and assembled itself into its characteristic working-class communities. As the leading historians of the coalfield comment, 'the sociological ramifications of the mining communities were, by no means, without complexity', but their fundamental feature was identified well enough by the miners' leader Will Paynter as 'the integration of pit, people and union into a unified social organism' (Francis and Smith,

1980: 34). Having grown up in the region, Smith provides his own personal endorsement of such a vision: 'I could define "my" Wales in terms of pit-head winding gear, domino rows of terraced houses falling down hills that pass for mountains, and the thin defiance of a brass band on the march. The clichés are too close to the truth for most of us to avoid them' (Smith, 1984: 3). Once again we see in this comment the almost imperceptible shift from direct individual experience to assumptions about what applies to 'most of us', as we are invited to participate in an act of shared recollection.

The reason why this particular image would attract specifically sociological interest is that it is already quite familiar. Such an organization of an entire community around a particular form of work and its demands has played a central part in the sociological construction of the idea of a 'traditional' working class, the general features of which are well-known and much described. Although the classic studies were produced outside Wales (Dennis et al., 1956; Young and Willmott, 1957; Jackson, 1968), the Welsh experience of industrialization fed, seemingly without difficulty, into the production of this wider sociological model of a distinctive class situation and pattern of communal organization. This was encapsulated brilliantly by David Lockwood in his classic article on working-class images of society (Lockwood, 1966) and explored further by Martin Bulmer and others (Bulmer, 1978; Davis, 1979) throughout the 1960s and 1970s. It was against this benchmark that Lockwood and Goldthorpe were to develop their account of working-class affluence and its effects. Part of the subsequent story of Wales is about how affluence and material change has rendered this vision obsolete, although in fact economic decline and deprivation have had at least as much to do with its demise.

The main characteristics brought together within the ideal type of the traditional working class included the centrality of male manual labour; subordination in the workplace and wider social structure; class consciousness; close family connections; and strong communities with a distinctive culture and pattern of social life. Along with other areas of heavy industry such as central Scotland and northern England, Wales provided the supporting evidence for this description, and Welsh workers in turn accounted for a significant portion of the British working class. Of course, it could be argued that there were aspects specific to Wales which had to be taken into consideration – including, for example, an especially well-developed sense of class solidarity, and a high degree of political unanimity. Francis and Smith note how

> this forging of a consciousness was hastened by the social geography of the narrow steep-sided valleys. Housing tended to be cramped and terraced and the ribbon development prevented the establishing of a physical civic centre to

> the communities, a feature which could have countered the hardening class
> identity. On the contrary, the few social amenities, particularly the institutes
> and their libraries, were overwhelmingly proletarian in origin and patronage.
> (Francis and Smith 1980: 8)

Not for the last time, we find the social features of life in Wales apparently
growing out of the landscape it inhabits. Furthermore, it is asserted, the
institutions of these communities remained firmly in the hands of the
working people themselves, since 'from the chapels to the free libraries,
from the institutes to the sports teams, the control was a popular and democratic one' (Francis and Smith, 1980: 34).

Compared to other areas, such features might lend working-class existence within Wales a special quality. Nevertheless, the fact that the greater
part of the account applied indifferently throughout industrial Britain (and
beyond) provided one reason to play down the possibility of a distinctive
Welsh sociology. If all the key features were common and only some of the
trappings were different, then there was little of real significance to say
about Wales as such: it merely exemplified in an especially stark, and
perhaps developed, way the general nature of a class and its historical
experiences. This was a view that could be taken even from within; one
autobiographical account discounts both the personal and the geographical
relevance of the events described because

> for the greater part of the story, the scene would differ little if it was set in any
> one of the older industries of the country ... the setting in the coal-mining
> industry and my personal involvement in it is not the important feature of the
> record; it provides the local colour only. (Paynter, 1972: 9)

This generalizing impulse, so central to the sociological perspective,
helps create precisely the expectation which led to predictions that, since
the whole working class of Britain shared a common fate, increasingly it
would leave its local variations, and 'regional' identities, behind, making
them of merely parochial or historical interest. The reasonableness of this
expectation is something which will have to be examined in due course, but
it suggests Wales holds a special place, if at all, only for its vanguard position in a wider pattern of change. Unsurprisingly, the notion of Wales as
the locus for a mature industrial proletariat which in its formation and attitudes conformed well to theoretical expectations has held a particular
appeal for sociologists with Marxist leanings, who have seen its 'militancy'
embodied most profoundly in its 'Little Moscows' (Macintyre, 1980).

We have here then one starting point from which to think about the
nature of Wales, what makes it different and how this has developed. The
idea of Wales in people's minds takes on a particular inflection because 'in
ways which have no real parallels in, say, England, an integral part of such

popular constructions embodies a powerful set of images of the social relations characteristic of the industrial Valleys' (Rees, 1997: 100). Put more
crudely, in the words of the Welsh Affairs Committee in 1988, we are
presented with an image of 'short dark men singing hymns in the shadow
of slag heaps' (cited Humphreys, 1995: 143). In other words, a part becomes
a token for the whole as the nature of Wales is read off from knowledge
(real or imagined) of the valleys. This is partly because these images correspond to a set of real and formative experiences, and partly because a
variety of individuals and groups have seen in them something which
appeals strongly to their interests and preferences.

From this initial sketch, we can identify a set of attributes which, for a
given period of time, appear to have defined some of the basic features of
Welsh society: predominantly working-class, well-organized, self-assertive,
intensely solidary and politically Labourist. With these go all the associated
characteristics of the conventional working-class way of life as depicted by
Lockwood and others: it is localized, strongly marked by gender divisions
and patriarchal power, with horizons restricted by the material limits of
powerlessness and subordination. It has the virtues of mutual support and
egalitarianism, but the vices of conformity and inhibited enterprise.

Ideal types of this sort are intended only to provide useful approximations to empirical truth, and they do so by accentuating key aspects and
stripping away the detail. Their drawback is that they tend to come as
complete packages which lead those who employ them to deduce the
remaining features from those which they are able actually to observe. They
encourage us to see the whole, when only the parts are present. We will see
that there is a strong tradition of sociological work carried out in Wales
which weaves around this core conception a variety of comparisons and
qualifications that do help to bring out some of complications that lie
hidden within it. Together with the contributions of Welsh historians, such
work serves to demonstrate that this preliminary typification is too simple
to do justice to the actual richness and variety of social organization in
industrial Wales, and therefore that it requires extensive modification and
elaboration. At the same time, if used with care and attention, it provides a
useful framework through which to consider some of the processes of
change and transformation which by now have made it largely redundant.

Rather than developing these possibilities for the moment, it is more
important to reiterate the point that this is only one of a number of possible
points of departure, and therefore that the extent to which it can succeed in
capturing everything that is (or was) interesting about Wales is strictly
limited. Apart from its temporal limitations – the image it presents having
been left behind by contemporary Wales, or turned into 'heritage' (Dicks,
2000) – large parts of the country, and large segments of its population,

never conformed to its characteristics, so that it produces a seriously distorted interpretation of their situation. Indeed, it is possible to conceptualize Wales in ways which, far from corresponding to this image, confront it with a competing version that has developed, in part, through a critical encounter with it. Reverse the terms of the description and you get something approximating to an alternative interpretation of the nature of Welsh society, which has its own dedicated adherents.

Quite obviously, industrial and proletarian Wales did not appear out of nothing. There was an earlier Wales, shaped very differently, some aspects of which have shown historical continuity through into the later developments. Pre-modern Wales owed its features to the conditions which predated industrialization; but they could be taken to have laid down some fundamental and lasting features that have never been eroded subsequently but which continue to define Wales's essential nature. Certainly features of an older, rural Wales were never wholly supplanted by industrialism, and there are many who have looked to the Welsh countryside, rather than the industrialized valleys, for a more authentic, deeper rooted, idea of Wales and Welshness.

Prior to the industrial revolution, Wales was almost wholly rural, without any substantial urban development. It was inhabited by a population of small farmers living in conditions of dependence upon large landowners and great estates which at times became almost feudal (Jenkins, 1971). The organization of social life at this time was on a much smaller scale, and far less populous, than the development of industry was to allow, though in its way equally communal. Prior to the explosion of industry, the population of Wales barely exceeded half a million. Most people lived in small and scattered settlements, under conditions of economic hardship, and in order to survive they had to develop both patterns of cooperation and qualities of independence, self-reliance and resistance to power, which could be seen to have become deeply ingrained in the Welsh character. Here too, it is not unusual to find these attributes explained in terms of the nature of the Welsh geography, as adaptations to an existence dominated by a relatively poor upland environment. Geographically and socially, the Welsh could be depicted as a marginal people in a marginal land, clinging on heroically against enormous odds – both natural and man-made. This provides a self-image which many appear to find attractive – for example, the historian Gwyn A. Williams closes his book *When was Wales?* with the poignant image of the contemporary Welsh as 'nothing but a naked people under an acid rain' (1985: 305): evocative, but hardly very convincing!

Nevertheless, there is some foundation for this conception of the Welsh as a people occupying a peripheral and pressured environment within which the society they had managed to construct, over a long period of time, was built primarily for defence and security, and so highly resistant to change. Its lineaments were etched virtually into the landscape itself. Rather than the dramatic history of disruption and change associated with the rise and dominance of industry, Wales in this account was marked by profound continuity and stability. Thus it could be claimed that in fundamental respects its features managed to survive unchanged over centuries: 'Rural Wales, the land of local cultures, supports a society as tribal in its organization today as that of the early inhabitants described in the Welsh laws' (Jenkins, 1976: 15).

Whereas the former frame of reference draws on a relatively truncated history, which begins no more than a couple of hundred years ago, and drives forwards towards a possibly predetermined destination linked to the destiny of a class, the alternative is grounded in a sense of permanency, and the emphasis goes towards the maintenance and preservation of what is already fully formed. Although neither is free of contradictions and inconsistencies, one vision is forward-looking, the other firmly grounded in the past. Among the main aspects of this more traditional, essentially rural society, attention could be drawn to the intimacy and cohesion of its small-scale communities, the centrality of kinship and neighbourly relations, the very limited local horizons of most people's existence, a powerful sense of belonging which this generates, and the organization of social life around hearth and home. There is an apparently organic unity to the pattern of social existence. The dominant economic conditions reflect the requirements of an agricultural way of life, set within prevailing power relations which governed people's access to control and use of the land. There are also dimensions of spirituality and religiosity which can be thought to infuse such an existence – close to nature and to the inheritance of untold generations. As the model unfolds, it comes nearer to a romanticized view, created in contrast to and in spite of modernity.

The contrasts between this description and the one preceding it open up the possibility of somehow locating Wales within a set of polarities that have exerted a great deal of influence upon sociologists in the past: urban/rural, modern/traditional, dynamic/conservative and so on. The attempt to interpret social organization and social change in the light of such dichotomies or continua has a substantial pedigree (Nisbet, 1966), and it has undoubtedly exerted an influence over interpretations of Wales, so much so that there is a recurrent pull towards a split conception in which Wales appears to consist of at least two parts, each defined by a distinctive clustering of these attributes: advanced/backward, industrial/rural, metropolitan/provincial, south/north. Even now, there are continuing arguments about which of the characterizations comes closest to the 'truth' about Wales. Each of the depictions has its advocates, organized into opposing camps; the value which one places upon specific aspects and developments tends to be reversed by the other. For example, Dicks (2000) provides an enlightening discussion of the way in which such competing viewpoints have informed the emergence of rival conceptions of Welsh 'heritage', which privilege different events, artefacts and locales.

Yet, as abstract criteria, it could be said that, while they provide us with a set of rather comfortingly conventional choices, there is still nothing about these contrasts which really manages to capture the distinctively *Welsh* character of the society, that which holds it together as Wales. Already it has been suggested that the major features of industrial Wales were common to a great swathe of districts across Britain, and indeed it has been usual in economic and social analysis to group Wales together with regions like the north-west and north-east of England, as part of the industrialized 'north' (Evans, 1989). Similarly, so far as the features just ascribed to non-industrial or pre-industrial Wales are concerned, they appear pretty much like those of other upland parts of Britain – so that Wales would belong together with places like Cumbria, Devon and Cornwall, and most of Scotland, to form an 'outer' or 'Western Britain', where there is a history of a similar kind of social organization and rural way of life (Frankenberg, 1966; Evans, 1998), and where present-day problems are also shared. If we want to pinpoint Welshness as such, maybe we have to delve further, and find something which so far is missing from either version: we have formed an impression of industrial and rural Wales, but where exactly can we locate Welsh Wales? This is a question which has fascinated many, and stimulated a variety of quests and expeditions to track down its elusive answer.

The two images discussed up to now have many elements in common, but also diverge at important points. They begin to suggest a fractured reality. However, all their substantive traits – including closeness of living together, family structure, sense of local belonging and political radicalism – are to be found elsewhere in other parts of Britain; unless it is in their combination, or their exceptional strength and clarity, none of them definitely sets Wales apart. Viewed through them, Welshness seems, at best, a matter of degree, an outcome of causal processes which are entirely general and operative upon social development more or less everywhere. In which case, maybe each provides no more than an outer shell within which the real 'essence' of Wales must be traced. Up to this point we have concentrated mainly on aspects of social organization, and the type of economy (industrial or agricultural) that supported them. Perhaps it is only when we turn towards more spiritual matters, such as values, and the subtleties of culture, that we can be said truly to begin to see what is unique about Wales. This indeed is how many would respond, arguing that Welshness is about 'being' Welsh, a question of personality and identity, rather than social structure. In fact, they might say, observable structures and patterns of living ought to be seen far more as the expression of Welshness, rather than its cause. Only because people have some vital inner Welshness, which they acquire from their origins and surroundings, can they externalize it in ways which become visible to us in their social habits.

For example, it can be argued that the closeness of community that has been so evident in both rural and industrial parts of Wales reflects an essential communitarian impulse that is part of being Welsh, and which goes along with the powerful sense of 'belonging' associated with Jenkins's 'land of local cultures' (Jenkins, 1976). So 'a very strong sense of place, a sense of belonging to a particular area – *brogarwch*' can be inferred as a characteristic of Welshness (Keen, 1999). This is what makes Wales into a 'community of communities' and leads Welsh people to respond to situations in ways which are typical of them, and different from the behaviour of others. Similarly, the lack of hierarchy, and democratic ethos remarked upon by many as features of society in Wales (in both rural and industrial contexts) can be held to represent qualities which are typically 'Welsh', as perhaps does a display of tolerance towards others, and lack of concern with material things. Some would root these attributes very firmly within the sphere of religion, and the legacy of Welsh Nonconformity and its history of revival, culminating as late as 1904–5. This tradition is seen for example as giving impetus to all the most noteworthy flowerings of Welsh culture (A. D. Rees, 1996: 111; cf. D. Ben Rees, 1975; I. G. Jones, 1981). A set of shared conceptions of this kind about what it is to be Welsh play an important role in both popular and academic analyses, from within Wales and from outside, although of course the exact qualities attributed to Welshness may differ considerably. As well as positive evaluations, there are among them also some highly negative characterizations, intended to denigrate Wales and its people.

There is nothing fundamentally strange about looking towards values of this sort to provide explanations of social relations. To do so forms the nub of idealist, as opposed to materialist, types of analysis, and there is no doubt that it has been an important aspect of the self-interpretation and external analysis of Welsh society. It assumes a variety of different forms which share the stress on ideas and cultural orientations, but disagree about their content. One important strand develops the conception of a Wales marked by tradition and stability, but extends the time-period back further still, far beyond modernity and rurality, into a remote and obscure past, highlighting the length of time during which the Welsh have occupied their land, and sustained their culture. In this account, historical continuity reaches back to a time when the Welsh emerged from their Celtic ancestry, and they are seen as distinguished right up to the present by those things they inherit from it. 'Celticism' of this sort has exercised an influence over some social scientific approaches, but is more omnipresent among literary and popular accounts of Wales. It is present in Goronwy Rees's use of the word 'tribalism' to characterize efforts to defend a Welsh way of life (Rees, 1972). The writer Jan Morris ventriloquizes such an idea of the inherent unity which has bound Wales together across the ages into a single identity:

> I am all Wales in one! The peasants are me, the miners, Rebecca's horsemen are me . . . the princes and their ladies, the bards, the priests – I am Owain himself, and the divine Dafydd, and Nest, and Hywel Dda, and before them I inhabited the ancient mysteries of stone and seer – myth-maker, shape-changer, there go I! (Morris, 1998: 458)

According to this vision, the 'natural' location of the Welsh is not with the rest of the 'British' population, but with other Celtic peoples, in Brittany, Cornwall, Ireland and Scotland, who share the basic inheritance. It is a point of departure from which we are encouraged to explore the *ethnicity* of the Welsh, rather than their history or economic situation, and which implies the ability to make distinctions between their particular ethnic and cultural legacy, as 'Celts', and that of other groups, such as (most obviously) the English – who are *Saes*, or Saxon, in origin. Aspects of Welshness said to derive from such Celtic roots figure strongly in the popular impression of Wales as a land of poetry and song, with a long and continuous literary tradition (Petro, 1998) and more negatively perhaps in attacks on eminent Welsh figures for being too much in love with words and rhetoric.

In these terms, it is apt that the picture on the front of a recent discussion paper on 'Our Welsh Heritage' is the Pentre Ifan burial chamber in Pembrokeshire (Keen, 1999). This image provides one answer to the question posed at the start of the paper: what is significant in Wales? By implication, it is the possession of a 'heritage' that goes back not just hundreds but thousands of years, and which links the modern Welsh to whoever erected this dolmen. The same image, from a different viewpoint, is used as the front cover of the paperback edition of Emyr Humphreys's text on *The Taliesin Tradition* (Humphreys, 2000). Rather differently, the *Western Mail* has suggested that in future St David's Day should be made a national holiday in Wales so that 'we could get back to our Celtic roots' (BBC Radio 4, *Today*, 1 March 2000). Here, even the meaning of Celtic appears to be contestable, implying Christian as opposed to pagan connections.

Transparently, however, there is more than a single way of responding to the question about the significant aspects of Wales, as the author of the heritage pamphlet is well aware. The chosen illustration could have been a castle, since we are informed that 'Castles are now powerful icons in the heritage of Wales and important parts of the heritage industry' (Keen, 1999:

2). Wales has plenty of castles to choose from; but of course they summon up a very different set of associations from a prehistoric megalith, ones that might be considerably more challenging because we know a great deal more about them and their histories, such as that most of them were built to subjugate the Welsh. As representations of modern Wales, pictures of industrial sites, or a modern office block, or Cardiff's Millennium Stadium, would be different again in their effects. As images, it has to be said, none of them is innocent.

The Celtic image of Wales is strongly imbued with overtones of romanticism. In many ways it is a product of the nineteenth-century imagination, and of the emotive responses of English travellers to Wales. In their minds, it was constructed largely in opposition to developing industrialism and all its rational, instrumental and mercenary aspects. The Wales they celebrated seemed untouched by these influences. It is therefore an anti-modern device, and continues to be deployed in ways that enable a critical stance to be adopted towards disfavoured aspects of the present. Within Wales, this opposition was realized especially in the contrast often posited between the industrialized south and an 'untamed' north and west, where the Celtic influence was said to have survived more or less undiluted. The Celtic image is much employed now on tourist brochures and in craft products, and reaches an apogee in the rituals and appearance of the Gorsedd of Bards at the annual National Eisteddfod. Although a relatively recent fabrication (P. Morgan, 1983), this ceremony is intended to put the Welsh in touch with their most deep-seated roots. As a vision, the Celticist version of Wales represents most clearly a tourist view, aimed towards outsiders, and encouraged by the proliferation of books on *Mysterious Wales* and the like, according to which 'Wales is the Celtic land of mystery par excellence . . . the mysterious land of Arthurian legend . . . a country of secret wells and buried treasure, of myth and magic, of sunken cities and forests, and lost lands under the sea' (Barber, 1982). The stock carried by Welsh tourist offices places Wales firmly within a circuit of cultural references which link it with Scotland, but more especially Ireland, and with prehistory, 'folk' culture, druids and dragons. Visitors are enticed in to 'Merlin's' realm in places such as Corris and Llanberis, and a major exhibition centre in Machynlleth presenting the story of Wales's history is known as Celtica.

Many within Wales would regard resort to these resonances as a mystification which obscures more or less everything that is important about real Welsh society, even if it succeeds in earning some useful revenue from the gullible and naïve. Nevertheless, its elements surface from time to time to exert an influence within other positions and standpoints; it has been significant in encouraging, for example, certain openings towards possible allies and affiliations elsewhere. In this regard, it has a weight within the

ways in which Wales is understood that is quite unlike the negligible significance attached, say, to 'Anglo-Saxon' or 'Norman-French' vestiges in the
culture and society of modern England.

Despite the fairy-like dancing children with their circlets of flowers and
the flowing robes of the Druids (so hot and heavy that beneath them they
may be wearing only boxer shorts), the National Eisteddfod, a peripatetic
festival held every August in a field somewhere in Wales, is mostly an altogether more mundane event, an opportunity to advertise, experience and
celebrate the whole range of activities and relationships that takes place in
the Welsh language (Trosset, 1993; C. A. Davies, 1998). Welsh is the tongue
of the Eisteddfod field, and the event provides an opportunity for a coming
together of all those who participate in and value a living Welsh-language
culture. If able to, many of those involved would wholly separate this
commitment from the strands of Celticism. Indeed, there are those in Wales
for whom the entire Celtic apparatus arouses a similar disgust to that which
Scots often feel for 'tartanry', as a stereotypical imposition that tries to force
people into a narrow and misleading set of pigeonholes which has little to
do with real life (McCrone, 1992: 174).

There is no need to dwell on the distant past in order to recognize the
presence of a very distinctive form of Welshness, which is centred upon
the language. Not only is there an undeniable historical continuity in the
development and use of Welsh, which can claim to be the oldest continu-
ously spoken language in Europe, but it is embedded inextricably into a
much broader set of social and cultural phenomena constituting something close to a separate 'way of life' which is indeed peculiar to Wales.
Hence 'the language is the truest badge of Welsh identity ... It gives
notice to all-comers that Wales is still a separate place' (Morris, 1998: 171).
The transformation of Welsh from a threatened and declining language
into what can be said now to be a 'normalized' vehicle of communication
within a bilingual society (C. H. Williams, 2000b), yet nevertheless
remaining incredibly vulnerable, is an indispensable part of the story of
contemporary Wales. The existence of the language very definitely makes
Wales different, and arguably unique, particularly if we concur with Lord
Elis-Thomas in his comment that 'the Welsh language is the common
property of all Welsh people, whether they speak the language or not'
(quoted from the Welsh Language Board's Annual Report and Accounts
1994–5). Within the British context this is certainly the case, since nowhere
else is there a setting for daily life which can be regarded realistically as
bilingual. By comparison, Scottish Gallic and Irish represent marginalized
languages with a strictly confined territorial base, and play a far less
crucial role in the articulation of Scottish or Irish national identities, while
the many other minority languages employed in Britain are confined in

their use to particular, usually urban, neighbourhoods and minority communities.

Definitions of Welshness which highlight the significance of language have been extraordinarily influential in recent years, and continue to exercise a major attraction for many. Its importance has been crucial to the evolution of Welsh nationalism. If pushed, many would assert that it is the survival of the Welsh language and the associated culture complex which, in the final analysis, makes Wales special: if the language goes, Wales as such would cease to be. This position has historical, as well as contemporary, bearing (Knowles, 1999; G. A. Williams, 1985). Placing such emphasis on the role of the language situates Wales alongside other examples of settings where questions of the social relationships between majority and minority language groups assume paramount importance (such as Quebec and the Basque Country). In the European context, for example, Welsh is one of the more prominent examples of the so-called 'lesser used languages' afforded recognition by the European Union. However, the brute fact is that – taking what is probably quite a generous estimate, derived from census evidence based on a very elementary test question – only 20 per cent of the people living in Wales can actually speak Welsh. By far the greater part of the population, in other words, cannot enter into the cultural universe that is defined by the language, even if they empathize with it and sincerely regret their exclusion. Hence a version of Wales and Welshness which privileges the language inevitably drives a wedge through the society, and risks the exclusion of the majority of Welsh people from full membership of their own society.

Here we have a key point, which should have been apparent throughout this chapter: these various images of Wales vie with one another. While there may be areas of overlap between them, and possibilities of synthesis, each can be upheld as *the* key to understanding the true nature of Wales. Each of them is designed to include and embrace certain ways of acting, thinking and feeling, which are designated as characteristic, but accordingly to exclude others. None of them is neutral, although all may advance themselves as objectively valid. Nor should they be dismissed as merely passive representations, which one can take or leave at will, according to inclination, since they operate as active shapers and determiners of outcomes. As has been pointed out, for example, they encourage certain alignments and comparisons, while creating distance from or opposition to other possibilities. They contain a normative as well as an informative/descriptive content, and a variety of actors (individual and collective) engage in substantial work to make them effective. In this sense they constitute ideological statements about Wales, which make declarations about where people stand, and how things should proceed. Arguments about their relevance and validity go beyond the merely intellectual or academic – they have meaningful social and political repercussions across large areas of everyday life in Wales.

What have been described are visions – glimpses – which carry meanings, but which need to be scrutinized and elucidated; they are all approximations. More will be said about them as we proceed, and hopefully this will include the provision of sufficient chapter and verse to demonstrate that they are not merely an arbitrary set of constructs, but have real foundations in the way significant numbers of people think and feel about Wales. None of them are 'real' in the sense that they correspond accurately and fully to what Wales is, or has ever been, like; but they do influence how reality is perceived, very frequently through confirmation/ contrast with one another. As was suggested earlier, they should not be regarded as rigidly compartmentalized viewpoints. Rather, they consist of elements which can blend and combine in a rich, and often heady, stew. As Humphreys (1995) warns, exploring these different images can often seem like entering a hall of mirrors, making it extraordinarily difficult to tell where reality ends, and illusion begins. Nevertheless, there has to be some underpinning conception of truth and falsity with which we can find our way through the dazzling maze. Faced by the challenge, everyone has to make some decisions about what to accept and reject, not least because aspects of the different conceptions are simply incompatible. The need to sort out where one stands is particularly strong when things are undergoing change: social transformation puts all such conceptions under stress, and in many ways how people respond, in hanging onto or amending the particular narrative to which they adhere, is probably more revealing than orthodox classifications of socio-political viewpoints as 'left' or 'right', 'conservative' or 'progressive', and so on.

For now, a final brief mention must be made of the fact that all of the above versions of Wales may be challenged and criticized, not just in the work of social scientists, but in the everyday perceptions and thought processes of (so-called) 'ordinary' Welsh people. In fact, once inspected, none of them provides anything like a sufficiently convincing depiction of what Wales at the start of the new century is actually like. Each is afflicted by 'lags' and delays in perception. This is understandable, because it takes time to formulate a view which carries significant weight, and by the time it has gained acceptance and currency, usually things have moved on. Consequently, those who are most actively engaged with the question of what Wales is 'really' like, now, are busy producing a variety of revisionist views which are intended to displace and correct the errors and misconceptions of the preceding accounts. For example, there has been a certain amount of excitement – not entirely spontaneous, but encouraged by a similar discourse about Britain as a whole – about the conception of a 'Cool Cymru', a modern twenty-first-century Wales represented in developments around the Welsh media, pop music and the economic and social regeneration taking place around Cardiff and the new Assembly. For a while, references to the band Catatonia and their delight in being Welsh, and the accompanying efflorescence of Welsh pop, including Welsh-language music, became almost obligatory, and were associated with other artistic and architectural achievements. The record has not been without its problems – Catatonia has broken up and, following the debacle of the Welsh opera house, arguments about the design and implementation of the new building for the National Assembly have taken still more of the heat out of being 'cool'. But while the record is patchy, there are enough noteworthy recent achievements in music, film and theatre to keep alive hopes of a 'reinvented' Wales with an emergent culture and identity that is young, literate and ironic (Blandford, 1999).

Of course, sociologists, naturally, would say that they are able to rise above any of these partial and inaccurate depictions. We can also play appropriately postmodernist games in which the various elements can be assembled and collaged into new and amusing combinations. A nice visual example was provided by the *Guardian* newspaper in 1994 as its illustration to part of a series on the break-up of Britain ('Lost For Words', *Guardian Weekend*, 30 July 1994): it incorporated the inevitable pit head, a red dragon, a map of Snowdonia and an ancient film camera linked by ropes to the logo of the Welsh-language television channel S4C. All that was missing to make the picture of a wholly imaginary and constructed Wales complete were a group of appropriately censorious-looking ladies in their 'traditional' flannel shawls and stovepipe hats.

2

Wales Remade? The Transformation of Economic Structures

The discussion in the preceding chapter provided support for Smith's characterization of Wales as 'a singular noun but a plural experience' (1984: 1). Its plurality consists of many layers of social meanings and relationships which are interdependent and interacting, but not reducible to one another. Wales is no different to any other society in this regard, although the extent and range of particular variations contained within it may be greater or lesser. For instance, setting to one side for later consideration the obvious and major demarcation which exists within Wales between those who are Welsh and the English, and allowing for the presence of a substantial but statistically invisible sub-population with Irish origins, the population has been and remains relatively ethnically homogeneous. Minority ethnicities make up only 1.5 per cent of persons resident in Wales (C. Williams et al., 1999), compared to some 6 per cent in Britain as a whole. Only Cardiff, with a 6 per cent ethnic minority population, comes close to matching the sort of mix found in other areas, but falls well short of most major metropolitan centres. This has resulted in questions of 'race' and multiculturalism emerging more slowly in Wales than elsewhere (C. Williams, 1999a). Politically, Wales has been unified by a tradition of radicalism and anti-conservatism which has narrowed the scope of the dominant definitions setting its agenda, as has been symbolized recently by the avowed 'inclusiveness' surrounding the creation of the National Assembly, a project in which all political parties except the Conservatives were able to cooperate. In Wales, the 'centre ground' is positioned differently from that in England and Westminster. The prevalence of left of centre attitudes has helped in turn to bring about a more uniform pattern of educational provision across Wales than is found in other parts of Britain, with the early adoption of the comprehensive principle during the 1960s removing the divisiveness of selection found elsewhere. With few exceptions, Welsh authorities had championed non-selective education for years, despite pressure from Westminster and its civil servants (G. E. Jones, 1995). Recent decisions from within the National Assembly of Wales show a continuing commitment to the comprehensive principle. On these grounds, at least, there is a commonality of experience, rooted in some form of shared history, which serves to unify the great majority of those who live in Wales.

At the same time, there are enough differences to render the nature of the unity of Wales contentious, and difficult to hold together within the limits of any simple shorthand description. Wales has to be deconstructed in order to be understood. At the very least, it requires a series of 'takes' on the nature and organization of Welsh society to put together anything like a comprehensive account of what, following Harvey (1985: 146), we might term its 'structured coherence'; that is, the arrangement of economic, social, political, cultural and other elements which make up its social distinctiveness. Harvey introduces this term in the course of a discussion of the nature of modern (capitalist) development to refer to a regional space within which 'production and consumption, supply and demand, production and realisation, class struggle and accumulation, culture and lifestyle, hang together as some kind of structured coherence within a totality of productive forces and social relations'. He suggests that the persistence of any such coherent regional formation is surprising, in view of the constant tendency of various economic, technical and political forces to undermine its limits. Consequently the boundaries of regions are highly porous; regional and spatial configurations are unstable, and there is a tendency towards a restless reformation of geographical landscapes and associated forms of regional consciousness and culture. These features are well exemplified by Wales.

As it happens, quite regardless of their currently fashionable status, deconstruction and reconstruction are entirely apt terms with which to describe the path taken by Wales over the past hundred or more years, both with respect to the changing reality, and to the way in which it has been perceived by commentators. Empirically and theoretically, Wales has been under construction for so long it begins to seem like a chronic condition. Almost every discussion makes reference to some state of transition, the disappearance of earlier certainties, the difficulty of being sure about the future; instability seems to be rife. Indeed, there has been a series of stages of transformation which historians and social analysts have tried to depict and explain. It has not been a smooth process in any sense – rather, there have been a number of sharp and often traumatic ruptures with existing conditions. The impression of plurality is enhanced by the disjunctures between these phases, posing the question whether it is the same Wales which concerns us throughout time, or whether and when it becomes something different: if so, just how many concepts of Wales must we deal with?

One of the essential points at issue throughout has been the question as to whether or not in this respect Wales was merely following the same course as the rest of Britain, under the influence of the same general forces, or whether there were exceptional factors and considerations which needed to be taken into account for a proper understanding. Much discussion has been couched in terms of positioning Wales as a 'problem region', thus placing it alongside a number of other regions faced with a common situation, and, by implication, distinguishing it from places which were unproblematic. To see it in this way suggests that the 'solution', if any, lies through action to be taken on the higher plane of some larger system to which the regions belong, to level out regional disparities and deal with the underlying problems. This view accepts that Wales's ultimate place is as a *part* of a larger whole, whether this be Britain, or, increasingly perhaps, Europe. Alternatively, it is contended that the difficulties reflect something intrinsic to the nature of Wales itself – the 'problem' either lies within Wales, or has to do precisely with its relationship to the larger system – and so can be tackled only by policies and actions which begin from Wales, and which treat it as the primary point of reference. While the emphasis moves between these two positions, the difference of perspective they entail has done much to organize debates about the sources and impacts of change, and to suggest competing policy directions.

THE FOUNDATIONS

The immediate post-Second-World-War period presented an opportunity to deal with the enormous problems which had beset Wales during the depression of the 1930s, chiefly mass unemployment and poverty. These had left deep scars in both consciousness and the social fabric, coming as a particular shock after many years of growth and comparative prosperity. The impression of dereliction and decline created during this time took several decades to shake off, and may not have been overcome fully even now, while the psychological damage done to people's self-confidence and sense of security has often been blamed for continuing weaknesses in their capacity to adapt to later change. In this, as in numerous other ways, the development of industrial Wales provides an instructive case of the problems and difficulties associated with industrialism and modernization. The prolonged dismantling and replacement of Wales's traditional industrial base has been one of the main structural parameters delimiting the shape and pace of subsequent development. Even now, some of the most intractable economic and social problems continue to reflect, many years later, the failure to deal adequately with that legacy. In parts of Wales, it is all too easy to trace a path that appears to have led directly from a confident, forward-looking working class towards a dispirited and excluded underclass.

Although there were important transformations in north and rural west Wales which must not be overlooked, the economic history of Wales during the nineteenth and early twentieth centuries was virtually synonymous with the development and change of the South Wales Coalfield, an area which, though it accounted for only a fifth of the total Welsh land mass, came to contain 70 per cent of its people, and nearly three-quarters of the workforce. This imbalance has had a seriously distorting effect upon later development, and the changing regional identity of south Wales *within* Wales has been as important a consideration as the influence which it has exerted over the rest of the country. The impact of its history as an industrial area was so decisive that the examination of economic change, and all the correlative alterations it brings about in labour-market conditions, local economic structures and occupational cultures, has remained the centrepiece for much of the best sociological work done on Wales, even to the extent that other equally important dimensions may have been relatively neglected. More than anything, it is the various contributions that have been made to Welsh economic sociology, and through this to the wider development of perspectives on economic and social change, which underpin the claim that there is a distinctive body of work worth studying. South Wales has also produced a crop of outstanding economic and social historians whose efforts to reveal and popularize the story of industrialization have been enormously vivid and illuminating (for example, Smith, 1984; G. Williams, 1978a; L. J. Williams, 1995; Daunton, 1977; Beddoe, 2000). Consequently our understanding of Wales is deeply influenced by an awareness of the tremendous impact the rise and fall of industrialism has had upon it, especially as that experience has been lived through and absorbed within a south Walian viewpoint. More narrowly, there has been a preoccupation with documenting the creation and dissolution of what are generally referred to as 'the Valleys' and all that they signify, and this has given rise to a coherent and quite focussed strand of sociological literature (Dicks, 2000).

THE FORMATION AND CRISIS OF MODERN SOUTH WALES

By the middle of the twentieth century, south Wales was stamped by the inheritance of successive phases of industrialization, beginning with the spread of the iron industry along the northern edge of the coalfield, which for a while made Merthyr Tydfil into the largest town in Wales, its population growing between 1801 and 1861 from 7,700 to 49,794. The export of Welsh iron across the developing world began a long and formative process of close involvement with the world economy. The subsequent development

of steel manufacture meant a shift towards more accessible coastal locations, including the construction of sites at Port Talbot and Margam,
followed by the establishment of the East Moors plant outside Cardiff. The
expansion of steam coal production in the latter part of the nineteenth
century saw the rise of Cardiff as a major export centre, with a ninefold
growth of population to 182,000 between 1851 and 1911, making it by far
the largest city in Wales. During the same period, the population of the
Rhondda valleys grew from under a thousand to more than 150,000, as an
unspoilt rural landscape became densely inhabited and totally polluted. As
one native of the district put it, quoting the title of a well-known novel
about the early development of the region, 'the rape of a fair country has
been a repetitive exercise against South Wales and still is' (Paynter, 1972: 43;
cf. Cordell, 1959). Further west, Swansea, Llanelli and Port Talbot saw the
development of substantial metallurgical industries. Urbanization became
a feature of Wales as new industrial centres came into existence (Carter and
Wheatley, 1982); almost all the really significant Welsh urban centres are in
the south. In all these localities it could be said that there existed 'a direct
and simple relationship between industry and the community' (Humphrys,
1972: 23), as south Wales was turned into a distinctive place possessing a
relatively straightforward industrial structure and a strong regional identity and solidarity based upon shared work experiences.

Industry was the *raison d'être* of the urban settlements, and their fate was
bound up inextricably with its successes and failures. When things were
going well, they expanded. Between 1881 and 1911, as the south Wales
economy let rip, there was net inward migration into the most industrialized county, Glamorgan, of some 330,000 people. This was the equivalent of
around 12 per cent of the total Welsh population at the time, and of these,
the 41 per cent who moved from elsewhere in Wales represented a substantial drain on the rural economy. They brought with them many elements of
an existing rural culture, planting the seeds of continuity with older Welsh
traditions. The remainder originated from various parts of England, especially the counties bordering Wales, as well as from Ireland and further
afield, such as Italy and Eastern Europe. Almost all were making the
personal transition from a rural, pre-industrial environment into previously
unknown urban/industrial conditions, although the expansion of Welsh
industry also required the import of a quota of technical and managerial
skills from other, even older industrial centres (for example, engineers and
miners from Cornwall and the Forest of Dean). In a study of the mining
villages of the Dulais valley, seventy or more years later, the impact of this
migration was reflected in the appearance among local families of names
like Tancock, Wonnacott, Trump, McCowan, Miller, Figoni, and Casimiro
(Sewel, 1975: 4). The rapidity of their growth, at a time when the experience

was so new, gave the settlements something of the character of frontier towns, with a similar reputation for lawlessness and chaotic disorder (G. A. Williams, 1978). Their expansion was an aspect of the generally unregulated development of the region, associated with the unorganized character of competition between enterprises. There were many small firms, with dispersed ownership, often acting as the focal point for highly localized sets of social relationships, and many small communities organized around particular places of work.

Despite its obvious shortcomings and the social costs that it incurred, those who describe this exuberant, frenetic phase of development in detail can hardly resist falling into a panegyric reminiscent of Marx's famous description in the *Communist Manifesto* of the revolutionary force of capitalism, which sweeps away before it 'all fixed, fast-frozen relations'. Witness Gwyn A. Williams's characterization of a 'society which was repeatedly modernizing and revolutionizing itself, planting communities and uprooting them, building itself into an export metropolis of a world economy' (1985: 180). There is a definite air of enthusiasm and excitement about such accounts, coupled with a positive celebration of the achievements of Welsh industrialists and their workforces – a kind of retrospective boosterism (for example, Smith, 1984; G. A. Williams, 1978). Driven forward by the profit motive, Wales helped lead the way into industrialism and modernity, full of vigour and confidence, creating as it went the institutions and structures that enabled its people to cope with the pressures and deprivations of working-class existence under industrial conditions; and in doing so it earned the respect and admiration of outside observers. This was a high point from which Wales made a real impact upon the world. Gwyn Williams held a plenary session of the BSA Conference in Cardiff in 1982 spellbound as he told a well-rehearsed joke about the Welshman who after extensive foreign travels decides it is time to return home and goes to Shanghai railway station to buy a ticket to his home town. As he states his destination, the helpful booking clerk asks 'Would that be upper or lower Cwmtwrch?' The historian Dai Smith concedes that it is still hard to determine quite what this process of radical social and economic change did to Wales, to the idea of Wales, to the Welsh and those who became Welsh, but he is clear that it made them into 'an industrial people' (Smith, 1984: 23).

As elsewhere, this was essentially a *regional* experience – industrialization in general had a regionalizing effect, through the way in which it brought about the development of clusters of specialized activities and functions. Almost by definition, this implied as well a growing inequality between conditions in the various regions. In fact, comparative analysis suggests that, owing to this massive and increasing specialization, the industrial profile of Wales a century ago was much more distinctive than that of Scotland or the majority of the English regions (McCrone, 1992: 68). Wales was comparable only to the north of England in the extent of its reliance upon heavy industry, predominantly coal and metals, and yet the vast bulk of this was located in its south-eastern corner. It did not see an equivalent expansion of textiles, clothing or other early manufactures; nor were the typical industries of pre- or early industrialism, such as brewing and foodstuffs, a particularly significant aspect of the Welsh economy.

It is no wonder that a particular image attached itself to the Welsh work-force: in 1911 no less than one in every three occupied males in Wales was a miner or quarryman; 30 per cent worked in coal. Employment in the industry peaked as late as 1920, at 271,516 (L. J. Williams, 1989). At that time half the male population were employed in an extraordinarily narrow band of occupations: coal, quarrying, metals and engineering, transport and agriculture. In 1913, coal, steel and tinplate together accounted for 70 per cent of all employment in Glamorgan; in 1929, the figure was still 56 per cent (Harris, 1987: 46). Relatively small proportions of the labour force were employed in manufacturing. The emphasis on primary production meant that in many ways, despite its early start, Wales was yet to be fully industrialized: many of the skills utilized, and conditions worked in, had changed little since their initial appearance, and both technology and 'value added' aspects of manufacturing were relatively poorly developed.

Specialization is always a risky strategy, and the consequences have dogged Wales ever since. As often happens, and as the inter-war period demonstrated all too clearly, an initial head-start proved to be a handicap in the long run; it left an accumulated burden of ageing investments and dated capital which has been a drag on later development, and which it has taken decades to remove. According to Baber and Thomas (1980), south Wales entered the twentieth century with an environment and physical and organizational infrastructure which was already 'overly narrow and largely inappropriate' to the circumstances of the time. Yet the demand for Welsh raw materials was so insatiable that there was little incentive to do more than ship them out as rapidly as possible: photographs of Cardiff and Barry Docks packed with railway trucks and ships poised to carry resources away from Wales are typical of the period. Rather than innovating and broadening the economic base, south Wales industrialists looked to get the most out of existing industries and production relations, by intensifying the demands made on their workforces. Levels of capital investment were low, and liable to flow out through company structures to benefit developments outside Wales. In a quite literal sense, through the exploitation of the natural resources with which it was favoured, Wales was working to energize the development of industrial capitalism beyond its borders.

It was this export economy which collapsed during the inter-war recession, transforming Wales from what had been a dynamic motor region for growth elsewhere into one of the most derelict and deserted parts of Britain. Its precipitate decline could be explained locally in terms of difficult geological conditions, and limited scope for technical adaptation, resulting in high costs of production and dependence upon labour-intensive methods (L. J. Williams, 1989). More globally, it was a victim of growing protectionism, and the emergence of economies which were able to out-compete Britain. As the international terms of trade shifted, demand for its products vanished, and unemployment rates soared to unprecedented levels: in 1932 the rates for the Rhondda and upper Rhymney valleys stood at well over 40 per cent, in Merthyr 59 per cent and a phenomenal 76 per cent in Pontypridd. This was despite the exodus of some 400,000 persons from the region between 1921 and 1939, making their way to more pros-perous places, a process neatly captured in the expression 'not dead but gone to Slough' (Harris, 1987: 13; Rees and Rees, 1983).

Along with other areas like the north-east of England, Wales gained noto-riety for its depressed and squalid state. The miners' leader Will Paynter records how shocked he was by conditions just a few miles from his native Rhondda during a visit in 1934: 'if the visual evidence of poverty was apparent in the Rhondda, it was ten times more so in the places . . . at the top of the valleys . . . I had not imagined that such poverty-stricken places existed' (Paynter, 1972: 95). When things were at their worst, proposals were made for the wholesale movement of populations out of towns such as Merthyr, Abertillery and Bargoed, now considered to be redundant and beyond saving (G. A. Williams, 1985: 252). In the absence of any such organ-ized policy, many made their own adjustments by leaving individually. Others, however, were fiercely resistant to such suggestions, and fought to ensure their communities had a future (Page, 1977). The crisis was also marked by high levels of industrial conflict, especially surrounding the coal industry, with major strikes and lock-outs throughout the period which left a legacy of bitterness and desire to settle scores. It was a trauma which affected an entire social class, as well as whole communities, and which was widely conceptualized locally as a struggle of the workers with their employers, fought mainly through the Labour movement.

Even more than other parts of Britain, Wales looked to the Labour Party to provide some resolution. Indeed, after the landslide victory of 1945, support for the party actually increased, until it was running at around 60 per cent of the electorate (K. O. Morgan, 1995), and the elections of the 1950s saw Labour winning even more parliamentary seats, as it ousted the remnants of the previous Liberal hegemony. The post-war Labour programme of nationalization and welfare provision seemed ideally suited to, if not grown directly out of, Welsh conditions, and Welsh politicians played prominent parts in its formulation. Aneurin Bevan, the architect of the new National Health Service, openly saw himself as someone who had been formed by a Welsh industrial civilization, and who was responding to its challenges. Labour was to remain the overwhelmingly dominant political party in Wales, especially in the industrial areas, right through to the 1990s, instilling a culture of Labourism which brought certain strengths, of collective solidarity and social consensus, but also imposed characteristic limits on the types of action favoured to deal with problems. The strength of the Labour Party machine created a degree of paternalism and exclusivity in many areas which fostered forms of conservative parochialism.

The traditional economic inheritance still dominated the region in the 1950s. According to an authoritative review of the situation produced as part of a series on industrial Britain, 'south Wales was still basically a nineteenth-century place in a twentieth century world' and its individual industries still wore their nineteenth-century forms, relying upon primitive technologies and outdated skills (Humphrys, 1972: 36). More poetically, the writer Gwyn Thomas excoriated the 'stupid horse-collar of nineteenth-century squalor and inadequacy that still hangs about our neck' (1964). The description of the Swansea valley as 'a lunar landscape of tips, a blitzed landscape of derelict industrial buildings, intersected by a nineteenth-century network of canals, railway lines and sidings' (Hilton, 1967: 33) could have been replicated for many of the other old industrial centres. Like the industrial structure, the communities of south Wales were obsolescent and there was an urgent need for renewal of their social capital. Housing stock in particular was elderly and decayed, its delapidation reflecting the haste with which much of it had been constructed. The image of row after row of identical houses, cramped and lacking basic amenities, strung out along the valley sides, was by now an indelible part of the iconography of Wales. Writing in the early 1980s, Carter and Wheatley (1982: 1) could still say that 'in spite of wartime destruction and postwar development, much of our townscapes and most of our urban problems are an inheritance from the last [i.e. nineteenth] century'. Industry itself was archaic, consisting of too many small units in unsuitable geographic locations. It was evident that, in south Wales at least, the end of an era had been reached, and that the need for modernization was urgent.

WALES BEYOND THE SOUTH

While the problems were concentrated in south Wales, the rest of the country was hardly immune from sharing in them. The expansion of the industrial economy had had its own effects upon the other parts of Wales.

As previously noted, one factor was the way in which population had been sucked south, often, to begin with, in a pattern of seasonal movement, which allowed people to remain engaged with their earlier forms of existence (returning home, for example, at harvest times), but eventually in a more permanent fashion. In the countryside, this resulted in the stripping away of a layer of farm labourers, for whom wage work in the industrial centres brought a better standard of living, leaving a predominance of small family farmers. Thenceforth the loss of young and active people became a routine feature of the Welsh countryside, and rural depopulation and the consequent threat to community viability became a problem in its own right. Wales had shared in the agricultural depression of the late nineteenth century, a period which set in motion the break-up of many of the large estates which had previously dominated the rural scene, and the relative poverty of its geographical and climatic endowment meant that the productivity and living standards of Welsh farmers remained low throughout the first half of the twentieth century. Where there had been earlier development of rural industries, chiefly various forms of mineral working and woollen manufacture, by the 1920s these tended to be either struggling or exhausted. In other words, the Welsh countryside underwent significant ruralization and seemed to be destined to follow its own separate route, allowing it to stay in contact with more traditional values and modes of conduct, and grow progressively further apart from developments in the industrial areas, until they came to be thought of as representing diametrically opposed possibilities.

Rural Wales remained a setting for small villages and market towns, few numbering above a thousand inhabitants, and widely envisaged as the stronghold of truly Welsh culture, remarkably unaffected by the intrusion of modern, industrial, Anglo-Saxon influences. There were many who saw this *lack* of development as the most reassuring sign that, notwithstanding the upheavals going on further south, an essentially Welsh way of life and culture would be able to survive. Meanwhile, in the north, there was something of a parallel pattern, albeit on a considerably smaller scale, to what had occurred at the opposite end of the country. In terms of the amount of attention it commands, even bearing in mind its far lower level of economic development, north Wales is a startlingly poor relation, although its history is locally just as rich and complex. For example, Smith (1984) devotes no more than a couple of pages to a discussion of the area, concluding that, despite having the potential for emergence as an integrated industrial region, the disparate industries of north Wales never managed to jell together sufficiently to bring about 'take-off'. In fact, they were stagnating or well into decline by the start of the twentieth century. Early initiatives in iron, copper, coal and slate had all given rise to localized economic centres, and despite great topographical difficulties, this had encouraged the development of the associated transport connections, especially a flourishing coastal trade, mainly devoted to taking products away from Wales to be worked on elsewhere. The major industries were coal, concentrated in the north-east corner, and slate, further west, each capable at their height of supporting labour forces of around 15,000–16,000 men. However, north Wales never accounted for more than a small fraction of the output of Welsh coal: it achieved its highest production in 1929, at around 3.5 million tonnes. By the late 1950s employment had dwindled to under 8,000, distributed among eight working pits, and producing some 2 million tonnes. By the 1970s only two pits, Bersham and Point of Ayr, survived. Bersham closed in 1986, and Point of Ayr was one of the last Welsh mines to cease production, in 1997.

The most distinctive economic feature of north-west Wales was its unique slate-quarrying industry, giving rise to the formation of such characteristic working-class communities as Corris, Blaenau Ffestioniog, Nantlle and Bethesda. Their rise, and collapse following the bitter industrial confrontations of the first decade of the twentieth century (I. G. Jones, 1981), essentially prefigured what was to take place shortly afterwards in south Wales, and produced very similar long-term problems of economic and social decline. The visible and lasting effects of productive activity upon a landscape and environment are as apparent in north-west Wales as they could possibly be, with entire mountains chiselled away by the workings of teams of men using a combination of handtools and explosives. However, despite their common reliance upon extracting their living from the raw physical environment, a considerable and often insurmountable spatial, social and cultural distance existed between the two sorts of industrial community in north Wales. Metal manufacture has also had a long-term presence in the area, with the existence of a major steelworks in Shotton, on the Dee estuary. Yet to a notable extent, the industrial developments remained superimposed upon rather than superseding an essentially rural foundation. More moderate in scope than those that took place in the southern counties, they did not stimulate the same kinds of population movement, and urban developments in the north were quite limited in scale: apart from the district around Wrexham, which grew into the main population focus, with more than 30,000 inhabitants, the largest settlements contained little more than 10,000 people. Their proximity to the attractions of Snowdonia and the north Wales coast ensured that even the most industrialized of them enjoyed some share in the area's popularity among tourists (R. M. Jones, 1989) and resorts like Rhyl and Llandudno leavened the local economy with an early, and successful, emergence of a service sector. On the whole, the occupational and employment profile of the area has appeared comparatively balanced and diversified; but this has not prevented it from encountering adversity, and its share of deprivation and economic uncertainty. However, it is symptomatic of the largely separate development of north and south Wales that the former is discussed far more often for its significance in the political and cultural life of Wales than for its economic contribution. Geography ensured that communications between the two were never easy, a large expanse of thinly populated hills and mountains intervening between the more developed and populated subregions. The historian Eric Hobsbawm sums up the whole picture in the following terms: as a consequence of these developments 'Wales was utterly transformed; or rather, divided into two culturally (but not linguistically) equal Welsh sectors, which had increasingly little in common with one another except the fact of not being English' (1968: 298).

DIFFERENTIATION AND DIVERSITY

Merfyn Jones, the leading authority on the development of the area, comments that north Wales is 'an elusive notion which lacks the regional coherence and cultural and other associations of "South Wales"; moreover, definitions which might apply to one part of the area are hard to enforce elsewhere' (R. M. Jones, 1989: 101). It is true that the conception of north Wales has not been anything like as elaborated and well-honed as that of the south; nevertheless this is a remark which could quite conceivably be applied even to south Wales, depending on the degree of specificity and precision one is seeking to achieve. Even from the brief account provided above, it is apparent that south Wales is nothing like a completely homogeneous, uniform entity, since it contains within it a number of vital differences and contrasts, which have had significant and lasting social effects. What happens, or has happened, in centres of mining is not identical with the situation of the steel towns, or the ports and docks, although they formed part of an interconnected industrial structure and exerted a strong influence upon one another. The pattern of their development across time differs as much as their distribution across space. Nor does the history of deep-mined coal coincide with that of areas of open-cast mining. In south Wales, there were always notable differences between the steam coal areas of the eastern coalfield, whose development was most closely tied to the export trade, and the anthracite beds of the western parts, which continued for instance to experience reasonable demand throughout the recession of the 1930s (Town, 1978). Likewise, the coal and the steel industries did not necessarily move to the same economic rhythms, and there were important structural differences between them with regard to their organizational and occupational formation. At the very least, the history of the south Wales economy is a tale of two industries, coal and metals, not just about mining.

Inevitably, the general picture which has been outlined conceals further significant differentiation – by area, by occupation, by form of economic life, by local community tradition and, an aspect particular to Wales, by language. The closer we look, the less accurate the general statements will seem to be. There are however certain broad themes that we can take away from the discussion so far, and which will be seen to resurface continually in later examination. Among them we must include: issues of economic and social development; of spatial and social differentiation and its local effects; the nature of communities and community change; transformations of identity and values; and the way in which experiences are absorbed within or wiped out by perceptions of change. The interplay between regional specialization and local differentiations is especially noteworthy, giving rise to host of questions about the definition and nature of particular localities. These may or may not correspond to the socially meaningful communities that people inhabit. Thus within south Wales there is subsumed the identity of the 'Valleys', and also a range of other spatial and social milieux, which might extend down into particular towns, villages or estates, each of which is regarded locally or from outside as constituting a distinct and significant social entity. Humphrys (1972) gives detailed information on six 'subregions' of south Wales, each of which is said to be 'readily identified' as possessing its own industrial character and prospects. Similarly, in north Wales, the characteristics of the slate communities are highly distinctive, and very unlike those of the more historic centres such as Caernarfon or Conwy, or the later seaside resorts, and different again from the remoter rural districts of Anglesey or the Llŷn peninsula. They have features in common with the more rural market towns, yet are set apart by their own peculiarities. Wales is at once an amalgam of all these differences, yet also, ostensibly, bound together by whatever it is that they all share. So much is dependent upon perspective, and a matter of the frame of reference that is adopted, that we need to exercise great caution when claims are made (as they often are) about the degree to which societies in the process of change are undergoing either integration or fragmentation (Nairn, 1977b; Osmond, 1988).

Unfortunately, but necessarily, if we are to grasp the overall movements, we have to reduce much of this variety to simplified accounts and broad generalizations; the rich detail which is produced by the historian or by the local expert or enthusiast has to be synthesized and summarized in our representations and conceptions. By its nature, sociology is engaged in a process of creating or ratifying typifications, models, idealizations. This means there is always a hidden side, and we see only the tip of an iceberg.

South Wales is such a model, as is Rural Wales: we say, it is like this, and try to provide the appropriate and adequately convincing sorts of information and backing to persuade others that this is so; but we do so at the risk of losing sight of the complexity of local variations, and the intricacies of the time scales involved. Recovering these involves doing some deep excavation. As Raymond Williams notes in his extraordinary work of cultural history, *The Country and the City*, the risk we run otherwise is that 'we fall back on modes of thought which seem able to create the permanence without the history' (1975: 347). Those engaged in digging the archaeological trenches will tend inevitably to see the sociological statements as excessively crude; and yet, without the framework of sociological generalization, we may be left only with unstructured particularities. As Runciman has put it, 'not all historians are closet sociologists. But then those who aren't don't explain very much' (1999: 147).

As has been suggested, though sharply contrasting, the different experiences across Wales can be seen within some frames of reference as both interconnected, and shared. From his vantage point as a man whose own biography was rooted in the border country between England and Wales, and between the rural and industrial, Raymond Williams was able to convey such a sense of their underlying unity. He contended (1981) that the differences that had been produced in a process of mutual interaction were being overtaken jointly by events:

> To stand on the Brecon Beacons and look south and then north is to see, on the ground and then very readily in history, the reality of this apparent abstraction. To the south, now, are the dwindling remains of that explosive development of the iron and coal trade. To the north are the depopulated but marginally surviving pastoral hills. It can be seen as simultaneous overdevelopment and underdevelopment, within the turn of the head. But the reality now is that both are old and both marginal.

As the final sentence of this quotation hints, from a wider 'British' perspective, while the most severe manifestations of industrial and economic decline were focused in the south, the whole of Wales presented a considerable challenge to prospects for future development. Everything about it seemed redolent of an episode that was drawing to its close, the phase of economic expansion organized around heavy industry. Wales was more and more evocative of the exhaustion of a once glorious and dramatic past, but without real indications of future promise.

THE 'NEW' WALES

The difficulties faced by all of Wales could be interpreted as the consequence of carrying out a regional role within Britain. By playing to its
comparative advantages, Wales had been storing up future troubles. This is
a view which has been reiterated recently by John Williams, who suggests
that there is no need for more grandiose explanations, since Wales had
performed as

> an integral but peripheral part of a general United Kingdom economy. The
> problem would then be simply that for a crucial period the Welsh role in that
> economy was so obviously best suited to primary production that no sizeable
> stable manufacturing was established. (L. J. Williams, 1989: 17)

With the sudden decline of that role in the context of the larger UK
economy, Wales was designated as a *problem region*, in need of support.
However, it was only one among several areas whose shared fate stemmed
from over-reliance upon the traditional industries: shipbuilding (Clydeside
and the north-east of England); mining (large parts of northern England
and central Scotland); metals/steel (Sheffield); docks (London, Liverpool,
Belfast). All these areas had undergone similar extreme patterns of boom
and slump, and to some extent had to compete now with one another for
attention and resources. Together, they had been formed as part of a period
characterized by 'distinct regional economies and identifiable regional civil
societies' commensurate with the domination of what has been termed
'organized capitalism' (Lash and Urry, 1987: 103). Among the main
economic features attributed to this era are:

> the concentration of capitalist industrial relations within relatively few
> industrial sectors;
> the development of extractive/manufacturing industry as the dominant
> sector with a relatively large number of workers employed;
> the concentration of different industries within different regions, so that there
> are clearly identifiable regional economies;
> the growth of numbers employed in most plants as economies of scale dictate
> growth and expansion within each unit of production. (Lash and Urry, 1987: 3)

In the Welsh case, it is south Wales which conforms most closely to these
criteria, and which thereby constitutes the basis for an identifiable region in
economic terms. The linkage between this region and the rest of Wales is
historical, political and administrative as much as it is purely economic,
and the way in which the south has grown 'away' from much of the rest of
Wales poses a question about the extent to which we are dealing with an
integrated and coherent whole. This becomes one of the defining issues for
Wales during the subsequent period. Within south Wales itself, the 'archaic'

quality of its industrial base set limits to the extent to which it was able to realize fully the economies of scale connected to concentration of employment and larger productive units.

Effectively, the inter-war period had witnessed the transfer of economic momentum from this first wave of industrial districts to centres of newer activities – chiefly the English midlands and south-east. Here the key industrial sectors included vehicle manufacturing, electrical goods and light engineering, chemicals and pharmaceuticals (so-called 'Department II' industries), rather than old-fashioned heavy industry. These industries, more closely related to final consumer demand, seemed to be set upon a virtuous cycle of growth, whereas the older districts of primary production were in danger of being caught in a vicious circle of decline. The result was a widening of regional disparities and the opening up of a 'north–south divide' (or more strictly, the reversal of an earlier north–south separation of the kind described by Mrs Gaskell and others during the nineteenth century). The economic initiative had moved south. During the 1930s, it was necessary for workers from the depressed areas to march from places like Jarrow, and south Wales, to bring home to the population of London and the Home Counties how severely they were suffering. It was this juxtaposition of growth and decline which set the context for the emergence of new forms of state intervention, including regional planning. Although geographically, the position of Wales was somewhat anomalous, economically and socially, it appeared to belong firmly with the north. Not only was it lacking in a significant share of the new manufacturing activity, but it had failed to gain any purchase on the expanding range of commercial services such as insurance, banking and finance which were playing an increasingly central role in the British economy. Despite the lively mercantile activity associated with the heyday of the export trade, there was no commercial centre in Wales able to bear comparison with the weight carried by Edinburgh, or even Glasgow, in the development of Scotland.

What emerged from the roller-coaster experience of Wales during the first half of the twentieth century was a determination to secure greater management of the development process, through the intervention of the state. This had begun already during the 1930s but with the advent of a Labour government it became the central plank in economic policy. It was no longer believed to be adequate to leave things to the unfettered operation of private decisions about investment or innovation. What was required instead was a policy for industry, and for regional development. This extended to the rural areas as well, since it was recognized that there was a vital need for a new approach to agriculture which would stabilize the industry and ensure that in future it would sustain the capacity to feed the population which had been put under threat during wartime, and again this implied extensive state involvement. Overall, there was a new readiness on the part of the state to act as the sponsor for change in the deprived regions, through the vehicle of an active regional policy.

THE REGIONAL POLICY PERSPECTIVE

The contribution which regional policy can make to solving the problems of 'imbalance' between areas has been extremely controversial, both theoretically and politically, and this has led to endless changes of tack in its implementation according to the prevailing currents of opinion and state of the economy. Periods of intensive intervention have been interspersed with spells of inactivity or even outright rejection (McKenna and Thomas, 1988; Hudson and Williams, 1986). There are those purists who adhere to the neoclassical assumption that a free market economy, left to itself, will level out in the long term. In their view, equilibrium is achievable because regional disparities, in wages and labour costs, will act to attract or deflect economic development. Responding to market signals, workers will move to wherever wages are highest, while firms will travel in the opposite direction in search of surplus labour and lower wage bills. Such movements will cease as wage differentials decline, labour supplies are exhausted and costs of congestion rise. Interference with this 'natural' process leads to distortions and inefficiency, making firms pay more than is necessary for labour, and subsidizing jobs in some places at the expense of others, where they might more 'rationally' be located.

Evidently there is some partial truth in this. As we have seen, the economy of Wales has indeed been influenced by very considerable movements of labour, both internally and across its borders, and these movements mostly reflect the 'voluntary' or spontaneous decisions of individuals and families made in the light of their calculations of economic circumstances. Because Wales forms part of a larger, open, economy and society, there are no formal barriers to such movement, and migration flows are an important feature influencing the changing nature of Welsh society. It is not possible to separate the strictly economic significance of migration from its broader social implications. Movements of population have far-reaching social consequences, setting in motion the dynamics of assimilation, integration or exclusion. Whichever direction migration flows have taken, these have been important and recurring issues with relevance for changing group relationships within Wales, and for evolving conceptions of 'Welshness' and belonging, not just in the recent past but over many centuries, and as we will see below, they continue to be actively debated at the present time.

The way in which processes of economic change and the workings of the market are embedded within social relationships of various sorts explains why few are able to remain wholly faithful to the tenets of neoclassical theory, an approach which relies upon an abstract and overly simplistic model of human behaviour. At best, the process of adjustment is inordinately slow. There is huge inertia to be overcome, since people do not find it easy to withdraw from existing social networks and commitments, and usually will do so only when impelled to by the sheer scale of the costs they are incurring. Otherwise, movement reflects the extent to which convenient channels exist – for instance, those with widely recognized skills and qualifications may be able to negotiate mobility more smoothly than those without, although this also depends on the kinds of opportunities that are available at any given time. Factors like age, family ties and responsibilities, educational achievement and attitudes towards risk will all influence people's preparedness to relocate. These social attributes represent advantages or 'hindrances' to free mobility which give rise to different streams of migration, structured according to variations by age, gender and social class. How people respond to inter-regional differences in costs and opportunities is therefore profoundly social, and cannot be reduced to a simple matter of rational individualistic calculation (Rees and Rees, 1983). Firms are just as constrained as individual actors by their existing obligations and by limitations on their knowledge and willingness or capacity to take risks; relocation is a costly and risky undertaking. These are among the many so-called 'market imperfections' which inhibit the operation of any automatic balancing process. While each of them could be regarded in isolation as a mere contingency, it is inconceivable that any actual market situation should be free of their influence. Consequently, the argument that it is best to leave things alone lacks plausibility.

Furthermore, leaving it to the market to produce a solution is also expensive in terms of writing off the sunk costs of existing physical and social capital. Private decisions to move may be made at the collective expense, when the material and social fabric of communities is left to decay. Such social costs borne by the community are not being fully valued within the market, and may be perceived as politically or morally unacceptable. The extent of regional inequality which arose during the 1930s was such that it was felt to be beyond solution at the level of the individual, and in reality, there was neither time nor patience to allow the system to grope its way towards some notional equilibrium. Already during the 1940s a number of government commissions had reported on the need to restore regional balance. They were part of the shift towards state interventionism associated with the rise of Keynesian and Beveridge-inspired approaches to the management of the economy. Wales would be a natural beneficiary of this policy because without corrective action it was so clearly in danger of becoming an economic write-off. There was also a clear political imperative, since the older industrial regions were strongholds of Labour support. This had been evident as long ago as 1910, when, in an early piece of political psephology, J. A. Hobson had noted that: 'Where industrialism is most highly organized and most concentrated, upon the great coalfields of Lancashire and Yorkshire, Derbyshire, Northumberland and Durham, *not to mention South Wales*, the greatest intensity of Liberalism and Labourism prevails' (Hobson, 1910; emphasis added).

There had been experiments in such state managerialism during the 1930s, and the necessity to act in wartime had provided some valuable practical experience. The decades after the war were a time when it was felt that governments *could* plan the way out of regional difficulties and bring about a more balanced national configuration. The keynote themes in doing so were modernization, diversification and rationalization. Putting these into effect was tantamount to a strategy of helping to bring the 'organization' of capitalism in Wales towards completion, by speeding up outcomes which sooner or later would have had to happen anyway. In line with this conception, Graham Humphrys described his examination of what took place in south Wales as a 'valuable case study of the effects of such things as rationalisation, increasing economies of scale, government involvement, structural change and the shift towards service industry' (1972: 35). In other words, it contained all the ingredients of prevailing wisdom – namely, the removal of the 'dead wood' of small, and uneconomic enterprises and the reorganization of the economy around a much smaller number of larger and more efficient units.

Obviously this had special application to the main industries: nationalization, and the transfer of control into the hands of government, with the explicit support of the trades unions, enabled a clinical execution of this strategy. In 1947 the mines were taken into public ownership; steel followed shortly after in 1949, was denationalized in 1953 and taken back into state ownership in 1967. By 1970, the number of pits in south Wales under the control of the National Coal Board had been reduced from around 300 to 50. Fifty small steel and tinplate works had been condensed to six, and three-quarters of steel production was now coming from just two plants. These measures were justified in terms of competitiveness and cost reduction, but in each case, closure and reorganization was hugely consequential for the immediate workforce and for the communities to which it belonged. The goal was to make the economy more viable in the long term by raising productivity and refocusing it around manufacturing industry, but it was quickly apparent that this involved a severe cost in term of jobs; a more productive workforce was invariably a smaller workforce, so the run-down in traditional forms of employment continued more or less unabated. The number of miners in south Wales fell from 110,000 in 1945 to 27,000 in 1978. The first symptoms of what was to become an increasingly familiar story of 'jobless growth' could be seen: for example, an investment of £38 million in the Margam steelworks in 1968–70 brought about a loss of 2,000 jobs. The promise was that, once this 'shake-out' was complete, then there would be greater security for those who managed to remain in the industries. Rather than their bloated and antiquated shape they would have achieved a more streamlined, modern, profile. It was part and parcel of this approach that great hopes should be attached to new 'giant' units involving the introduction of high levels of technology – super-pits and integrated steel plants.

The expectation was that the contraction of the coal and steel industries would be complete by the mid-1970s, and things would be set then for a regional boom. This however was conditional upon continuing success in attracting new jobs, in new industries, to Wales. Regional policy was intended to enable this by providing funding for infrastructural developments that would make deprived regions more attractive to investors, and by helping where possible to redirect 'growth' industries from areas which were already doing well. Government had at its disposal a variety of instruments to assist in achieving this. A precedent had been set before the war, with the creation of industrial estates supported by a Special Areas Fund. One of the earliest was at Treforest, opened in 1937, and the provision of subsidized sites and factory buildings subsequently became one of the main inducements for inward investment. Wartime dispersal of industries such as munitions and vehicle parts had shown that new kinds of work could be introduced successfully into previously neglected areas (Lovering, 1983b). After the war, a number of these factories continued to operate, and others became available to businesses which were looking for premises in which to expand. A range of financial incentives – grants, tax and rent rebates, investment allowances, and payments linked to the numbers of jobs created – could be offered to firms, while disincentives and controls such as the use of Office Development Permits and Industrial Development Certificates could be used to discourage further expansion in southern Britain. More directly, government also engaged in the decentralization of some of its own activities: Wales gained new employment with the transfer of the Royal Mint to Llantrisant, and the Driver and Vehicle Licensing Centre (DVLC) to Swansea; Newport acquired offices to issue passports and to process government statistics.

Such measures were subject to continual revision and modification, and the map of areas deemed to be worthy of 'assistance' was constantly redefined (McKenna and Thomas, 1988). There were times during which the whole of Wales qualified for some form of regional assistance, whereas at others policy was 'targeted' to more narrowly defined localities, identified by indicators like local unemployment figures. Such adjustments were related to the general performance of the UK economy, levels of unemployment and shifts in government agenda. Regional policy as such was phased out progressively by the Conservative governments of the 1960s, and eventually became overtaken by European policies following Britain's membership of the European Community.

Wales gained considerably from these activities. Indeed, the combined effect of nationalization of its key industries, government involvement in shaping the distribution of private industry and the expansion of public-sector employment was so influential that it led to south Wales being described classically as 'the closest to a nationalised region that existed in Britain' (Humphrys, 1972: 64). The vast majority of employees, either directly or indirectly, owed their job to the intervention of the state. Having apparently taken responsibility for the region's future, successive governments met with an appreciable degree of success. The growth of manufacturing employment at least kept pace roughly with the loss of jobs in the traditional sectors, so that manufacturing employees eventually overtook the numbers working in coal and steel. By 1968 the total manufacturing workforce in south Wales stood at just under 195,000, of which metal manufactures accounted for 69,000. There was particular growth in the vehicle and light engineering sectors, with examples like Hoover in Merthyr, Prestcold in Swansea (a short-lived success, but the plant was then taken over by Ford) and British Leyland in Llanelli. Even so, there was some way to go before the composition of the labour force in Wales matched that of other regions: employment in coal and steel in 1968 still amounted to a fifth of the south Wales labour force, compared to a UK figure of less than 5 per cent. Total manufacturing employment, including metals, at 39 per cent of the labour force, was just above the national rate. There had also been growth in services, the employment figure for south Wales reaching 203,396; however, only a tiny proportion of these, just over 6,000, were working in the financial service sector.

Before long Wales – especially south Wales – was being hailed as a prime example of successful regional policy. In what looks like a well-orchestrated publicity campaign, the *Guardian* newspaper (2 March 1963) described how,

> of all the depressed areas Wales has been by far the most successful since the war in attracting new industries and in creating for itself a new economic base capable of sustained growth in the future . . . the long-term outlook is more hopeful than it has been for a half a century . . .

while on the same day a leader in *The Times* praised Wales as a 'great success story' that set an example to other parts of the country. Academics joined in this celebration of renewal. In a book with the positively charged title *The Welsh Economy: Studies in Expansion*, Brinley Thomas welcomed an end to the 'creeping paralysis' of mass unemployment and anticipated instead the 'growing pains associated with technical progress' (1962: 197). Humphrys's immensely detailed discussion of south Wales sounded a number of important cautionary notes, but nevertheless accepted that the 'inertia and gloom of the pre-war depression have disappeared' from a Wales modernized beyond recognition into a 'model of rejuvenation'. The most significant single symptom of this change was that unemployment had fallen from the dramatic heights of the inter-war period to around 4 per cent.

At the time when he was writing, Humphrys believed the transformation he was documenting was almost complete. The economic base had been rearranged, long-standing defects had been addressed, and Wales was now possessed by a spirit of optimism. There was much talk of the 'new Wales' (Humphreys, 1995), symbolized by such physical features as the Severn Bridge, M4 motorway, Heads of the Valleys road and new town developments in Cwmbran, Llantrisant and Newtown. By 1970 it could be claimed that 'virtually everyone who is employed in South Wales is now in a new job, either a job which did not exist in 1945, or which did exist but in a different location' (Humphrys, 1972: 71). These economic changes of course were the underpinning to more extensive social alterations, with far-reaching consequences; but it took a while before analysts woke up to the implications of such a fundamental shift in the nature of Welsh society. By the late 1960s, a modernized Wales could be hailed for having left its past behind. Unfortunately, this was just when the first signs began to appear of 'an array of interconnected processes which disorganize or literally deconstruct social and political life in modern Britain' (Lash and Urry, 1987: 99). Like Britain, Wales was once again on the move.

3

'An Ideal Research Site': Wales and the Problem of Development

What happened in Wales during the 1950s and 1960s has to be put in the context of wider processes of economic and social change operating on a national and international scale, or what at the time appeared to be an almost unlimited prospect of 'growth' and social improvement for the industrial nations. This was the 'golden age' of the long boom (Hobsbawm, 1994), a worldwide phenomenon stimulated by making good the destruction of wartime, and carried forward by increasing production and mass consumption through the extension of what came to be known as Fordist principles throughout manufacturing industry. The central features of this phase of development can be summarized as follows: (i) mass production of durable consumer goods, (ii) mass consumption, (iii) state management of the economy and state provision of a wide range of collective means of consumption and general conditions of production, (iv) major transfers of workers from peripheral countries and areas, and of women, into the modern branches of industrial and service-sector employment (Dunford and Perrons, 1983: 355). The crisis of the 1930s represented the hesitant, and extremely painful, emergence of this new economic order, which came into its own after the war. Manufacturing output increased fourfold, and world trade in manufactures by a factor of ten, between the 1950s and 1970s (Hobsbawm, 1994: 261), with most of the benefits accruing to the 'advanced' industrial economies of North America and Western Europe. As Hobsbawm comments, nothing like it had been seen before, and solving problems seemed so much easier to contemplate in conditions of general optimism and economic buoyancy. It was a time when theories of 'trickle-down' growth, and the diffusion of expansion and modernity from better off to poorer areas and social groups seemed to carry considerable weight, both internationally and on the domestic scene (Day, 1980). The assumptions of regional policy sat easily within these circumstances: the state, acting on behalf of the general social interest, merely needed to give a helping hand to the process – which, as we have seen, was done in Britain with the minimum of compulsion and the maximum of exhortation and inducement (lots of juicy carrots, few sticks).

Confidence in the ability of regional planning and state intervention to bring about the necessary modernization and revitalization of Wales provided a temporarily unproblematic frame of reference for economic and social policy. Difficulties would be tackled within the framework of general British policy-making, and the perspective of national regeneration and development. In the long run, it was hoped, regional policy would be self-liquidating, since the diversion of growth industries to assisted areas would eventually establish the basis for self-sustaining growth, and thus eradicate the regional problem altogether (McKenna and Thomas, 1988: 283). In other words, planning and active state involvement would help speed up and smooth out the underlying self-balancing tendencies assumed by liberal and neoclassical approaches to the regional question. Realistically, the implementation of such a policy was concerned as much with relieving expanding areas like south-east England from the pressures of 'excess' growth as it was with raising living standards in the deprived regions, but at least this ought to bring benefits to outlying areas. There was a strictly limited sense of how radically society might need to be changed to deal with its underlying problems: the talk was in terms of creating additional jobs, via the spread of new industries and types of employment. Dev-elopment was viewed as essentially an economic question, with almost accidental consequences for social structure. As far as possible, the objective was to sustain existing communities and patterns of life, lifting them all together on the incoming tide of prosperity. This would enable the satisfac-tion of the most insistent demands, from the most organized and needy (or vociferous) sections of the population, while ensuring that everyone shared to some degree in the general well-being. With the attainment of full employment over a sustained period, it was even plausible to contemplate the elimination of poverty. It was certainly possible to forget that it existed.

Despite quite far-reaching but often unnoticed social and cultural changes which accompanied these influences, the basic nature of industrial society seemed secure. There would continue to be a strong and substantial working class, though focused more in engineering and 'metal-bashing' jobs and in technologically advanced sectors like chemicals than in the old heavy indus-tries. If anything, with the backing of full employment, this class could face the future with greater self-assurance and engage more effectively in its long-term project for social reform and equalization (Goldthorpe et al., 1969). With the emergence of new types of manufacturing employment, and a shortage of labour, women would play a larger part in the workplace than in the past, and their incomes would help lift standards of living. At the same time (and somewhat inconsistently) with the growth of professional, tech-nical and managerial employment, the middle classes would see expanding opportunity. Following the introduction of the tripartite system in 1944 and the extension of the school-leaving age, educational standards were rising, and there was some increase in general chances for social mobility. Under the twin inspirations of Keynes and Beveridge, the welfare state and the mixed economy seemed capable of providing an adequate safety net for the disadvantaged. Altogether, conditions were ripe for the promulgation of influential theses relating to the affluent society (Zweig, 1952), 'embourgeoisement' (Goldthorpe et al., 1969), and the withering away of class (Westergaard, 1965). A formidable social consensus formed around a rather narrow conception of social engineering, which was essentially economistic in tone, with widespread acceptance of Fabian beliefs in gradual and progressive social amelioration underpinned by a benign state. There was no reason to think that Wales would not share in these trends, as indeed for a time it did.

THE LIMITS OF REGIONAL PLANNING

Although there were significant forerunners, sociology really enters the scene in Wales with a mounting critical response to, and critique of, what had been achieved in the post-war 'settlement'. There had been earlier reservations. Given the enormous part played by regional assistance, the *Guardian*'s view that Wales had been able to create change 'for itself' was puzzling, and there was bound to be a worry about what would happen if, for whatever reason, the state withdrew its sponsorship. Yet suggestions as to how this could be avoided seemed to amount to little beyond aspirations for more of the same. For example, Humphrys concluded his book on the modernization of south Wales with a plea for better and more coherent planning (Humphrys, 1972). The closest Wales came to achieving this was the publication in 1967 of the Welsh Office document *Wales: The Way Ahead*, which for many epitomized the limitations of indicative planning, setting an unfortunate precedent for several subsequent reports that were equally long on hope and weak on delivery (for example, IWA, 1993). Drawn up in conditions of semi-secrecy within the newly formed Welsh Office by civil servants who seemed reluctant to consult with informed opinion, the plan was generally felt to be ineffectual and duly attracted heavy criticism from the bulk of expert commentators, including the government's appointed advisory body, the Welsh Economic Council. Rees (1980: 198–9) describes it as a highly conventional piece of analysis, which played down the persistence of social and spatial inequalities within Wales by treating them as residual problems, consisting of no more than isolated pockets of disadvantage left behind by general progress, largely owing, it was suggested, to the region's own inadequacies. The report failed to relate its forecasts adequately to the changing nature of the Welsh economy. In particular, by simply extrapolating current trends and assuming the continuation of existing regional policies, it seriously underestimated the number of jobs which needed to be created in Wales to maintain full employment. The report's deficiencies stimulated a reaction from Plaid Cymru, the Welsh national party, which 'turned regional economics inside out' (Clavel, 1983: 108) by producing its own alternative document *An Economic Plan for Wales* (1970). This used similarly orthodox methods, but rested on quite different premises, namely the importance of protecting existing Welsh communities and retaining population in Wales. The chairman of Plaid Cymru at the time commented that

> the government wants to maximise the mobility of labour to solve economic problems which they see from the point of view of Britain as a whole. We on the other hand want stable communities in Wales and so we are against labour mobility and in favour of the direction of industry. We want to limit the migration of Welshmen (sic) out of Wales. (Clavel, 1983: 13)

The lesson which many took from this debacle was the importance of relating planning issues to 'the economic and political imperatives which underpin them and which derive from the particularities of the way in which British society is currently organised' (Rees, 1980: 198). At the political level, Plaid Cymru had managed to mount a very effective challenge which exposed the government's pretence of making a purely objective, technical assessment of economic and social needs through the planning process. Clavel analyses the whole episode as an example of 'oppositional planning', highlighting the growth of territorial consciousness in Wales and the inability of government to respond to it (Clavel, 1983).

As was the case with the rest of Britain, it is possible to characterize this period retrospectively as a time of undue complacency, a wasted decade (Massey, 1984: 131) during which genuine advances in material prosperity encouraged people to overestimate the extent to which the economy could be managed indefinitely in ways that would ensure the ability to meet welfare needs and bring about sustained social progress. By the end of the 1960s, however, there were mounting signs that this confidence was misplaced.

Britain's economic performance compared rather poorly with its international competitors and its share of world trade and manufacturing exports was in decline (Gamble, 1981). Demands made on government expenditure, including the costs of regional interventions and transfer payments to support the worse-off areas, were beginning to escalate but attempts to cut back on them risked offending heightened expectations about what the state could achieve. Low levels of economic growth, pockets of persistent unemployment and a sense of the inability of redistributive policies to bring about real social levelling presaged the 'rediscovery' of poverty and the exploration of new forms of social inequality, which became key socio-logical themes for the 1970s and 1980s (Westergaard and Resler, 1975; Robbins et al., 1981). All this found echoes in Wales.

By the early 1970s the British economy had entered a decisive new phase. Aggravated by the shock of an unprecedented increase in the cost of oil, it was a time of mounting inflation, wage pressures and growing social conflict. The challenge was no longer to distribute the benefits of growth but to cope with the effects of dramatic *de-industrialization* as British manu-facturing industry proved unable to withstand overseas competition (Blackaby, 1979; Martin and Rowthorn, 1986). This stimulated the realiza-tion that, despite surface appearances of social and economic improvement, Wales was still confronted by deep-seated structural weaknesses, and that the modernization which had been brought about, at considerable indi-vidual and social cost, was still incapable of coping with the changing demands of economic survival. The failure of the post-war consensus to deliver all that it had promised led to a considerable theoretical reorienta-tion, which challenged the depiction of Wales as a region which just happened to be bedevilled by the legacy of a particular kind of economic and social history, and suggested instead the need for a more systematic explanation of its situation. This was associated with the rise of a wider intellectual challenge to prevailing notions of how 'regional' issues should be interpreted and dealt with.

NEW CONCEPTIONS

An example of the changing climate of opinion is found in the work of Stuart Holland who, in a couple of influential books (Holland, 1976a, 1976b), introduced ideas and concepts drawn from sources in European socialist and Marxist thought, and from theories of world development, into the examination of regional issues. Holland attacked the orthodox model of regional balance, which appeared to deny the reality of any entrenched regional problem. Drawing on experience from across Europe, Holland had determined that indicative planning had little impact on leading capitalist firms. Regional incentives tended to be insignificant in relation to the other costs and benefits which dominated their calculations. In any case, plans for problem regions took too long to prepare, and had not been effective in establishing regional development as a national priority (Holland, 1976b). Nowhere did he consider regional policy to provide an adequate response to the needs of regional development. Instead he claimed that imbalances were integral to the nature of capitalist societies, and that their current configuration could be understood as the consequence of the 'mesoeconomic' role of large, multi-product, multinational corporations which tended to be located in, and so favour, the more developed areas. Responding to their growing economic domination required forms of analysis and political action that would go beyond the accepted limits of liberal capitalism.

It was characteristic of this phase of reorientation that Holland should highlight the need to relate regional outcomes to the activities of firms, and to the ways in which they were organized, and also that he should emphasize the significance of placing regional questions within a broader analysis of the nature of capitalism as an economic and social order. In both these respects, his arguments implied the need for a more sociological approach which would pay attention to the social relationships and forms of organization embedded in the prevailing political economy, an aspect which hitherto had been missing from most analyses of Wales. It was this focus which provided a point of entry for a new generation of researchers whose background lay in the fields of geography, planning and sociology, and in the expansion of British social science during the 1960s. Holland was also typical in drawing upon lessons from other parts of Europe and the world to make sense of British conditions, and again there was a similar impetus within Wales.

Holland's arguments elicited an extremely hostile response from the doyen of Welsh regional economists, Brinley Thomas, who wrote in a review that it would be better simply to accept that differences in regional rates of growth were a necessary feature of development, whether capitalist or not, due to disparities in factor endowments, market imperfections and differences in relative stages of economic development. Holland's analysis was dismissed as 'a purely political argument resting on Marxist premises. Confirmed believers will swallow it. Those who are not believers will regard it as stale ideology warmed up to taste like economic analysis' (*Times Higher Educational Supplement* 20 August 1976). By now, however, Thomas was swimming against an increasingly powerful tide of criticism which was rejecting established neoclassical tenets on the grounds that, contrary to their avowed intentions, they served to maintain a status quo which perpetuated rather than corrected regional inequality. More radical solutions seemed to be required to bring about the economic and social transformation that so far had failed to materialize.

Conventional regional economics, and the closely affiliated branch of geography which dealt with the location of industry, came in for attack from a panoply of critics, including Massey, who accused it of exuding a spirit of 'cheery empiricism' unencumbered by serious theoretical reflection or attention to conceptualization (Massey, 1984: 12) and Cooke, for whom it displayed an uncritical and unreflective attachment to functionalist and reductionist modes of theorising (Cooke, 1983a). The latter noted how planning was invoked principally to 'clean up market failures and secure a degree of spatial orderliness to the disorderly forces of the market-place' and concluded that the impact of such action was essentially marginal (1983a: 25). In other words, it left the basic framework of the social order unaffected, and did nothing to bring about significant long-term change. Likewise, Rees and Lambert (1985: 6–7) attribute to academic examinations of state intervention a poverty of theoretical analysis whereby

> there is no attempt to formulate the wider role of the state in British society. Ironically then the development of *policy* is presented without serious reference to *politics* [emphases supplied]. The analysis ignores the complex determinations of state intervention out of conflicts of interest between social groupings with varying political power and access to the policy-making process.

Each of the authors mentioned was to make important contributions to the investigation of Wales. All take as their point of departure the imperative to remedy the weaknesses of orthodox social and political analyses of supposedly 'regional' matters by developing alternative approaches.

The intervention of Holland and numerous others into the field of regional analysis around this time signalled the search for a new paradigm which would deepen the understanding of spatial inequalities and provide a basis for more profound policy solutions. A shift in perspective is indicated by the changing use of language, incorporating new concepts and frames of reference such as 'uneven development', economic and social 'restructuring' and, with a greater spin on the political aspects of relationships, 'internal colonialism' (Day, 1980). More generally, we can see the growing influence of conceptions of political economy linked to a wider ascendancy in social science of radical perspectives derived from Weber and Marx, supplanting the earlier dominance of British empiricism and Parsonian structural-functionalism. Though these new influences encompassed a great diversity of approaches and theoretical stances, they have in common a move towards a more holistic perspective in which the emphasis is not placed solely upon a narrow set of 'economic' variables but embraces their social, political and cultural concomitants as well. In differing ways, they direct attention towards the importance, which has been basic to sociology, of examining the characteristics of the whole social system. The influence of such ideas is evident in the theoretical statement which accompanied the formation of a Wales Regionalism Group among members of the Planning Department at UWIST in 1980. Proclaiming that it accepted 'neither the division of knowledge into fragmentary disciplines nor the immutability of existing social relations', the group offered assistance to those who sought to 'transcend, in collective ways' the inequalities result-ing from uneven development. To this end, Wales provided the locale where 'for reasons of concern and curiosity as well as convenience, the group tries to observe the effects of processes of change which are largely unconstrained by geographical space'.

INTEGRATION OR INEQUALITY?

The publication in 1980 of a volume on *Poverty and Social Inequality in Wales* edited by Rees and Rees played a valuable role in pulling together some of the emerging work, making explicit a focus on Wales and its continuing problems, and encouraging contributors to examine competing explana-tions for why these were so persistent (Rees and Rees, 1980). At a time when Britain was undergoing a rapid and accelerating collapse in manufac-turing employment, the depth of which was not paralleled anywhere else in the world (Martin and Rowthorn, 1986), social researchers in Wales could hardly fail to register some of its effects closer to hand. Between 1966 and 1984, there was a 35 per cent decrease in the labour force in British manu-facturing, involving the loss of three million jobs. Half of this loss occurred between 1979 and 1984. Such was the gravity of the crisis that it constituted a pervasive problem throughout all regions of Britain, including the previ-ously impervious midlands and south-east (especially London), and thereby appeared to undermine the entire rationale for regional policy (K. Morgan, 1986). There was no justification for directing help to specific areas if the entire economy seemed on the brink of collapse. Yet although Wales was no longer special in experiencing such economic difficulties, it was certainly not exempt from taking its share of them. In the two decades up to 1986, 125,000 out of 331,000 manufacturing jobs disappeared, a 38 per cent loss whose suddenness is graphically illustrated in the near-vertical plummet of the figures for manufacturing employment in Wales (McNabb and Shorey, 1988: 119). Not only were there massive losses in the industries that had 'traditionally formed the very basis and character of the Welsh industrial economy and the whole structure of the region' (McNabb and Shorey, 1988: 121) with losses of 50,000 jobs in steel making a particularly hefty contribution, but Wales was also witnessing the run-down of much of the new manufacturing base that had been so painstakingly established during the post-war years, and the demise of many of the young enter-prises which had been expected to safeguard the Welsh economy for years ahead. It was not long before a leading comedy programme of the period, *Not the Nine O'Clock News*, could parody a 'Made In Wales' advertising campaign by setting a long list of company names to the tune of 'Men of

Harlech' with the caption 'Failed in Wales'. As ever, the local effects could be devastating, as key employers shed labour at unprecedented rates. The return of substantial and rising levels of unemployment was the most obvious effect, but there were many other major implications which took time to work their way fully into the consciousness of social analysts, including the shift towards part-time employment, the associated deskilling of the workforce and the decisive feminization of the Welsh labour force. It also took a while to assimilate the crucial lesson (Martin and Rowthorn, 1986: p. xvii) that de-industrialization was 'not a single or mono-causal economic mechanism with undifferentiated social or geographical consequences, but rather a diverse set of complex processes affecting different social groups and different localities in different ways'.

Prevalent assertions about the possibility and likelihood of economic convergence occurring between regions had tended to carry a much broader sociological implication, that removal of the regional problem would ensure greater or total integration and assimilation of local populations into the wider society. Conventional economics and political science both supported this conclusion (Day, 1980). As expressed by one commentator, 'if one theme dominates Western policy and theory towards regions, it is the inexorable disappearance of local territorial consciousness and organization' (Clavel, 1983: 39). There was a strong undercurrent of rather crude economic determinism in this view. It was as if, without tangible differences in material quality of life, there would be no particular reason to anticipate the persistence of other aspects of 'regional' differentiation – such as variations in cultural traits, political loyalties and so on. Helped along by appropriate policies, over time regions would lose their identities within the context of prevailing national patterns. Questions of place, territory and local belonging would fade into the background, compared to the remaining unfinished business of variations around such 'national' categories as class and gender. A stark expression of this dominant view was advanced by Westergaard, who contended that in modern societies identification with class transcended loyalty to place (Westergaard, 1965) and therefore that, while differences undoubtedly existed between the various parts of Britain, 'it is the horizontal divisions of class, not the vertical divisions of region, which are the crucial breaks in British society by criteria of welfare, opportunity and influence' (Westergaard and Resler, 1975: 355–6).

Obviously this raises a whole bundle of questions to do with the priority attached to class, and economic matters, over other dimensions of social organization, the way in which nation-states are formed and held together, and the role in modern societies of identity politics and social movements concerned with local, regional and national aspirations. It also sets up a questionable opposition between 'class' and 'regional' characteristics which needs to be examined. Indeed, following the loss of confidence in the older forms of regional analysis, this was precisely the agenda which began to unfold. As concern increased about the re-emergence of patterns of regional disparity, and as this was accompanied by a new restiveness about the extent of regional and national autonomy, it became obvious that there were some major gaps in prevailing theoretical approaches. Clavel (1983: 52) for one noted how the inability of both liberal and more radical theories to make space for territorial movements and variations meant that analysts were forced back on *ad hoc* explanations, so that 'Conceptually, local experience is relegated to reports of case studies, incorporated through ad hoc theorizing only loosely connected with the main theory, and given inconsistent, pragmatic treatment in policy'.

Contrary to Westergaard's position, and predictions, the de-industrialization of Britain during the 1970s sharpened old divisions between north and south while opening up new rifts between urban and rural locations. Far from experiencing growing homogeneity, the country seemed to be fragmenting, and there was a reawakened interest in issues to do with spatial and geographical differentiation and division (Massey and Meegan, 1982; Martin and Rowthorn, 1986). Furthermore, there was evidence from many directions that this was not a process peculiar to Britain; new forms of regional awareness and action were appearing throughout the developed world (Esman 1977). The re-emergence of significant regional differences and interests in the context of new economic pressures showed that the attempt at a technocratic and conflict-free management of spatial inequalities had failed. Wales in particular was still relatively poorly off. Even while it had been enjoying historically low levels of unemployment, there had been a nagging discontent that it was not sharing fully in the good fortune of other areas. Now, with the down-turn in prospects, there was a growing sentiment that somehow or other Wales still suffered from inbuilt disadvantages which were dragging its performance downwards. A number of substantial commentaries from outside Wales lent support to this view, and thereby encouraged local researchers to feel that their preoccupations were not parochial after all, but could teach some valuable social scientific lessons to others. In terms of its impact within Wales, the most important of these was undoubtedly Michael Hechter's work on internal colonialism, which used Wales along with Scotland and Ireland to develop an argument about the relationship between economic and social development and the resurgence of nationalism.

THE QUESTION OF INTERNAL COLONIALISM

As an American sociologist, Hechter came to the question of Wales and the other 'Celtic' countries from the perspective of a need to account for racism and ethnic conflict as it affected black Americans. However, in his own words, the very different setting of Britain provided him with an 'ideal research site from which to explain some fundamental issues in sociological theory' (Hechter, 1975: p. xiv). His work on Wales was therefore strongly theoretical in orientation, rather than driven by any personal or institutional commitment. It revolved around the contest between two rival models of explanation for the way in which ethnic differences persisted even within the boundaries of advanced industrial societies. The two models were labelled as diffusionism and internal colonialism. The former is an approach which generalizes many of the elements already uncovered within the orthodox response to regionalism. It adheres to the view that there is an evolutionary tendency within societies for the degree of economic, political and cultural integration to increase, as they progress towards homogenization. This position had the backing of the vast bulk of the literature produced during the 1950s and 1960s in conjunction with theories of modernization and westernization, and was strongly endorsed by key aspects of American structural-functionalism (Parsons, 1966; Kerr et al., 1964). Hence, the process of diffusion was believed to operate globally, as well as within the limits of single societies. Effectively, within any coherent system of social relations, a set of dominant influences was regarded as spreading outwards from a centre towards the periphery. In economic terms, this meant that regional differences would be progressively muted, while cultural variations would diminish in the face of assimilation and acceptance of dominant social norms. Among the differences which would be expected to disappear were so-called 'primordial' attachments to ethnicity, locality, and nation (Hechter, 1975: 313). In Parsonian terms, these were forms of 'particularism' which would tend to be displaced by the increasing prevalence of universalistic codes and values. In fact, it would be true to say that, for much of conventional sociology, the loss or suppression of such 'differences' has been a leading aspect of what it means to belong to a 'society'; the rise of functional distinctions representing positions within a single system of relations, such as those of social class, was said to leave no room for these more primitive loyalties. Historically, the creation of national societies had involved the assimilation of such differences into shared homogeneity (see, for example, Weber, 1979; Smith, 1991).

In challenging this perspective, Hechter's analysis ranges well beyond consideration of just the economic aspects of social organization. In fact, the discussion is more centrally concerned with issues of culture, ethnicity and politics. Nevertheless it contains a set of statements about the economic trajectory followed by Wales, and the other Celtic 'peripheries', which was highly influential in helping to change the way in which many viewed both the history and contemporary situation of Wales. *Internal Colonialism* was a solid and ambitious piece of academic investigation, in which a systematic examination of Wales and its historical development came replete with an extensive scholarly apparatus of footnotes and some relatively sophisticated statistical analyses. It showed how sociologists could take Wales seriously, and gave rise to a quite heated debate about its accuracy and relevance. For a time the notion of Wales as an internal colony gained currency among politicians and activists, as well as among academics (P. Williams, 1977; Evans, 1974), just as in Scotland, the idea of a colonial status echoed many of the political concerns of the time (McCrone, 1992: 55).

The two models propounded by Hechter constitute crucially different ways of making sense of the relationship between Wales and the wider British economy and state. Within the diffusionist framework, there was an expectation that different areas within a cohesive national territory should experience substantially equal rates of social and economic development. Where there were significant differences, then the problem was thought to lie with lack of integration and the failure of developmental impulses to flow freely to all places. The answer would be to ensure closer ties with the centre; regional policy would make its contribution to this, by bringing areas under the grip of a common set of aims and programmes. There are obvious affinities between this view, and the neoclassical framework in which the logic of the market is seen as tending to level out differences as it progresses towards equilibrium. This type of diagnosis was associated with frequent references to the remote, malintegrated, even 'backward' nature of the deprived areas. More generally, the model relied upon a contrast between 'traditional' and 'modern' sectors. The kind of analysis which attributes the failures of Third World development to the backwardness and need to modernize of the less developed countries (LDCs) could be extended readily enough to less 'developed' parts of a given society, with the same implication: that their problems were explicable largely in terms of their own characteristics and defects. To overcome them, they needed to be 'modernized' to become more like the advanced areas and societies.

By contrast, the internal colony approach attributes the persistent under-performance of a particular region to the relationship it has with an external, dominant, partner. Joined together in a way which ensures that the interests of the latter take precedence, the weaker partner finds itself driven by external considerations to play an 'instrumental' role in meeting those interests; it is fixed in a dependent, exploitative situation. What this means is that its development will tend to be complementary to that of the 'centre', and in practice this usually means concentrating on certain narrow activities at the expense of a more rounded development. In effect, peripheral products are exported to the more favoured areas, and this will be reflected in their spatial as well as economic organization – the layout of transport routes and urban centres, for example, will be shaped by export activity. In the British case, the majority of manufacturing, processing and distribution would take place in the English metropolis, with the outer peripheries specializing in labour-intensive primary production (Hechter, 1975: 148). Under such conditions, the scene is set for the exacerbation of differences and worsening of inequalities; thus Hechter predicts that 'the 'backwardness' of peripheral groups can only be aggravated by the systematic increase in transactions with the core' (1975: 32). According to this line of argument, the prolongation of regional disparities constitutes a 'failure' of British national development, that eventually brings about resistance and opposition from the periphery. Hence Hechter links this underlying colonial situation to the survival, and reawakening, of regional and nationalist sentiments and identities. In Britain, the end result of internal colonialism is Celtic nationalism.

Hechter puts the contrast as follows (Hechter, 1975: 343–4): according to diffusionism, 'heightened core–periphery interaction and ongoing structural differentiation, should encourage the development of regional economic equality, national cultural homogenity, and a national politics dominated by functional, rather than status group, orientations to political action' whereas

> the internal colonial model posits altogether different consequences . . . structural inequalities should increase, as the periphery develops in a dependent mode . . . the bulk of the peripheral population will be confined to subordinate positions in the social structure. In sum, a cultural division of labour will tend to arise.

Developing this insight, Hechter suggested that there were a number of 'significant analogies' between the condition of Wales, and the rest of the Celtic fringe, and the experience of LDCs within the world system. Even when the level of industrialization was controlled for, his analysis indicated that Wales had suffered a persistent shortfall in income levels compared to England, over many decades. It was not possible to explain this as resulting from any lack of economic integration, since England and Wales had been part of the same economy for centuries; rather it appeared that there was some blockage or deliberate interference with the diffusion of economic advantages from the centre. His own explanation was that Wales and England were in an essentially colonial relation, the benefits from which went to England. Profits from Welsh industry were exported along with Welsh labour and raw materials, and political measures were designed to ensure that this continued. As well as its political content, there was a heavy cultural overlay to Hechter's theory of colonialism. Drawing on the historic record of European colonial development and expansionism, he envisaged colonialism as involving contact between culturally distinct groups, bolstered by dogmatic assertions of racial, ethnic or cultural superiority. These distinctions would be maintained through processes of ethnic stereotyping and cultural oppression within a cultural division of labour. Wales, like other colonies, was therefore a victim of institutional racism (1975: 133).

CRITICAL ASSESSMENT

Obviously there is much here which needs to be unpacked, but for the present the significant point is that Hechter's intervention had important theoretical as well as political consequences. The argument locates Wales within a framework of theories of development in which the key points of reference are Wallerstein's world systems theory (Wallerstein, 1974) and a number of Latin American studies (Gonzales-Casanova, 1965; Furtado, 1967; Dos Santos, 1970). This had the merit of lifting Wales out of the limited terrain of regional analysis and inserting it into the mainstream of sociological debate (Day, 1980), while encouraging a more thorough examination of the way in which economic, political and cultural relationships were intertwined. It also situated Wales as an example alongside numerous other instances where the notion of internal colonialism seemed to have some explanatory purchase. Robert Blauner had already made use of this framework to throw light on the position of black Americans (Blauner, 1969), while others had applied it to the case of indigenous, or native, Americans in both the USA and South America (see Khleif, 1978: 111–12). Claims about the internal colonial status of regions had aroused interest not just within Wales but in other places similarly gripped by the prolonged and intractable nature of relative deprivation. It was one of the strengths of the model that it highlighted the extent to which people in many regions had been experiencing a sense of loss of control over their own lives and economic and social fortunes in the face of contemporary economic developments.

Through association, Wales became open to the same kinds of arguments and analyses that were being pursued by radical and critical intellectuals elsewhere, while those who saw themselves as advocates of the interests of Welsh people could draw parallels between their circumstances and those of other minority and oppressed groups, including those who were being racially or ethnically victimized. In the United States, for example, the Appalachian region, which had become the principal focus of the anti-poverty programme (Harrington, 1962), was seen as a good instance of an internal colony (Lewis et al., 1978). Hence its description by a prominent local minister of religion as 'a colony which America has exploited . . . used, stripped of her wealth, raped and reamed and reduced to ruin' (Weller, 1978: 49). Although the devastation this had wrought was if anything yet more drastic than what had happened in Wales, the comparison with the way in which Alexander Cordell and others had written about south Wales is indeed striking. Like Wales, Appalachia was also widely considered to be somewhat set apart from the social and cultural mainstream, a 'strange land inhabited by a peculiar people' (Shapiro, 1977). Together with the economic dominance of coal mining, the existence of extensive areas of relatively unspoilt countryside or 'wilderness', and the strength of community bonds, as well as certain direct influences from and connections with Wales, this made it very tempting to see the two places as belonging together within the same analytical category, and therefore, potentially at least, making common cause politically as well (Clavel, 1983: Lewis, 1984: Day, 1987). However, rough and ready applications of labels such as 'internal colony' were no substitute for precise analysis and before long numerous objections were being levelled both at its general coherence, and at Hechter's work in particular (Lovering, 1978a, 1978b; Day, 1978, 1980).

A Welsh historian dismissed the whole proposition as an 'enfeebled allegory, devoid of theory and crippled by innumerable errors of fact' (Smith, 1980: 12), while scrutiny of the underlying economic model found that, on any of the accepted economic meanings of the term, it was impossible to uphold the claim that Wales was suffering 'exploitation' (Lovering, 1978b). In particular, the attempt to apply the term in its Marxist sense to relationships between countries was declared totally illegitimate, except in cases where 'the colonised nation is homogeneous and exclusively proletarian while all capitalists live in the imperial core' (Lovering, 1978b: 91) – a description which would fit neither Wales nor England. Otherwise, it could not be demonstrated convincingly that Welsh workers were subsidizing the wages of their English counterparts, nor that there was an outflow of capital from Wales to support English business; in fact, on balance both public and private funding appeared to be moving in the opposite direction. The omission from the internal colonial model of any reference to the transfer payments made by the British state to support living standards and welfare in Wales was an especially glaring weakness. At the very least, it was arguable that through welfare payments and other forms of state-sponsored investment, Wales was being subsidized by other parts of Britain, rather than the reverse. This cast doubt on the validity of equating relationships between regions within an established nation-state to those which existed between separate states linked by world imperialism (Massey, 1978: 2).

Although the concept of the internal colony was helpful in bringing into focus issues of power, decision-making and control of everyday life, there were alternative formulations which could do this equally well, or better. The idea of an internal colony proved vulnerable to 'conceptual confusion or carelessness' (Walls, 1978: 323) as it was stretched and diluted by its application to more and more situations, until it was being used to refer not just to regions, peoples, and ethnic groups, but also social categories like homosexuals, the elderly, even women. Conversely, more rigorous attempts at definition meant that it had a much more circumscribed relevance. Unsurprisingly, since he was aiming to explain the relationships between 'racially' defined groupings in America, Blauner's use of the term had made the presence of racism one of its essential features – that is, social domination premised upon the existence of certain biological differences between powerful and powerless groups. Similarly, as Walls pointed out, exponents of the term in the South American context had also conceived of it applying to relationships that involved the domination and exploitation of the whole of one population by another, each having its own internal social structure, including class composition. According to this account, internal colonialism arose from an encounter between 'distinct races, cultures or civilizations' (Gonzales-Casanova, 1965). Thinking of African examples, Van den Berghe distinguished internal colonialism from 'mere differences in economic development' by the existence of four ideal type conditions: the rule of one ethnic group (or ethnic coalition) over other ethnic groups within a given state; territorial separation of subordinate groups into 'homelands' or 'reserves'; a specific internal government ruling over subject peoples with a distinct legal status; and unequal economic relations that consigned subject peoples to inferior positions in a division of labour (van den Berghe, cited by Walls, 1978). Plainly, most examples of regional deprivation and disadvantage fell far short of meeting such tight conditions. In other words, although the idea of the internal colony had some appeal as a political metaphor, and means of mobilizing action, it lacked sufficient clarity and precision to be entirely satisfactory as a sociological concept.

WALES AND UNDERDEVELOPMENT

Hechter's own field of reference, of course, was the Celtic countries. His discussion is premised on the fundamental comparability between the three peripheral zones of Britain – Scotland, Ireland and Wales – and the fact that their populations shared a common subjective awareness and identification. His book opened with a contention that, whereas the great majority of people in the British Isles, despite some quite mixed ancestry, had come to define themselves as British, the one group which stood apart was the 'so-called Celts' (1975: 10). Both these claims are highly dubious in fact, but the distinction, which was essential to his argument, was never closely examined. At the cultural level, the way in which the opposition between the British and Celts was said to have been deployed, to the advantage of England and the English, was central to the claim that the peripheral nations had been 'colonised', and that this continued to be the decisive factor shaping their development. The assertion that 'the Celts are an internal colony within the very core of (the world) system' (1975: 348) indicated that in this respect Wales had undergone the same essential experiences as Scotland and Ireland. Unfortunately, there is a striking inconsistency in the usage of the labels 'British' and 'English' in the discussion, and a dearth of evidence to show how people in the three countries actually thought of themselves, and their 'Celtic' identities.

Appearing within months of Hechter's book, Tom Nairn's *The Break-Up of Britain* (1977b) occupied some common ground, in that both showed the influence of Ernest Gellner's seminal work on nationalism, in which he relates the rise of national sentiment to the impact of the uneven spread of modernization and industrialization. Gellner conceptualized this as a kind of tidal wave which moved outwards from its point of origin, causing a set of encounters between those at the forefront of development, and those who came to see themselves as lagging behind. The mobilization of national consciousness was a response to these modernizing tensions (Gellner, 1964). This model provided Nairn with the underlying material basis for his examination of contemporary manifestations of nationalism in parts of the 'advanced' world. While Nairn's primary focus was his native Scotland, he makes frequent comparative reference to Wales, along with Northern Ireland.

By and large Nairn endorsed the impression of Wales as suffering from relative underdevelopment, seeming to place it among those regions which had been 'thrust back' by uneven development, with ensuing 'depopulation, cultural impoverishment, a psychology of powerlessness and dependency, and ... particularly fragmentary or distorted kinds of economic growth' (1977b: 203, 208). While at first sight this account, as he admits, is difficult to square with the exceptional part Wales had played in the history of industrialization, he argues that since this was overwhelmingly guided from outside, its impact upon Wales can be likened to an 'invasion' (1977b: 209). However, Nairn objects to the conclusion that all regions showing a revived sense of national awareness are in the same position, or engaged upon the same struggle – to him, this smacks of a 'new political romanticism'. Scotland in particular does not fit this story, because it represents an *over*developed, potentially more modern, place, which was being held back by its submersion in the British state. Relatively speaking, Scotland was a success story, not a developmental failure; Wales looked more like a failure.

In an address to a Plaid Cymru summer school in 1976, Nairn (1977a) agreed that it was important to find some unifying theory capable of explaining both kinds of situation, but was inclined to discount theories of internal colonialism and cultural oppression as misleading. Hechter's work in particular, although 'impressive', is finally dismissed as too abstract, and weak on historical detail. Instead the preferable approach is to follow Gellner's lead by examining how exactly the process of uneven development bears upon 'real and diverse places', taking due note of both their similarities and differences, and their exact location in modern processes of socio-economic development. So far as Wales is concerned, Nairn finds the stress which tended to be put upon cultural matters suspect, but acknowledges that it reflects how in Wales 'the usual forces of uneven development have been tied together unusually closely and graphically' (1977b: 211). Distorted economic and social development, it appears, is reflected in warped analysis and explanation. Nairn's approach, though idiosyncratic, was basically anchored in neo-Marxism and an understanding of economic development, whereas Hechter's work drew more heavily on Weber and aspects of cultural change.

The perception of Wales as figuring among the 'underdeveloped regions of the overdeveloped world' (Khleif, 1978), or forming a part of the Third World situated within the First World, was taken on board by several other writers. Khleif saw such regions as being embarked upon a shared process of asserting their autonomy in response to global structural changes, and related the occurrence of territorial and ethnic mobilizations within them to a whole series of social upheavals and new social movements brought about by major economic and social shifts towards post-industrialism. Reactions in Wales, he suggested, were increasingly influenced by the articulation of an awareness of exploitation by a foreign power (1978: 108); the Celtic fringe was taking up positions against the English centre. Drawing on Wallerstein's depiction of a world system within which Britain could be seen as relocating from the historic centre towards the semi-periphery, with knock-on effects for its peripheral regions, Rawkins comments on the growing marginalization of Wales, and its 'accentuated economic dependency' (1983: 219). In his view there is a definite relationship between uneven development and minority nationalism, although it is one which displays considerable intricacy, and several intervening variables require specification. G. Williams (1981) adopts a similar standpoint, prefaced by a thoroughgoing critique of the predominance of diffusionist explanations which treat territorial separatism as an expression of cultural conservatism, the 'traditionalist' response to the onward movement of modernization. The suggestion is that insistence in such work on the 'primordial' quality of ethnicity obscures its ongoing relationship with existing social structure, and the impact upon it of the unequal relationship between core and periphery, and thereby consigns it to a residual category. Ethnic identity becomes something odd and unexpected, which requires special explanation. For Williams, such treatment has an air of 'arrogant ethnocentrism' (1981: 278) which permeates much of the writing on Wales. His aim is to provide an alternative analysis which brings ethnicity fully into the picture as a normal part of social reality among categories of actors 'differentially located within the economic order, struggling for control in a local order which is integrated into the dynamics of the state' (1981: 282). Finally, Clavel reiterates the conception of Wales as having been subjected to an externally dominated 'hegemony', thus suffering from externally induced development, leading to distorted planning. The upshot is that it continues to be a poor region in a rich country (Clavel, 1983).

These, along with other similar interventions, represent a formidable conceptual and methodological barrage that encouraged efforts to reconstruct the economic and social history of Wales in the light of contemporary theories and concepts of underdevelopment and dependency. From this there emerged two main questions: whether the characterization of Wales as underdeveloped and/or dependent was adequate; and, if so, how this related to the generation of movements of ethnic or nationalist solidarity. As was noted at the time, bringing together the themes of economic development and cultural distinctiveness in this way lifted the potential for a sociology of Wales to a qualitatively new level, making a comprehensive approach to Wales seem possible (Day, 1979: 467). At the same time, it was very evident that a good deal of work would need to be done to test and refine the ideas which were being introduced from elsewhere. It was always going to be a debatable matter how far perspectives which had emerged from very different contexts, and which formed part of complicated intellectual and political lineages, could be transferred, willy-nilly, to new settings (Day, 1978). As some of the definitional points cited above suggest, it was particularly controversial whether or not the experiences of societies in the Third World, which had been coercively incorporated into empires and colonies at a relatively late stage, really matched those of places with a far longer history of integration into the frameworks of established nation-states. No matter how poorly people in Wales had fared compared to those elsewhere in Britain, there was literally a world of difference between their situation and circumstances which prevailed in LDCs. Williams (1977) suggested that among those who responded to the challenge of such analyses were some whose hackles had been raised by the assertion that Wales had a colonial status, and who had been stung by it into developing a critical perspective on Welsh society and culture. Consequently new energy was devoted to the examination of relative deprivation, within the parameters of Marxist-style theories of 'uneven development'. These could be conducted either in relation to ideas about the evolving nature of the capitalist world economy as a whole, or apropos more specific effects observable at local level.

FROM UNDERDEVELOPMENT TO DEPENDENCE

The theory of underdevelopment grew out of a devastating critique of modernization theory and its policy implications launched by people like Frank (1971) and Amin (1976), primarily with reference to the Third World. The essential idea was that it was principally through their relationship with a larger system that particular areas or populations suffered disadvantage and impoverishment. Frank stated that, in order to understand how this worked, one had to search out and refer to 'the systemic whole in terms of which the reality . . . can be explained and changed' (1971: 14). There was, of course, considerable scope for debate and disagreement about the actual nature of the system in question. For Frank, underdevelopment was a process which involved the transfer of surplus through a chain of connections from the most remote, peripheral parts of the system to its very centre. Wealth and power accumulated there, at the expense of poverty and oppression elsewhere. This particular version of the theory could be criticized for its lack of specific detail, for overgenerality in its application and for its tone of fatalism (Day, 1979). It appeared to offer less developed places, once they had become caught up within the system, the prospect only of stagnation or regression, unless they contrived to bring about a rupture with it. In this respect, Frank's argument had clearly revolutionary implications, encouraging those experiencing underdevelopment to take drastic action to rectify it. Other approaches were less definite in making underdevelopment a necessary consequence of existing relationships, and were prepared to countenance some chance of forward movement, although this would remain constrained within a 'dependent' mode (Day, 1978). That is, so long as the underlying relationships within the system remained unaltered, whatever development did take place would have to be adapted to meeting the needs of the centre, as well as those which were determined from the periphery itself. Change would be biased away from what might occur under conditions of autonomy.

There had been some early applications of this kind of approach to Wales (Buchanan, 1968, 1970) in which its position had been presented as that of a 'satellite' undergoing economic exploitation as well as being threatened by 'cultural liquidation'. There were also some influential examples of the use of underdevelopment theory to interpret the situation of other parts of the British Isles, showing how they had become entangled in processes which were detrimental to their long-term interests, even if they brought some short-term gains to local population in the form of jobs or new kinds of industry. New developments could take place without altering the essentially subordinate and disadvantaged situation of those subjected to them (Carter, 1974; Regan and Walsh, 1976). In similar fashion, it was suggested that the skewed and disjointed development of Wales reflected the external pressures exerted by the British and world economies, which had produced a pattern whereby a succession of industries had been intensively exploited and then abandoned, resulting in a series of transformations of social and community structures (Day, 1978, 1979). Examples affecting different parts of Wales included woollen textile production, lead, slate, coal and more recently steel manufacturing. In each case, their decline or exhaustion had left behind districts marked by decaying infrastructure, struggling communities and 'redundant' populations.

Aspects of underdevelopment theory were also deployed in a number of articles by Glyn Williams exploring the sources and significance of Welsh nationalism (Williams 1981, 1985). Among the many features of historical and current change which were examined, he gave particular stress to the process of marginalization. This was a term that had been introduced into Latin American sociology to refer to the way in which specific kinds of economic change could produce a cleavage between the dynamic features of new development, and the stagnation of previous forms (Williams, 1986: 191). In other words, it was a particular type of uneven development which resulted in some being left out or excluded from the benefits of change. According to Williams, the marginalization of both space and people was a leading characteristic of development in Wales, and one that was becoming more marked over time. In his words, 'marginalization derives from the inability of most of the population to participate in new developments while also being made even more remote from the scarce infrastructural resources' (1985: 324). A wide variety of processes were shown to contribute to this outcome, operating at a number of different levels within the labour force, productive organization, and state policies, and the concept was helpful in organizing a good deal of empirical material pointing to significant elements of polarization within the economy and society of Wales. However, picking out the bare bones of the argument, there was also a certain ambiguity or elusiveness about the way in which the concept worked.

Thus if we follow Williams's discussion of polarization (1981: 291–300) we come across references to a marginalized sector, consisting of a particular group which is not relevant to accumulation at the highest level; a large marginalized area, within which housing conditions are among the worst in Britain; a marginalized sector providing limited job opportunities at low wages; an emerging picture of a marginalized area, as borne out by statistics from mid-Wales, relating to the marginalized sector of the economy. There is also an associated contrast drawn between the situation in the marginalized sector, with its high indices of deprivation, and an industrialized enclave, or set of growth poles, where comparable indices are low. In other words, there is a systematic compounding of spatial and sectoral categories, with the latter referring to both population groupings and branches of the economy. The relatively better-off 'enclave' can be either or both a place and a particular economic segment. All this was seen as part of the process of uneven capitalist development, in which leading and lagging sectors were interrelated, and the disadvantages going to some derived from the benefits which accrued to others. Finally, not only was there a correlation between spatial and social deprivation, but it was also said to be the 'indigenous' population which was overrepresented in the process of marginalization, thus yielding cultural polarization as well. Ultimately, this seems to bring us back to the problematic of the cultural division of labour posed by Hechter, for which indeed Williams was a significant protagonist.

Williams warns explicitly against the danger of overemphasizing the spatial dimension of inequality and polarization, but to say the least there is also a certain untidiness about the way in which spatial and social aspects appear to elide in his account. However, he is by no means unique in this regard; indeed, it is an underlying issue in much of the work I have been discussing. One of Hechter's reviewers pinpointed the problem when he noted how the thesis of a cultural division of labour presupposed the coincidence of regional economic disparities with ethnic and cultural boundaries (Luke, 1976). To what extent can we assume such a coincidence between spatial, social and cultural boundaries in our investigation of Wales and its formation? If it does exist, how can such a correspondence be explained? It is evident that much of the work on Wales revolves around just these questions – the extent to which an understanding of 'regional' disparities involves one in unpicking aspects of cultural, ethnic or other social differentiations. How such questions are answered is extremely important, because this helps to shape the type of explanation we will adopt. For instance, in the movement from analysis of what was seen as a regional problem to the adoption of the language of core–periphery, satellite–metropolis, and internal colony, a significant theoretical alteration occurs. We are taken from what is basically an empirical conception of regions, in which they can be defined either pragmatically or by following some existing convention, such as administrative frontiers or units designed for the collation of official statistics, to a stronger assertion which treats regions as real entities, or actors in their own right. As noted elsewhere, once we begin to think of regions as 'dependent' upon or 'oppressing' one another, then 'the risk of reification is acute and the illumination given . . . may be more than outweighed by the mystification of the processes it seeks to capture' (Day, 1980: 237).

There was a looseness in the theory of underdevelopment which allowed this type of confusion to thrive. Politically, it might very well serve a useful purpose. After all, writers like Frank were engaged upon what has been described as 'political writing' in which the use of social scientific theories and historical analysis was combined with the activist pursuit of reformist or revolutionary goals (Preston, 1987). Something similar could be said of some of the contributions to debates in Wales, including the work of Glyn Williams. Daily experience teaches us that there are often sound political reasons for cultivating a degree of ambiguity and fuzziness around concepts in order to maximize a message's appeal. However, this can also be a major hindrance to clarity of analysis and create confusion or uncertainty where it is not intended. During the 1980s, there was a strong impulse within sociology, which sometimes took the form of an extreme theoreticism, to insist that the concepts used were anchored properly in consistent theoretical perspectives. This was especially prominent in and around Marxist theorising, where there was an acute awareness of the possible political repercussions of ill-defined concepts and confused analysis (Hindess and Hirst, 1977). Frank's image of the chain of exploitation reaching from the most degraded Third World rural peasant to the most bloated first world plutocrat, or from the Amazon jungle to the stock exchanges of New York, Tokyo or London, was very effective in conveying the impression of a single 'struggle' in which everyone was involved. Yet it is obviously incoherent to lump together individuals, countries and institutions all within the same categories of 'satellite' or 'metropolis'. In what sense can a person be a 'satellite' in a chain of exploitation? How can that individual's situation be equated with that of a multinational company, a national government or a colony? The trick could be worked only by leaving key terms – such as 'exploitation', 'surplus', even the central conception of 'dependence' – very vague and ill-defined; but this becomes a problem once one starts to probe more deeply beneath the general categories and relationships of the theory.

Lessons drawn from development studies were important because they helped to provide a 'totalizing' perspective, one which sensitized analysts to connections between the social, political and economic contexts for development which had not been taken on board fully before. However, if followed seriously, they demanded a level of conceptual and empirical care that was sometimes missing from their initial reception. Thus it could be said that Wales satisfied the broad description of an 'underdeveloped' social formation when compared to a checklist of relevant criteria: export orientation, reliance on narrow markets, external control and so on. But in doing so there was a danger that underdevelopment would be treated as a set of pick-and-mix attributes, rather than a coherent syndrome, and that it would be detached from its meaningful location within a specific historical context (Day, 1978: 106). Appropriating models and concepts to apply them to settings for which they were not intended originally was a risky business. Indeed, one of the leading dependency theorists warned social scientists in the advanced societies that over-enthusiastic adoption of such ideas might blind them to the complexities of the social and spatial differentiations within social formations, encouraging them to fall prey instead to the '"vulgar" current [that] was predominant in analyses that regarded imperialism and external economic conditioning as the substantive and omnipresent explanation of every social or ideological process that occurred' (Cardoso, 1977: 12). Rather than putting all the emphasis on 'outside' forces, the same author stated that it was essential to examine how the relationship of dependence was established and maintained, since 'What was significant was the "movement", the class struggles, the redefinitions of interest, the political alliances that maintained the structures while at the same time opening the possibility of their transformation' (Cardoso, 1977: 14).

In just the same way as the wider sociology of development moved on to new and more precise perspectives which entailed clearer and more elaborated analytical concepts (Taylor, 1979), so the vogue for 'underdevelopment' approaches to Wales was relatively short-lived, although significant. This does not mean that dependency theory has no further relevance to the analysis of Wales. It continues to offer insights and stimulate research with respect to particular aspects of Welsh development. In a recent examination of labour-market conditions in north-west Wales, for instance, attention is given to the need to consider how economic peripheralism affects patterns of development. Arguments which blame limited growth within the area on its 'isolation' from centres of dynamism are criticized for substituting geographical distance for political control (Williams and Morris, 1995). To explain things in such a way is challenged for taking the relationship between core and periphery for granted, as if it were a natural configuration. This encourages proposed solutions in terms of measures to enhance spatial articulation with the core (such as improved road links) while at the same time divesting the local population of those attributes thought to be responsible for holding back development. Investments in 'human capital' would be among the steps commonly put forward, and designed to correct alleged deficiencies in the local labour force. However, this position is seen as adhering to diffusionism, treating social and cultural homogeneity as a desirable outcome. Instead it is suggested that the relationship between core and periphery is fundamentally exploitative and dependent, so that increased connections with the core will merely complicate and enhance the problems of the periphery. The existence of peripherality in a fixed, geographical sense is seen as lending itself to the formation of unstable relationships between core enterprises and those locations which they regard as 'remote'. Their 'fickleness', and readiness to withdraw as soon as any perceived advantage is exhausted, undermines attempts to maintain sustainable development, and so perpetuates dependency. The similarities between this argument and Hechter's work should be obvious, but its application has shifted now from Wales as such to the explanation of differences which exist within Wales, differences which harm the prospects of particular areas that have come to be defined as peripheral to dominant economic and social relationships.

4

Enclaves, Archipelagos and Regions: Rethinking the Regional Problem

As well as enabling some significant advances in understanding, the application to Wales of approaches from the sociology of development also raised some profound questions. The most important had to do with the need to clarify just what was the object of analysis for a sociology of Wales (Day, 1979). By this stage it was apparent that at least three distinct possibilities were contained within the framework of developmental analyses, and that specific contributions tended to slide between these in often uncontrolled and confusing ways. In effect, Wales could be addressed as a place, as a people or as a complex social formation. Each of these positions carried with it a particular set of related disciplinary connections, assumptions and problems. The manner in which Wales was inserted into one or other of these varied discourses was bound to influence the direction taken by any subsequent discussion.

PEOPLE, PLACE AND SOCIETY

An examination of the condition of Wales as a place, area or territory could be conducted most readily through approaches taken from human geography and spatial analysis, including some aspects of planning. There was a particular appeal in doing so, because some of the earliest and most influential contributions to Welsh social science had been produced from within an explicitly geographical context, and the personal and institutional connections between sociology and geography in Wales have remained relatively strong. Superficially, much development theory seemed to couched in terms of relations between places – 'countries', 'regions' and so on. The long-standing treatment of Wales as a 'problem region' also encouraged an areal focus. Approaching the issue of Wales as a matter of how a particular 'place' had fared in the development process meant that commentators quickly became embroiled in some of the most vigorous debates in sociology during the 1980s, those which were concerned to clarify the relationships that exist between society and space. These occurred at the interface between sociology and geography (Gregory and Urry, 1985), and raised some fundamental issues about the meanings of place, region, communities and localities.

On other occasions, however, it is plain that the expression 'Wales' is used as a means of referring indirectly to the condition and prospects of a particular human population, or group, the Welsh. So when Wales is said to be oppressed by England, or is depicted as a particularly deprived region, often what is really being scrutinized is the situation of the Welsh, vis-à-vis other groups. Assertions about the significance of a cultural division of labour are like this: it is not 'England' as a place which is alleged to be dominant, but English people who are seen as exerting control over those who are culturally different. They might be doing this from outside the place called Wales, or while actually inside it. As noted before, in the Welsh context it is extraordinarily difficult to separate arguments about uneven development and economic inequality from considerations of nationalism and national identity, and this takes the debate into the realms of cultural analysis, political sociology and theories of nationalism and ethnicity. Among topics which are relevant here we could include the disagreements which arise between 'primordialist' conceptions of identity and different forms of social constructionism. Lessons from anthropology as well as sociology have a bearing on how such debates proceed (Jenkins, 1997).

The third possibility, which might be thought to come closest to a fully fledged sociological viewpoint, is to see 'Wales' as a shorthand description for a social formation of some kind. Since this is the standard sociological point of departure, thereafter it could be construed in any number of ways, but it would involve some notion of exploring the interconnections among a set of institutions, or networks of social relations, patterns of class formation and so on. The majority of conventional sociological contributions are concerned to develop this type of approach, and in passing many would aim to demonstrate that ordinary ideas of 'place' and 'people' are grossly simplified ways of talking about complex social structures of one kind or another. For instance, a 'people' rarely if ever consists of individuals who are identically positioned socially, so it is only in extreme circumstances (such as genocide) that an entire people is likely to confront the same situation or undergo the same experiences. Examination of the internal differentiation and structuring of different peoples, and their relationships to one another, would be one way of describing the subject matter of sociology. Perhaps unfortunately, because there is such a wealth of possible ways of conceptualizing such differentiations and structurings, this is only the beginnings of a sociological analysis. Among the forms of social variation which have attracted most attention, and been seen as having the most general bearing, are class, gender and ethnicity.

That places, people and social formations cannot simply be mapped onto each other is one of the main conclusions of a vast array of sociological work, more or less since the discipline began. *How* they relate to one another, on the other hand, is among the most intriguing fields of social investigation, and if anything has become more explicit with the extended perception of social diversity, multiculturalism and hybridity in recent sociology. Hence whichever of these directions of inquiry was pursued was bound to present a considerable degree of complexity. None provided the key to a straightforward characterization of Wales, as was becoming increasingly apparent with the accumulation of evidence to suggest that the underlying social reality, always varied, was fragmenting further in various ways. This made Wales more difficult to encapsulate within the bounds of any single, simple description. Indeed there is an interesting paradox in this regard: as Wales grew more diverse and disjointed, so the awareness of it as an entity seemed to grow. It was only from the late 1960s onwards that there seemed to be a social scientific community prepared to devote attention to Wales as a significant phenomenon in its own right, and to engage with analytical perspectives that were 'premised on the existence of a real object corresponding to Wales' (Lovering, 1983a: 49). Prior to this, it had been claimed, only geographers had taken a global view of Wales (Williams, 1983a: 1) – a claim which certainly does not do justice to the work of Welsh historians (Williams, 1950; K. O. Morgan, 1981). But sustained sociological attention was new, and this change of focus is itself related to a rising political consciousness of Wales, with more compelling attempts being made from a number of directions to mobilize opinion and action orientated specifically to Welsh issues, such as the fate of the Welsh language and the future of the Welsh economy. Naturally, individual social scientists occupied a variety of positions in relation to these political questions; many took part in debates about them being aired in different Welsh magazines and journals, including *Radical Wales*, *Arcade* and *Planet*. Conversely, political or policy implications were rarely far from the surface in the more academic literature, which occasionally openly avowed the hope that research and analysis might contribute towards defining the limits of legitimate political action (Rees and Rees, 1980: 30).

The apparent inconsistency between a dissolving reality and heightened efforts to articulate a more unified perception of it can be resolved by grasping these responses as being *about* fragmentation, or stimulated by it. Wales presented an increasing puzzle to social analysts; as some of the previous certainties dissolved, so there was more that needed to be explained. Meanwhile, politically speaking, growing divisions compelled people towards some kind of reactive mobilization. This could take defensive forms, involving resistance to change, and efforts to reassert the integrity of the 'old' Wales. It could also assume more progressive shape, in efforts to exert control over new developments, and to improve the capacity of Wales to compete for the associated benefits and escape the costs. Either way, there was something of an identity crisis to be confronted, which among other things provoked a preoccupation with key problems of definition (Day, 1987) – when it came to the crunch, what exactly was Wales? And who were the Welsh? Comparative use of developmental frameworks was helpful here in demonstrating that these processes of self-examination were not exceptional to Wales, but quite normal features of modernization. Under the pressure of rapid social and economic change, people have to grapple with finding appropriate and useable frameworks of meaning which enable them to understand what is going on. This includes taking stock of where they belong and how their interests and aspirations compare to and align with those of others. More recently, arguments have been put forward which make a similar point about 'globalization' as a contemporary process: on the one hand, it integrates and assimilates, promising to abolish differences on a world scale, yet at the same time it somehow also precipitates local differentiation and variety, including new kinds of territorial politics, as people respond reflexively to it (Albrow, 1996; Giddens, 1999).

Some of the earliest intimations of this view could be absorbed from development theory, since one of its lessons was the importance of examining how general processes of development contributed towards creating and maintaining local variations. For example, the suggestion that development brings about marginalization already implies a growing separation between life at the margin, and what goes on somewhere else, at the centre or core. Dualistic models of this type ran through much development analysis, setting two distinct sectors against one another in a way which basically reworked the old distinction in modernization theory between the modern and the traditional. Since the mechanisms of development were considered by many to penetrate into the furthest corners of the world, the contrasts drawn between developed/less developed, advanced/backward, centre/periphery could be projected onto the less developed societies as well. It was suggested that they also would take on a dual character as they were brought within the range of the underlying relationships; thus development had divisive, as well as integrative, effects.

A contrast of this sort emerged within the theory of internal colonialism, for example, when development was seen as responsible for creating 'small urbanized enclaves oriented to English and international markets which featured cosmopolitan life styles. With the passing of time the social and cultural gap between enclave and hinterland grew steadily wider' (Hechter, 1975: 143). It is not easy to identify precisely which small urban centres the writer has in mind, but generally speaking, enclaves are depicted as sites which have little or no intrinsic connection with the economy or society surrounding them, because their *raison d'être* is rooted elsewhere – in one formulation, they are dependent upon neither local resources nor local markets, and give the host country a minimum of control over their activities (Williams, 1981: 291). The use of the word 'country' here conveys an impression that such enclaves are in some sense 'foreign', and Hechter's description bears this out by treating them as little bits of England, or the metropolis, dropped down into Wales. Students of development in southern Italy coined the term 'cathedrals in the desert' to describe the way in which large industrial plants had been established there without forming any significant local links. The rise of the multinational company was instrumental in ensuring the proliferation of such enclaves, since large-scale organizations could deposit bits of their operation wherever it suited them, without needing to make connections locally; their activities did not grow up organically from local soil. Large corporations therefore were an important factor in creating dualistic patterns within local economies (Hymer, 1979). Taking up this line of argument leads into consideration of the organizational logic governing such corporations, and its social effects, and the relationships that exist between external and indigenous businesses (Lovering, 1978a, 1983a). These were to become major issues within Wales during the 1980s.

Hechter's approach is rather different. His picture of territorial fragments of Wales pulling away from the prevailing norm is the reverse side of the coin of 'marginalization', and suggests again that there is a spatial (urban/rural) as well as social and cultural dimension to internal differentiation. While this makes a useful gesture towards the analysis of differences within Wales, it throws up further questions about the somewhat elusive nature of the internal colony: is it the whole of Wales which is internally colonized? If not, how are the boundaries to be drawn around its parts? A possible answer would be that it is the growing rift between different parts of Wales which furnishes proof of its colonial dependency. This would presume that similar differences would not arise where there was no equivalent condition – for example, within England, which is seen as the agent, rather than the victim, of colonization. Even then, one would need to provide reasons as to why fragmentation should be seen as a problem, rather than simply the inevitable outcome of 'progress'. The term 'marginalization' does identify a problem, by implying that a wholly different pattern of development would be in the best interests of those who are marginalized. In other words, dependent development is a problem because it increases inequality. Glyn Williams's claim that marginalization was specific to the 'indigenous people' of Wales adds a further complication, as now these have to be defined. On his definition, indigenous essentially means those who speak Welsh; where then should we place non-Welsh-speaking Welsh people? Must they be considered automatically to form part of the 'enclave'? Are they exempt from marginalization? In view of some of the other comments Williams makes, it seems reasonable to conclude that the marginalized area or 'hinterland' really means rural Wales. Where then do the derelict industrial Welsh valleys fit in? Once again, it is evident that to make progress it is necessary to untie some knotty problems to do with the extent to which people, places and social categories can be assumed to overlap with one another, or not. While these distinctions conform to the image of an endless 'chain' of relationships of exploitation and subordination, they also tend to support McCrone's opinion that dependency may be only a pseudo-concept which 'explains everything in general and nothing in particular' (McCrone, 1992: 49). There is certainly something very slippery indeed about the shape-shifting nature of the topic of discussion.

NEW PERSPECTIVES

Despite the weaknesses and limitations that beset the development approaches, they helped to bring about an almost complete transformation in the way in which Wales was conceptualized sociologically. This can be seen by comparing the three edited volumes which emerged from or in close connection with the activities of the BSA Sociology of Wales Study Group. Even the titles reveal something about how ideas had moved on: _Social and Cultural Change in Contemporary Wales_ (G. Williams, 1978a); _Poverty and Social Inequality in Wales_ (Rees and Rees, 1980a); _Crisis of Economy and Ideology_ (G. Williams, 1983a).

Whatever the strengths of individual contributions to the first volume, it is difficult to discern any consistency of approach among them, although some underlying themes can be drawn out which are quite revealing about the state of sociological knowledge at the time. There is far more unity of purpose and vision in the other two volumes, partly because there was greater scope for editorial control in defining an agenda, but mainly because by now many of the authors were participants in a set of ongoing debates, both among themselves, and in relation to the wider sociological world. As is customary, each volume comes with its own overview of the contents, and together these identify a number of strong lines of argument: a desire to theorize Wales; to situate it within its wider economic and social context; to see where it resembles and where it differs from other social settings; and a growing emphasis on doing so within a framework of political economy, coupled with an interest in the role of the state. These aims are bound up with preoccupations about the nature of Welsh identity and the significance of national consciousness which run through many of the discussions.

Social and Cultural Change in Contemporary Wales is a collection of papers originally delivered at a conference sponsored by the then Social Science Research Council (SSRC) and held at the University of Wales Centre in Gregynog in 1976. As such it represents a snapshot of research which happened to be in progress at that particular time, and includes contributions by authors from a range of disciplines, including geography, psychology and political science as well as sociology. In a brief reflection on the conference, Coxon notes that it brought together two diverse research traditions, each able to give a coherent account of itself, but not meeting one another until a final 'confused, but exhilarating', encounter (Coxon, 1978: 270). The two streams Coxon identifies were the ethnographic and the structural – that is, research which pays close-up attention to everyday life in Wales, usually centred on accounts of particular local communities, and more wide-ranging attempts to analyse some of the basic dimensions of Welsh social organization. Chapters by Emmett on 'Blaenau boys in the mid-1960s' and Winrow on 'Social deprivation in Wales: 1961–71' typify this contrast, which is not at all unusual in sociology. However, in his introduction to the book, Glyn Williams, who was the moving spirit behind the conference, provides a rather different reading which is perhaps more specific to Wales. In its contents he discerns a latent distinction between those whose work is organized around one or other of two allegedly alternative 'principles of inequality', class and ethnicity. Much of his introduction is taken up with exploring the relationship between these two conceptions, and giving what amounts to a push in the direction of the latter, when he attributes the previous paucity of work on Wales to tendencies among sociologists not to take ethnicity sufficiently seriously, or to fail to see its relevance for Wales (unlike its ready application to migrant minorities in British cities). In other words, according to Williams, the 'puzzling blind-spot' which afflicts Wales is related to the way in which its special nature has been played down by sociologists whose propensity was to 'neglect the concept of culture as a relevant tool of analysis and to regard Wales as merely a region within a homogeneous Britain or alternatively as a rapidly disappearing linguistic minority worthy of neither a theoretical consideration nor a research focus' (1978a: 1). This attitude, he argues, is an expression of a prevailing ethnocentric centralism that makes Wales vanish as a topic which merits inquiry. Sociology had not responded adequately to its existence as 'a nation with a unique history and a distinct social organization'.

Coxon and Williams are correct in seeing the germs of a lively debate or contest between differing sociological perspectives, although nowhere in the book is it clearly pursued. Actually the distinction goes considerably further. Out of sixteen substantive contributions, seven deal with aspects of rural Wales and no less than nine focus on questions to do with language and/or ethnic identity. By comparison, only one chapter, a study of networks of influence in Llanelli, touches specifically upon social organization in south Wales. Thus there is more to the skewed nature of the discussion than simply the impact of methodological or theoretical differences. Rural is accentuated over urban, north and west Wales over the industrialized south, and linguistic divisions and changes over other key features of Welsh society. Therefore, despite its title, the book gives only a limited insight into the current condition of Wales. Day (1979) locates this bias in a prior tradition which concentrated attention on a version of Welshness that stressed language, rurality and community as prime features, and suggests that it had had the effect of creating a separation between those who were sociologists *of* Wales, and who were content to follow in these earlier footsteps, and those who did their sociology *in* Wales without being part of the older tradition. As it happened, the ethnographic style of research, which drew on the methods of social anthropology and 'community studies', was more attuned to studies of rural Wales, whereas the structural approach had been more prominent in examinations of the industrial areas. Hence, while there were researchers whose interests lay in industrial Wales, and its changing nature, or who were working on urban matters, they did not appear to consider themselves to be orientated towards Wales, and so had not taken part in this conference.

For a fuller account of Wales to emerge, it was vital to overcome this restrictive definition of areas of interest, and bring work on the different geographical and social segments closer together. Lessons taken from the sociology of development were invaluable in this regard, because they helped bring about a widening of viewpoints which showed these emphases need not be incompatible; indeed, they suggested quite the opposite, that previously disconnected issues formed part of the same real, and explanatory, universes. The state of rural Wales could only be understood properly in relation to industrial and urban change; ethnic questions could not be detached from the analysis of class inequalities; and culture and structure did not have to be treated as if they were antithetical. Nevertheless, there were obvious points of continuing disagreement. For example, whereas Williams was stressing the need to pay greater heed to culture than in the past, Day's argument pointed more towards obtaining a firmer structural grasp. At the same time, they also seemed to be adopting opposed positions on the 'choice' between class and ethnicity as vectors of analysis (G. Williams, 1977; Day, 1979).

The coming theoretical reorientation in Welsh sociological work just about makes an appearance in the odd footnote of the SSRC volume; but, more significantly, the practical outcome of the Gregynog conference was to stimulate a further approach to the SSRC which, together with the BSA, gave funding for a seminar series, to support what became the Sociology of Wales Study Group. This met at regular intervals between 1978 and 1985, and it was in discussions within this group that Coxon's 'exhilarating' encounter could be taken further. As it transpired, it proved to be the structural rather than the ethnographic style of work that tended to win out among the participants. An obvious factor which had contributed to the rather fragmented nature of research up to this time was the considerable isolation in which researchers worked, both from the sociological mainstream, and from each other. They were in a variety of different educational establishments, and different academic disciplines, and this created considerable barriers to communication. By contrast, the Sociology of Wales Group provided a regular meeting point and forum for an active network of researchers; it also produced a newsletter which contained brief research reports, book reviews, and conference notices of interest to members. In due course, this newsletter mutated into a journal, *Contemporary Wales*, which, from 1987 onwards, was funded by the University of Wales's Board of Celtic Studies. Although the Board took considerable persuading that there would be enough material of suitable quality on Wales, by now more than a dozen editions of the journal have appeared. Cooperation within these settings, albeit short-lived, encouraged the formation of a set of shared perspectives and interests which stimulated a phase of highly productive research activity.

There is a remarkable difference in the way in which Wales is approached by most of the contributors to *Poverty and Social Inequality in Wales*, published in 1980. Whereas the papers delivered at Gregynog had an air of introspection, rarely attempting to provide a broader context (the principal exceptions are chapters by Khleif and Madgwick, which do introduce some international comparisons), the editors of *Poverty and Social Inequality* develop a general framework for analysis which immediately homes in on the question of uneven development and its relationship to the economic and political transformations affecting Britain as a whole. Poverty is identified as a particular manifestation of inequalities which are endemic to capitalism, unequally distributed across space, and with determinant consequences for class formation. Class appears to be prioritized over ethnicity as the chief vehicle for comprehending the nature of inequality; the primary task is to grasp how such inequality is rooted in the characteristics of a capitalist economy. Finally, it is noted that the operation of these characteristics produces significant divisions within Wales which must not be ignored (Rees and Rees, 1980b). While not every subsequent contributor endorses all of these points, there is a considerable unanimity of approach. By 1983, when *Crisis of Economy and Ideology* appears, this brand of analysis seems to have become well entrenched. The editorial introduction (Williams, 1983a) opens immediately with a reference to Marx and the concept of modes of production. Wales is seen as going through a period of radical change, as significant in its way as the industrial revolution, whereby fundamental economic structures are being reshaped, leading to major changes in social formation, and increasing pressures on prevailing forms of ideological legitimation. Within the context of this general 'crisis', a variety of social fractions, including fragments drawn from different social classes, are regarded as battling for power and hegemony. In every respect, this overview bears the hallmarks of the Marxism which was at the forefront in British sociology at the time.

THE RESTRUCTURING APPROACH

The 1970s and early 1980s were the highpoint of Marxist influence in British sociology. Whereas an eminent forerunner, T. H. Marshall, is reputed once to have remarked that the task of sociology was to provide students with the facts so that they could interpret them according to their Marxist instincts, this was a period of intense theoretical debate during which it was felt to be essential to get one's conceptual framework into good order, before (if ever) engaging with the messy empirical world. The influence of Marxist ideas extended across all the social sciences, and it was almost inevitable that when approaches to the 'regional question' were reformulated, this should occur within the general ambit of Marxism. Particular inspiration was taken from the work of the geographer Doreen Massey (1978, 1979, 1984), and there were close links between developments in regional analysis, and the appearance of a 'new urban sociology' (Pickvance, 1976; Harloe, 1981; Rees and Lambert, 1985) which shared similar concerns with getting to grips with the processes which lay behind spatial patterns of social organization. Massey says that the key innovation was 'to get production itself into the equation' (1985: 13).

The starting point for Marxist analysis is the conception of the modern economy as a productive system which is directed primarily at the accumulation of capital and the making of profits. This is achieved by organizing the productive efforts of wage-workers so that they continually produce a surplus, over and above the costs of production. This constitutes a system of exploitation of their labour power, and generates a basic conflict of interests between labour and capital which provides the underlying dynamic of relations between the social classes. Within this context, the main thrust of analysis is to comprehend the general processes of capitalist political economy in order to explain a variety of 'local' effects. This stance could be adopted with varying degrees of determinism, positions differing according to how much room was made for local or 'relative' autonomy, such as the extent to which outcomes were viewed as predetermined or open to the contingencies of class struggle, the political process, or uneven effects across particular industries and local economies. Marxist analysts on the whole were less concerned with whether or not capital wore a particular 'national' face; anyway, in a world of multinational corporations and global economic processes, this was considered to be becoming less important. Where development theories sometimes spoke of the role of 'countries', Marxism referred to 'capital'; it was not 'countries' which did the exploiting, but capital in general, through the specific means of capitalist industries, firms and employers (Harvey, 1982).

Production, of course, is organized into a myriad of different kinds of unit, which can be grouped and classified in numerous ways. There are the different economic sectors, such as services and manufacturing; different industries, such as clothing or electronics; and different organizational shapes, ranging from the single-unit, one-product, local enterprise to the worldwide multidivisional conglomerate. These different types of productive structures are arranged by the forces of competition and cooperation into highly complex chains, networks and clusters, including those that are laid out across geographical space. Massey's interest lay in describing and explaining some of the most significant of these spatial arrangements. This built on earlier work she had carried out on location decisions and the employment effects of firms as they expanded and contracted (Massey and Meegan, 1982). As Massey puts it, 'much of the history of capitalist societies so far has consisted of the opening up, domination and subsequent desertion of areas by particular industries' (1984: 100). In effect, this reiterates the sentiment of development theory, but grounds it in the nature of capitalist society, while at the same time enabling a more disaggregated form of analysis. Rather than the over-simplifications of 'underdevelopment' or even 'dependence', the suggestion is that attention should be given to the movements of the various units of capital, and the forces to which they have to respond. For example, they are involved in an incessant quest for profit which means that they need to react – among many other things – to changes in technology, new organizational devices, alterations in the availability of suitable kinds of labour and adjustments in political regimes. This results in both small-scale, constant adjustments which take account of 'market' signals of various kinds, and also larger shifts in the nature of capitalism, and its prevailing forms of production. Over the long term, the latter would include the impact of factors such as mechanization, automation, the advent of information technology, the rise and fall of trade union powers, state regulation and deregulation. Different phases of laissez-faire capitalism, Fordism, neo-Fordism and 'flexible specialization' would each entail a distinctive kind of organization of production, with its own typical relations of production, and its particular spatial effects. These changes would be associated empirically with the rise and decline of different industries, and the successes and failures of specific firms, all with their local repercussions.

Massey lays heavy emphasis on the importance of specificity in analysis and the need for empirical investigation. In her view, there are no inexorable laws such that these results can be simply read off from the theory: thus 'behind the whole notion of uneven development is the fact of highly differentiated and unique outcomes' (1984: 49). Therefore one has to deal with the real historical diversity. As for local, or regional, consequences, 'geography matters' (1984: 51). There is a crucial interaction between society and space, such that essential social processes are constructed across space, with fundamental consequences for the significance of place. The most distinctive aspect of Massey's theory is the contention that economic and social divisions of labour can be viewed as a series of layers superimposed upon one another over time. Each new phase of development occurs in ways which react to what is already there, so that there is an interaction between successive layers. The popular use of terms like 'greenfield' and 'brownfield' sites to describe new industrial locations is an expression of this: some developments are attracted to 'virgin' places where there is no previous history of industrialization, whereas others can be sited literally on top of the remains of earlier development. Understanding how things have come to be as they are at present requires a process of excavation. It is not just the physical environment or infrastructure which acts like this – the existing state of the labour market, the availability of forms of 'social capital', the skills and reputation of local populations all enter into enterprise calculations which decide whether or not firms will expand or contract in a particular location.

A very similar perspective is offered by Dunford and Perrons (1983) as the culmination of their historical review of capitalist development from feudalism to Fordism. Like Massey, they take the argument well beyond the limits of the productive process alone, into the realm of social reproduction and cultural change. The formulation applies both to entire countries and to regions within them:

> in each country the arena of capital is in fact a palimpsest, in which each new layer of human social activity and each new structure is shaped by those with

whose erasing they are associated, while an examination of space also reveals elements of continuity whose roots lie in the modification, reproduction, or preservation of historically given conditions, as a result, it must be emphasised, of a new logic of development ... [T]he process as a whole results in the production and reproduction not only of the material basis of society and of its individual members, but also and simultaneously, of the social relations and social classes of which the society is composed, and of the ideas and meanings through the medium of which human experience and the processes of material and social reproduction are lived and understood. (1983: 351)

This passage is nothing more than an elaboration of Marx's famous dictum that people make history, but not under conditions of their own choosing – they have to act within the constraints inherited from the past.

RESTRUCTURING AND WALES

Massey provides a number of illustrations of the way in which her arguments clarify and explain changes affecting particular industries and areas. One of these 'applications' deals at some length with the example of the changes taking place in the old peripheral coalfield areas of south Wales, north-east England and central Scotland (1984: 195–223), drawing out both similarities and differences among them. In doing so, Massey is able to make effective use of the work of a number of Welsh scholars, including Humphrys, Lovering, Rees and Lambert, and Rees and Rees. In this way, work that had been done on Wales was feeding into the broader reconstruction of some significant aspects of sociological analysis, while the general approach being developed by Massey provided stimulating guidance for further work on Welsh issues (Rees and Rees, 1983; Rees, 1984: Day, Rees and Murdoch, 1989). Massey notes that her analysis is not intended to apply to entire regions, but mainly to certain labour-market areas or contexts that are typical of them. This is a significant assertion, because it is one of the tenets of her approach that 'regions' and other seemingly 'coherent' local areas cannot be predetermined before analysis, nor do they have an unchanging reality; they must be viewed instead as being continually reproduced in shifting forms as part and parcel of the kinds of process under examination (1984: 195). In the case of coalfield areas, industrial change had brought about a loss of coherence and homogeneity, making them less marked as distinctive 'regions'. They were losing their 'identity' as separate places and fragmenting as they were absorbed into new, and qualitatively different spatial divisions of labour. Pursuing this line of argument has implications for the way in which all such 'local' settings, including 'Wales', are understood.

Adopting this broad approach leads to conclusions such as the following: that 'the restructuring of the economy in South Wales is a consequence of the region's position within a national and world-wide economy, the *raison d'être* of which is production for private profit' (Rees, 1980: 203). The same of course could be said for the other parts of Wales as well. Given the propensity of capital to seek out advantages wherever they exist, and to make use of space accordingly, it could be expected that the differences which already existed within Wales would confer upon it a variety of opportunities and disadvantages. In responding to the legacy of earlier rounds of investment, capital would be prone to amplify such differences, thus contributing towards a pattern in which it was asserted that spatial and sectoral differences appeared to be gaining in intensity as a feature of the current phase of capitalist development (Urry, 1981, 1984). Processes of economic and social restructuring would eventuate in a series of locally orientated vicious and virtuous circles of development, creating widening disparities among the respective winners and losers.

From this vantage point, the proclaimed 'modernization' which had been accomplished in Wales could be disclosed as nothing more than the latest phase in an unceasing process of change and reorganization aimed at maintaining the overall viability and profitability of the dominant economic system. Presenting it, as in official government commentaries, in the more optimistic terms of how Wales was succeeding in getting to grips with its past and moving forward to a more secure future helped to conceal the nature of the underlying relationships, dressing up as a general benefit the extent to which the gains made by some imposed severe costs upon many others. Seeing it as a pattern of 'restructuring' which served particular interests opened the way to a more critical and reflective mode of analysis. Certainly, there was a danger in this alternative perspective of taking an unduly functionalist view of the essential relationships, inferring for instance that one could somehow 'derive' the particular changes taking place at local level from an appreciation of the nature of economic production alone (Rees, 1980: 203) or that the role of government and the state in assisting and regulating the process was entirely predictable (Cooke, 1980). This would be to underestimate the importance of providing an account which did justice to those features of the situation that were specifically and uniquely Welsh, and which made allowance for the ways in which the interests of capital could be resisted and even sometimes defeated. Nevertheless, it was reasonable to seek to identify a set of prevailing conditions within which change was being shaped, according to the dominant tendencies of production at the given time. This provided the framework in which a number of authors, including Cooke, Lovering, Morgan, and Rees, could proceed to carry out research at varying levels of detail on the economic and social restructuring process in Wales. An important theme which united their work was the recognition of the internal heterogeneity of Wales.

Once the overall process of 'development' was broken down into specifiable patterns of causal influence operating within the productive system, it was unavoidable that there should be a recognition that this had differing consequences for different parts of Wales. Part of the argument about relative beneficiaries and victims had to do with the impact on different places: growing prosperity for some areas coming at the expense of the decline of others. So Cooke, for example, writes of the 'changing regional fragmentation of geographical space in Wales' (1983b: 74), while Rees and Lambert (1985: 53) comment more generally on how 'this diversity of specific trends implied . . . the emergence of often very local patterns of change, with each area experiencing the effects of economic reorganization in quite distinct ways'.

In south Wales, Rees describes how the older industrial centres of the valleys, and the coal and steel communities, were undergoing decimation of their employment structures, whereas new work opportunities were emerging at the valley ends, and along the coastal plain (Rees, 1980; see also Rees and Rees, 1983). Between 1961 and 1971 the population of the valley areas of Gwent and Mid Glamorgan grew naturally by 23,000, yet an overall loss of 21,000 was recorded as people moved out in search of better economic prospects. As well as migration to new locations, large numbers were having to commute to jobs in such places as Llantrisant, Pontypridd and Cardiff. As the previously relatively self-contained nature of valley communities was shattered, some individuals and families found themselves possessing the capacity to exploit the new possibilities while others, including those least well resourced to begin with, were trapped into diminishing life chances. New social divisions and inequalities emerged to erode established social relationships and undermine the collective defences built up by preceding generations. At the macro-level, this reflected the changing industrial and employment structure of the Welsh economy. Even prior to this period, it was noted, adjustments towards a broader manufacturing and service base 'were not painless. There was much social stress in particular localities' (George and Mainwaring, 1988: 2). As economic conditions worsened during the 1970s, and job loss became more familiar than employment growth, such 'stress' became a chronic feature of life in Wales.

The major shifts taking place included a rapidly changing balance of manufacturing industry, associated with quite radical alterations in the pattern of skills and occupations, and the general expansion of the part played by the service sector within a de-industrialised or possibly emergent 'post-industrial' economic order (Carney and Lewis, 1978; Massey, 1984;

Rees and Lambert, 1985). So far as manufacturing was concerned, it was tending to avoid or abandon the older centres, including both the regions of heavy industry, and the inner cities, in favour of fresh pastures where there was scope for the construction of new and more efficient infrastructure, and an untried and more pliant labour force was available. This meant a 'relocation' of manufacturing out towards the more rural areas, and back into some of the more 'peripheral' parts of Britain. Innovations in technology and the workplace division of labour, combined with pressures to raise the level of productivity to stave off falling profit margins, encouraged processes of 'deskilling' which led to an expanding role for semi-skilled workers, and the weakening or disappearance of older forms of skilled manual employment. Together with the expansion of light engineering work, especially the assembly of new consumer durables, this afforded far greater possibilities for the employment of women. Massey characterized the shift as involving a transfer from skilled male manual employment to semi-skilled or unskilled work for females (Massey, 1983). As well as less skilled work, this also helped bring about more part-time work, more casual employment and a general increase in the instability of the labour force. These were the early symptoms of what came to be hailed as a more 'flexible', casualized, and insecure workforce in which earlier conceptions of skill, career, and stable employment were being destroyed, with far-reaching and as yet undetermined social consequences. These processes have continued to the present day, with ever widening implications for the nature of contemporary work (Sennett, 1998). The expansion of the service sector also generated greater demand for women workers, who for a variety of reasons (including gender stereotypes of various sorts) were regarded as particularly suited to jobs in personal services and some of the rapidly expanding clerical and administrative spheres of employment.

In Wales, the feminization of the labour force attracted considerable attention. From a situation in which barely a quarter of Welsh women had been in paid work by the mid-1960s, rapid expansion in female employment took place during the 1970s and 1980s (Winckler, 1985; Rees, 1999). Indeed, some rather over-excited claims were made about how the entire working population was beginning to take on the character of women's work, as women entered the labour force *'en masse'* (G. A. Williams, 1985: 298); before long, it was suggested, women would constitute the majority of the labour force, and the bulk of the Welsh working class, signifying nothing less than a social revolution (G. A. Williams, 1984). Claims of this sort had to be tempered by a more realistic appraisal which noted both that women's historical contribution to the Welsh economy had been systematically underestimated, and under-recorded, and that the extent of the contemporary change was being exaggerated (Rees, 1988). While numerically women were making considerable gains, these were not matched by progress on other fronts. The proportion of women who were in part-time work rose steadily as the numbers of women in paid employment increased. In 1975, 37 per cent of working women were in part-time jobs; by 1994 this had risen to very nearly half (Rees, 1999). By that time, there were almost as many female as male employees in Wales, but they worked on less favourable terms, and were less well-paid, and less likely to reach the higher and better rewarded positions.

Reviewing the situation in 1988, Teresa Rees noted that

> The strategies used by employers to ensure a flexible workforce, the recalcitrance of trades unions to involve their female members at decision making levels, and the persistence of the traditional patterns of domestic divisions of labour combine to ensure that women, rather than being the vanguard of the labour movement, are likely to remain a numerically substantial, but distinctly disadvantaged section of the workforce. (Rees, 1988: 127)

Winckler (1985) describes how, even in the relatively benign area of civil service employment, the dispersal of public-sector jobs from the south-east of England had brought substantial numbers of low-skilled, low-paid and basically unattractive 'paper factory' jobs to Wales. These had contributed to the reinforcement of regional inequalities by installing 'new and deeply entrenched differences both between Wales and the rest of Britain, and between men and women' (Winckler, 1985: 217). In general, the Welsh workforce remained subject to rigid divisions along gender lines (Rees, 1999), with men and women working in different industries and, even when in the same industry, in different occupations. The main increases in women's employment were concentrated heavily in two sectors – distribution, hotels and catering; and 'other services' – in which there were particularly large numbers of low-paid and casualized jobs (Walker, 1992). Eventually these two sectors accounted for four out of every five women who were working part-time. By contrast, women in Wales have made very limited progress into top jobs (Rees and Fielder, 1991) and in this regard continue to lag behind what has been achieved in other parts of Britain.

The position Wales occupied within the newly evolving spatial division of labour corresponded to its particular combination of advantages and disadvantages. One of the main developments in industrial structure to which Massey had drawn attention was the extent to which larger and more rationalized organizations permitted the hierarchical separation of different functions, which could then be located in different places. It was no longer necessary for a business which had grown up in one place to exercise any preference for local labour, local markets or contact with other nearby companies. Capital had always enjoyed the advantage over labour with regard to mobility, but now industries, or large parts of them, were increasingly 'footloose'. Improvements in communications and transport obviously played a part here as well. Thus the higher order functions of management, research and design could be physically distant from the more routine productive activities, such as mass assembly work, without losing touch with them. Each aspect of the organization could be driven by its own particular logic, for example by the need for suitable labour, or for close proximity to intellectual hot-spots, or whatever. This created the potential for the formation of areas which specialized in high-grade technical, scientific and managerial work, while elsewhere the need was only for people who could fill mundane, low-skilled jobs.

Wales was widely thought to fall into the latter category: among its main assets was an ample fund of under-employed labour capable of meeting the demand for relatively lowly skilled, 'screwdriver' type jobs. This was available through a combination of reasons: excess labour in places where the existing industrial base could no longer provide enough work for the local population; areas which had never been developed for industrial employment; and, most prominently, large reserves of female labour-power which had not yet been drawn into the workplace. Conversely, numerous reasons could be adduced for suggesting that Wales was not best placed either to provide, or to accommodate, the skilled and expert kinds of labour needed to staff positions in the top tiers of modern organizations. Like other areas whose previous economic role had been exhausted, or which had never been fully developed, Wales appeared vulnerable to being treated mainly as a reservoir of cheap labour, filling undemanding jobs. In the words of Rees and Rees, 'the hierarchisation of production results in regions such as south Wales becoming focuses of the "bottom rung" of assembly work' (1983: 114).

This possibility had further ramifications. The higher-status jobs in question were those most closely associated with corporate control functions; it was the company headquarters which tended to be located in the geographically most 'favoured' places. Thus the vast majority of major British companies had their control centres in or close to London. Wales, on the other hand, attracted activities at the opposite end of the corporate hierarchy – the controlled, low-status kinds of work. Rather than the core aspects of business, it was over-endowed with 'branch plants' – those bits of companies which were least vital to operations, and most in danger of being lopped off if times got rough. There was much discussion of the effects of this 'branch-plant syndrome'. Cooke (1983b) among others described the pattern whereby Wales had been increasingly penetrated by branch plants of firms in the vehicles, electrical engineering and plastics industries, whose centres were most often located in southern England or the midlands. They were being joined as well by growing numbers of branches of overseas firms. This had made parts of the former coalfield into an 'intensive branch plant region' while the spread of such units across mid and south-west Wales had introduced an 'archipelago' of branch plants throughout the country (Cooke, 1983b: 78). Appropriately to the Welsh context, these units were not so much cathedrals in the desert as a sprinkling of scattered chapels, made up of relatively small and often isolated manufacturing operations. Recession had a drastic impact upon these, producing an 'employment switchback' as different parts of Wales recorded losses of between 15 and 25 per cent in manufacturing jobs between 1975 and 1981. Only the north Wales coast, with tiny proportions of employees in manufacturing, escaped such heavy losses. In total, Wales saw 75,000 jobs go in just five years, and it did not escape attention that the key decisions about this were being made elsewhere, among people who had little concern for the impact of their actions upon Wales, or upon the Welsh workforce.

Given that firms had been splitting up various stages in the process of production and locating them where local conditions were most favourable to minimizing their overall costs (Cooke, 1983b: 73), this was not really surprising. However, the results should have carried an official health warning: economic development can be negative as well as positive, and branch plants can damage your health. The degree of separation or 'disarticulation' between different levels of the Welsh economy had increased, as contrasting sectors appeared which moved to very different rhythms. The 'enclave' pattern discussed by Lovering stemmed from the way in which many of the more recent developments owed very little, if anything, to their specifically Welsh environment. Thus the number of overseas manufacturing establishments had grown from just sixteen in 1949 to 177 in 1977; employment in them had expanded from 14,000 to almost 53,000. These were often high-productivity plants, mostly located within easy reach of the main transport routes out of Wales, and it was estimated that no more than 4 per cent of their output went to other firms in Wales, compared to as much as a fifth which was directly exported out of the UK (Davies and Thomas, 1976). Half undertook no research and development activity, and 58 per cent of the jobs created by them were unskilled. These were enterprises which had only a vestigial connection to Wales. Another two-thirds of manufacturing employment in Wales was traceable to firms which had their origins in other parts of Britain. Together, these British and foreign companies made up what Lovering termed the 'monopolistic' or internationalized sector of the economy (Lovering, 1983a). They provided many of the better-paid Welsh jobs, but remained in Wales mainly because wages were lower and labour was better behaved than elsewhere. They had no particular attachment to being part of the Welsh economy, and were increasingly orientated to European and worldwide market conditions.

By contrast, there was a more localized, 'competitive' sector, which was far more tied to local conditions and local markets, in which wages were even poorer, labour productivity was low and prospects for growth very limited. Leading examples were small and medium-sized firms in tourism, construction and some branches of retail. Although they generated less prosperity, these businesses were altogether more committed to continuing in operation locally, and far more dependent upon economic circumstances within Wales. Which of these sectors individuals ended up working within could be extremely fateful for their future chances; likewise, local economies were strongly influenced by the particular mix of the different sectors which they happened to contain. At the very bottom end of the distribution, Lovering suggested, there did indeed exist a 'marginalized' sector consisting of those who were liable to unemployment, seasonal work, casualization and so on, and who were therefore only weakly attached to the labour market. Such marginalization was a product of changes affecting labour markets, not just in Wales, but throughout the advanced economies; however, the way in which different sorts of jobs and labour-market positions were distributed between geographical areas did have major repercussions for particular populations. By now, others (McNabb, 1980) were also warning that far too many of the jobs being created in Wales bore the stigma of the 'peripheral' or secondary type of employment – part-time, insecure, with high turnover – which, as labour-market theorists had been demonstrating, were a poor substitute for 'primary' employment closer to the heart of the contemporary economy. As noted above, the occupants of many of these positions were Welsh women.

These considerations were extremely instructive so far as future policy developments were concerned. More and more it was becoming apparent that it was not enough to aim simply to attract more jobs to Wales, without giving close attention to what kind of jobs they were, and how they fitted into the changing nature of economic organization. Quality, as well as quantity of employment, counted, and to achieve this it was necessary to position oneself carefully within the evolving economic and social division of labour. Furthermore, as Cooke rightly emphasized (1983b: 74), the processes which were being uncovered were of interest not just to econo-mists alone; they presaged instead a thoroughgoing recomposition of Welsh social structure, with particular significance for patterns of class and gender division. This was because, as Massey had insisted, changes in the social organization of production were only part of the story. They provided an important way in to an understanding of how social structures were changing, but there was a great deal more to social structure than could be learned from production alone. The restructuring framework offered an approach to the examination of the real world, not a substitute for it. The whole aim of the reconceptualization was to reinstate, in a more theoretically informed manner, an awareness of regional and local particularities, and how these came about. Analytically, as well as practically, the process was iterative: in Massey's words,

> Historically, of course, the whole process is a circular one. Distributions of class relations and different social groups over space are in part a product of these processes and operate as location factors in subsequent periods of investment. Reserves of labour, for instance, are the product of social relations; they don't just happen. And such local variations in class and social structure can in turn have significant effects on location. (1984: 55)

5

Divided and Dividing Wales?
Explorations in Geography and Class

In an examination of trends affecting the regional division of labour in the 1980s, Cooke (1983b) produces a fourfold grouping of regional patterns which conforms roughly to a breakdown of the geography of Wales at the time. The four areas thus defined are: (i) the emerging major service area centred on Cardiff, which as well as seeing an expanding service sector had also been undergoing significant de-industrialization; (ii) the urbanized centres of the coalfield and in other parts of Wales, which were increasingly becoming focal points for public services together with some limited manufacturing development – for instance, an outer ring of places around Cardiff such as Caerphilly, Cwmbran and Bridgend was witnessing some significant industrial developments; (iii) the so-called 'leisure reserves' along the north and west Wales coast, whose resort areas specialized in tourism and associated services; (iv) in central Wales, the erstwhile agricultural economy was being converted into a combination of services and manufacturing developments which Cooke terms a 'state managed branch plant outpost of the midlands and south of England' (1983b: 85). While the precise specifications of each of the areas might be queried, these different types of setting undoubtedly constituted very disparate contexts, within which people typically faced quite distinctive sets of opportunities and challenges. From the standpoint of each of them could be derived a certain sense of what Wales was about, and where it was headed, but since the differences between them were at least as striking as anything they had in common, it was no easy matter to form an overall impression that would do justice to the diversity they represented. Furthermore, just as in other parts of Britain where, under the influence of social and economic restructuring, different areas seemed to be becoming more distinct, the signs were that these differences would increase, rather than diminish. Cooke himself notes how these and other changes suggested increasing social and geographical polarization for Wales, taking Wales 'ever further from the mystical image of a classless society' (1981b: 1).

Cooke's classification of Welsh subregions fits into a tradition of such attempts to delineate the country's various spatial and social zones. In 1921 Sir Alfred Zimmern had distinguished between three versions of Wales which he claimed were representative of 'different types and traditions', moving historically in different directions: Welsh Wales, Industrial or 'American' Wales, and upper-class or English Wales (Smith, 1984: 100; Zimmern, 1921). Some sixty years later, memories of these 'impressions' of Wales were stirred by Balsom's 'three Wales model', in which three distinct 'primary social groupings' were identified, each with its corresponding territorial 'enclave' (Balsom, 1985). Derived mainly from survey data collected in 1979, this classification distinguished between the two English-language areas of 'Welsh Wales' and 'British Wales', and separated them both from the Welsh-speaking territory of *Y Fro Gymraeg*. Whereas Cooke's classification was based principally upon economic function, and Zimmern and Balsom were highlighting cultural and political factors, all three were acknowledging the split geography of Wales, which, in various forms, has been an omnipresent consideration in much of the discussion so far.

Such obvious spatial and social fragmentation elicits contrasting responses. On the one hand, it helps explain the reluctance many commentators show towards generalizing about the society as a whole. Among many students of Wales, it produces a commendable sensitivity to place, and a preference for focusing on the local, particular and communal, which means that generalities are often criticized for exceeding the limits of their applicability. Some of the most impressive social scientific pieces on Wales have taken specific communities or localities as their focus, and it is not too fanciful to link this academic inclination to a strong tendency among ordinary people in Wales to express a sense of identity and belonging which is closely related to a particular place or locale. Harris (1987: 13) observes that it is one of the distinguishing characteristics of the Welsh to structure their social world in terms of relations between particular persons, places and events, producing a strong attachment to those locations within which their relationships have been formed. Similarly, Cole (1990: 3) notes that 'much of the strength of Wales lies in its community structure and the sense of loyalty of its people to concepts of place and distinctiveness'. On the other hand, and perhaps also because of this, it happens from time to time that aspects which really are applicable only to parts of Wales are extrapolated to the whole, elevating a limited vision as if it was universal. The balancing out of these two tendencies is one of the several forms taken by the 'schizophrenia' which is frequently spoken of as a feature of the Welsh situation.

Hence a social science text published in association with the Open University in Wales begins with the proposition that Wales is itself primarily a geographical expression (Hume and Pryce, 1986: p. xvi), and rapidly moves on to the exploration of those spatial divisions which make it difficult to treat as a single whole. Thus Pryce (1986) uses primary historical sources to demonstrate how records of the language of worship employed in the provision of church services can help to define Wales as a 'culture region'. Their inspection over time shows how the English language gradually infiltrated a key institutional domain, that of religion, in ways which distinguish a core region of 'Welsh Wales' from a sphere of growing Anglicization. It is in the bilingual domain between the two that the dynamics of language change are played out. According to Pryce, language usage is associated with distinct 'ways of life', with Welsh carrying the 'old' ways and English representing more modern intrusions; the inner area of Wales corresponds to what is known as *Cymru Gymraeg* or the Welsh 'heartland'. Class influences – especially through the impact of prominent landowning gentry families – and migration patterns associated with industrialization are seen to be important among the factors bringing about these changes. Thus spatial, cultural and economic variations all conspire to set different parts of Wales apart from one another, and to raise questions about the 'authenticity' of different forms of Welshness.

As a geographer, Pryce is sympathetic to the well-respected work of Emrys Bowen, who set out under the influence of French regional geography to identify the entity which he labelled the 'Pays de Galles' (Bowen, 1959). In a radio lecture given in 1964, Bowen gave credence to a significant degree of geographical determinism, in describing how the 'lie of the land' was reflected in the divisions of Welsh culture and society. Taking language, religious affiliation, education and prevailing types of agriculture as his indicators, Bowen mapped out a very long-standing distinction between 'Inner' and 'Outer' Wales, with the mountains and uplands providing the defensive perimeter behind which inner Wales could persist and, eventually, retreat over the centuries. For him, geographical conditions furnished an underlying continuity within which new actors could come and go on what remained basically an unaltered stage. Bowen noted the 'irony' whereby, for geographical or geological reasons, industrial development in Wales came to be concentrated in the 'outer' areas, where it was most susceptible to the influence of non-Welsh, Anglicizing or cosmopolitan forces. Hence industrialization tended to increase the pressures pitted against the Welsh heartland, setting the strength of economic forces against the maintenance of cultural and linguistic characteristics already eroded by political influences. Bowen's own standpoint is unequivocal, when he writes that 'in the end it is the *culture* of Inner Wales that has given Wales its personality, its language, its religion and song. These survive into the modern epoch and represent the real Wales' (1986: 85; stress added). In which case, 'outer' or industrial Wales has to be viewed as either not having a 'personality' or as having one that is not 'Welsh'; apparently, in some way or other, its status as part of Wales is illusory.

It is contentious assertions of this kind which spurred the historian Gwyn A. Williams (1985: 236) to castigate a version of Welsh historiography through which

> large numbers of people, who in fact constituted a majority, were perceived as in some basic senses, un-Welsh, and the perception acquired retrospective force. . . . The more arrogant, extreme or paranoid exponents of Welshness simply refuse to see any 'culture' at all in English-speaking Wales, or else they dismiss it as 'British' or even 'English'. The victims of this myopia cultivate an equally contemptuous and dismissive response.

Like Hobsbawm's comments quoted earlier, this statement points to a very deep and traumatic schism which has occurred over the years in the formation of Wales, and which continually echoes, in a characteristic dualism, through attempts to describe and explain what Wales is really about. Even the most fleeting acquaintance with writing about Wales makes one quickly aware of disputes about what exactly constitutes Welshness, and who can be regarded legitimately as Welsh. Aspects of geography, history, class and personal identity all become caught up with the way in which these questions are addressed and answered.

THE *GWERIN* AND THE WORKING CLASS

The precise juncture at which Williams makes his acerbic remarks comes when he sets out to deal with what he presents as two great components in the Welsh mythological pantheon: the working class and the *gwerin*. These present themselves as sociological categories which encapsulate, to a great extent, alternative, and frequently opposed, world-views, supported by sections of the Welsh population who, according to Williams, have been living for decades in increasing mutual alienation. 'Working class' of course is a term which is utterly familiar as part of the general vocabulary of both politics and sociology, albeit one which is used nowadays with far more reservation than in the past. The nature and fate of the working class in Wales forms part of the much larger story of class transformation over the course of the twentieth century, not just in Britain but on a world scale. *Gwerin* by contrast is a specifically Welsh expression meaning, more or less, 'the people' (*y werin*), those ordinary folk who make up the mass of society (P. Morgan, 1986). These are identified by Williams as being 'cultivated, educated, often self-educated, responsible, self-disciplined, respectable but on the whole genially poor' (1985: 237). Revealingly, this is an essentially behavioural description, which singles out certain traits of conduct as characteristic of the group in question. It bears at least some resemblance to the Scottish notion of the 'lad o' pairts', the individual from humble origins who through education and individual effort can rise to leading social positions without losing touch with the community of origin. In Scotland, this is said to form part of 'a conservative ideology which congratulated itself on the openness of Scottish (essentially rural and small town) society and its social institutions' (McCrone, 1992: 98) and which attached social identity to its roots in community, rather than class. Something similar can be said about the signification of *gwerin* in Wales, although it sometimes proclaims itself as a radical, rather than conservative, conception.

'Working class' has been employed more often as a structural concept, signifying the occupation of a particular social position, although again, it must be admitted, one that frequently triggers certain presumptions about corresponding sets of attitudes and values which form part of an accompanying class culture. The reason that these appear to be opposed rather than compatible ideas is that *gwerin* has been used in ways which tend to deny the relevance of class considerations for Welsh society, proposing instead what might be regarded as a focus on differences of social status, whereas the working class as a category transparently belongs within an analysis of a broader structure of social classes. As Williams notes, without being totally confined to it, *gwerin* is redolent of a rural milieu, whereas the existence and nature of the working class is normally centred on the fact of industrialization. Through the use of these terms, therefore, rural Wales stands counterposed to industrial/urban Wales, with inevitable geographical associations, and at the risk of reproducing this separation, the terms will be discussed here in the setting of rather distinct bodies of work and literature.

Since Williams places the notion of the *gwerin* back pretty firmly at the turn of the twentieth century, while Morgan (1986) sees its roots going back even earlier, it might seem completely irrelevant to any examination of Welsh sociology a century or more later, except that from time to time the concept still pops up as a working element in sociological discourse. Furthermore, Williams attributes some of the main turns taken subsequently by Welsh society to its influence, especially in the spheres of politics and education. Thus it has more than an antiquarian interest. In a recent discussion of race relations in Wales, for example, the term is said to evoke an idyll deeply embedded in the national consciousness, which prompts 'imaginings' of a community built on mutual understanding, harmony and tolerance amongst a upright and cultured people that has little place for the recognition of 'racial' difference or for a self-critical awareness of racism (C. Williams, 1999b). Very similar notions have been projected from other 'folk' societies, at or around the transition to modernity, and they have made an important contribution to the development of ideas of national identity, enabling people to mobilize around beliefs about the things they have in common, rather than what divides them (Gellner, 1983). The maintenance of the myth of a classless *gwerin* is seen by some as fundamental aspect of nationalist ideology in Wales (Adamson, 1988: 7; Evans, 1974).

As indicated, among the divisions which tend to be denied by adherence to the notion of the *gwerin* are those of class. Since from this standpoint the 'people' are considered to be a homogeneous mass, united by their similarities, when class differences are acknowledged, they tend to be externalized, and identified with those who are not 'of the people'. Consequently class and ethnic, or national, divisions are assimilated to one another, along lines already familiar from our discussion of the literature on internal colonialism and the cultural division of labour (Day, 1979). Morgan, who has given close historical attention to the idea of the *gwerin*, concurs with this when he interprets it as a component of cultural nationalism, rather than class struggle (1986: 135; see also Morgan, 1983). Well aware that the idea has been extensively mythologized, he nevertheless finds some support for its validity in the work of Welsh rural sociologists, whose studies of small communities in the Welsh heartland provide some 'real elements' to back a notion that is otherwise 'a little bit too good to be true' (1986: 150). Further consideration will be given to these studies later. For now, it can be noted simply that they reiterate the linkages between the social depiction of the *gwerin*, the significance which is attached within it to culture and to language, and the nature of 'inner' or rural Wales as a fundamentally classless society. As Gwyn Williams comments, whereas the idea might seem well-attuned to aspects of rural, north and west Wales, it is wholly unable to incorporate the complex reality of industrial Wales. Instead this has produced the rival 'myth' or archetype, of the Welsh working class.

The extent to which the two ideas can stand in for opposed points of view is highlighted by another writer, who contrasts

> on the one side a revolutionary working class internationalism with no sense of Welsh identity and on the other a national consciousness which shuts out the historical experiences of its own working class and therefore largely excludes the politics of the working class. (Davies, 1976)

This stark opposition considerably over-simplifies the range of positions to be found on either side of the equation, and it also overlooks a critical common aspect of the way in which these two 'myths' have been deployed: namely, that both have been used to propound an essentially egalitarian view of Wales, minimizing the importance of those differences which existed within the society. Whatever truth there may once have been in this, it is an assumption that has been decisively discredited by processes of change, as already implied in the following passage, written nearly forty years ago (Rees, 1964; cited in Bell, 1968):

> A new world and a new society are coming into being as a result of the industrial renaissance of South Wales. Even the democratic class structure of Wales is changing. It is losing its homogeneity and uniformity, based on the preponderance of a single class whether the peasant or proletariat and tends increasingly to adapt itself to the subtly graded social hierarchy which provides the anatomy of modern industrial society.

THE FATE OF WORKING-CLASS WALES

If, as Harris suggests (1987: 229), sociology is 'about' class in the same way that anthropology is about kinship, then the sociology of Wales undoubtedly suffers certain handicaps. Investigating social class in Wales is like utilizing the exploratory trenches dug by archaeologists to provide information on what might lie hidden beneath the surface; no one yet has attempted a full-scale excavation. Instead we have a number of significant 'case studies' undertaken at different time points, dealing with different circumstances, usually in different places. In most instances, they are linked to research agendas which are not oriented primarily to Wales. Yet they all form part of the same story, with hidden connections and continuities. To some extent we are required to make speculative leaps to bring these into the open. In this regard perhaps we are little worse off than sociology as a whole, since knowledge has usually been garnered in the same piecemeal way, and the recurrence in this field of the names of certain individual sociologists (Harris, Rees, Adamson) provides at least an element of coherence. But there are certainly some very large gaps in our knowledge, such as the almost total lack of examination of the characteristics of Welsh elites, and of the activities of the powerful in Wales. Attention has been directed far more systematically towards the working class, and the relatively powerless, although even here various threads need to be drawn together.

As noted in Chapter 1, the centrality of the industrial working-class experience to both the image and reality of Wales is beyond question. Historical meanings and inheritances which derive from the years preceding the Second World War are extraordinarily hard to shake off, and up until very recently there were many for whom it could be said that '"Wales" equals mining valleys; miners; slag heaps; Aberfan; socialism; chapels; Labour party stronghold; rugby football; Dylan Thomas and nowadays, I suppose, Max Boyce' (Harris, 1987: 12). Without saying as much, what is being described here is working-class Wales, and, as is hinted, it is an image upon which many have traded, for a variety of purposes, but which carries some powerful negative as well as positive connotations. Quite literally, large parts of Wales were created by the efforts and energies of its industrial workers, so that

> South Wales's gaunt landscape of high moorland divided by deep, once beautiful, valleys lined with tight rows of terrace houses, roads and railways and scarred by mining and industrial decay speaks of the hard labours and poverty of a classic industrial working class, a class whose legendary communal solidarity now seems oddly anachronistic to most English people. (Morgan and Sayer, 1988: 149)

These characterizations are taken from texts which are concerned above all to provide up-to-date knowledge of the forces which have been driving the real economy and society of modern Wales in a different direction, taking them increasingly further away from the truth and relevance of these kinds of image. In each instance, it is suggested that the features described have become a source of estrangement or embarrassment to outsiders, helping to define those parts of Wales which tourists will choose to avoid (Harris, 1987), and those places 'rarely given a thought by the English middle classes' (Morgan and Sayer, 1988), except when they present themselves forcibly as a problem that must be solved. As well as indicating the time-lag which affects people's perceptions, such remarks catch something of the peripheralization and isolation undergone by once dominant sets of social relations. Far from being typical any longer, it is suggested that these are places and relationships stranded by the tides of change, as a once solid base for social existence has melted away.

Writing in 1987, Harris points out that by this time only a tenth of employment in south Wales was attributable to coal and steel; the bulk of the population were a generation or more removed from these former basic industries and what had once been a majority experience had become of relatively marginal concern. Nevertheless, he accepted that the two industries still had a vital significance for the region, since they provided the only feasible basis for the maintenance of the traditional settlement pattern and associated way of life. As he put it,

> delete mining and the whole economic base of the South Wales valleys is undermined ... Remove employment in heavy industry and mining and you sever the links of the working class with its own past and its present culture and thus threaten the basis on which Industrial South Walian men construct and negotiate their identity as competent working class people. (Harris, 1987: 14–15)

History has performed precisely this excision, removing for ever the material basis on which so much of the deeply engrained social and cultural nature of Welsh working-class life had rested. The effects bear out Massey's thesis that economic restructuring is simultaneously and integrally the reorganization and recomposition of class and gender relations (Massey, 1978) and, in line with Harris's predictions, the repercussions for conceptions of Welsh identity have been enormous, not just for men, and not only in the industrial areas.

THE WORKING CLASS IN DISINTEGRATION AND DECLINE

The dismantling and demise of a 'traditional' working class has been a major topic of sociological inquiry and debate for at least fifty years, and accounting for its fate has been intrinsic to the attempt to understand the wider transformations of class structures and relationships in contemporary capitalism (Crompton, 1993; Bradley, 1996; Lee and Turner, 1996). While theoretical and empirical arguments on the matter abound, at least there is fairly good agreement about the main characteristics of the working class as classically conceived. It rose to prominence as a conscious and assertive social actor on the back of the collective strength of masses of male employees, assembled together in particular industries and workplaces where they were subjected to a common framework of control, and where their conditions and attributes were largely homogenized in order to ensure the continuing advancement of the accumulation of capital. The combination of the structural pressures of economic position, and the communal relationships that grew up around them in order to enable the workforce to survive, and reproduce itself, gave rise to a 'strong idiom' of class analysis (Holton, 1996) in which economic, political and cultural influences were all held to flow together. This is not to deny the complexities involved in tracing their connections, nor the room this gave for research into and discussion about the exact way in which the various aspects were melded; but there was a powerful overall sense of a distinctive, organized and coherent form of existence, a 'way of life', which could be identified as that of the industrial working class, and which was marked off firmly from that of other social groups and classes. This persisted well into the post-war period, when if anything it appeared for a time to be growing in strength, the labour movement having won grudging acceptance as a legitimate partner in the regulation and government of society (Hobsbawm, 1968; Middlemass, 1979).

At this time, the working class, consisting of manual workers and their families, still accounted for something like two-thirds of the population. Although this included many elements which were only loosely incorporated, and which did not necessarily behave 'reliably' in the standard ways expected of them, their role was compensated for by the existence of other sectors which provided the leadership, organization and combative spirit required to carry forward a collective class project of material advancement and social improvement, of the kind alluded to in prominent sociological studies conducted during the 1960s and early 1970s (Goldthorpe et al., 1969; Brown and Brannen, 1970). Miners were invariably listed as among the most militant and determined elements of the class, as were ship-builders, transport workers and other employees in 'heavy industry' in general.

The Welsh case conforms well to these general principles. Enough has been said already to indicate that accounts of the working class in Wales have been constructed primarily with south Wales in mind; after all, during the first half of the twentieth century this was a prime candidate for being seen as the 'proletarian region' *par excellence* (Rees and Rees, 1980b: 24). Stamped with a massive working-class presence, driven by the vicissitudes of the economic cycle, its inhabitants underwent an overriding set of experiences which contributed to the formation of a very powerful conception of Wales as home to a nation of radical proletarians, forcefully represented in literary as well as political expression (L. Jones, 1937). If anything, with the triumphs of Labourism, the prevalent working-class ethos of south Wales retained and increased its power as a structural and cultural phenomenon through into the 1950s, when it could be described as displaying a highly organized and well articulated democratic class culture (R. M. Jones, 1999).

Socially, industrial Wales remained a relatively undifferentiated society, organized around the essential terms of employment of wage-labour, and cross-cutting gender divisions. At its heart the economy consisted of large blocks of male manual workers, doing jobs in basic industries where they met broadly similar conditions and opportunities, and encountered similar situations of subordination and disadvantage. Significant among them, of course, were more than 120,000 miners, already much depleted from their peak of a quarter of a million at the start of the century, but given renewed confidence for a while by the state's apparent readiness to assume responsibility for their future. A further 40,000 men were employed in metals. They were surrounded by the necessary infrastructural employment in transport, docks and ancillary services required to support them in their work. These had been the essential industries of Wales for more than a hundred years, and much of the social framework had been formed around them and their requirements. Yet for such a dominant reality, the Welsh working class has attracted surprisingly little close sociological attention. Its study has been assigned mainly to historians and students of politics, while sociologists have opted mostly to treat it as a background, 'taken-for-granted', feature against which to carry out their own more narrowly focused researches. However, in common with the rest of Britain (Bradley, 1996), the history of the second half of the twentieth century is that of the disintegration of the main outlines of this formation, and its break-up and reorganization into a number of quite distinctive fragments. Cooke's account of class structure in Wales at the start of the 1980s, for example, is insistent on the extent of 'fragmentation, diversification and segmentation of the working class in Wales which is under way as capitalist social relations are extended and reproduced and the class is recomposed' (1981b: 27). Nevertheless, Cooke still contended that 'a process of proletarianisation has been underway in recent years over large parts of the territory of Wales', and he anticipated that these tendencies would continue further.

With its mass of workers in coal, steel, quarrying and transport, it was predictable that Wales would provide at least its quota of working-class heroes and villains, and make a distinctive input into the development of modes of working-class organization and politics, as has been documented extensively by Welsh labour historians (for examples, see Smith, 1980; Francis and Smith, 1980; and *Llafur*, the journal of Welsh Labour History). Through the influence of prominent Welsh Labour politicians and trade unionists, Wales punched above its weight in the contribution it made to the British labour movement and the formation of the distinctive British welfare state. The National Health Service, for example, is still seen as a peculiarly Welsh possession because of the leading role played in its inauguration by Aneurin Bevan. Wales was also marked by the features of spatial concentration, and prevalence of one-class communities, organized around work and its routines, which have been assumed to foster especially strong forms of identification with a class and its representatives (Kerr and Siegel, 1954). The effectiveness of the local Labour Party machine in parts of Wales has been legendary, as has its propensity to substitute patronage for popular participation. Arguably then, Wales is among those places that have witnessed the dominance of a 'regional class' – that is, the formation of patterns of class politics and culture distinctive enough at the regional level to demand separate definition (Massey, 1984: 59). There has been no shortage of people ready to uphold such a claim, and prepared to celebrate the special quality and aura of Welsh labour, with its seemingly 'natural' allegiance to the union, the Labour Party and to such local institutions as the miner's lodge, the working man's club, the chapel and the choir (R. M. Jones, 1999). In south Wales, at least, being working class was not to belong to some residual category but to lay claim to an honourable status, and a source of pride (Harris, 1987: 15).

A more down-to-earth expression of this view is found in the comment of a shop-steward in the Ford Motor Company, explaining why he was able to contemplate strike action with more enthusiasm than colleagues in other plants:

> It's not the fault of the Dagenham lads. All working class blokes are the same basically. It's the leadership that's at fault . . .We've got a whole history of working class militancy behind us in Liverpool and South Wales. We've got the tradition, the equipment . . . everything. And we're cashing in on it too. We're going to take over this show. We're off. (Beynon, 1973: 216)

There is bound to be a risk that such generalizations will take on mythic proportions, leading to the overstating of the levels of solidarity, militancy and consistency of action associated with class membership. This is a mistake that has been made not only by commentators, but also by activists. Behind the abstractions of the 'working class', we are usefully reminded, it was the identity of workplace, trade union and community that constituted the reality (Williams, 1985: 239). As is plain from the shop-steward's statement, this always resulted in a critical combination of general characteristics, shared among workers everywhere, with definite forms of localism, which could as easily generate divisions as unity between them (Nichols and Beynon, 1977; Nichols and Armstrong, 1976). Typically, the working class has been formed around involvement with *particular* industries, and its character has varied according to the nature of the work, and the way in which it has been organized. This has meant that pursuing the interests of a given industry and occupation has often taken precedence over the wider prospects of the class as a whole, a point that sometimes has been forgotten in discussions of Wales. Attachment to specific sites, and their populations, has divisive as well as integrating effects; community is an exclusive, as well as inclusive term.

The two dominant local industries of south Wales, each in its own way, were able to impress upon the workforce numerous styles of conduct, organization and experience which were peculiar to them. Beynon notes how although steelworkers and miners lived in the same areas, they inhab-ited different economic and social worlds (Beynon, 1985: 18). Similarly Sewel sees it as an aspect of the exclusiveness of miners that they believed no steelworkers could really understand them (Sewel, 1975). The same can be said for the quarrymen of north and west Wales, that the world they inhabited was well-defined and distinctive (I. G. Jones, 1981). In reality, therefore, the 'proletariat' of Wales cannot be treated simply as uniform, but must be seen as made up of a number of discrete elements, each meriting specific attention. This is because 'while heavy industry regions may be thought of as archetypally the locations of the core elements of the classic working class, the practices often associated with such formations are highly unevenly developed' (Cooke, 1985: 230). In the same way, while all industries must respond to the general movements of the economy, each industry (with its myriad decision-making units) reacts in its own particular way. The formation and decomposition of the Welsh working class is thus the result of complex patterns of change in a number of separate industries, which has resulted in experiences which are differentiated both objectively and subjectively.

In an account of industrial relations trends and class recomposition affecting south Wales, Cooke (1981a) draws attention to some of the inherent differences between its core industries. As had been noted in some earlier classics of industrial sociology (Scott et al., 1956; Trist et al., 1963) there were significant contrasts in the way in which the labour-force profile for each industry was shaped by the actual organization of the labour process. In coal mining, the underground situation of the 'collier' tended to transcend differences of skill between jobs, and create a common bond throughout the workforce which overrode variations in job description. All miners were alike, in that their ability to deal with safety issues was paramount. Although working conditions in the steel industry were also extreme, and set steelworkers apart from the mass of other employees, there was not the same premium on shared qualifications and abilities; instead older craft skills were consolidated into a hierarchy of grades, which were reinforced further by organization into multiple trade unions. Intra-industry battles between occupational grades consumed as much energy as confrontations with employers. Thus the two industries developed different forms of collective bargaining, along with different reputations for conflict. Cooke contrasts the level of precariousness associated with working in coal, and the frequent outbreaks of intense conflict to which it gave rise, with the relative security of steelmaking, and its ability to sustain long-term rises in wage levels. Both industries produced attitudes of collectivism, and loyalty to unionism, but the detailed variations in levels of control exerted within the labour process, and in the extent of homogeneity between workers, contributed towards what he terms the 'complex determination' of regional unevenness in intensity of class consciousness, organization and solidarity. A practical expression of this was that workers in the two industries did not automatically support each other at times of conflict – in 1980, for instance, the south Wales miners refused to help striking steelworkers, recalling that on previous occasions when they themselves wanted assistance, it had not appeared (Cooke, 1981a: 174). Cooke suggests that the 'militant' reputation of south Wales, from which the rest of Wales has often borrowed, was based upon relatively rare but dramatic wage struggles, especially in coal. However, for would-be employers a more influential consideration might be the high level of support for unionization expressed among the Welsh workforce in general.

That differences of this sort could be observed in south Wales was not unique to the area: coal mining has been known worldwide for its militancy, whereas the steel industry has gained an international reputation for being relatively orderly. At the same time, it is not just a matter of uncovering the 'determining' nature of a given industry, since the development of industrial relations in south Wales coal followed a quite distinct path from that which occurred, for example, in the north-east of England (Daunton, 1981; Moore, 1974). Following the guidelines provided by Massey, it is a question of the interaction between a number of 'layers' of causation, and different factors which come together locally in a unique combination of the general and the particular. In a later version of his analysis, Cooke spells out five main types of structural influence which help to determine the appearance of distinct socio-spatial formations at regional level, and these clearly have a bearing on our understanding of Wales:

1. The productive base – what commodities are produced, under what conditions, and how labour is organized to yield surplus value
2. The labour process – with its incumbent forms of autonomy, supervision, skill, mechanization, and resistance
3. Ownership of capital – variations in size, type, sectoral distribution, and site of ownership (local, national, foreign)
4. Specific social relations – including cleavages of interest along lines of gender, wages, consumption, and 'popular' or ethno-regional mobilization
5. Institutional specificities – forms of cognitive, intellectual, and cultural practice, distributions of information and knowledge. (Cooke, 1985: 222)

Together these provide the parameters from which, it is claimed, there emerge sets of social practices sufficiently distinctive to constitute separate regional formations, with relatively sharp-edged frontiers. Variations in such practices become the 'markers' of different regions, and quite probably exert a major influence over how they impress themselves upon people's consciousness, leading to some regions having rather clear and well-established identities, while others lack comparable presence.

A good deal of the literature on economic and social restructuring involves the exploration of changes in the first three factors, as they work themselves out through the various relationships and practices identified in the other two. In this formulation, there are strong echoes of Marxist economic determinism, or the base/superstructure distinction, through which the productive system is taken to 'explain' social organization. However, the way in which Cooke seeks to integrate the analysis of production relations with aspects of the organization of civil society, such as family, locality, ideological and cultural practices, reflects the work of Gramsci and others in constructing a less deterministic form of Marxism, which could help elucidate variations in regional development in Italy and elsewhere without pretending to 'deduce' them from the nature of the economy alone (Gramsci, 1971; Kenny, 1999).

Cooke argues that, in the South Wales Coalfield, economy, culture and history combined to produce a wealth of everyday and taken-for-granted practices which made it an arena of relatively strong resistance to the dominant power structures. Local institutions of education, health and culture were imbued with a spirit of popular socialism, so that the region figures historically among the 'red zones' of Europe. Others endorse this vision of a 'radical region' marked by its industrial militancy and readiness to engage in class struggle (Rees and Lambert, 1985: 29), on behalf of its own alternative and autonomous vision. Francis (1990: 109) lists as component parts of 'all this proletarianism' coal, community, Nonconformity, trade unionism, self-education, democracy and socialism. As Lovering points out, the capacity to sustain such a radical culture over a significant span of time casts doubt on arguments that Wales was ideologically subjugated to the demands of 'the centre' (Lovering, 1978a: 92); in many ways it presented instead a standing challenge and rebuke to what that 'centre' desired.

CLASS AND CLASS CHANGE IN SOUTH-WEST WALES

The population of south Wales and its valleys was among those 'self-regulating' working-class communities, capable of mounting an effective collective defence against economic and social change, which grew up with an earlier phase of industrialism but which has been superseded by subsequent economic and spatial restructuring (Lash and Urry, 1987; Calhoun, 1982). The dissolution of its class base has meant the slow but inevitable evaporation of the 'proletarian' tradition. An early whiff of this can be captured from the single most impressive sociological study of class carried out in Wales.

Appearing in 1965, *The Family and Social Change* was one of the first fruits of the newly established School of Social Studies at University College Swansea. It reported on research initiated in 1959 as a direct follow-up to the famous Bethnal Green investigations of Young and Willmott (1957), and its main orientation is therefore towards examining changes taking place in the structure and role of the family, especially the question of the changing nature of the 'extended' family. Although it is addressed to a far wider sociological audience than those interested in Wales alone, it owes something to the 'communities studies' approach which Young and Willmott had pioneered, and the book therefore also contains numerous indications of the social alterations then taking place in Wales, and their effects upon the social organization of the country's third largest urban centre, Swansea. A central theme was defined early in the volume, with the repeated depiction, derived from an extended case study of 'Mr Hughes' of Morriston, of the disappearance during his lifetime of a 'traditional' working-class pattern of social life. This entailed the transition from a close clustering of kin in a limited locality, with a high degree of social and economic homogeneity and complex ties of mutual cooperation, into a far looser structure, marked by heterogeneity of occupation and income, and diversity in social and cultural values (Rosser and Harris, 1965; cf. Goldthorpe et al., 1969: 86).

In the past, it is suggested, Swansea had contained a population which was typically unified by constant interaction, and multiple social relationships built around work, neighbourhood and chapel, engendering shared moral values and cultural uniformity. Material possessions differed little among its households and families, and its compact industrial communities formed

> (s)trongholds of Welsh-speaking and nonconformity, with crowded chapels and a multiplicity of splendid choirs and working-men's clubs and rugby teams, they displayed a vigorous working-class culture and a deep-rooted community cohesion affected by periodic waves of economic adversity, religious revival, and political radicalism. (Rosser and Harris, 1965: 57)

Evidence to support this had been provided by an earlier investigation of the area conducted by a specially created research unit at the university between 1949 and 1953 (Brennan et al., 1954). This had considered south-west Wales to be 'a community with a distinctive unity of its own', but also containing some fifty-five more local communities, each with its own boundaries and identity. Despite a long history of industry, the area's ecology could still be described as a quasi-agrarian mosaic of small settlements and open country, and the outlook of the people was also characterized as semi-rural. The population was homogeneous, at least 80 per cent belonging to the working class, with a limited range of skills and occupations. Unlike other parts of south Wales, industrial relations in the surrounding anthracite coalfield had been paternalistic and relatively non-militant, and the attitude of workers in the steel and tinplate industry was also said to be 'conciliatory'. Brennan et al. provided a thorough account of a well-integrated local system of linkages between chapels, unions and political associations, with overlapping leaderships upholding strong codes of social behaviour. This was seen as supporting a definite and distinctive way of life and local culture. However, this was said to be weakening under the pressures of material improvement, secularization and the encroachment of a variety of 'English' influences. The advent of new kinds of light industry in particular was having major consequences for the employment of women and for the prestige of men, changing both the skills required in work and the power relationships in the home. The intense local patriotism which had made people react to an offer of new houses 3 miles away as if it were a plan for 'uprooting people from the land of their birth' (1954: 6) was being undermined by growing commuting and criss-crossing movements to and from work.

Brennan et al. describe many of the main characteristics of the local economy and society. They note the deficiency of 'good jobs', which they attribute to both the structure and organization of the major industries, and also refer to the increasing significance of employment in branch plants offering limited prospects for promotion and high-skilled work. Yet the local labour force is seen as resistant to the growth of jobs in places they disparaged as 'dolls-eyes' factories' (1954: 4), where work was cleaner, less strenuous and involved shorter and more regular hours, but did not have the traditional attributes of hard physical graft. However, despite its high degree of integration, the social system of south-west Wales lacked the power to exercise any real control over such economic changes. In fact, it was suggested that the backward state of industry in the region smothered individual enterprise and confined local influence to seeking to extract subsidies from the rest of Britain (1954: 108). The legacy of older industrial conditions was a workforce lacking in transferable skills and therefore in danger of being trapped into disadvantageous labour-market positions – a theme which still has considerable resonance almost half a century later (Rees et al., 1999).

According to this study, the population of south-west Wales at the time could be subdivided into four main social class categories. The backbone of the local system of associations was 'the characteristically Welsh working class', solid and respectable people based in the traditional industries, who were often ready to accept the leadership of an equally Welsh middle class, active in the chapels and other local organizations. These groups were being challenged from two directions: by the rise of an 'unoriented working class', outside the local network of associations, and based mainly in the towns and in the newer industries, and by an Anglicized middle class located in the expanding professions. These changes were considered likely to disintegrate the local social order, and weaken the existing Welsh way of life (1954: 181–7). These predictions were borne out by the later study by Rosser and Harris, whose account shows that growing differentiation by education, occupation and income was encouraging the emergence of more individualistic and self-centred attitudes, and bringing about the fragmentation of previously strong communities into more isolated elementary families, with fewer effective links between them. In this way, the study touches upon a number of themes which were of central interest to British sociology at the time, and foreshadows a good deal of the discussion of changes in class formations that was to follow.

SOCIAL CHANGE IN SWANSEA

As a regional metropolis, with a population of some 166,000, Swansea could hardly conform to the stereotype of the narrow one-class, one-job community. Nevertheless, historically it had been shaped around the limited economic base of tinplate, iron and steel manufacture and this meant a restricted set of occupational and economic experiences. In the words of one of those interviewed, 'all the men were working class'. Furthermore, as the authors point out, many were still only one or two generations removed from what they describe as the 'rural peasantry' of west Wales. Swansea itself was said to consist of a collection of relatively self-contained 'urban villages', a total of more than twenty named neighbourhoods and localities. By the 1960s it was changing rapidly, as it became more economically diverse, with expanding commercial and service activities and the replacement of some of the older industrial jobs by new forms of light engineering, including many more jobs for women. Post-war urban regeneration saw the replacement of older housing by newer estates, and eventually new tower blocks. Responding to greater security and relative affluence, the population was moving westwards, away from the original sites of industrialization to the 'promised land' of more wholesome and scenic districts towards Sketty, West Cross and the Mumbles. This was associated with a pattern of social mobility which represented the local version of 'embourgeoisement'. The bonds between work and residence were also broken by daily commuting which took some 3,000 workers out of the city to the newer, and larger, steelworks of Port Talbot, Margam, Trostre and Velindre. Consequently, neighbours were no longer workmates, sons did not automatically follow fathers into the same jobs, and increasingly employed women were making an important contribution to both the labour force and the household income.

Swansea is described nicely by one informant as having the usual complement of social classes: working class, middle class and those who were kidding themselves. Rosser and Harris found that 60 per cent of their survey sample identified themselves as working class, 30 per cent as middle class. Likewise in their own classificatory schema, intended to discriminate as far as possible between groupings that were economically and culturally homogeneous, they placed the bulk of people firmly in the working class. However, it also yielded a sizeable 'intermediate' cluster or halfway house consisting mainly of routine white-collar employees; more than a third of the local population were said to fall into this 'vague interstitial area' between the traditional social classes. Considerable occupational and educational mobility, together with 'mixed' marriages across class lines, were making for far more fluidity and blurring of class boundaries than in the past, introducing more hesitancy and confusion about subjective class location. Even so, Rosser and Harris are pretty unequivocal about the continuing significance of social class; not only does it provide the 'central sociological problem of modern urban society which underlies and pervades all social research whatever the actual topic selected' (1965: 81), it is also 'everywhere, pervasive, intangible, recognizable, but hard to define' in the life of Swansea (1965: 115). As well as shaping family organization, it is shown to be related to a wide variety of general attitudes, and to what nowadays we might call 'lifestyle' variations, evinced in cultural contrasts between dance halls and dinner dances, bingo and premium bonds, holiday camps and private holidays. Overall, Rosser and Harris assign 11 per cent of Swansea's people to the middle class, and another 12 per cent to the lower middle class; 24 per cent are described as upper working class, leaving the remaining 53 per cent to form the working class. On these figures, despite its changes, Swansea was still predominantly a working-class town, albeit one in which there was more room for ambiguity and variation than in the past.

There are several points in their study where Rosser and Harris opt not to pursue the 'anthropological' depth that might have told us more about the specifically Welsh character of Swansea. It is noted that, while there are subtle differences between the expressions of class in Wales and in England, it is exceptionally difficult to say what they are, or to demonstrate their existence statistically. An example given is the lack of interest shown by the Swansea (or Welsh?) middle class in sending their children to public schools. In general we get rather mixed messages about the ethnic or national placing of Swansea: it is a Welsh town, 'at least to the extent that it is located in Wales' (1965: 115) and the centre of a characteristically Welsh region; yet in itself it has always been at heart 'English or Anglo-Welsh' (1965: 41). Indeed, many of the features of its 'Welshness' appear to be particularly under threat from processes of change: thus the dispersal of population from the most Welsh neighbourhoods, and the rising tide of Anglicization, were putting the Welsh language under pressure and making its future an issue of growing intensity. The hold of the chapels over the younger generation was loosening, and religion was becoming less central to their lives. Cultural distinctiveness had been further diluted by a recent referendum vote to allow Sunday opening, in which fewer than half of the inhabitants were moved to vote. Even so, in 1961 streets could be filled with people mourning the death of the conductor of the Morriston Orpheus Choir. The vast majority (almost 90 per cent) of Swansea residents were Welsh-born, and most had had remarkably limited social contact outside Wales.

The changes taking place within the town are regarded by the authors as part of a far wider transition discussed by Raymond Williams (1961), through which Britain was witnessing the break-up of 'old' community patterns; like Williams, the authors show some uncertainty as to whether or not this transformation is permanent. We are left with the impression of Swansea as a loose federation of more or less distinct and dispersed communities, divided along class and status lines, a place of social and cultural contrasts. Economic fragmentation was beginning to disrupt some of its previously dominant cultural and social characteristics, including both its traditional class alignments and cultural identity. The old centres of industrial activity which had brought about its growth had been reduced to a 'vast and bleak lunar landscape' of waste tips and deserted sites, comprising one of the worst areas of industrial blight in the whole of Britain. In a final comment, the authors acknowledge the emergence out of the abandoned background of an older social tradition of a new and more modern society, better adjusted to the needs of a physically and socially mobile population. Whereas the former cohesive society was stable and enduring, so that 'people knew where they were', it also seems to have been a stagnant society; for all its old-fashioned cultural virtues, we are told, it is simply out of date (Rosser and Harris, 1965: 299).

A subsequent study of social transformation in one particular street in nearby Llanelli bears out this general picture (Rosser, 1989). Among its population of 330 in 1950, three-quarters had been born within a half-mile radius, and 69 per cent had lived there for twenty years or more; almost all were fluent Welsh speakers, and everyone would have described them- selves as working class. Three-quarters of the male occupants worked in the heavy metals industries, and their occupational status diffused into the total status system of the community, generating a sense of belonging which 'riveted and reconciled the inhabitants to the community'. The result was a localized way of life expressed through chapel, family connections and the Welsh language. There were especially close connections amongst women, and mutual help between mothers and daughters. However, between the 1960s and 1980s, mobility linked to educational success, marriage and career moves took many of the younger people away, leaving their places to be filled by new incoming households. The number of these in which English was the sole language rose from four to thirty-seven. As even the ties between female relations weakened with new-found affluence and social mobility, so a coherent community was replaced with its residue, 'a fractured and linguistically polarised social milieu' (Rosser, 1989: 135). Rosser's interesting reconstruction of social organization in this single street shows the simultaneous loss, or weakening, of the underpinnings of both working-class and ethnic Welsh identities, which previously had been inextricably fused together.

In a study related to that of Rosser and Harris, Bell (1968) examined social relations on two private housing estates in west Swansea in order to explore some of the effects of social and geographical mobility. Although the study is only tangentially concerned with probing 'Welsh' issues, it does provide evidence of the seeds of an important 'service class' presence in Swansea, while also showing how local relationships were affected by both class segregation and the everyday use of 'ethnic' labels and categories. As well as the break-up of its established working class, the expansion of new industries and services meant that Swansea was experiencing a considerable inflow of managers, technicians and other middle-class professionals, many of whom originated from England. Bell found that among these many were 'spiralists', whose careers involved movements from place to place as they progressed through the organizational hierarchies of their employing companies. They included a sizeable fraction whose educational achievements had opened a route from working-class backgrounds into these middle-class careers. Living side by side with them were other middle-class people whose roots were more local, and whose class position had not changed; these were more often involved with smaller indigenous businesses. Neither group had much social contact with the working class within the town.

The most significant organizing feature of life on the estates proved to be the distinction between locals and non-locals. This was shown by the way in which individuals lined up to support (non-locals) or oppose (locals) plans for nearby expansion of university halls of residence. A graphic illustration of the different life worlds of the respondents was provided by case studies of three christenings, one involving a local family who were able to invite more than a hundred relations to the ceremony, whereas between them two non-local families could muster only seven invited kin. In general, however, Bell notes that kinship, regardless of its importance to individuals, was by now a minor feature of social structure in Swansea. Locals on the estates were known colloquially as 'the Welsh', but inspection of their backgrounds showed that ability to speak Welsh cut across the local/non-local division. On a measure counting as 'Welsh' all those who could speak some of the language, or who had a parent who could do so, 20 per cent of those living on the estates were Welsh, compared to 46 per cent in Rosser and Harris's broader sample. According to Bell, Welsh speaking did not appear to be a significant aspect of the structure of social relations, either on or off the estates (Bell, 1968: 184).

The Swansea studies made an early and justifiably celebrated contribution to the theme of 'fragmentation' and diversity which has run through much of the subsequent work, with the implication that it is ever harder to produce simple generalizations about Wales and Welsh ways of life. In terms of how we should understand class in Wales, they pointed towards the increasing separation of various dimensions which had once seemed inextricably bound together. Subjective definitions of class, and the shared sense of class identity, were beginning to lose their clarity because the objective aspects of class situations were becoming more confusing. With hindsight, Rosser and Harris's description of Swansea can be seen to contain many of the leading elements which were to become familiar from later accounts of economic and social restructuring. These include: the advent of new forms of work, associated with the general development of modern industry and the specific diversification of the Welsh economy; the expanding role of the service sector, especially important in, but not limited to, urban centres; the geographical relocation of work to new local areas, stimulating connected residential movements; and the recomposition of family and community life which this entailed, along with major redefinitions of gender divisions. There is also evidence among those surveyed of a new orientation to consumption and commercialized entertainment, which reflected an unfamiliar sense of relative security and prosperity, enabling people to engage in new sorts of individual and household projects. Together these influences were working to bring about an extensive remaking of class identities, stretching the limits of the old working class and encouraging the formation of new fractions and class boundaries.

It is worth noting here that this was neither an entirely new nor unusual phenomenon; a historical perspective bears out the assumption, inherent to the restructuring approach, that the 'working class' has always been a fluid reality, continually kneaded and reshaped by the changing demands of capital (Blackwell and Seabrook, 1985). Still, the changes in the post-war period were exceptionally sharp, and they have generated a voluminous literature dealing with the mutation from the apparent solidity of traditional class patterns grounded in industries like steel, coal, iron and cotton to the 'ambiguities and volatility' (Blackwell and Seabrook, 1985: 17) of a class whose members are more typically employed now in hotels, shopping malls, leisure centres, fast food outlets and the communications industries. Wales has participated fully in these changes, although as elsewhere the extent and speed of the transformation has sometimes been concealed behind images that had congealed some time in the past. Attempts to prolong the old realities have also led to some of the fiercest social and political struggles taking place at local level. Nowhere has this been more so than in relation to the collapse of the Welsh mining industry.

6

Beyond the Basics

COAL AND THE FATE OF THE VALLEYS

As the epitome of classic proletarianism, and the repository of a particular type of Welshness, the fate of the coal-mining communities of Wales has assumed an exceptional significance. The case of mining has been gone over so thoroughly by sociologists that its special features barely need stating. It is among that select band of 'extreme' occupations which are so all-pervading in their impact that entire modes of life appear to be dictated by them. At the level of the local community, this has meant the overlapping of ties of work, leisure, neighbourhood and friendship, to form close-knit collectivities of people with a shared history of living and working, heightened by a strong degree of physical danger and collective insecurity (Bulmer, 1975). This has been said to promote intense feelings of mutuality, and a tendency to be inward-looking, often enhanced by geographical isolation and separation.

The classic local British study, of a Yorkshire mining community (Dennis et al., 1956), notes how everything about it seemed to conform to a plan, dictated by the requirements of money-making. This conclusion is elaborated by Allen:

> In what might appear to be an incredibly uncanny fashion every detail of the immediate environment of the miners – their leisure, their homes, family relationships, wives and children – has served the structure of their existence, namely the provision of labour power with given skills in required quantities at the requisite times. Nothing and no one has been spared: no humanity has been allowed to intrude . . . It has been simply a case of the basic structural needs of the situation dominating everything else, moulding everything to suit its own peculiar requirements. In this process women and wives have been adapted to meet the needs of mining as effectively as miners themselves. (Allen, 1981: 74)

This picture is over-drawn to the extent that it ignores the way in which miners and their families have been active participants, rather than passive victims, in deciding the shape taken by their communities (Williamson, 1982). Although mining villages must surely figure among those 'communities of the oppressed' identified by Raymond Williams (1973), their occupants have been renowned for the ways in which, as well as having to collude with the demands of the workplace in the evolution of characteristic patterns of social life, they have resisted, culturally and politically, the demands placed upon them by their employers. Indeed, coal mining has often seemed synonymous with militant bloody-mindedness, and high levels of industrial conflict, while 'the themes of discipline and collectivism run deep and strong in the political atmosphere' (Massey and Wainwright, 1985: 149). As well as the overwhelming dominance of male, manual labour, and the lack of white-collar work, mining communities have also been typified as predominantly white, socially conservative and exhibiting very clearly demarcated sexual divisions of labour (Massey and Wainwright, 1985). Others also note how the characteristic features of both production and social reproduction within them have combined to produce solidary social relations, industrial militancy and 'macho' cultures (Rees and Thomas, 1991; Waddington et al., 1991). Such descriptions approximate to the perfect realization of a proletarian work and class situation and it is not surprising that Lockwood (1966) incorporated mining communities into his analysis of working-class social organization as strongholds of 'proletarian traditionalism'.

However, this conventional account can be criticized for relying heavily on a small number of rather dated case studies and for failing to respond adequately to the actual diversity of local coalfield conditions and historical experiences, and to those changes which took place in such localities in the period after nationalization (Rees and Thomas, 1991). The impact of general social developments, as well as technological and organizational changes within the industry, served to weaken many of these traditional attributes, which were often adopted by members of mining communities themselves as idealized standards against which to express their own sense of the actual 'decay' of community over time. Even so, until fairly recently Welsh studies offered some backing for the generalized account. In his study of the mining communities of the Amman valley, for example, Town (1978) was able to describe a stable population structure with a strong and intricate network of kinship and friendship ties. Around 80 per cent of inhabitants had been born locally (within 10 miles of their current home), and most had married locally as well. The majority of residential movements took place within the restricted valley area, which was where people normally looked for alternative job opportunities. They shopped in their own village, or in Ammanford, with only occasional trips the extra few miles to Swansea for larger items.

Such localism was a very important component of respondents' sense of personal identity; and even among those who were not actively part of the

industry, there was an extensive shared knowledge of mining and its conditions which brought people together. Sewel (1975) presents a very similar
picture of life in the Dulais valley, noting how, with the exception of a small
'Jet Set' of local shopkeepers and businessmen, an individual's status in the
community tended to mirror the occupational hierarchy of the pit. Male
activities focused around work and the pub, women's around home and
family. For both, social ties with the community made for strong resistance
to any pressure to move, and there was general agreement that the texture
of community life was dictated by the means of getting a living: hence, 'our
village life will be destroyed if the collieries are closed. Somehow people
change when they start working in a factory; they're not as close then'
(Sewel, 1975: 22). The research bears out this view, showing how, as pits
were closed, so the mutually reinforcing bonds of community loosened:
chapels, union, party politics and welfare provision grew apart from one
another, and each became weaker as a result. The loss of its productive
centre removed much of the meaning and purpose of the community. As
the artist Howard Riley wrote with irony, apropos one such affected place,
Glyncorrwg, 'this village attracts the attention of sociologists and architectural schools in the way pathologists gather around a unique corpse. Of
course it's easier to handle and dissect now' (Riley, 1978: 97).

Although Sewel insists that the world of the Dulais valley was neither
self-contained nor self-sufficient, it is clear that, for many purposes, each
mining community constituted its own self-enclosed social milieu, and this
helps explain the often-noticed reluctance of miners and their families to
relocate even comparatively short distances when the state of the industry
has required it. Such localism is not unique to mining communities; as
already noted, in their study of the iron-working villages around Swansea
in the 1950s Brennan et al. had remarked on the occurrence of 'an intense
local patriotism' which made people hostile to geographical movement. But
for miners, removal carried special risks, since it would involve them in
working among strangers, in an unknown setting, at a personal cost:

> It was terrible. I was working with people I didn't know. None of my old
> butties were working with me. You get used to a colliery, you know which parts
> are dangerous and what to look out for, you can feel when something is going
> to happen. (Sewel, 1975: 25)

More succinctly, we are told, there is 'nothing like your home pit' (Thomas,
1991).

Up until the 1960s, most men in such areas would expect to enter the
mines. Town (1978) notes how the National Coal Board was virtually the
sole employer of male labour in the Amman valley. Subsequently there
had been economic diversification, resulting in a very limited growth in

manufacturing jobs, generally of more benefit to women than men. Men from mining backgrounds found it difficult to adapt to the disciplines of factory routines, and labour relations in the new firms tended to be poor. However, by the 1970s manufacturing work had become the preferred local employment option for men, as well as for women. Unfortunately, the local mix of light engineering, motor components, clothing, shoe and knitwear companies did not provide a particularly stable employment base, consisting almost entirely of branch plants which were often highly vulnerable to external market fluctuations. Given the shortage of alternative work, employers were able to control wage rates, and hand-pick the best of local labour. This meant that older men, those with disabilities and the less qualified tended to face exclusion from the labour market. Younger, more qualified, people were leaving the area, finding work in the coastal towns, or undertaking daily commuting to them. Thus the pattern of employment was much more fragmented than in the past, destroying that element of common experience which had underpinned the sense of community and cohesion for which the valleys were celebrated. Cooke (1981b, 1983b) considered the valleys to be a 'paradigm' branch plant economy, where manu- facturing jobs involved unskilled and semi-skilled labour, and routine assembly work for women, often done part-time. Compared to its earlier marked homogeneity, the class structure of the valleys remained 'overwhelmingly proletarian but differentiated and segmented along occupational and gender lines'.

With increasing industrial and social diversification, it was no longer possible to pass off the wishes of any single occupational group as those of the locality; instead the emergence of different, and conflicting, interests could be anticipated, until 'the local interest will be as difficult to define as the national interest' (Sewel, 1975: 81). Change was also likely to dilute the largely homogeneous class nature of the villages; as the economy changed, so the class composition of the coalfield communities was rearranged (Rees, 1985). Processes of change within the mining industry itself added to this dislocation. When pits closed, miners were offered transfers to other sites, sometimes in other regions. Although often this occurred as a group, it broke the intimate connection with a particular place of work and its surroundings, and resulted in criss-cross patterns of daily travel around the coalfield, sometimes adding several hours to the working day. The mixing of miners from different home locations weakened solidarity at the workplace. Despite all the changes, the local economy still placed most people in situations of subordination, doing low valued jobs for poor pay. They were still undeniably part of the working class, although now with a more diverse profile and, as Town puts it, still subjected to 'the continuing exploitation of a local labour force by external capital for its own ends . . .

They take what they can from the valley and leave the labour force to fend for itself' (Town, 1978: 123). What had changed was the ability to empathize with one another, and to mobilize around a common cause.

By the 1970s the coal industry had already been reduced to a relatively small role in the Welsh economy. Between 1960 and 1973 the number of pits in south Wales had fallen from 118 to 51, and the number of miners from 87,000 to 35,000. In the north of the country, by the end of the 1960s there were just three working pits, of which one, Gresford, closed in 1974. Welsh coal was meeting strong competition from alternative energy sources, especially oil, and was handicapped by low productivity and severe technical limitations. Its economic viability depended closely upon the performance of other key industries and cutbacks in steel production during the 1970s put added pressure on the price of coal. A combination of rising productivity, falling demand and competition from cheap imports following relaxation of government controls, precipitated a general crisis of the British coal industry in the 1980s, coinciding with the imposition of aggressively Thatcherite free-market policies which insisted that industries must 'pay their way'. The years after 1979 were marked by recurrent conflict around plans to close pits, and the south Wales miners were at the forefront of attempts to mobilize resistance. In 1983 there was an underground sit-down strike to protest the closure of the Lewis Merthyr pit. On the whole, they met with little success in gathering support from other areas (Howells, 1985). However, proposals to decimate the number of UK collieries culminated in the National Union of Mineworkers (NUM) strike of 1984/5, a period of intense industrial and political conflict, during which miners were defined politically as the 'enemies within', and represented by government and media as militants who were not just protecting their own narrow industrial interests, but also sustaining a blinkered and outdated conception of the working class and its future.

Given the generally bleak economic climate of the times, the prospect of further contraction created an understandable sense of desperation. During the 1980s, male unemployment in the main coalfield areas of south Wales was running at or above 20 per cent; a tenth or more of the men had been out of work for at least a year. Mining still accounted for almost a fifth of male employment locally (Wass and Mainwaring, 1989), and therefore remained a mainstay of the economic life of the valley communities. Some 22,000 jobs had already been lost to the area between 1978 and 1984, equivalent to one in every five, and there was little prospect of their early replacement; further losses in mining would bring the whole local economy to the brink of collapse. Hence the strike came to be defined as a battle for jobs (rather than the more usual objectives of industrial action, wages and conditions) and for the very survival of the communities: 'coal not dole' and 'close a pit, kill a community' were slogans with a very clear message, while 'the NUM fights for Wales' signalled an even bigger claim, that the industry was an irreplaceable component of the nation itself. As might be expected, both during the strike and afterwards, the circumstances surrounding it generated a rich body of writing and analysis. Many of those describing the events had in varying degrees been participants as well as observers (Beynon, 1985; Howells, 1985; Rees, 1985) and the access they had to opinion and incidents, as well as their own political, and often family commitments, helped colour their interpretations.

Economists engaged in a highly technical argument about how 'profitability' ought to be calculated but agreed that the industry was paying the penalty for the historic costs which had been incurred in obligations to the workforce (such as pensions and compensation for ill-health) and for repair of the environment, and that the true extent of the social costs and benefits of mining were not being taken fully into account (George and Mainwaring, 1988; Cooper and Hopper, 1988). It was recognized, for example, that it was extremely difficult if not impossible to evaluate social stress and environmental change – major considerations in such a basic industry (George and Mainwaring, 1988: 172). Even if it had been possible to arrive at some agreed economic calculus, it would still be the case that no 'purely' economic judgement could have done justice to the enormous range of social effects. As George and Mainwaring noted, pit closures had a devastating impact on the social fabric of mining communities, and this was not just a short-term problem but one with consequences for years ahead. Such arguments had a much wider resonance within Wales, where the society as a whole was faced with coping with a fundamental shift from older to newer industries; very similar debates focused around the future of agriculture and rural Wales throughout the 1980s and 1990s, and helped bring about an unprecedented alliance between representatives of mining and farming.

The central question was raised by one ex-miner: 'how do you weigh up the cost against the social destruction of the communities? . . . the social costs to a community against the economic costs to a pit?' (M. Thomas, 1991). This man was part of the workforce at a colliery estimated in 1977 to have a working life of 100 years, but closed in 1986 because suddenly it was declared 'uneconomic'. As frequently happened, the deep lack of trust which permeated industrial relations in the industry led the workforce to accuse management of making perverse decisions designed to prove that the pit could not thrive. Arguments about whether or not closure was justified tended to reflect radically different rationales, the claims of the market on the one hand versus a strong conception of 'social contribution' and human need on the other (Town, 1978). For many, closure meant early withdrawal from the labour market, or prolonged unemployment, with all the costs occasioned by loss of a valued identity, stress and boredom. In a study of the effects of one closure, Markham colliery, only a third of those actively seeking work had been successful within eighteen months (Wass and Mainwaring, 1989). Miners were ill-suited to the types of alternative work that were available; they lacked factory experience, and were viewed with suspicion by many employers as not having 'appropriate' behaviours. They were used to determining their own pace of work, and did not take kindly to close supervision. There is later evidence that displaced miners have been prone to unusual levels of absenteeism and turnover (Rutherford, 1991). In line with Massey's argument about how the consequences of one round of investment become the conditions for the next, the reputation miners had earned for militancy in their own industry also became a very real hindrance to getting access to other types of work. Men who had previously enjoyed relatively good earnings within an industry which had prestige and respect for its manual skills found themselves limited to semi-skilled and unskilled work that carried fewer financial and status rewards. For many, the construction industry was the nearest valued alternative to the kind of work they respected.

Although there was no great enthusiasm in for the manner in which the strike had begun, Welsh miners lived up to their reputation for solidarity. In the south of the country, no more than 1,500 out of the NUM membership of 20,000 returned to work during the year-long strike, and at its end the miners of Maerdy marched back to the pit without having formally conceded defeat, with a crowd of supporters accompanied by the colliery band (Rees, 1985). The strike had shown the folly of treating all miners, and all coal-producing areas, as if they were the same; instead, their different circumstances and histories had produced radically different, and divided responses, which indeed proved to be the miners' downfall. A rare examination of the strike in the North Wales Coalfield warns against allowing facile images of solidarity, and celebratory accounts of past struggles, to obscure the reality of complex and distinctive local responses (Howell, 1991). As was true throughout Britain, the Welsh coalfields adhered to separate, and durable, cultures. In north Wales the history was one of relatively right-wing accommodation, which included the formation of a breakaway union during the inter-war period. The workforce was drawn from a scattered, rather than concentrated area, and the strike divided opinion, with many, including local leadership, standing by the local tradition of caution. Workers at the Point of Ayr colliery were split throughout the strike; those at Bersham voted against strike action, yet showed considerable unity in refusing to cross picket lines. Strikers and their supporters in the area spoke of how they had to 'build' a community during the strike, rather than being able to simply enact a predefined unity. The efforts undertaken by strikers and women's groups to mobilize support entailed them in a novel exploration of the complications of the north Wales identity. Support was more readily forthcoming in Liverpool, across the English border, than it was in nearby Welsh seaside towns; yet there was also strong backing from the Welsh-speaking slate quarry communities further west, and representatives of the strikers were invited to address a Plaid Cymru conference. Howell (1991: 86) comments that

> The dispute was fought by a National Union, where 'nation' referred to Britain; the search for support from other industrial workers, the links with other striking miners took north Wales men out across the border. But equally there was a Welsh dimension to the dispute, involving not just the search for economic aid within Wales, but also appeals based on a shared national community.

The same observation about the national (Wales) dimension of the strike is made by Kim Howells, with reference to the support given to the men in south Wales from various groups in north and mid-Wales: 'for the first time since the industrial revolution in Wales, the two halves of the nation came together in mutual support' (1985: 147), while within the coalfield people had developed 'a new collective spirit which revived community life'. Thus, for many of those involved, the strike brought a rediscovery of the significance of both community and nation.

In 1981 the South Wales Miners' President Emlyn Williams had called for a 'demonstration for existence' (Francis, 1990: 112). The miners' strike, with its call to rally to the defence of communities, provided such a demonstration, and turned out to be a final paroxysm of classic proletarianism. As a result of the defeat, cost-cutting policies were implemented, large numbers of pits were closed and extensive reserves of coal were abandoned. Despite brave words about continuing 'guerrilla action', the stuffing had been knocked out of the workforce. Interviews with those affected suggested that the ability to mount effective resistance to further closures had been undermined by the infiltration of miners from other pits who had already experienced closure and adjusted to it. Most were persuaded to accept seemingly generous redundancy pay-offs, which offered a good deal when balanced against the personal and social costs of transfer to work elsewhere. Thus the labour force was whittled away, until by 1987 only fourteen pits remained in operation, and the workforce had shrunk to 10,000. Even this was not the end of the story. By June 1990 there were just five pits, and 2,792 miners in south Wales, and one colliery in the north. With the exception of the Tower colliery, bought out by its own workforce and successfully maintained in operation, deep mining was defunct and the figure of the Welsh collier had marched over the horizon into the past. Henceforth, nearly all the mining taking place in Wales was opencast, capable of even more environmental damage, but without the mystique and historic symbolism of underground working.

The inexorable decline of the mining industry took the heart out of the south Wales valleys, confirming only too well that 'communities that grow up around extractive industries face calamity when the industry ends, unless there has been forward government planning of alternative industry' (Paynter, 1972: 19). Since mining communities are located for obvious geological purposes, they are usually in places which are not conducive to other forms of development; the exposed upland villages of the South Wales Coalfield are no exception. Their demise presented the recurrent problem faced by every decayed industrial area and derelict inner-city district: to what extent should effort be devoted to shoring up and preserving the legacy of past economic and social investments, rather than encouraging people to adapt to new circumstances and new opportunities? Whichever option is taken, there will be those who benefit and others who lose out. Local interests also have to be balanced against wider definitions of the social good. These tensions had been present in the 'strategic' thinking of *Wales: The Way Ahead* (1967). On the one hand, reassurance was offered that no policy permitting the disintegration of the 'substantial' valley communities would gain government support; yet at the same time the plan looked to steer future development towards the coast and valley mouths. This was because these areas had the advantage of easier access, greater potential scale of operations, including a larger pool of labour, and proximity to other developments. From now on, the valleys had to compete for their survival. By the end of the 1980s, the proposition that they should be assimilated into an area known as 'greater Cardiff' could be seen as putting the final nail in the coffin of the Welsh proletariat (Francis, 1990).

It had been an essential feature of the dominant Labourist ideology that the miners should look mainly to the state to provide remedial solutions. After all, south Wales was among those regions 'owned, regulated, fed and watered by the central state' (Massey and Wainwright, 1985). Over the years, numerous calls were issued for governments to make good their promises; otherwise, it was feared, the valleys would die. 'The year of the valleys' was declared in 1974, and the following year a conference was convened bringing together activists and academics to make the case for their future (Ballard and Jones, 1975). Instructively, this was put in social, or even sociological, terms to do with the importance of sustaining a distinctive character and way of life, something that admittedly was hard to put into words but 'made up of an extremely complex and interlocking array of customs and traditions, patterns of behaviour out of which some tangible manifestations emerge' (Carter, 1975: 368). The maintenance of this pattern was felt to be significant not just in itself, but also because it was 'a rich contributor to the national character of Wales' without which 'the whole life of the nation would be impoverished'. Not only was the link asserted between a particular social formation and the interests and very nature of the Welsh nation, but the implication was that the valleys had to be saved, as near as possible, in their existing form; this presumption was accepted by most as 'axiomatic' (Rees, 1997). This meant that the search was mounted for a production-based 'solution' that would ensure 'proper jobs' suited to male wage-earners, able to exercise satisfactory levels of skill and/or autonomy in their work, an aspiration which unfortunately was increasingly out of step with the direction being taken by economic change. After 1979 it also collided with the impact of policies driven by a Thatcherite agenda to 'roll back the state'. As well as making a direct attack on organized labour, this meant that a more insidious threat was posed by the abandonment of all pretence at regional intervention, and a new-found dedication to 'self-help' solutions relying upon individual and community enterprise. Here, positive images of valley life, drawing upon traditions of social cohesion and neighbourliness, could be mobilized against contrasting conceptions of the region as 'economically out of date and socially disorganized', and thus liable to 'excrescences of social pathology' such as family breakdown, educational under-performance, crime, drugs and lawlessness (Rees, 1997: 99). Unfortunately, over a period of more than three decades, including two rounds of a Welsh Office 'Programme for the Valleys' inspired by Secretary of State Peter Walker (Rees, 1997), and numerous other interventions, it could be said that little had been achieved (Dicks 2000). In 1999, government ministers were still launching documents hopefully called *The Valleys: New Opportunities, New Future*, and the National Assembly was getting into the act by debating motions on revitalization calling for integrated and comprehensive strategies for regeneration of the valleys. Yet the valleys were no closer to escaping from the legacy of industrial decline and social disorganization. Indeed, maps produced as part of a study documenting the existence of multiple social deprivation in Wales makes this very evident; the south Wales valleys are picked out in the purple or dark blue coloration indicative of deep deprivation (NAW, 2000).

WALES IS CLOSED? THE CONDITION OF STEEL

Following post-war reorganization, the steel industry in Wales enjoyed a period of relative boom. Reorganization and modernization had seen the closure of many of the smaller, obsolete plants and the expansion of production in more technologically advanced sites in Port Talbot and Llanwern, bringing the promise of a good future. Renationalization in 1967 brought most steelmaking within the framework of a single organization, the British Steel Corporation (BSC), although it left stockholding and finishing mostly in private hands. Workers in the industry appeared to have the prospect of secure employment in well-respected, skilled manual occupations. However, the 1970s saw a steady trimming of the numbers of employees, as the industry was driven to reduce manning levels and raise productivity. There was enormous excess capacity throughout Europe, which the EEC was attempting to remedy through managed contraction, and growing competition from new producers, particularly in the countries of the Pacific rim, which were not only competing on price, but also showing themselves to be capable of yielding better quality. By the end of the 1970s, British governments were demanding radical action to restore profitability in the industry. It has been calculated that reductions in employment in steel between 1974 and 1986, with their knock-on effects for other employment, accounted for about half the job losses in Wales (Baber and Mainwaring, 1988: 207). The East Moors works was closed in 1978, and 'heavy end' steel production finished at Ebbw Vale in 1975 and Shotton in north Wales in 1979. As part of a national restructuring programme, the decision was taken in 1979 to implement the Slimline agreement, which would maintain production in both Port Talbot and Llanwern, but at the cost of cutting numbers employed from 22,000 to 10,600. This coincided with a debilitating defeat for the steel unions in a national strike over pay in 1980, which made those returning to work far less ready to fight any proposed cutbacks. Negotiations to implement Slimline had been going on even while the strike was in progress.

At various points both before and after the war, governments had intervened to deploy changes in the steel industry as instruments of regional policy. Usually this meant channelling developments where possible towards places where there was surplus labour, or to mop up rising unemployment. Frequently, decisions made for social reasons contradicted economic rationality. Thus the development of Llanwern in Wales in the 1960s had to be balanced against the needs of Scotland and the promotion of a rival facility at Ravenscraig; and rather than achieving fully integrated production on one site, strip milling at Port Talbot was separated geographically from tinplating at Trostre and Velindre. Old patterns of industrialization were being perpetuated by such decisions, probably at the long-run expense of the places they were intended to serve; certainly, dependence on steel proved to be a very dubious proposition. What happened in Port Talbot became symbolic of de-industrialization more generally (Fevre, 1989). The building of the Abbey works in 1947 and the modernization of nearby Margam had rejuvenated the old steel centre, and soaked up labour made redundant by rationalization elsewhere. At its peak, BSC employed 18,500 workers in the town. They had been recruited widely from both inside and outside Wales, many, including former miners, commuting to work from Llanelli and the valleys. There was talk of a 'gold rush' to get the benefits of working in 'Treasure Island'. Unlike the area around it, Port Talbot saw comparatively little expansion of service jobs, and continued to be a town dominated by manufacturing, and above all by the production of steel: in 1978 BSC accounted for 39 per cent of its employment. Between 1971 and 1978 the town lost more than 7,000 jobs, mostly in construction and mechanical engineering. On top of redundancies already in hand, the Slimline agreement meant the workforce at BSC would be slashed from 11,259 to 5,701. More or less overnight, Treasure Island became 'Giro City'. In words echoing those of Harris cited earlier, Fevre (1989: 37) states that, for many people, the scale and suddenness of this collapse was enough to destroy any link with the past, throwing them into a totally unknown situation. Alongside BSC, almost all other sectors and firms in the town were laying off workers. In three years from 1980, nearly 19,000 jobs disappeared from Port Talbot, not just in manufacturing, but also across retailing, leisure and the service industries. There was very little success in finding work to replace them. Fevre graphically describes the forlorn efforts expended on building industrial estates and advance factories to attract new industries as practices tantamount to a modern cargo cult that was expected, somehow, to magic a solution. He estimates that by late 1985 each new job created had cost something like £2 million in public money. By this time, no less than ninety-five different grants were on offer to encourage small business, and Port Talbot was also able to access funding through its Special Development Area and Inner Urban statuses (Fevre, 1989: 47).

Working with a group of associates in the Swansea Redundancy and Unemployment Research Group, who produced a substantial cluster of research papers and two full-length volumes (Harris, 1987; Fevre, 1989) dealing with the impact of these job losses, Chris Harris was able to continue his interest in social change in industrial south-west Wales into the 1980s. What started out as a study of the way in which a local labour force adjusted to large-scale redundancy proved to be a valuable opportunity and context from which to analyse some major changes in the nature of labour markets; these were associated with what the team came to see as a significant social transition. When they occurred, the steel redundancies coincided with a period of extensive unemployment and labour-market turbulence. Between 1979, when the Slimline redundancies were announced, and 1981/2 when they were implemented, unemployment in Wales surged from 6.9 per cent to 12 per cent. However, instead of the anticipated outcome, whereby workers would be forced to deal with their loss of employment by moving elsewhere to find work (a solution famously urged upon them by a prominent government minister of the time), the local economy showed a remarkable and unexpected ability to absorb the redundant individuals. Movements both out of *and into* work showed a sharp increase.

Closer inspection showed that, in fact, a substantial proportion of those laid off had exited the labour market altogether, either by taking early retirement or by declaring themselves unfit to work through sickness or disability. Typically these were older workers. Of the remainder, those who were still looking for work, a significant part had been taken up by unexpected changes in the way in which work itself was organized. BSC responded to government pressures for restoration of private control by moving the boundaries between public-sector and private work. Many of the jobs taken off the books of BSC reappeared in the form of contract work, often performed by the very same individuals, on behalf of private companies (Fevre, 1986, 1991). This was particularly true of such 'peripheral' tasks as construction and transport, but increasingly privatization penetrated into the steelmaking process as well. The demand for and supply of labour were linked in a reciprocal process whereby the availability of a pool of experienced and competent workers enabled employers to redesign work into novel forms, so as to cut costs, increase 'flexibility' and raise productivity. As a result, there was extensive disorganization of previously reliable male working-class career patterns. Information collected on labour-market histories revealed the 'complex and shifting experience of bewildered subjects striving to make sense of what is happening to them' (Harris, 1987: 178). Fevre cites the example of 'Frank' who had eleven separate jobs, interspersed with eleven periods of unemployment, in six years; all the jobs involved contract work with BSC, and all the contracts were fulfilled satisfactorily. Frank had entered a new 'life' involving recurrent episodes of short-term employment which bore little connection to his own commitment and competence. He was one of a growing category of workers displaying such 'chequered' work patterns.

The disintegration of prior kinds of work organization and the emergence of this new employment pattern were seen as having consequences at three distinct levels. For the individuals involved, it meant new levels of disorder and uncertainty, even if some were able eventually to learn to cope with frequent change as a normal feature of their lives. Meanwhile they were experiencing what appeared to be a 'social nightmare' induced by far-reaching rearrangements of social structure (Harris, 1987: 10). Like the sociologists studying them, they were taken by surprise when the situation failed to be resolved by restoration of the *status quo ante*; even after the recession was over, things did not return to 'normal'. For the labour market, this led to a far more variegated structure, with the labour force dispersed across a greater range of different situations so that its structure became more complex, and more difficult to grasp. For the working class, it meant the emergence of new divisions, and less probability of shared consciousness and experience. The changes in work organization observable in Port Talbot and the surrounding area were part of a much larger process of 'flexibiliza-tion' (Atkinson, 1984; Fevre, 1991) whereby management pursued workforce strategies which increased the proportion of part-time, short-term and casu-alized kinds of employment. It also deepened divisions between 'core' and 'peripheral' labour – those fortunate enough to get themselves into the most stable, well-organized sorts of work, usually linked to the internal labour markets of large organizations, and those who were left out in the cold of the external labour market. In Port Talbot, steelworkers expelled from the former ended up, if they were lucky, in the latter. Compared to previous experience, this represented significant downward social mobility, and the loss of recognition as skilled individuals. Reproduced across many work-forces, throughout Wales and the rest of Britain, these changes added up to a redefinition of the boundaries of economic and social classes.

Harris and his colleagues explore a number of facets of this change. Much of the discussion is couched in terms of abstract typification, trying to draw out the broad connotations of various social types and situations, with little direct reference to such concrete aspects as the Welshness of those involved. But since the research was conducted within the context of Port Talbot and West Glamorgan, it had evident, if understated, implications for the analysis of class in Wales. The economic changes occurring during the 1970s and 1980s had thrown into reverse the assumptions of full employ-ment and security which had prevailed during the preceding couple of decades. With rising unemployment and instability, it was found, new importance came to attach to variations in social identity, and the posses-sion of different forms of social capital. Depending on their social positions, individuals might or might not be able to make use of their networks of social and personal contacts to gain (or regain) access to work. Within the informal labour market, where opportunities came about by word of mouth and personal contact, and might well present questions of legality (working 'off the cards', drawing benefit, doing 'hobbles'), a person's perceived moral identity, with the elements of trust and familiarity, could be crucial. Employers and workmates wanted 'tidy boys' (Harris, 1987: 131) who could be relied upon to do decent work and keep their mouths shut. In situ-ations where work was in short supply, the readiness of others to vouch for someone in these terms could be the vital ingredient in finding a job. Hence, along with general considerations of age and skill, where people were located within the local social structure and the sort of social identity they were able to present to those around them proved to be key determinants of labour-market position and success.

Fevre's (1989) analysis of these processes is concerned less with the immediate impact on Wales and the locality of Port Talbot than with the wider implications for the changing nature of work and employment in Britain. For Fevre, neither 'de-industrialization' nor a 'regional problems' framework offers a satisfactory explanation for what was taking place. Rather, he emphasizes the way in which a general reconstruction of the form of work was doing away with the 'solid working class' of the past. For years Port Talbot and other places like it had been heavily dependent on state intervention for their existence, and when this was withdrawn, the workers paid the price. Those who ended up doing contract work in and around BSC were doing so for lower earnings, fewer bonuses, more cash in hand and no holiday pay. In this way, BSC played its part in what Kevin Morgan describes as a classic capitalist displacement mechanism, through which the company's financial crisis, precipitated by government action, was 'displaced and translated into an acute social crisis for its redundant workers and their host localities' (Morgan, 1983: 194). In a situation where 40 per cent of those surveyed in Port Talbot had experienced redundancy, and 10 per cent had been out of work for more than two years, the town had also lost its solidity as a working-class community (Fevre, 1989: 98).

In the crisis presented by the new situation, a leading response for those affected was to struggle to maintain their identity and social relationships within the working class, so as to use them positively to find a way back into work. Becoming a 'chequered' worker was one way of holding on to class membership (Harris and Lee, 1988), albeit as part of a new, peripheral-ized, class fraction. Those who were unable to break out of unemployment faced the steady attrition of their social relationships and the loss of social support. As their social identity became 'spoiled', so they were pushed back on the household as their main arena of interaction and relationships, rather than either class or locality. Substantial numbers were confronted by this situation: two and a half years after the Slimline redundancies occurred, only 29 per cent of those affected had actually managed to get back into employment. In class terms, this encouraged fragmentation, since

> poverty, unemployment and geographical stability push in the same direction as affluence and mobility insofar as they both increase the tendency to the isola-tion of the nuclear family and the child-centredness it already exhibits. The net result is the segregation of the unemployed from the social life of their own locality and class . . . There is a sense in which the unemployed have 'fallen' out of the local social structure. (Harris, 1987: 226)

Thus the discussion ends on a troubling note, pointing to the possibility of the continual recreation of a class or class segment that is excluded from sharing in the benefits of productive development. While not fully developed, the problematic of 'social exclusion' that emerged during the 1990s is very firmly suggested. As in the earlier Swansea study, the working class in south-west Wales is shown to be 'stretched' at both ends, making it a much less solid and consistent foundation for identification and action.

A 'NEW' WORKING CLASS?

According to Harris (1987: 217), it was 'a strong sense of belonging to both regional and class categories, and of interconnections through a network of ties focussed on locality and spatially extended through kinship' which for many years gave south Wales its fundamentally working-class character. Our examination of the fate of the two great south Wales industries leads inexorably towards the theme of the diversification and disintegration of this class identity, and with it the loss of the associated sense of belonging. This local experience forms part of the wider pattern of disruption of 'traditional' working-class communities registered by Goldthorpe et al. (1969: 13), when they note how

> It was through the network of kinship, the pattern of neighbouring, the collective activities and rituals of communal solidarity which characterised such districts that working-class culture was transmitted and preserved. Once this basis is gone, therefore, the local and particularistic nature of working-class life is immediately threatened.

As well as changes in the labour market, processes of urban planning and redevelopment, and enhanced geographical mobility, contributed to this weakening of the impact of local ties. Although it was possible to imagine that the end result of these processes would be the expansion and extension of working-class identities into new areas, signifying the growth of a 'proletarianised population thoughout Wales of potentially enormous significance in the development of class relations' (Cooke, 1981a), much of the emphasis of the research which has been discussed rests instead on the disintegrating effects of these changes. For Harris and his Swansea colleagues, it appeared that the older patterns of local 'community' had been replaced by a variety of kinds of network relationships, and that the differences between these now played a key role in deciding personal and social identities, access to essential resources and rewards, and general social location. There were no longer common features binding whole populations together, and participation in local pubs, clubs, chapels and other associations had become a differentiating, rather than unifying, factor. This left many whose social relationships were limited to 'neighbouring within the urban sprawl'. Similarly in the formerly solidary coal-mining communities, although the population remained overwhelmingly 'proletarian' in general outlook, it had been decomposed and diversified in such a way that variations in life-cycle stage and new forms of gender differentiation had assumed central importance as dimensions of working-class existence (Rees, 1985; Rees and Thomas, 1991). In particular, substantial numbers of the elderly and the young had been marginalized by their isolation from opportunities within the labour market, and were experiencing growing personal and associational exclusion, while new types of employment seemed more adapted to the skills and competences associated with women than those of the 'redundant' male workforce. Furthermore, the response from policy-makers and government was increasingly liable to individualize the treatment given to different people, through the appeal to market-led solutions and strategies. In the coalfield, for example, efforts were made to foster greater personal 'enterprise' through schemes to promote retraining, managed workshops and loans for business start-ups. The aim appeared to be to bring about 'the effective reconstitution of the local class structure through the significant expansion of an entrepreneurial stratum of self-employed and small-scale capitalists – class places which had been markedly underrepresented . . . hitherto' (Rees and Thomas, 1991: 65). In reality, most of those who took up the the offer of support for the formation of a new business turned out to be relatively well-educated and securely placed individuals from outside the affected areas. Few among the displaced local manual labour force did so, probably preferring wisely to put their redundancy money to 'safer' uses by paying off debts and reducing their mortgages or improving their homes. Given a surfeit of similar skills and work experiences being released into potential competition, the chances of them succeeding through the small-business route realistically were quite small. Consequently the researchers suggest that, for the majority, the future appeared to be one of continuing problems with employment, and further de-industrialization.

An awareness that the variety and complications of modern work and market situations make it meaningless to equate different experiences merely because they all involve wage-labour, or are in some sense subordinate to managerial authority, lies behind a good deal of the agonizing about the meaning and significance of class that preoccupied twentieth-century sociology. Adamson (1991b) makes the point when he contrasts a miner and a female clerical worker, whose experiences differ in so many respects that it seems facile to treat them as occupying the 'same' class position, or as having the same kinds of social attitudes and expectations, even though both are fundamentally propertyless and powerless. The shift from large workforces performing very similar (or at least, closely coordinated) tasks to highly diversified forms of labour working in very varied settings is an aspect of the 'disorganization' of late capitalism (Lash and Urry, 1987) which has made such contrasts more significant, bringing about a proliferation of distinctive class positions. There have been many competing attempts to work through the implications of all this for class analysis, which battle with the complexity of the resulting categories and groupings, including trying to cope with large numbers of positions which have to be regarded as ambiguous or contradictory in key respects (Marshall et al., 1988; Wright, 1985; Poulantzas, 1975).

In an analysis which is anchored in a predominantly theoretical survey of some of the main contributions to such class theory, Adamson (1991a) arrives at the position that social classes in Wales have to be grasped in terms of the 'totality' of economic, political and ideological relations within which their members are embedded. Even employing economic criteria alone will rarely produce an unequivocal verdict about where people belong; but added to this, Adamson is led to conclude that there is little or no correspondence between classes as they might be defined economically, those social class groupings which are demarcated as forms of life by mixtures of cultural, market and status distinctions, and the alignment of political forces. It is not possible to translate between the economic, social and political in any straightforward way (Cottrell and Roslender, 1986). The same contention underlies Rees's attempts to derive lessons from the miners' strike, when he says that the time has come to move away from theories embodying purely structural determinations and pay greater heed to specifying those processes by which class and other political actions actually come about, including the role of class and other social groupings in shaping industrial and political conflicts (Rees, 1985: 390). Class practices and forms of struggle cannot be 'read off' from the social structure of mining communities any better than levels of militancy or radicalness can be attributed to 'regions' as a whole.

The relevance of this for Wales is that the underlying alterations in economic and social life which have been outlined have had profoundly destabilizing consequences for earlier patterns of class relationships. They have enabled the appearance of a number of new class groupings, while also ensuring that alternative forms of social organization compete strongly with class as possible sources of membership and identification. Among the possibilities is the development of what Adamson (1988) terms a 'new' working class, consisting of people who have been cut loose from their previous class moorings by changes of job, location and social environment. Whereas at one time everything about their lives might have confirmed their membership of, and identification with, a particular class, now there are sufficient inconsistencies or discrepancies to create doubt, and open up a degree of choice as to how they see themselves. Politically, for example, this means the emergence of 'cohorts of voters (who) no longer experience a reinforcement of familial, political socialization in their work and community experiences. The totality of socialization in Labour politics has been broken' (Adamson, 1991a: 165). The effects are not just political, since culturally and socially as well, there has been a dislocation of the previous working-class 'habitus' (Blewitt, 1983). So, for example,

> Many of the Welfare Halls, previously famous for their high level of cultural and political activity, their debates and libraries and dramas, became little more than drinking clubs and many of the amateur societies and voluntary associations which had previously blossomed within the cultural space they provided withered with them. (Jones, 1999: 18; cf. Francis and Smith, 1980)

Thus the fact that large numbers of people continue to frequent the old haunts of traditional Labourism does not mean that the social meaning of their behaviour is unchanged. The rupturing of previous social ties and conventions leaves the individuals concerned free to make political choices, or prone to ideological drift, which can take them in new and unexpected directions. As noted before, the shake-up in existing patterns permits a growing distance to develop between those who can 'make out' within the new array of opportunities, and those they leave behind, both physically, through migration, and mentally, through their adaptation to new values and ideas (Rees and Rees, 1983). Those who are already thoroughly endowed with 'traditional' work and community experiences are perhaps less likely to transfer their political allegiances; but in the long run, they are a dying breed.

Adamson's argument is that these developments throw up strange combinations, in which the circumstances seem 'proletarian' – low pay, low skill, low status – yet the conceptions and attitudes associated with them are more 'middle class' or even 'bourgeois'. Emphasis on the mental, rather than manual, nature of the labour required, for example, permits people to keep a working-class identity at arm's length, and identify themselves with others who are further up the managerial and class hierarchy. In this way, the erosion of the social bases of Labourism creates room for the promulgation of alternative ideologies; this may include variants of nationalism, which draw heavily on the residues of 'radical' sentiment, as well as on the Welshness which was previously part of a taken-for-granted working-class consciousness. While strongly critical of the determinism and reductionism associated with orthodox Marxist analysis, the analytical sequence Adamson employs is still obviously inspired by Marx, and by his successors, such as Gramsci and Poulantzas: economic restructuring conditions class recomposition, which permits ideological and political repositioning. At the same time, he acknowledges the importance of moving beyond the workplace, and the changes occurring within it, when he turns to consider some of the cultural changes that have helped to enlarge the gap between old and new forms of working-class existence (Adamson, 1991b). The rise of the out-of-town store, and DIY centre, offering a wide selection of 'lifestyle' commodities, has contributed to the privatization of family existence for many, at the expense of the exclusion of others, who lack the means – including the possession of private transport – to enjoy access to it. Thus variations in consumption patterns reflect and reinforce the divisions which have been promoted within the working class by changes at work, while enhancing the poverty of those at its lowest levels, whose prospects for employment are most limited. In an era of expansive credit-based consumption, differences of diet, dress, car ownership, holiday and leisure activity all become important signifiers of relative social position. These forms of consumption are related closely to changing patterns of ownership of housing, and also, it could be added, to movements of residential location. Former collectivist traditions can be undermined by rampant individualism. Cooke (1981a) saw the 'radical' tradition of south Wales fading under the impact of restructuring and the integration of the region into these new modes of mass consumerism. For him, the spread of consumer values marked a crucial stage in the penetration of new modes of existence into traditional communities, and the institutions of the working class proved defenceless to resist their 'anaesthetising' effects (Cooke, 1981a: 168). However, Adamson contends that, while these changes ensure backing for the old politics of Labour is less guaranteed than in the past, they also make for a relatively open-ended political future. In addition to the scope for new variants of nationalism, he also sees potential links between modern consumerism and an emergent 'green' politics, and the potential for new varieties of radicalism, as well as for privatized complacency.

Without explicit acknowledgement being made, it is possible to see some major continuities between this conclusion and the much earlier work carried out by Rosser and Harris in Wales, and Lockwood and Goldthorpe and their collaborators in England. The latter research grouping were particularly preoccupied with the significance of 'affluence' and employment security which was bringing about the emergence of a privatized, instrumentally orientated stratum at the top end of the established working class. In many ways this formation prefigures Adamson's 'new' working class. Over the same period, however, there has also crystallized towards the lower end of the working class an increasingly dispossessed, socially excluded layer, sometimes characterized as an 'underclass' (Mann, 1991;

Roberts, 2001). The presence of such a layer has been noted within Wales (Campbell, 1995; Adamson, 1997, 1999). While much of the traditional Welsh working class has found itself left behind by the forces of economic change, yet remained loyal to and supported by its existing community and political structures, there are elements among the less well qualified and less skilled who have found themselves subjected to growing practices of social exclusion and marginalization. In this sense, the existence of 'a significant population with no experience of work, few qualifications to offer an employer and no experience of the confidence and sense of capability that work experience brings' (Adamson, 1997: 3) is an obvious legacy of decline. Throughout the process of economic transformation, and the decline of the traditional industrial economy, large numbers of employees have been discarded from the workforce whose previous skills and qualifications have lost all value. They in turn have been unable to pass on to later generations the necessary attitudes and competences that would fit them for new kinds of work. Consequently among the working-class communities and estates of south Wales there are many which suffer from exceptionally high levels of unemployment, benefit dependency, lone parenthood and physical and environmental decay (Adamson, 1996, 1998); these places have their counterparts in north and west Wales as well, wherever the economic basis of particular localities has been superseded and displaced. This includes the slate communities of north-west Wales, many small market towns and coastal ports and harbours. Adamson (1999: 46) points to the emergence of a growing internal divide within Wales as the valleys and rural regions fell increasingly into a spiral of economic decline. Such places can become stigmatized as 'dangerous' locations, riddled with crime, substance abuse, family breakdown and youth disaffection, and this adds to the likelihood that those who inhabit them will be denied access to the material, social and environmental rewards which others take for granted. In particular, they become almost wholly cut off from access to the political system, either in terms of having effective representation within it, or from participating in its processes. Indeed they may come to see political agencies, including local authorities, as in part responsible for their difficulties, for example through the housing and rehousing policies which create areas known as 'sink' estates. Despite this, such evidence as there is suggests that they continue to aspire to essentially the same sorts of opportunities and choices as are available to mainstream members of the community.

Data collected at local authority district level provides confirmation of growing social polarization across Wales (Morris and Wilkinson, 1989a, 1989b). More close up, extreme differences of relative wealth and poverty can also be observed at ward level within local authority districts. It would seem therefore that the benefits of economic change and development over recent years have been limited to certain segments of the population, who have accelerated away from those who have not been able to share in the gains, or who more directly have paid the price for them. Spatially, the winners have included a number of prosperous small rural towns, especially those which serve as dormitory areas for commuters who work in desirable jobs and occupations in the larger towns, and the large urban centres of south-east Wales, especially Cardiff and Newport. At the opposite end of the spectrum there is a 'black hole of deprivation' which centres on the northern valley communities of Rhondda, Merthyr Tydfil, Cynon Valley and Blaenau Gwent. Despite serious job losses during the 1980s, north-east Wales has performed relatively well, whereas there are pockets of severe deprivation further to the west, in Anglesey and south Gwynedd. The more prosperous areas are occupied by a burgeoning Welsh lower middle-class and upper working-class population, consisting of home-owners whose living standards have improved markedly, although still not reaching levels to be experienced in other parts of Britain. A typical example is said to be the district of Creigiau in Taff Ely, characterized by 'pleasant, spacious housing, extremely low unemployment, a low sickness rate, a high percentage of social class I and II types, and extremely high car ownership. Moreover, it is spatially and socially isolated from the area of deprivation' (Morris and Wilkinson, 1995: 44). Overall, the extent of social distance and 'ghettoization' to be seen among both the better-off and the 'new' poor suggests that the time has come to finally put to rest the myths of the *gwerin* and a classless Welsh society (Morris and Wilkinson, 1995: 43).

The presence of persistent problems of poverty and multiple deprivation in Wales today implies that things have not necessarily changed that much from the circumstances which inspired 'radical' young sociologists to engage with the sociology of Wales twenty years earlier (Rees and Rees, 1980a). It is also the case now that there is a growing body of opinion in Wales which doubts the ability of conventional anti-poverty and economic regeneration strategies to bridge the gap between aspirations and delivery (Adamson, 1997). The language of 'social exclusion', which has largely replaced that of 'poverty' and 'deprivation', does help focus attention on the practices and barriers which serve to prevent large parts of the population from exerting any influence over, or sharing in the benefits of, change. These include barriers in the design and execution of social and economic policies aimed at securing development. In his more recent work, Adamson has suggested that, in the absence of satisfactory help and support from outside, some of the most socially innovative attempts to overcome these barriers of separation and exclusion have begun to emerge from within the 'economically and socially distressed communities of the marginalised working class' (Adamson, 1998). Others have made very similar claims in relation to the need for, and capacity of, rural communities in Wales to deal with their equally deeply entrenched economic and social problems (Wales Rural Forum, 1994; Day, 1997; Cloke et al., 1997). Whether they prove to be correct will depend greatly on the extent to which there remain sufficient residues of community spirit and social cooperation in those parts of Wales and Welsh society which have been most battered by the processes of economic and social transformation. Meanwhile it is evident that the problems encountered by such marginalized populations are compounded by the readiness with which others, including the media and often their better-off near neighbours, seek to apportion blame and to attribute general moral decline, loss of community values and social pathology to those who have been sidelined by economic and social change.

CHANGING GENDER PATTERNS

Although he noted a lack of relevant research evidence, Rees (1985) suggested that changes in gender relations would be among the most significant effects of the recomposition of the working class taking place in the coalfields. However, we have referred already to the way in which economic restructuring within Wales made use of, and to some degree reinforced, existing gender differences. Historically the pattern of industry had helped produce a strong dominant gender ideology centred on a rigid division of labour between men and women, and a conviction that men should be the natural breadwinners. The conventional bases for female identity were child care, domestic work and the home (Rosser and Harris, 1965; Leonard, 1980; Harris et al., 1987; Rosser, 1989). The domesticity of women was often celebrated in the figure of the Welsh 'Mam', but for most purposes Welsh women remained culturally invisible (Beddoe, 1988; Pilcher, 1994). Many spheres of public activity, including the organizations and institutions of the labour movement, were accessible mainly or only to men (John, 1984), with women relegated to supportive roles. Recent years have seen attempts by feminist scholars to recover some of the hidden voices, and stories, of Welsh women (Aaron, 1994; Betts, 1996), and to question the extent to which Welsh society and its history has been presented solely from the point of view of Welsh men.

The entry of women into the labour force in rapidly growing numbers from the late 1960s onwards, and more particularly the increasing participation in paid work of married women, inevitably put the traditional arrangements between the sexes under pressure, but change has been slow to occur. For example, it might be reasonable enough to expect that women's added commitments to paid work, often associated with extra time spent on travel, would lead to some reorganization of the domestic workload. However, using information from the steel studies, Morris (1985) found little direct relationship between the experience of male redundancy and changes in either women's involvement in the labour force or their role within the home. That is, women did not undertake paid work primarily in order to compensate for the loss of male incomes. Instead they responded to the increased availability of what were considered to be appropriate forms of work, in services and manufacturing, according to whatever information they happened to be able to gather about it. In many cases, in fact, the loss of a male job resulted in a calculation that the household would be better off, in benefit terms, if a woman stopped work as well. There was evidence that male unemployment could lead to tensions within the home, since men had lost the accepted source of their dominance, their ability to command a wage sufficient to support the family, and were forced to live more within the arena in which it was women who made the key decisions. Yet in the context of highly traditional conceptions of the household division of labour, men showed only a very limited readiness to take on such tasks as child care, cleaning and cooking; for the most part, their contribution was restricted to giving occasional 'help' in what was still regarded as the woman's sphere of work. There was no clear relation between men's work situation and the 'flexibility' they displayed within the home; in the face of economic uncertainty, the general tendency was to maintain or even strengthen existing gender patterns. Thus while there was evidence of some blurring of domestic roles, there seemed to be no strong challenge to the maintenance of the existing division of labour between the sexes.

Similarly, in a study of household adaptations to youth unemployment, Jenkins and Hutson (1990: 104) report that it continues to be the mother who has 'prime responsibility for looking after the house and those who live within it. She expects and receives little help, even when she is working full or part-time'. More generally, they state that, while some changes have taken place, as yet Wales has achieved no revolution in gender equality. As the foremost commentator on the position of women in Wales puts it, patterns of gender segregation remain 'astonishingly rigid' and far more will need to be done to change prevailing attitudes, culture and organization if equal opportunities for the sexes are to become part of the mainstream of Welsh life (Rees, 1999; Williams et al. 2000). Within the workplace for instance, it is still standard for women to hold positions at lower, more routine levels, where they are subject to the authority of male supervisors and bosses (Winckler, 1985; Rees, 1999), a contributory factor in ensuring that women's earnings on average remain well below those of men. A variety of factors contribute to the maintenance of a 'glass ceiling' which inhibits women's prospects of making it into senior management and professional posts (Rees and Fielder, 1991; Charles et al., 2000), one of which is the expectation that women should put the family first and carry out those obligations associated with a very traditional image of a 'woman's world' (Charles et al., 2000: 126). As Beddoe (2000: 180) puts it, Welsh women appear to be subjected still to a particularly virulent strain of patriarchy.

Younger women appear more likely to reject these assumptions. Nevertheless, the very limited inroads that have been made into traditional gender differences have raised anxieties and debate about the impact upon Welsh masculinities, a topic that has barely begun to be researched (Scourfield and Drakeford, 1999; Thurston and Beynon, 1995). As Scourfield and Drakeford show in their analysis of the selection of a millennium project 'appropriate' to Wales, the aspirations and interests of Welsh women, as distinct from those of Welsh men, hardly entered into the discussion. In this regard, as in so many others, a preoccupation with class, and the alleged differences between middle-class and working-class tastes, was used in a way 'which marks, overlooks or denies other forms of difference' (Scourfield and Drakeford, 1999: 9). Briefly, the miners' strike in Wales did produce a notable shift in the balance of relationships between men and women. As in other coalfields, women played a very prominent part in the activities of the many local support groups, and were particularly instrumental in mobilizing much of the response at community level, including the supply of food and other essentials. They also showed themselves to have previously unsuspected skills in leadership, organization and public speaking. In doing so, they were able to take inspiration from earlier action by Welsh women in helping to set up the anti-nuclear peace camps at Greenham Common. Developments subsequent to the strike, however, supported those who were less than optimistic about the prospects of maintaining this level of independence and confidence once 'normal domestic service' had been resumed (Rees, 1985: 404; Massey and Wainwright, 1985; Loach, 1985). Towards the very end of the twentieth century, there were some notable breakthroughs as women began to appear in some prominent public positions: in the National Assembly, the cabinet actually had a majority of women members. But perhaps the main factor affecting the situation of Welsh women was the weakening of the traditional family structure. For some, this was a liberation, whereas for others it brought added trouble. By 1991, 13 per cent of Welsh families were headed by lone parents, 93 per cent of whom were women. Single mothers were largely excluded from participation in full-time, or even part-time, work; like the growing number of teenage mothers, especially in the more deprived areas, they continued to be marginalized.

7

Rural Wales: The Sociological Account

RURAL WALES – 'THE WELSH HEARTLAND'

Up to this point the discussion has been preoccupied mainly with developments that have occurred in the more heavily populated industrial centres
of Wales, and with the way in which they have helped entrench particular
images and emphases within the various discourses of Welsh life. This
emphasis is justifiable in that it corresponds to the experience of the
majority of the Welsh population, three-quarters of whom live in the towns
and cities which take up less than a third of the country's geographical
space. In many respects, the major challenge to the ascendancy of this
perspective has come from an alternative set of themes and images associated with rural Wales. Those who seek to establish long-term continuities in
the nature of nations and peoples often find them in the characteristics of
rural living, and Wales has been no exception (Gruffudd, 1995). If coal and
steel were the twin pillars of modern Wales, then the connections between
Wales, agriculture and the rural economy seem to reach far deeper, into the
legacy of pre-modern and ancient times. The identification of true
Welshness with rurality, and its presumed social characteristics, has been a
recurrent discursive theme with significant repercussions for conceptions of
national identity, as well as for the preferred direction of future development. Recent controversies about contemporary changes in rural Wales
show this still to be the case.

   In the words of Gwyn Williams (1985: 197), history left rural Wales
bounded by a linguistic–religious demarcation line which was also very
clearly defined in class terms, a richly suggestive combination of factors.
Towards the end of the nineteenth century, the Welsh countryside had come
to be seen as the homeland of the *gwerin*, the 'common folk', a Nonconformist people who thought and socialized more or less exclusively in
Welsh, and who were free of any seriously damaging internal social divisions. During the preceding decades, they had been united in a successful
social and political struggle against an alien-seeming landowning class,
which spoke English and worshipped in the established Anglican Church.

The story of the mobilization of popular opposition under the banners of Nonconformity and resistance to 'Englishness' has been told often, and from varying points of view (Morgan, 1963; Evans, 1974; Day, 1984). Employing his Althusserian framework, Adamson (1991a) presents this as a classic instance of the 'overdetermination' of dominant economic or class issues in the Welsh countryside by cultural and political struggles, sufficient to result in an exceptional rupture of existing social relations. Despite real and exploitative differences between rural labourers and tenant farmers, the mass of the rural population was able to combine against what appeared to be an overwhelmingly powerful class of landlords, and bring about its defeat. Howell (1977: 21) notes that in the middle of the nineteenth century 60 per cent of Welsh land was under the control of just 1 per cent of landowners, each of whom possessed estates of 1,000 acres or more. Yet by the 1920s these great estates had been sold off, and passed into the ownership of hundreds of small family farmers (Davies, 1974). The ejection of the landlord class from the social structure of rural Wales was completed by the impact of prolonged agricultural recession and the effects of the First World War.

With the principal economic and social division resolved in this way, rural Wales could be conceptualized as essentially 'classless', and the outcome of social struggle interpreted in predominantly nationalistic terms; the removal of the landlords had made the countryside of Wales even more Welsh than it had been before. As Adamson puts it, 'The imagery of resistance is of a Welsh tenantry oppressed and exploited by an English landed class. That class imposes a foreign religion in an alien language on a culturally and religiously homogeneous people, the Welsh' (Adamson, 1991: 106). None of this is necessarily exactly true, but the combination of religious dissent, class war and radical politics which flourished for a while in Welsh-speaking rural Wales gave rise to an immensely powerful construct of what this Welshness comprised. Its features were associated so strongly with the idea of the *gwerin* that 'everything outside them came to seem only half-Welsh' (Williams, 1985: 206). As Williams reminds us, it was by contrast with this construction that 'large numbers of people, who in fact constituted a majority, were perceived as in some basic senses, un-Welsh' (1985: 236). Among the excluded majority were the working classes of industrial Wales. To some extent, the exclusion of the 'Anglicized' gentry was also a function of the way in which the notion of the *gwerin* took shape, since their social features and organization came to be seen as increasingly incompatible with what it was to be really Welsh. Thus the existence of a classless *gwerin* provides the foundations for one of the dominant versions of Welshness and Welsh nationhood, and it makes frequent appearances more or less at the margins of social science writing on Wales.

As summarized elsewhere, the ideological themes of this essentially nineteenth-century construction of Welshness were

> drawn from nonconformist religion, rural social relations, and Welsh-speaking. They stressed the centrality of community rather than class, the absence of marked social distinctions in Welsh society, and the capacity of ordinary people to make themselves through education, hard work, and thriftiness. So vigorously articulated was this idea of Welshness, so sharply drawn the lines of inclusion and exclusion, that for significant sectors of Welsh society it has subsumed all subsequent developments. (Day, 1984: 41)

The first generation to make a significant contribution to a sociology of Wales (though see Michael (1983) for a qualifying view) were largely preoccupied with celebrating and memorializing just such a conception of Wales and Welshness. The vehicle through which they chose to convey this viewpoint was the Welsh community study.

WELSH RURAL SOCIOLOGY – A CLASSIC TRADITION

The work of the small band of scholars led by Alwyn D. Rees (Rees, 1996; Davies and Rees, 1960; Jenkins, 1971; Owen, 1986) constitutes the most celebrated, distinctively Welsh, contribution to the formation of British sociology, and it is significant in a number of ways that their attention should focus so much upon the nature of the Welsh countryside and its changing social characteristics. Several of those who worked with Rees, and who followed like him in the footsteps of such pioneers as Daryll Forde and H. J. Fleure (Forde, 1934; Fleure, 1926; Carter, 1996), went on to become important figures in the development of human geography in Britain. Right up to the present there have been continuing links between the activities of members of the department of geography of the University College of Wales, Aberystwyth, and the development of rural studies, within and beyond the British Isles, which add up to a distinguished record of cumulative social scientific research. Inevitably, the analysis of Wales and Welsh issues has played a key role in this.

In the years before and after the Second World War, with the encouragement of the then Principal of Aberystwyth, Alwyn Rees sketched a programme of organized research into the nature of Welsh rural life, only part of which was brought to fruition. The linchpin is his own investigation of the settlement of Llanfihangel-yng-Ngwynfa (Rees, 1996). The other main published source is the collection of essays derived from similar community studies carried out by four of his postgraduate students (Davies and Rees, 1960). As has been argued elsewhere (Day, 1979, 1998a), although the content of each of these studies was shaped according to the interests and convenience of the particular researcher, together they represent a body of writing with considerable coherence, unified by a shared vision which ensured the predominance of a number of selected emphases. The republication in 1996 of Rees's *Life in a Welsh Countryside* shows that the exploration of these themes is still considered to have value for the academic, and wider public, audience in Wales.

In his foreword to the reprint, Harold Carter describes the study of Llanfihangel as 'totally innovative' in conception and execution, a pioneering attempt to provide a holistic account of the nature of rural community in Britain. The point is frequently made that Rees had no explicit theoretical base for his analysis of Welsh community life (Carter, 1996; Owen, 1986). In this regard, he was simply typical of his time and place. However, lack of conscious theoretical awareness is not the same as having no theoretical position at all. Rees was entirely conventional in the manner in which he chose to present rural social existence as offering the possibility of a traditional, integrated way of life, setting it in opposition to an increasingly dominant urban social world which he castigated for its supposed inability to give its inhabitants 'status and significance in a functioning society' (Rees, 1996: 170). In the Welsh context, this implied a criticism of the way in which life was evolving in the more industrialized, urbanized, districts, one which at times became quite explicit, and scathing (Gruffudd, 1994a). The communities of rural Wales were upheld throughout as models of effectively functioning local societies, complete and warm in their human relationships, and able to give those who inhabited them an unequivocal sense of belonging. Carter correctly notes how Rees wrote from 'an entirely engaged position' in this respect (Carter, 1996: 3), and how he and his associates could all be described as 'committed Welshmen'. Their commitment was to a particular conception of Wales and its relationship to a natural environment, a view which still finds contemporary echoes (Wyn Jones, 1991: 41).

Among the main themes they address are the extraordinarily potent historical continuity of the traditional Welsh way of life, and its adaptation to the land it occupies; the centrality to it of the Welsh language; the significance of religion and its social organization; and the lack of materialism and essential unpretentiousness of Welsh rural culture. As depicted in these studies, Welsh rural communities exhibit all the classic signs of the *Gemeinschaftlich* social world defined by Tönnies (1955); additionally, they are regarded as bastions of authentic Welshness. Carter echoes this when he draws attention to the way in which these studies, once justly celebrated, have been struck from the record of sociological research into community, and laments the resulting absence thereby of 'Welsh Wales' from the most comprehensive recent review of the field (Crow and Allen, 1994). The reasons for their dismissal have been widely rehearsed. To many later critics they exemplify all too clearly the limitations of the consensualist, functional style of social anthropological analysis which prevailed in the 1950s, and the associated 'idyllic' mythology of rurality (Day, 1979; Harper, 1989; Wright, 1992). The communities investigated are presented as vibrant examples of organic development, established over a very long period of time to exist in close harmony with their immediate environment (Owen, 1986). Their members, whose local roots generally were held to go back for several generations, are bound together in a deep web of social reciprocity, cemented by shared values and a common world-view. Such signs of social division and differentiation as appear among them tend to be absorbed back into the generally integrative framework of analysis. Consequently as social worlds the communities can seem at times so self-enclosed and self-reinforcing as to be almost suffocating. While it can be argued that there is considerably more to be said on behalf of this tradition than this impression would suggest (Day, 1998), even Carter does little to refute such objections.

The Aberystwyth studies undoubtedly cast Wales in a particular mould. By singling out for investigation a 'relatively secluded and entirely Welsh-speaking area which could be expected to have retained many features of the traditional way of life' (1996: p. v), Rees helped set the terms on which rural existence would be understood for some years to come. Of a dozen related studies carried out between 1940 and 1968, all but one were located in Welsh-speaking west and north Wales (Lewis, 1979). In most of them, the image of the traditional Welsh rural community provided an idealized standpoint against which later developments could be judged, and invariably found to be disappointing. This perspective is employed repeatedly within Rees's own text on Llanfihangel, where contemporary changes are assessed negatively by contrast with the 'old ways' and ancient tribal traditions. Life in this tiny Montgomeryshire community, with a diminishing population of some 500, is held to be both representative of Welsh society at its best, and indicative of its parlous situation. From the author's observation and reportage of its daily life, judgements can be made about loss and decline. These include the encroachment of materialistic values, the weakening of religious conviction and, hovering always in the background, the threat to the status of the Welsh language. Overall, a unique and valuable social order is shown to be threatened imminently by linguistic and moral anglicization, along with commercialization and urbanization. Thus the defence of the nature of rural life is made synonymous with the defence of Welshness, and the interpreters of Welsh community are also its advocates.

The dedication Rees and his epigones show to mapping vanishing ways of life leads a recent commentator to refer to their work as a project of 'rescue ethnography' (Dicks, 2000: 87). In spirit it is closely linked to the physical rescue of homes and rural artefacts for relocation to the Welsh Folk Museum in St Fagans, near Cardiff, set up in 1948 under the supervision of Iorwerth Peate and later Trefor M. Owen, both of whom passed through Aberystwyth as students. Peate (1940) was himself a noted celebrant of the longevity of the material culture of the Welsh countryside, and prominent among those who endorsed 'the subtle persistence of Ancient Ways' among the people of rural Wales (Parry-Jones, 1952), and the need to ensure that they were not simply forgotten. The attempt to document and explain in sociological terms the virtues of rural ways of life before they were lost forms just part of this highly influential current in Welsh social philosophy, which saw the Welsh countryside as a reservoir of civilized moral values, which if possible must be preserved (Gruffudd, 1994b). There have been later, even more skilful, attempts at reconstructions of the same kind. David Jenkins makes extensive use of oral history and recollections to retrieve the social patterns prevalent in south-west Cardiganshire at the very start of the twentieth century, a time when it was possible to

> see the why and wherefore of the social structure in that the ways in which people were related to one another were on a local basis, and that these ways are intelligible when seen in relation to the needs of the land upon which the community lived. (1971: 251)

However, by then there were already extensive relations with wider society, and as a result the local community was becoming increasingly subject to external influences and relationships which were pulling it apart.

RURAL WALES FROM THE INSIDE OUT

The Aberystwyth tradition proved short-lived, passing out of fashion along with the wider demise of British community studies (Bell and Newby, 1971; Crow and Allen, 1994). There were other significant contemporaneous contributions to the analysis of Welsh rural society written from contrasting perspectives. Frankenberg (1957) and Emmett (1964) both used insights derived from Manchester anthropology to highlight some of the differences and divisions within rural communities that were missing from most of the other Welsh studies. They showed that alongside friction between insiders and outsiders, English and Welsh, there were also significant age and gender distinctions which needed to be considered. In their preface to the volume on *Welsh Rural Communities* (1960), Davies and Rees noted the discrepancy between studies conducted 'from within' the culture, and those carried out by researchers who are external to it, a point repeated by Lewis (1979). On the one hand, there is a preoccupation with religion, the social structure of the chapels and a literary and poetic tradition centred on the home and the hearth, while on the other it is the more secular concerns of football, carnival and intra-community conflict which come to the fore. The former are said to correspond more closely to 'the Welshman as he sees himself' (Davies and Rees, 1960: p. xi), since they form part of the 'essentials' of a culture, to which the latter aspects are merely peripheral. Like the other features of Welsh rural community, 'culture' is treated in this comment as something homogeneous, while those who are not participants within it are set up to fail to grasp what it is really about.

The issue of the accessibility of a particular way of life to those who do not actually belong to it has been a familiar debating point for social anthropologists. Rees contended that the norms and values to which a community like Llanfihangel adhered were immune to scientific appraisal in terms of standards applicable in other societies; they could only be understood fully from inside. For example, farm practices could not be assessed according to the same measures of 'efficiency' used elsewhere. At the time when he carried out his research, Welsh farmers might consider writing poetry or attending a prayer meeting a more worthwhile use of time than working their land, while few would contemplate working on a Sunday, no matter how efficient or productive that might be (Rees, 1996: 144). This assertion of the need to be part of the value system in order to understand and comment upon it has been reiterated ever since with reference to Wales (see, for example, Jenkins, 1980; G. Williams, 1994). In fact, despite the sharpness of tone taken towards them, the 'outsiders' who attempted to document and examine Welsh rural life were by no means wholly antagonistic towards it. In her account of *A North Wales Village* (1964), Emmett made a determined attempt to explicate local attitudes and values from within, especially the stance taken towards 'ruling England' and the impact competing criteria of social success and achievement were having upon local young people, as they were faced by choices between loyalties to local Welsh values, and the lure of educational and social mobility through English. Frankenberg (1957) displayed great sensitivity towards the subtlety with which notions of 'belonging' and identity were deployed to distinguish 'Pentre People' from those who were not part of the community of Glynceiriog, showing that the boundaries of community were actually negotiable, according to circumstances. Such accounts opened up important questions about place, community and belonging which remain quite central to attempts to understand social relationships in rural Wales (Day, 1998a).

Indeed, it is in the investigation of aspects of rural Wales that divisions between 'insiders' and 'outsiders' and their respective sets of perceptions have been most controversial. The disjunctions which arise between external 'observers' models' and local 'actors' models' are explored most fully and systematically in this context by David Jenkins (1960, 1971, 1980). Jenkins is interested especially in the local idioms through which people make sense of their own social experiences. His impeccable historical reconstructions hark back to a time when a county such as Cardiganshire could be seen as a 'natural community' in which the vast majority of people spoke Welsh and were either engaged in or familiar with agriculture. This familiarity pervaded their every turn of phrase. A similar pattern of small local communities each with a relatively stable population and a common base in working the land was reproduced throughout the rest of rural Wales. As Jenkins notes, this meant that the ways in which the society was conceptualized tended to be particularistic, specific to individual communities and so did not allow direct comparisons to be made between one community and another (Jenkins, 1980: 117). So far as he is concerned, it is doubtful whether much value could be attached to a study which did not concern itself with such 'folk' concepts – the terms and categories, classifications and evaluations, used by those individuals who constitute the society. In the setting of rural Wales, this would necessitate understanding the Welsh language and the concepts embedded in it. This had a bearing on what came to be referred to as 'the *Buchedd* controversy' (Coxon, 1978: 269).

RELIGION AND SOCIAL STATUS IN RURAL WALES

The problem of generalization to which Jenkins animadverts has been one of the persistent stumbling blocks of community study methodology, and the tension between the wish to provide a detailed and specific account of how particular communities tick, while at the same time drawing wider lessons and conclusions, runs through the Welsh studies. Later critics (Bell and Newby, 1971; Harper, 1989) concluded that this could not be done, due to differences in theoretical perspective and lack of comparability of data. However, in *Welsh Rural Communities* Davies and Rees confidently asserted that the various aspects discussed 'although in detail particular to their localities, are not peculiar to them. They are characteristic, *mutatis mutandis*, of rural communities throughout Wales' (1960: p. x). A specific case in point is the 'fundamental social division', said to be more or less evident in all such communities, between distinct status groupings, which Jenkins labelled *Buchedd A* and *Buchedd B* (Jenkins, 1960). It is true that most of the collected essays make some reference to such distinctions, linking prestige and position within the community to the place an individual (or family) occupied within local religious life. The status system of each community appeared to match the hierarchy found within the Nonconformist chapels, and between 'believers' and non-believers, who constituted groups set apart by distinctive styles of living.

The importance of this distinction connects very closely with claims made about the social nature and role of the *gwerin*. As we have seen, it was widely argued that rural Wales dealt successfully with its class divisions by ousting the landowners. This left a basically egalitarian milieu within which distinctions centred on personal respectability and compliance with the normative expectations of religious organizations could substitute for the kinds of class differences found elsewhere. Among the 'English' influences Rees believed to be percolating into the Welsh countryside, and undermining its Welshness, was class consciousness, which replaced these locally generated prestige ratings with 'cruder' judgements of wealth and possessions (Rees, 1996). For him, this represented a form of cultural invasion which was inappropriate to the actual circumstances of Welsh rural life. Jenkins (1980) observed that common local linguistic expressions did reflect a classification of the population into three main class groupings: the gentry, farmers and cottagers. The two latter groups were often collapsed into a broader category of 'ordinary people' (*pobl gyffredin*), distinguished from the (by implication 'extraordinary') 'great people' (*y gwŷr mawr*). In other words, there was an acknowledged framework of rural social stratification; but for everyday purposes this took second place to a classification which originated in the religious rather than the economic domain, as Jenkins had explained in his earlier work (Jenkins, 1960). Those who lived up to the ethos and values of the Nonconformist denominations earned social respect and standing; they exemplified the lifestyle of *Buchedd A*, and conformed to the characterization of the *gwerin* as 'cultivated, educated, often self-educated, respectable but on the whole genially poor' (G. A. Williams, 1985: 237). Those who comprised *Buchedd B* however fell short of these standards, and exhibited a more secular lifestyle which earned the disapproval of the community. In an interesting twist, the leading historian of the *gwerin* and its mythology finds supporting evidence for its existence in the rural studies. On the strength of their accounts, he typifies *Buchedd B* as consisting of 'merry happy folk who are prepared to accept the leadership of others in the varied activities of life . . . gladly accepting (their) drive, resourcefulness and leadership' (P. Morgan, 1986: 148).

Jenkins's influential interpretation of these community patterns was challenged when Day and Fitton (1975) drew attention to the close correspondence between these 'subjective' conceptions of social status and more objective economic distinctions within the local population. Upon inspection, the superior status grouping, *Buchedd A*, tended to be made up of elements drawn from the local middle class and better-off working class, while the *Buchedd B* group consisted of unskilled workers. Rather than a peculiarly Welsh social classification emanating from the cultural sphere of organized religion, Day and Fitton suggested this bore a distinct resemblance to the separation between 'rough' and 'respectable' segments of the working class observed in many other local British studies, which also tended to be drawn according to behavioural or 'lifestyle' differences. Instead of representing a community-wide consensus, they proposed that the *Buchedd* classification was an ideological apparatus reflecting the views of some sections within rural society – in fact, the very rural elite of teachers, ministers and professionals to which the authors of the Welsh community studies themselves belonged. Hence, by playing down the inequalities and class divisions which existed among the Welsh, their analyses could be interpreted as endorsing the viewpoint of a particular segment of the local population, and legitimizing some of their exclusionary practices.

As an able social anthropologist, David Jenkins himself recognized the risk of slippage between everyday social understandings and analytical categories: both sides in the argument were vulnerable to his accusation, that 'when we discuss a society which is familiar to us we operate with concepts which are little removed from those of the people we study so that we may unwittingly slide over from one type of concept to another' (1980: 116). The issue is pursued further by Glyn Williams (1978b, 1983b) who considers Day and Fitton's contribution to be a 'highly motivated critique' driven by an 'overriding commitment to class analysis'. The suggestion is that, given their own personal origins outside Wales, they might be victims of a peculiarly English disease, the obsession with class. This leads them to view 'native' sociologists as lacking objectivity, and having an irrational attachment to the idea of Welsh culture. In fact, Williams goes still further, to make the somewhat extraordinary allegation that Day and Fitton treat Welsh culture as 'relatively unimportant in the life of rural Wales' (1983b: 141). This reaction illustrates just how tightly questions about rurality, Welshness and particular types of traditional values had come to be tied together. Critical inspection of any of these elements was immediately interpreted as an attack on all of them, and the ability of the outsider to apprehend the real meaning of local social organization was denied.

Williams's own reading of Jenkins's work is that it was not directed towards an analysis of stratification, or class, in rural Wales, but was about appreciating the way in which members of Welsh communities were differentiated by varying degrees of conformity to the set of values embodied in *buchedd*. Essentially these comprised the virtues of Christian Nonconformism: 'knowledge, education, brotherly love, cooperation, unselfishness, humility, frugality, forgiveness, perseverance, honesty and concern for the less fortunate' (Williams, 1983b: 138). Adherence to such values militated against any conspicuous display of wealth and helped to defuse potential economic differences within Welsh society. Williams contends that, during the course of the nineteenth century, these values became so firmly established that conformity with them was seen as 'an essential ingredient of Welshness with members of the secular *buchedd* being regarded as less worthy of being defined as Welsh'. Thus ethnicity, rather than economic position, became the basis of status group formation. This begs the questions: less worthy in whose eyes? And where then were the boundaries of 'ethnicity' to be drawn? What was the ethnic destination of those whose failure to abide by dominant local values resulted in their exclusion from genuine Welshness?

Glyn Williams's namesake, Gwyn Alf, took an altogether more sceptical stance towards the elision of the social attributes of the *gwerin* and the realization of ideals of virtuous conduct. He emphasized the need for extreme caution when approaching a concept that has been promoted so consciously within a context of political and cultural struggle. In his view, the idea of the *gwerin* had shown itself capable of infinite extension, serving among other things as a mobilizing myth for a rising middle class who claimed to speak on its behalf. In reality the situation was more diverse. Even at the height of the power of Welsh Nonconformity, it seemed that substantial sections of the population remained outside the orbit of the chapels; not even the vital civic ceremony of marriage came wholly under their control. The image of an overwhelmingly united population moved by religious conviction obscured these actual local and historical variations, just as the frenzy of competitive chapel building among denominations and communities during the nineteenth century had vastly exceeded the numbers of believers who needed to be accommodated.

THE DEATH OF 'RURAL' WALES?

Debate about the validity of ideas of the *gwerin* and *bucheddau* formed part of a generally more sceptical stance which emerged during the late 1960s and 1970s, a time when, according to Carter (1996: 7), aspects of the earlier researches began to be deconstructed as part of 'the myth of a wholesome rural Wales which had been invented by nationally minded Welshmen'. Among sociologists, there was growing critical analysis of notions of the 'rural idyll' and the general tendency to romanticize the nature of rural communities (Bell and Newby, 1971; Newby, 1979). The understanding of rural life was 'normalized' by being brought into the framework of mainstream sociological analysis, through the application of Weberian and neo-Marxist ideas (Newby, 1978). Meanwhile sociological research in Wales remained somewhat preoccupied with the cluster of topics derived from the classic rural studies: language, community, religion and rurality (G. Williams, 1978a). Yet as many of these accounts indicated, the social and cultural nature of the Welsh countryside was changing quite profoundly. Thus Carter and Williams (1978) point to the steady and continuous erosion of the traditional aspects of the 'Welsh culture complex' with its basis in the rural areas. Using information on the pattern of voting in repeated referenda about the acceptability of Sunday drinking, they show the retreat of the 'dry' region from 1961 to 1975, the frontier of 'wetness' moving progressively westwards. Their prediction that by 1990 only the district of Dwyfor would remain dry was borne out by events. This shift matched the pattern of decline in the proportions of the rural population speaking Welsh, where there was evidence of 'decline, retreat, and fragmentation'. 'Suburban' expansion around the rural–urban fringes, and 'intrusive' economic development in rural areas appeared to be among the factors responsible for this shrinkage. In the same collection, Day and Fitton (1978) report evidence from one rural community that routine attendance at religious worship had fallen to below 20 per cent of the adult population, and that of those attending more than 40 per cent were aged 60 or more. They anticipated a 'syndrome of collapse' which would bring about further secularization and closure of many chapels and churches. Writing about a 'border community' in north-east Clwyd, Wenger (1978) notes how the fading influence of the chapels was a cause of regret to those involved in the movement to defend the Welsh language. The English tongue was increasingly making its way into domains of activity which had previously been the preserve of Welsh: even in chapel Sunday schools, for example, more and more of the children had Welsh as their second language. Culturally, it was apparent that the framework of life in rural Wales was going through an intense transformation, very much in line with the pessimistic expectations of Rees and his associates, as previously integrated elements were split apart; inevitably, as further research was to show, this culture shift was intimately related to major changes occurring in the broader economic and social conditions of rural life.

Although theoretical perspectives and policy agendas have since undergone several mutations, social research into rural Wales has continued to show definite thematic and even stylistic continuities with the classic community study tradition described above. No full-blown examinations of specific communities have been carried out in recent years, but many of the key texts draw heavily on local-level case studies to develop and illustrate general theses, and the preoccupation with the nature and significance of 'community' has rarely been all that far from the centre of attention. The various strands identified as relevant in the earlier studies have largely dominated subsequent discussion, albeit against a background of concern to grapple with broader questions of economic and social change. They include: the shifting distribution and strength of the Welsh language; the consequences of patterns of migration; encounters among diverse social groups and types; and the nature of local and 'ethnic' identities. Much of the work has been carried out with at least one eye on the 'problem' of rural existence and the difficult adjustments required for it to be sustained, amidst not infrequent assertions of 'crisis'. More or less routinely, rural Wales has been presented as standing at a crossroads, needing urgent decisions to be made about what sort of Welsh countryside, and indeed what sort of Wales, can survive. Confirmation that these questions are far from resolved is contained in a recent statement that 'rural Wales is currently experiencing a period of profound upheaval and structural change' (Bristow, 2000: 71). Very similar words could have been written at almost any time during the past fifty or more years!

For a lengthy period it seemed that some sort of terminal resolution to the crisis of rural Wales would be achieved as the Welsh opted to vacate their rural territory. Prolonged exodus from the countryside forms the backcloth to many of the anxieties expressed by the rural geographers and sociologists. The rural Welsh counties had been losing population steadily since the 1840s, and towards the end of the nineteenth century this was happening at a tremendous rate; during the 1880s alone, around a quarter of the rural population, 100,000 people, went from the area. Much of this migration was necessary to furnish industrial Wales with its labour force; arguably it also provided a safety valve for excess rural numbers (Jenkins, 1971: 250). For several decades it enabled close connections to be maintained between rural and industrial Wales, as individuals and families circulated between the two, and made direct links through trade and income transfers. It has been argued that the Welshness of industrial Wales, including its use of the Welsh language, turned on this importation of people from rural backgrounds (Thomas, 1962). But increasingly it became a one-way traffic, as those unable to make a living in the countryside found their way to the 'bright lights' and wider opportunities of urban south Wales, or the English cities. One effect was a simplification of the rural social structure as mass emigration removed many of the layers that previously had given it some complexity – craft workers, artisans, shopkeepers, small professionals, those working in the quarries and other industrial trades – making it appear more uniformly 'petty bourgeois' than before, a universe of small family farmers (G. A. Williams, 1985: 208; Adamson, 1991a). Despite significant pockets of industrialization in north and west Wales around coal, and slate, which had given rise to distinctive working-class communities very much like those of the south, the limited scale and scope of industrial development meant that rural Wales became increasingly marginalized and subordinate to the more prosperous and advanced urban areas. By the mid-twentieth century it was perceived as remote and peripheralized, isolated not just geographically but also socially from the mainstream of British life. Frankenberg's use of Alwyn Rees's work to encapsulate the 'truly rural' end of an implied evolutionary spectrum seemed to reflect this (Frankenberg, 1966). Rural Wales was a region of deprivation, economic marginality, falling population and lack of growth (Priestley and Winrow, 1975; Wenger, 1980).

The widening gulf between patterns of existence in town and country that developed in Wales during the nineteenth and twentieth centuries was merely a particular instance of a much more pervasive trend, which created the basis for distinct, and often disconnected, rural and urban sociologies. For many years these differed with respect to prevailing theoretical perspectives and substantive issues (Newby, 1980). The real marginalization of rural societies was aggravated by the diminishing intellectual interest shown in them: the sociology of rural life itself was a minority interest. Efforts to understand and react to rural change were handicapped by the dominance of urban attitudes and theories, and an urban bias in policies, coupled with the absence of any clear strategy for social, economic or industrial development in rural areas (Grant, 1978). The situation in central Wales was quite typical in this regard: by 1971, with 40 per cent of the land area of Wales it contained fewer than 7 per cent of its people. For the most part they lived in very small and scattered settlements and were dependent on farming and related occupations. What happened to them was of major concern to agricultural economists, and a subject of some fascination to folklorists and enthusiasts for the Celtic fringe, but otherwise appeared old-fashioned and somewhat quaint to most outsiders (Frankenberg, 1966). Such an impression was reinforced by the decaying social fabric and evidence of physical dereliction that surrounded a rapidly ageing population, whose habits and social relationships seemed frozen in time. The characteristic images of the period were of deserted farmhouses and redundant chapels. Young people continued to leave the area in large numbers, taking with them the promise of new ideas and energies (R. H. Morgan, 1983). There was a growing sense that this could not be left unchecked any longer, because it threatened the viability not only of a distinctively Welsh, Welsh-speaking 'way of life', but of large tracts of the countryside as well (Beacham, 1964).

THE 'MODERNIZATION' OF RURAL WALES

By the 1960s there were the beginnings of some positive responses to the needs of rural Wales, which took differing forms according to the value those involved placed upon the attitudes and social structures traditional to the area. The formation in 1957 of the Mid Wales Industrial Development Association, bringing together business leaders and representatives of local government to promote economic change, signalled a new awareness of the need for the area to take action to 'develop' out of its perceived backwardness and stagnation (Broady, 1973, 1980). This could be seen as a 'grassroots' initiative by a ginger group who had become impatient with the lack of momentum. As its title suggests, the Association's objective was to achieve some industrialization of the region, which had seen a number of its established craft and industrial occupations disappear. The industrialization of the British countryside was a prominent feature of the period from the 1960s onwards, and had as its obverse the 'ruralization' of industry (Healey and Ilbery, 1985).

The aim of attracting new firms and industries became a central strategic imperative for the Association's successor bodies, the Mid-Wales Development Corporation and eventually the Development Board for Rural Wales (DBRW). The headquarters of these organizations were located in Newtown, Montgomeryshire (later Powys), and the Newtown/Welshpool area became the nub of attempts to apply 'growth centre' theories of regional planning to rural areas. The intention was to bring about a bigger concentration of business and commercial activity within modernized urban centres, the success of which would enable benefits, especially employment, to spread to the more remote hinterland. The main instruments were branch plant development, on subsidized industrial estates, together with the provision of new housing suitable for attracting key workers. Henceforth, estimates of the number of new jobs created in return for public investment became the talisman of successful rural development (Law and Howes, 1972; Law and Perdikis, 1977; Thomas and Drudy, 1987).

An Act of Parliament in 1976 conferred powers on DBRW to 'promote the social and economic well being of the people of mid Wales'. However, these powers were restricted in the main to industrial development; the Board had no authority to act in respect of agriculture, or the development of tourism and other services, and very limited capacity to pursue its social goals. Its principal focus became the attraction of manufacturing employment to rural Wales. It was an important part of the Development Board's ethos that it viewed the area as a place without any history of entrepreneurship or industry, other than farming (Pettigrew, 1987: 104). This perception was factually inaccurate, since in Newtown and other nearby towns there were visible remnants of a quite sizeable woollen industry; but it was important ideologically for the Board's role as a modernizing agency. As well as providing direct incentives for industry to locate and grow in the area, by the provision of advance factory space and infrastructure, it also undertook action to stimulate entrepreneurship and to change attitudes towards business and industrial employment, including sponsoring educational projects with local schools. By the end of 1985 the Board had nearly 500 factories either in operation or under construction, totalling approaching 3 million square feet of floor space, and it laid claim to the creation of some 7,425 'job opportunities' (never quite the same as actual jobs). At this time, DBRW was still proclaiming that new factory building was the 'backbone' of its activities.

Supporters of the approach contended that by building on earlier efforts DBRW was furthering a 'robust regional strategy' that had acquired a 'familiarity that feeds the momentum for development' (Pettigrew, 1987). Relations between the Board and other agencies, including local authorities, were said to be excellent and its role within the region uncontroversial. To meet its objectives, the Board took on the task of championing the region, and one aspect of this was an attempt to eliminate the effects of the past, with all its unsuitable connotations. The slogan 'Mid Wales – a New Wales' and other marketing tags such as christening mid Wales 'The British Business Park' were intended to serve this purpose (Howe, 1999). They formed part of the 'place marketing' and branding process through which planners and others have sought to position areas and regions so as to increase their appeal to potential users and consumers, such as footloose industries and tourists (Philo and Kearns, 1993). They also indicated a conscious attempt to redefine the nature of rural living and values, away from its predominantly agricultural and traditional bias.

Wenger (1980) documents some of the initial results of this development strategy. The change in perspective from the earlier community studies is obvious from the emphasis now placed upon analysing the nature of local labour markets and the problems of rural employment. Rural Wales is described as a marginal economy to which people were compelled to make a series of 'untypical' adjustments; otherwise their main option was to move to more prosperous locations. Many of the topics touched upon in Wenger's report were to become the staple fare of debate for years to come: diversification of the rural economy; the necessity for multiple job holding in a situation of scarce opportunity; success and failure in business start-ups; and the social and cultural strains between 'old' and 'new' aspects of rural society. Even if doubts could be raised at times about the objectivity with which they are described, the vignettes Wenger provides of the development process in her half-dozen selected study areas are very revealing of the ongoing struggle to contain new developments within established cultural, environmental and aesthetic codes. Without question, numerous clashes of values and aspirations occurred among the diverse variety of entrepreneurs, local notables, officials, 'hippies' and visitors who became caught up in the process. In the town of Bala, for example, Wenger describes the ultimately unsuccessful effort to develop a craft centre against the resistance of certain members of the town council and local religious leaders, who claimed to know what was in the best interests of the town, and what, or who, was 'undesirable'. Wenger does not quite use the language of *bucheddau*, but in her account there are strong indications of the battle being waged locally to maintain the norms and standards, and privileges, associated with *Buchedd A* against hostile forces regarded as emanating from beyond the community. The strength of opposition to unwanted development meant that Bala was taken out of DBRW's list of potential growth centres.

Commenting on the Development Board's work Wenger remarks that the 'same policies may produce entirely different results due to intangibles, which can be hard to predict, particularly since the responses are cumulative' (1980: 39). For example, the way in which different local communities chose to define themselves proved to be a major constraint upon the type of development which was seen as appropriate and viable. According to such local conceptions, a place could be seen primarily as a resort, needing to cater for visitors; as an agricultural community; or as a Welsh-speaking environment. These definitions elicited different responses to possible economic and social changes, and gave rise to disputes and disagreements comparable to those seen in Bala. Attitude surveys carried out during this period produced consistent evidence of substantial local disapproval of plans for advance factory building and for the recruitment of labour from beyond the area, on the grounds that it would have a deleterious impact on quality of rural life, and also force up local wages. Farmers and small-business proprietors certainly had mixed feelings about the merits of such 'development', fearing that it would create a more competitive labour-market situation which would disadvantage them. At the same time, there were many who attached priority to the need for new, and more varied, sources of employment, and saw this as the only way out of conditions of low pay and restricted choice. Behind these differing group interests could be discerned some quite fundamental questions about the nature and future direction of Welsh 'rurality', as well as radically contrasting perspectives on development (Wenger, 1982).

The choice Wenger seemed to be posing in 1980, between deprivation and development, was obviously not realistic. Some form of development had to happen, since without extensive change depopulation would have

continued to the point where rural Wales, for all its worthwhile social qualities, would have ceased to exist, except possibly as a museum piece. The
issue posed therefore was about what sort of place it was, and could
become. Absence of change would have left the region to slip further into
the past, earning the label of backwardness which some critics were only
too eager to pin on it. The struggle has been to find instead a way of
securing survival, without sacrificing altogether the valued legacy of the
past, including crucial elements of rural Welshness. The modernizing thrust
of the rural development agencies, backed by innumerable reports, treated
the task as one of wrenching rural Wales forward into the twentieth (and
now twenty-first) century; and this meant diluting or discarding much of
its traditional base. In their view, as with other peripheral areas, its remoteness and relative detachment from the wider world needed to be overcome.
For them, rural Wales was not a 'heartland', but located at the margins,
and at risk, if neglected further, of degenerating into the badlands.
Modernization implied integration, and a process of 'catching up' with the
characteristics of modern industry. However, agreement about the plausibility of this case was not universal. There were those who were suspicious
of the motives and likely outcomes of such top-down, externally directed,
strategies for change. The introduction into rural Wales of new forms of
industrial employment, and the values associated with it, could be
regarded as a way of adding to its dependence, merely another version of
internal colonization. Raymond Williams provided a fictionalized account
of such fears in his novel *The Fight for Manod* (1979), in which the plot
strongly echoed a proposal to expand Newtown into a substantial urban
centre, housing overspill population from the English midlands.

The readiness with which the agents of change dismissed the value of
past patterns and social structures, or saw them indeed as the problem
which needed to be solved, resembled an evolutionary enthusiasm for
change. Theorists of modernization usually have proclaimed the inevit-
ability of the 'progress' they represent, and cast opponents into the role of
reactionaries. In the Welsh context, this tendency inevitably became linked
to arguments around the promulgation of and resistance to 'English'
(synonymous with urban/metropolitan) culture (G. Williams, 1980).
Warnings were issued that, far from resolving difficulties, this approach
would bring about the creation of new structures of inequality and impoverishment, while destroying much that had made the area precious. Rather
than deprivation *or* development, it pointed to the probability of development *with* deprivation.

THE PROBLEM OF AGRICULTURE

As we have seen, the conventional image of rural Wales, endorsed by an influential body of research, has been that of a primarily agrarian economy, with a social structure made up of small family farms and relatively self-contained communities, highly adapted to its physical environment. Wales shared these characteristics with other parts of upland Britain, and like such areas everywhere has been under the most enormous pressure to change. The time is long gone when the 'traditional' type of rural economy could sustain anything like the depth of social and cultural relationships it upheld in the past. Indeed, by now it is possible for some to assert that the industries on which it rested – agriculture, forestry and fishing – have come to be only of relatively marginal importance to the fabric of rural society (Bristow 2000: 199). This puts a question mark over the entire meaning of 'rurality' in the twenty-first century, a topic which has been hotly debated for some time (for example, see Murdoch and Marsden, 1994; Cloke and Little, 1997). Newby (1978) has argued that all meaningful definitions of 'the rural' hitherto have had their basis in agriculture, and therefore that rural sociology has to remain centred upon the specificities of agricultural production. However, as the foot and mouth crisis of 2001 demonstrated so brutally, farming is only one among a number of vital industries upon which the rural districts of Wales depend. Although its importance remains absolutely central for the landscape and environment of the country, the Welsh agricultural industry has proved poorly equipped to compete successfully in the modern world, and its significance for the Welsh economy has been in substantial decline for well over a century.

Of agricultural land in Wales 80 per cent qualifies for less favourable area (LFA) status; its soil quality imposes limitations that are graded as 'severe' or 'very severe'. The climate is poor, with high rainfall, and about a third of the land is hill or mountain grazing a thousand feet or more above sea level. Hence, except for limited areas of dairy farming in the south-west and north-east, crops are restricted mainly to potatoes, barley and animal feed-stuffs and the principal activity is beef and sheep production. Even if there have been times in the past when their agricultural products, especially wool, have been in great demand, Welsh farmers have never enjoyed the prosperity experienced by their counterparts in the English lowlands, something that is made visible in the quality of their farmhouses and outbuildings. Much of the added value derived from agricultural production has been, and continues to be, exported from the country to create wealth elsewhere. Nevertheless, agriculture has made a notable contribution to economic and social development and even as late as the mid-1980s it was counted among the most important Welsh industries (George and

Mainwaring, 1988). While at that time it contributed only about 4 per cent of total Welsh GDP, its role in the rural counties was enormously more important. Farming provided 15 per cent of employment in Dyfed, and almost a quarter of the jobs in Powys. Altogether there were some 57,000 agricultural employees, of whom 32,000 worked in the industry full-time. Estimates of the total contribution, direct and indirect, that farming made to the rural economy were invariably very much higher. Like any other industry, farming requires a wide range of inputs which also create additional jobs and revenues (for example, sale of agricultural machinery) and its products leave the farm to become raw materials for processing into consumer goods and other commodities (see Midmore, 1991).

Together with the rest of rural Britain during the twentieth century, Wales came under the influence of an irresistible productivist orientation towards agriculture, strengthened by the formative experiences of war, which made food production a national priority. Despite the power attaching to ideological conceptions of independence and competition with which farming has been imbued traditionally, agriculture has been arguably the most heavily supported and state-dependent of all industries throughout the post-war period, and has become entirely dependent upon subsidy. Following Britain's entry to the European Economic Community (EEC) most of this support has been channelled via the Common Agricultural Policy (CAP). At its peak in the mid-1980s, Welsh farmers were in receipt of some £25 million per annum in European subsidies for hill livestock production, the bulk of which (£19 million) was attributable to headage payments for sheep. They were eligible for a further £27 million in capital grants, equivalent to 44 per cent of all agricultural investment (George and Mainwaring, 1988: 146). Such favourable incentives encouraged the extension of the amount of land given over to livestock, and led to ever-growing numbers of sheep on the Welsh hills. The structure of support has also been one of several factors encouraging consolidation of holdings. Between 1971 and 1985 more than half the holdings of 40 hectares or less disappeared (a reduction from 36,557 to 17,168) while the number larger than 40 hectares increased correspondingly from 7,778 to 11,844. As noted before, the great majority of Welsh farms have been owner-occupied since the early 1900s, and the reduction in their number has had obvious implications for the possible demise of family farming, the mainstay of traditional rural social organization.

The aims of the CAP, like those of government intervention more widely, have been to ensure the productivity and profitability of farming, and also to maintain the valued aspects of rural social and community life. Yet the verdict delivered by two senior economists on the effects of such regimes for Wales could hardly be more damning: 'The picture that emerges is of high prices, overproduction, generally low and unstable incomes, declining full-time employment, resource wastefulness, and negative environmental effects' (George and Mainwaring, 1988: 154). According to figures calculated by Bateman and Midmore, by the early 1990s GDP per head from agriculture was substantially below that generated by other rural economic activity, so that with roughly 19 per cent of the workforce in rural Wales working within agriculture it was producing only some 5 per cent of locally generated GDP. The industry's net product had declined by a fifth between 1986 and 1991. This leads them to comment that agriculture, although 'traditionally spoken of in hushed tones as "the backbone of the economy"', would be 'at least superficially better described as the engine of rural decline' (Bateman and Midmore, 1996: 15). The work done by Midmore and his colleagues is aimed primarily at estimating the economic role and performance of Welsh farming, but they acknowledge the much wider impact the industry has in social and environmental terms. They note that the majority of Welsh farmers now are engaged in 'pluriactivity', supplementing their generally meagre farm incomes with other types of employment and business. For a combination of attitudinal and situational reasons, such as their geographical location in the less populated and economically diverse areas, this is less common among Welsh-speaking, and Welsh-born, farm households. The interaction between agriculture, the Welsh language, and other aspects of 'traditional' Welsh rural culture is complex, and profound. In 1991 farming accounted for 10 per cent of employment among Welsh speakers, contrasted with only 2 per cent for the rest of the population. Very nearly half of those working in agriculture spoke Welsh (Hughes and Sherwood, 1996); thus the continuing decline of agriculture poses a major threat to the reproduction of Welsh in the rural areas. But efforts to regulate the spiralling costs of the CAP have meant the steady withdrawal of subsidy, and various steps have been taken to target support more closely to economic and social policy objectives. The economic pressures bearing upon Welsh agriculture have created a continual awareness of the precarious nature, not just of the industry itself, but of the whole of Welsh rural society, and a sense that far more is at stake than a way of making a living; in many eyes, it has been an entire way of life, one that is close to the very heart of what Welshness is really about, that has been put under threat by the withdrawal of agriculture from its previously leading role in the rural economy and its communities.

8

Contemporary Rural Wales: Via Development to Dependence?

Discussion of the nature of rural change in Wales since the 1960s has reprised many of the same arguments and debates already discussed in relation to more industrial settings, especially with regard to the extent to which local people can be said to be able to exert any real control over what occurs. Williams (1980) identifies two common modes of development applicable to peripheral rural areas, both of which he sees as harmful. One involves large projects, with significant capital investment, designed to take advantage of the prime rural asset base, its natural resources, in circumstances where popular resistance is likely to be muted, or manageable (Davies, 1978; Rees, 1984). Examples would be the location of nuclear or other power stations – in Wales, Trawsfynydd, Wylfa, and the hydro-electric scheme at Dinorwic would be examples – harbour developments or, more recently, the installation of wind farms. These enable the exploitation of geographical conditions and raw materials, and bring short-term employment benefits during the construction process, but in the long run make a very limited local economic contribution; meanwhile they can be highly disruptive of existing economic and social relationships. Local gains tend to be restricted: for example, farmers with wind turbines on their land will be paid a premium but there are no other direct local beneficiaries (Hedger, 1995). Williams (1980) suggested that most of the benefits of such developments were either exported (as revenues) or went to an elite of skilled and technical employees, mostly recruited from outside the area. True to his predictions, after an (extended) operational life of some thirty years, the actual or proposed closure of the older generation of Magnox reactors has created major problems of job loss and uncertainty for local communities in Wales. Hence both the short- and long-term consequences of this type of development have been destabilizing, with rather mixed benefits in between. Even activities which might seem more 'naturally' attuned to the countryside can have similar effects. The covering of large parts of Wales with extensive and uniform conifer plantations has resulted in a product which has inherently low value being transported long distances for processing (Midmore, 1996). The local economic returns have been negligible, and have to be weighed against the visual harm done to the environment and the additional burden placed upon country roads by huge loads of logs which often pass one another travelling perversely in opposite directions.

The alternative pattern, of far more general relevance, was the policy of 'regional development' already outlined: the use of a variety of inducements to encourage new businesses, and new workforces, to relocate to country areas, so as to improve the mix of economic activities and create a more diverse and 'modern' profile by stimulating a movement away from dependence upon agriculture and related activities. In effect this has constituted a system of extended subsidy to private enterprise, especially small and medium-sized businesses, and an added encouragement for business to make the most of the opportunity provided by underemployed, low-wage, labour tied to rural locations. In practice, this often consisted of female employees, whose prospects previously had been limited to unpaid family labour on the farm (Ashton, 1994) or to poorly rewarded jobs in the service sector. Information on women's participation in the rural labour force is sparse for Wales, as for other rural areas (Little, 1991; Walker, 1992). Rural women have been added to the workforce in considerable numbers, but for the most part they have been confined to low-paid jobs requiring little skill. The emphasis placed on providing work 'suitable' for rural conditions has favoured firms with relatively few employees, operating in light manufacturing, craft and service provision. The limited choice available within the labour market has been restricted still further by expectations that women's primary responsibility is to home and family, and by practical constraints such as limited access to private transport (Day, 1993).

The approach to rural development which prevailed during this period has been accused of major weaknesses in both execution and conception. In crude terms, its effectiveness was judged by the supposed numbers of new, non-agricultural jobs created, based on estimates of factory floor space let or on survey responses by managers. Calculations of the number of new manufacturing jobs tended to lapse into arguments about the technicalities of measurement (see Thomas and Drudy, 1987; Willis and Saunders, 1988; Day and Hedger, 1990). This preoccupation with a rather limited form of development precluded adequate discussion of more fundamental points to do with the impact the policy was having on the economic and social character of the region. As well as the quantity of jobs created, this could be assessed in relation to their quality, the specific kinds of work involved, and the differential spatial consequences of their distribution, with all the ensuing effects these had for rural people and places. Criticisms of the dangers of undue reliance on branch plant development could be extended to rural Wales, where it was noted that there was a continuous turnover of businesses, such that closures needed to be offset against new ventures; as a result, the numbers of new jobs expected to flow from inward investment usually failed to materialize. There was scepticism about the staying-power of many of the small and medium-sized enterprises attracted by the lure of subsidy, and their ability to establish genuine local roots. Furthermore, people in rural Wales were being supplied with jobs which were at the bottom end of the labour market, and which therefore tended to perpetuate many of their existing disadvantages. After all, the fact that they were cheaper and less troublesome to employ than competitors elsewhere was being advertised as their principal attraction! So far as manufacturing employment was concerned, the majority of jobs gained turned out typically to be fairly routine tasks requiring little training or expertise. Many of the more skilled jobs went to 'key workers' and managerial staff attracted into the area, whose presence added to pressures in local housing markets as well as introducing novel and sometimes challenging social and cultural elements into the local social mix.

An obsession with manufacturing growth blinded many to the fact that it was never going to be a mainstay of the rural economy. Compared to employment in services it was a minor influence, accounting for only around 10 to 15 per cent of the jobs in rural labour markets (Thomas and Day, 1991). With upwards of 70 per cent of employment in the service sector, changes affecting tourism, social care and welfare, developments in the retail sector and reorganization of public administration had the most far-reaching repercussions, bringing about a wholesale reshaping of social patterns, lifestyles and cultural values. Yet the decisions governing most of these factors were being taken outside the area, usually by those who were quite oblivious to their local effects.

For the most part, the problems this brought for rural Wales have been shared with most other rural areas, and more especially the remoter, upland parts of north and west Britain. These include issues to do with the steady centralization and 'rationalization' of various services and public utilities to bring them more firmly under the influence of the twin logics of profitability and efficiency. The result has been a steady loss of local control, and the weakening of local interdependencies. Successive governments and planning authorities have had to wrestle with the costs of providing for small and scattered populations. As far as possible, they have encouraged services to 'regroup' into larger units, serving bigger catchments, and this has brought the closure of village schools, 'cottage' hospitals and rural post offices, and a reduction in the number of medical and job centres. These changes have helped transform the nature of most small rural communities, removing from them many of the sites of social interaction and cooperation which previously held them together.

The same kind of concentration has occurred with regard to retail services, with the decline of the village shop and the development of shopping centres and trading estates on the edges of most of the small market towns. Few influences have been more powerful than the encroachment of national supermarket chains into rural space, with drastic consequences for local economy and society (Day and Jones, 1995; Guy, 1995; Monbiot, 2000) as well as for the fortunes of agriculture. Rural producers have been subsumed into extended chains of supply and processing which have rendered them increasingly unable to decide matters of price, quality or even production methods, and they have seen much of the value of food production captured within large corporations and enterprises, very few of which have any distinctively Welsh identity or frame of reference. Here, too, key decisions are taken in places remote from those who will be most affected by them.

Some efforts to alter the pattern of rural spatial location were more deliberate than this. They followed the recommendations of the 1964 Beacham report, which argued the need to rectify an obsolete settlement pattern by encouraging the expansion of growth centres and the redistribution of people into larger units. Manufacturing employment in the Welshpool labour market grew by 50 per cent during the 1970s, whereas during the same period it declined in Aberystwyth by almost a third. Aberystwyth also suffered major losses of public-sector employment through administrative reorganization, and educational cutbacks. Hence its role as a regional centre, with a predominantly Welsh-speaking population, underwent significant demotion (Day and Hedger, 1990). Similar patterns of growth and decline occurred throughout rural Wales. Detailed analyses of labour-market data revealed the extent to which different localities were following distinctive economic and social pathways (Day, 1991; Wales Rural Forum, 1994; Cloke et al., 1997). Taking the rural county of Dyfed as an example, it was possible to see the emergence of highly differentiated local economic configurations. Travel-to-work areas centred on Lampeter and Cardigan remained strongly oriented to agriculture, forestry and fishing; Aberystwyth kept its concentration of public administration, education and other services; Carmarthen showed strength in communication, banking and finance. Whereas the fastest-growing local labour market in the county showed an employment increase of 19 per cent between 1981 and 1987, with female employment growing astonishingly by very nearly three-quarters, at the other extreme there were areas showing losses of 8 to 11 per cent. In absolute terms, these trends affected modest numbers of people; but relatively speaking, they produced dramatic swings in fortune between different locations, often achieved apparently by stealth. During this period, two of Dyfed's districts, Pembrokeshire and Cardigan, joined Holyhead in north Wales among the five worst performing local labour markets in the whole of Britain (Champion and Green, 1988), and it was symptomatic that all three of these struggling localities were to the west of the country. In general terms, the more Welsh-speaking, westerly areas fared less well than districts closer to the English border (Morris and Wilkinson, 1989a). The disproportionate emphasis on development in the 'accessible' eastern half of the region gave rise to increasing local discontent, and posed mounting questions about the accountability of those responsible, and the way in which economic objectives should be balanced against social and cultural considerations. It was evident that a policy of rural industrialization and diversification was increasingly at odds with conceptions of the Welsh countryside which revolved around the centrality of farming and a 'traditional' rural way of life, and also with alternative frames of meaning which emphasized the need to preserve a specifically Welsh, and non-urban, mode of existence (Day, 1999). Yet at the same time a steady stream of economic and social reports since the 1980s have provided depressingly ample evidence that the problems this policy was supposed to solve have persisted largely unchanged.

THE RURAL RESTRUCTURING PROCESS

Bringing all these considerations together suggested the need for an adjustment of perspective going well beyond the orthodox framework of 'modernization' and the importance of achieving closer integration with the world beyond. Such an adjustment was proposed by Gareth Rees (1984), who used rural Wales as a case study to show how the then emerging restructuring framework could help make greater sense of what was going on. Outlining some of the theoretical developments taking place around the 'new' rural political economy and sociology, Rees brought rural areas under the microscope as examples of the way in which different fractions of capital were making changing use of space to meet their own objectives. Each new round of investment undertaken by them would bring about a different spatial configuration, among other things changing the relative significance and meaning of 'rural' and 'urban' environments. Viewed in this way, one could see how the changes taking place in rural areas were reflective of 'profound shifts in the nature and organization of capitalist production' at a given time (Rees, 1984: 27). Rees suggested the framework would also help show how alterations in rural employment were related to adjustments in rural class structures, gender divisions and forms of political conflict, as well

as the complex processes by which 'rural cultures' were produced and reproduced. Changes affecting agriculture were to be treated simply as a special
case of these more general processes, whereas an 'overly exclusive' focus on
agriculture, such as had tended to prevail in the past, would result in only a
partial understanding of how particular rural localities acquired their
distinctive characteristics (Rees, 1984: 35).

A virtue of Rees's analysis was that, instead of treating rural Wales as an
isolated unit into which change had to be introduced from outside 'by invi-
tation', its underlying contention was that the region was already
thoroughly bound up with, and shaped by, developmental processes. Quite
independently of any conscious policy or strategic intent, these had been
making it a very suitable place for investment. Local experience therefore
was just a small aspect of a far greater urban–rural shift which was seeing a
rapid decentralization of employment and industry away from urban/
metropolitan centres to more outlying districts, producing a pattern of
'urban decline and rural resurgence' in Britain and other advanced
economies (Fothergill and Gudgin, 1982; Champion et al., 1987). In the
Welsh case, it was an added bonus that extra incentives could be made
available to help channel 'footloose' firms away from other competing rural
areas, but even without them Wales would have got some share of the new
developments. As confirmation of this, others have also noticed that a
reversal of fortunes in mid Wales actually predated the formation of the
DBRW and its strategic overview (Bateman and Midmore, 1996). While this
is not to discount entirely its ability to influence events thereafter, it does
imply that change would have happened even without the help of the
agency, just as those parts of rural Wales which fell outside DBRW's sphere
of action nevertheless showed some of the same tendencies.

In an elaboration of the restructuring analysis, Day, Rees and Murdoch
(1989) sought to contextualize these contemporary changes more historically, as the latest in a series of phases of capitalist development in the
Welsh countryside, during which it had moved away from its predominantly agricultural base to become considerably more diverse. Attention
was drawn to the extent to which various branches of the state had taken
the lead in assisting and encouraging the region's economic reorganization,
as well as to the way in which successive waves of investment had built
upon the legacy of earlier social and economic patterns. Most recently, the
region had proved attractive due to its possession of such dubious 'assets'
as 'developable space, surplus labour, low wage rates, and weak trade
unions' (Day et al., 1989: 232). Its future still seemed extraordinarily
dependent upon the continuation of high levels of subsidy and support,
which the state was proving less and less ready to allow to persist. As we
have seen, a significant consequence of the current phase of development

was the fragmentation of rural Wales into a patchwork of local labour-market patterns, each shaped by a complex set of determinants, which included the interaction between new influences and the residues of earlier developments. These were the 'intangibles' of which Wenger (1980) had spoken when describing local variations, and the way in which they inter-acted with policy measures to produce 'unpredictable' results. In other words, general policies produced a range of specific local consequences, including discriminating between places and groups of people which were beneficiaries, and others which were net losers.

With respect to the diversity, and complications, of current economic and social structure, there was clear evidence from earlier patterns that the interaction between different forms of rural economic activity was not something new. In some respects, there had been a return to a previous situ-ation in which, in order to survive, rural people in Wales often became involved simultaneously in two or more sets of economic and social rela-tionships. Smallholders and tenant farmers who engaged in mining or quarrywork during the nineteenth and early twentieth centuries were a prominent example (Jones, 1982a; N. Jones, 1993). Now, with pressure to 'diversify' and become 'pluriactive', individuals and households were once again finding themselves at the point of intersection between different, and often contrasting modes of economic and social organization, as they engaged in various kinds of multiple job-holding. This was because they were being asked to fill relatively large numbers of precarious and poorly rewarded occupational places, which were viable only in combination. Such complications were likely to be significant for the way in which those concerned saw themselves, and their conceptions of 'rural' identity. Hence the conclusion that 'the particular forms of restructuring which have occurred in rural Wales exert an important influence over the ways in which people think about their social world and what is possible and appropriate within it' (Day et al., 1989: 240).

As with studies of urban and industrial districts, attempts to apply a restructuring approach to rural areas have attracted criticism on a number of grounds (Day and Murdoch, 1993). Since economic change was usually treated as the prime mover, they have tended to be weaker in following through all the implications for social organization, civil society and the role of the state (Newby, 1986). Yet, while this may be fair comment, it is an objec-tion that could have been levelled even more emphatically at the bulk of the writing done on change in rural Wales during the 1980s, which had remark-ably little to say about how the social costs and benefits of economic change were, or should be, allocated. The question of which particular social groups or categories stood to gain from, or lose by, the transformations taking place was hardly pursued. Instead, the adoption of spatial and administrative frames of reference meant that changes were presented either at the aggregate regional level, or in terms of distributions among different rural subareas. Rather than providing knowledge of genuine places and communities, information was organized according to such artificial constructs as labour markets and travel-to-work areas. Critics might have pointed out that this type of analysis risked reifying spatial categories, and creating or encouraging spatial competition, whereas in reality it was only people, acting individually or collectively, who could carry out social acts (Duncan, 1989: 110). Another danger was that, in redressing the bias towards exaggerating the influence which various agencies and actors within the area were able to exert over events, the restructuring analysis lent itself to going too far in the opposite direction, putting too much weight on external forces alone, even though it was a basic tenet of the approach that development was *'combined* and uneven'. As Day et al. (1989) comment, localities were arenas in which social processes were not simply manifested, but also shaped. The delicate balancing act attempted by Massey, to understand general underlying causes while at the same time recognizing and appreciating the importance of the specific and unique (Massey, 1984: 300), depended upon being able to say just how local factors made a difference. In other words, there was some room for choice and for local action, for example in developing alternative strategies for development (for an exploration of some of the possible directions this could take, see Day and Thomas, 1991).

These defects were not peculiar to work on rural Wales. McLaughlin (1986: 292) makes the point more broadly when he says that

> By focusing the problem, analyses and subsequent policy prescriptions on the issue of rural *areas* as poor places . . . the policy debate on rural deprivation has largely ignored crucial questions about the particular groups and individuals *within* rural areas who gain or lose as a result of policies.

Others (Lowe et al., 1986: Cloke and Davies, 1992) drew a distinction between a planning perspective which tended to concentrate on the spatial effects of decisions made beyond the area concerned, and a more sociological approach which explored decisions made locally, within a context of relationships of power and inequality. The latter approach was more likely to take an interest in what the people affected actually wanted, and whether they were served well by the outcomes, rather than following the consensual view propounded by the agencies that the 'experts' knew best. However, the distinction is too sharp, since policies and processes affecting rural Wales were shaped by both external and internal relations, and by their interactions. This became very apparent as soon as researchers made closer contact with the way in which people actually perceived and responded to the changes going on around them.

THE CONTINUING PROBLEMS OF RURAL WALES

Despite significant alterations in the balance of the Welsh rural economy, the incidence of low wages, irregular employment, poor working conditions, and hence rural poverty and deprivation remains acute and continues to affect large sections of the rural population (for examples, see IWA, 1988; Day, 1991, 1997; Cloke et al., 1997; Williams and Morris, 1995). Incomes in rural Wales, for example, remain significantly lower than those in the rest of Wales, and therefore well below British average levels: average gross weekly earnings in rural Dyfed and Gwynedd in 1996 were only just over 80 per cent of the figure for England and Wales, while Powys, on several measures the most rural of the Welsh counties, was even further behind. In this sense, the strategy of rural 'development' appears to have failed. This conclusion might seem difficult to square with far more optimistic assessments which have emerged from the agencies and from official and governmental sources, but the paradox is easily explained once related to the unevenness of development and social polarization which has afflicted the Welsh countryside. Rural deprivation exists side by side with rural prosperity, and by focusing only on one or the other it is easy to arrive at misleading or selective impressions of the current reality (Day, 1997). Even the majority of those who actually live in the Welsh countryside seem unaware of the extent of the poverty experienced by something like a quarter of the neighbouring households (Cloke et al., 1997).

More fundamentally, the entire policy approach pursued through into the 1990s appeared deeply flawed, since almost by design it ensured that development was not properly integrated, but separated and layered. The exclusion of agriculture from the framework of regional development strategy meant policies often worked in opposite directions. Efforts to maintain and increase rural employment were undercut by the continual expulsion of labour from the land, as encouragement was given to farmers to adopt more technically efficient and specialized systems of production. This favoured those with larger holdings, and encouraged the 'rationalization' of farms, making it harder for farm families and households to find a foothold in the industry (Hutson, 1990). Similar observations were made about the way in which policy shifts around defence and military requirements had unanticipated consequences for rural areas, as weapons establishments and bases were run down (Lovering, 1985; Thomas and Day, 1991). More centrally, it was questionable whether the emphasis on attracting inward investment had done enough to secure a economic and social future for rural Wales that was sustainable. According to one summary,

The diminished reliance on primary industry has, through increased manufacturing activity, merely traded one form of vulnerability for another. Industrial relocations, aided by grants and subsidised factory accommodation, attract either marginal firms or branch plants. Their main economic linkages are with urban markets . . . and in the main they fail to establish links with local businesses which would prevent their predominantly 'footloose' behaviour. (Asby and Midmore, 1996: 108)

By the beginning of the 1990s there were signs of a shifting emphasis in strategic thinking about the needs of rural areas (Thomas and Day, 1991; Day and Thomas, 1991; Wales Rural Forum, 1994; Asby and Midmore, 1996). A series of 'new rural initiatives' placed greater stress than before on integrated approaches to rural development, local enterprise and community-based initiatives, and on doing more for the western parts of the region. The development agencies, DBRW and WDA, were being encouraged by the Welsh Office to work together more closely in their ambition to create a 'thriving self-sustaining market based economy' which would bring prosperity to rural Wales. European funding was playing an increasing part in setting the terms on which this could be done, and much of the pressure for rural 'self-help' was coming from Brussels. It was given a further boost by the withdrawal of Development Area status from rural Wales, which no longer stood out from the general run of a weakened national economic performance as deserving exceptional help. To this extent, the 'quiet convergence' which had brought rural economies and employment structures somewhat closer to national norms (Townsend, 1991) worked against maintaining a consistent focus on rural problems and issues.

Data for 1991 showed that by now the traditional rural industries accounted for around 10 per cent of employment, and manufacturing for another 15 per cent. The remaining 75 per cent worked in services. Between 20 and 25 per cent of economically active people in rural Wales were self-employed, which could be interpreted either as evidence of significant individual enterprise or as a symptom of coping with limited work opportunities. The picture overall was one of marked diversity, with parts of rural Wales figuring at both extremes of the rankings for employment and unemployment. Significant local prosperity was matched by some acute pockets of deprivation, with considerable hidden poverty and unemployment. The future of the rural economy still gave cause for grave concern. Outmigration of young people, coupled with the vulnerability of Welsh farming, made it entirely possible that there would be a continuing spiral of decline and further peripheralization. DBRW was still working to an agenda which focused effort on half a dozen 'growth areas', although for local political reasons the majority of reasonable-sized towns were deemed 'special' enough to merit some support. It would be tempting to conclude that, for all the efforts of the preceding three decades, nothing much had been achieved. While in an optimistic moment the hope was expressed that with 'strategic coordination, adequate funding and long-term commitments free from external distractions' (Thomas and Day, 1991: 47), rural Wales could escape its difficulties, severe doubt was cast on the capacity of the various agencies and authorities to work together effectively (Murdoch, 1988). There were many who voiced growing reservations about the depth of genuine commitment on the part of policy-makers to the future of the countryside, and who argued the need for a change of direction. In a later comment, Midmore (1996) typifies the region as continuing to suffer from 'economic weakness and environmental pressure'. The threat of declining employment is still real, while the standard response has changed little except in detail: the essential 'problem' is still seen as one of remoteness, to be overcome by better communications and financial compensation. The answer is said to lie with a package of infrastructure investment plus incentives for light 'clean' activities, information industries, tourism and diversified agriculture. The view that, despite all the changes, long-standing problems remain unresolved is reiterated by Cloke et al. (1997: 73). Attempts to apply an industrial logic to both the land and people of rural Wales seemed to have done little to alter the fundamentals, or to remove the threat to survival. By the end of the decade, there was a growing clamour for the needs of rural areas to be taken more seriously, and major efforts were being made to mobilize 'rural' against 'urban' interests on a range of issues, from hunting to access to the land and the costs of rural transport. Protagonists from Wales played an influential part in instigating and coordinating this activity, which usually took the form of asking the state to intervene yet again to give special support to rural needs, in the form of subsidies or tax concessions. This bears out the conclusion that rural Wales has not yet succeeded in escaping from its 'clientalist' position of dependence upon external support and welfare payments (Marsden, 1998), even if the terms of the debate have changed somewhat to give greater stress to the environmental and ecological contribution which rural people can make, rather than their role as producers of foodstuffs and raw materials.

CULTURE WARS IN RURAL WALES

The long-drawn-out process of rural change which has been described above has raised deep questions about the very meaning of rurality in the contemporary world. Like other rural areas in the advanced economies, Wales has witnessed the transformation from a situation in which most

people living in the countryside had some close connection with agriculture and the farm economy, and were anchored in highly stable rural
communities, to a far more mixed reality in which different people, living
side by side, are engaged in very different kinds of economic activity and
ways of making a living, which may or may not link up with one another.
Consequently, like Wales as a whole, life in the Welsh countryside has
grown socially more fragmented, and fractured. Whatever the truth of the
situation in the past, it is impossible now to imagine that when people talk
about the importance of maintaining a rural way of life, or safeguarding
rural values, they necessarily all mean the same thing. Instead the nature of
the rural has become almost inordinately contestable. Recent studies of
rural Wales make this extremely evident, in pivoting around the contrasts
between a number of different visions of rural living. Much of this has to do
with the complex confrontation that has arisen between social groupings
that can be defined as 'indigenous' and those which in some fashion or
another have been 'migrant'. These are sometimes referred to as 'adventi-
tious', as if they had no reason to be part of the rural social landscape; but
this is to ignore the extent to which that landscape has changed. It is no
longer so easy to be sure about who 'really' belongs in the countryside,
and whose voices therefore represent 'authentic' rurality (Halfacree, 1995;
O. Jones, 1995).

A major goal of the interventionist policies previously described was to
stem depopulation, and stabilize or regenerate rural Welsh communities.
The degree of success this yielded has been obscured by a much bigger
phenomenon, the 'population turnaround' which has seen a transfer of
substantial numbers of British people from urban to rural locations.
Between 1971 and 1981 population growth in the most rural parts of
Britain exceeded the national average by 8.9 percentage points (Champion
and Watkins, 1991: 8). After a lull, the upsurge of the early 1970s was
followed by another widespread acceleration during the 1980s. Explanations for this shift include the attraction exerted by images of the 'rural
idyll', growing discontent with urban problems and congestion, the impact
of differentials in costs and qualities of living between different types of
area, and the need for people to follow the movement of jobs and opportunities as industries dispersed from metropolitan locations. These pressures
had their specific counterparts in Wales, such as its exceptional scenic and
environmental values, low living costs, and the in-migration of key workers,
including managers and professionals, to staff newly locating businesses.
From the 1960s onwards, population figures for rural Wales started to grow,
as the numbers migrating inwards began to exceed the rates of natural
population decline and outward movement. During the 1970s the rural
population grew by nearly 10 per cent, and some communities faced the

novel experience of having to absorb significant numbers of new arrivals. Earlier depopulation had created the niches which could be filled by incomers – including empty housing and vacant school places; but absorbing them socially and culturally was an altogether more taxing proposition. The conversion of former chapels and abandoned farmhouses into gentrified residences, holiday homes and commercial purposes had obvious symbolic as well as material importance, in that traditional religious and agrarian uses were being usurped by 'alien' secular and non-traditional roles. Coping with the effects of inward migration has been a recurrent theme of studies of rural Welsh social life ever since.

Some of the earliest alarm bells sounded in relation to an explosion of second-home ownership, a by-product of rising levels of affluence among key sections of the British population. Wales was one of the main recipients of this trend, especially in coastal locations on the north and west, so that from the 1970s onwards it became a cause for concern that sometimes as much as half the housing stock in certain settlements was being transformed into second and holiday homes, making them into ghost villages for much of the year. Apart from arousing the supposedly 'natural instinct of the human group to fear and feel threatened by the incursion of aliens', commentators pointed to the real worries this engendered about 'the dilution of Welsh culture, the impact on the Welsh language and the lack of appreciation of Welsh country ways' (Bollom, 1978: 7; de Vane, 1975). Although easily stereotyped as affluent professionals, the presence of skilled manual workers was noted amongst owners of second homes in north Wales, reflecting that, for a while at least, properties were exceptionally cheap (Bollom, 1978). Though few of these incomers were Welsh-speaking, or particularly familiar with local mores, many claimed family links with Wales. Quite a high proportion expected to transmute into residents on retirement. Survey findings in the most affected communities evinced little awareness of significant 'class' differences between established residents and the newcomers. Instead the main lines of polarization were perceived as ethnic, between Welsh 'locals' and English 'incomers'. Anxiety about the impact on Welshness was widespread, and the ability to resist it and maintain a well-organized local social life seemed to hinge on the capacity of communities to maintain active local leadership. Fears were expressed that this had been weakened by previous depopulation, and the continued tendency for some of the 'brightest and best' to move away from their rural places of origin.

Like ownership of second homes, migration to take up permanent residence in rural areas tends to be selective by age, class and ethnic origin. From the 1980s it began to supersede second-home ownership as the main issue. With a widening chasm between property values in different parts of

Britain, and especially soaring house prices in the south-east of England, inward movement reached new levels. Individuals were able to make substantial financial gains, while simultaneously achieving access to the sort of rural assets which had long been valued as worthwhile goals in a complex game of social and geographical mobility (Pahl, 1970). Some calculations put the total numbers of people flowing through rural Wales during the decade at as many as a million – a figure greatly exceeding the actual rural population (Day, 1989). The result was a profound social and cultural recomposition which entailed the reshaping of many local communities. It was easy to assume that this was a uniform process, mainly involving monied English people, from the 'home counties' of south-eastern England, converting rural areas into middle-class enclaves. In other parts of the British countryside it was certainly the case that there was a form of geographical colonization under way, as middle-class people, pursuing their largely imagined constructs of rurality and community, initiated a cumulative process, whereby new residents seeking a particular form of communal life which they believed to exist in rural areas moved into places where they expected to find appropriately 'rural' communities, often with a very poor knowledge of what they would actually find there (Murdoch and Day, 1998; Boyle and Halfacree, 1998).

To some extent, this happened in rural Wales as well. Symonds (1990) distinguished two main social types having this effect in rural Dyfed: retired people and younger craft-orientated entrepreneurs. Both were overwhelmingly English by origin, and their actions had similar consequences of bidding up house prices, and contributing to the area's gentrification and cultural dislocation. As a result Dyfed appeared to divide into two distinct communities, Welsh and English, separated by background, values, social class and, very often, language. Jones (1993: 9) backs up this viewpoint when she writes of the 60,000 or so people who entered Dyfed during the 1980s as a flow 'whose arrival changes the character of entire villages and hastens the demise of a fragile Welsh rural culture'. However, by ignoring the way in which social change has helped splintered the 'rural' into many competing ruralities (Murdoch and Day, 1998), this conclusion rather oversimplifies the situation. Even the two migrant groups just mentioned were likely in practice to gravitate towards slightly different places, and seek to make different kinds of adjustment, partly because they would not always make comfortable neighbours. The so-called 'Woodstock' generation of middle-class 'drop-outs', with their craft shops, wholefood restaurants and ethnic clothing designs (Symonds, 1990: 29), were by no means identical in their tastes or aspirations to the 'early retired' couples living in bungalow developments and seaside properties. Day (1989) attempted to disaggregate such inward flows into a number of distinct streams with varying motives, attitudes and demands, differences all too easily obscured within simplified categories of 'locals' and 'incomers'. The hope was that to break down migration patterns in this way might facilitate the development of a more sophisticated calculus of positive and negative effects, instead of encouraging a reductionist tendency to set all the costs of change against one particular faction of the population.

Similar arguments about diversity are put forward by Cloke et al. (1991) who provide a specific example of the use of planning guidance and controls relating to the Gower peninsula to ease the way for quite narrowly defined categories of middle-class personnel – senior managers, technicians and business people – to gain access to an area well-known for its beauty and rural charm. In this instance, the planners' objective was to assist the regeneration of south Wales by easing development close to Swansea's urban fringe. The authors suggest that their example points to the existence of complex local variations in the access points available to different fractions even within the middle class, as well as strong possibilities of intra-class conflict between those who wished to defend or improve their privileged access to such 'positional goods' as rural values. Rather than treating this as the behaviour of a single social group, it was important to recognize the presence of a 'complex heterogeneous set of middle class fractions' engaged in competition for desirable rural space. For example, it is quite normal for those who are among the first to arrive in such an area to seek to put up barriers to others who might join them later, thus reinforcing opposition to expansion which stems from elements of the older local population. Consequently there are interesting, and varied, possibilities for local alliance-building and division.

The end result of these processes of mobility and population exchange has been to ensure that, as well as those who are rooted in the area of rural Wales, and in its history, there are increasing numbers whose attachments to particular rural places and sets of social others are recent, temporary or provisional. Such complexity was bound to be reflected in the contrasting definitions of rural Wales taken up by the various groups. For some, as we saw earlier, a sense of Welshness and its corresponding social relations constitutes the very essence of the 'rural', whereas for others this would be no more than a contingent, or even irrelevant, accretion to their conception of what counted as 'truly rural'. Predictably, the encounters which have occurred at local level between groups supporting such very different conceptions have proved to be a major source of political and cultural disturbance, which still reverberates powerfully through Welsh country areas. They also furnish rich material for the most recent set of rural studies, in which rather than being treated as the phenomenon which has to be described and explained, knowledge of the restructuring process provides the backdrop for the investigation of changing social situations, relation-ships and meanings in rural Wales. In line with more general developments in rural geography and sociology, rather than maintaining the pretence of rural homogeneity and consensus, these studies have also shown a greater willingness to examine the realities of social conflict and disagreement as they impinge upon different social groupings.

One such study (Aitchison et al., 1989) of an unremarkable part of the 'quiet' Welsh countryside, the Ithon valley between Newtown and Llandrindod, found that around 40 per cent of the local households were still involved in some way with agriculture, and that these formed the established social core of local community life. At the time of study (1988–9) the area was showing signs of levelling out from a typical history of popu-lation decay, and there were the beginnings of significant inward movement. Just over a third of households consisted of people who were locally born, the majority of whom were long-term residents who had close kinship ties with near-neighbours. Part of the remaining population hailed from other regions of Wales, but otherwise the largest contingents came from the English west midlands and south-east, drawn to the area by its desirable environmental and locational qualities, and by the developing opportuni-ties for work in nearby towns. With the development of manufacturing and office jobs, women were succeeding in finding new sources of work outside the valley, albeit at the cost of severe difficulties with travel and child-care arrangements. However, young people were still moving away, about equally for reasons of education, work or marriage. Shortages of suitable local housing, and the constraints of planning control, were adding to the pressures forcing them out of the locality. The ambiguous identity of the place was captured by one respondent who said that 'English people tend to regard this area as Welsh; Welsh people regard it as English; it is caught in the middle but has its own identity. However, the place is losing its uniqueness, the transient population is increasing.'

In fact, within even this tiny space, evidence was found of several distinct local identities and communities, each with its own imputed characteristics. The sense of 'belonging' expressed by many informants was exceedingly local. Despite this, the population remained unified, so far, by some strong local institutions, in which there were high levels of participation, and projected a broad consensus about the virtues and benefits of rural life. Incomers became accepted slowly, if at all, only providing they assimilated on terms set by influential members of the local community. Opinions were least unanimous with regard to the value placed upon development, and access to local housing, with some factions opposed to further growth, which they saw as likely to destroy rural tranquillity, while others felt it was vital for the good of local people, especially the young. Reflecting on this study, Day and Murdoch (1993) argue that it demonstrates the continued relevance of popular conceptions of 'community' for the interpretation of rural change in Wales, since it was largely in terms of competing definitions of community that people locally negotiated their identities and sense of belonging. Some of the definitions they used were very tightly drawn, in effect excluding most of those actually living in the area; others were much more relaxed and inclusive. Farmers in the Ithon valley, firmly embedded in their own networks of social relationships, appeared to have managed to retain control of the main local institutions and elective offices; but they faced a growing challenge from those regarded as 'newcomers' and 'outsiders', who did not always share or empathize with their particular aims and interests. If the established pattern was to be sustained, the economic viability of family farming was crucial; further attrition of Welsh agriculture would enfeeble the social underpinnings upon which local power and influence rested. Meanwhile, different groups were able to draw upon differing resources to pursue their varied ends. In determining the direction likely to be taken by local society, the strength of traditional local networks was pitted against skills and life-experiences which had been brought in from elsewhere, including new forms of knowledge and technical expertise. It was not unusual to find families working farms which had been in their possession for several generations living alongside computer programmers or workers in arts and crafts whose working life involved routine contacts and travel across the British Isles, or even internationally.

Discussing the framework of institutionalized connections through which such relationships within and beyond the Ithon valley could be maintained, Day and Murdoch write in terms of the deployment of various 'resources'. Addressing similar issues, Paul Cloke and his group of colleagues have taken up the theme of the 'cultural competences' displayed by different sets of actors on the contemporary rural scene (Cloke and Milbourne, 1992; Cloke et al., 1998). These competences derive in part from ideas of what is acceptable and welcome behaviour contained in the various cultural constructs of rurality which fill people's imaginations. They provide sets of cultural expectations that people can carry around with them from place to place. English migrants to Wales are described as importing them in their packing cases when they take up residence in the Welsh countryside (Cloke et al., 1997: 106), along with particular visions of the rural idyll. These may be modelled upon familiarity with specifically English situations, whether real or as portrayed through a variety of cultural media. Cloke et al. posit the existence of a range of such constructs, operative at local, regional and national levels. Their work on rural lifestyles shows that there are many thematic similarities in the contents of these constructs across Wales and England. For example, outsiders, however defined (it may be that they come from the next village, or from much further afield), invariably fail to 'fit' with expected forms of behaviour; they are viewed as unable or unwilling to adapt themselves to local conventions, and are either (or often, both!) accused of being too apathetic to play their proper role in local life, or too assertive in wishing to 'take over' leading roles. Since the pioneering work of Pahl (1965) and Newby (1979) there has been a solid stream of rural research which has given backing for the existence of such mental models of how people conduct themselves in rural situations, and their impact on village and community life (see also Rapport, 1993; Bell, 1994). The amazing flexibility and adaptability of such notions means that it is always possible to find fault with those who do not 'belong'; thus one informant quoted in Wales can berate incomers for driving the wrong cars, putting up the wrong curtains and creating the wrong sort of gardens (Cloke et al., 1998: 143).

In Wales, however, such conceptions take on a specific inflection because the 'national' constructs of Welsh and English rurality butt up against one another. So, incomers are said to bring with them ideas of 'village England' which are historically and contemporaneously inappropriate to Wales, for instance by making assumptions about local status hierarchies, while for their part, locals look for and erect barriers around ideas of English affluence, arrogance and insensitivity. The stage is set for an outbreak of cultural warfare, in which the nature of rural Wales is exceptionally contested. The clash among such perspectives provides the setting for Cloke's study of 'rural lifestyles' in Wales (Cloke et al., 1997), carried out alongside a parallel study in England (Cloke et al., 1994). Like Wenger's earlier discussion of development in mid Wales, the research makes use of particular local case studies in order to reach generalizable conclusions. The research team is adamant that, no matter what specific local variations appear, the work could have been carried out in almost any part of rural Wales and arrived at similar findings. Thus on the basis of survey evidence from four chosen localities, Cloke et al. seek to produce a comprehensive discussion of the current state of rural Wales, particularly in relation to key areas like housing, employment and access to rural services. In these respects, they highlight the increasing difficulties faced by many subgroups among rural residents as they come under increasing pressure to cope with changing circumstances through their own individual and household arrangements, including making heavy use of private transport to gain access to facilities which are increasingly distant from their homes. Neither the public authorities nor the local community seem able or prepared to make the same level of provision for them as in the past. Despite high levels of car ownership in rural areas, this leads to marginalization and isolation for many rural people, especially the elderly and the very young, and contributes towards wide divergences in living conditions and quality of life. Although in fact these do not appear to be quite as extreme in Wales as they are in some other parts of rural Britain, there are individuals and households who enjoy considerable personal afflu- ence, living close by others whose incomes and lifestyles are pitifully constrained. Part of the argument put forward is that these differences usually stay hidden behind a fog of idealized sentiment and belief about the 'idyllic' nature of rural society (cf. Day, 1997; Milbourne, 1996a).

Two aspects of the Welsh part of this research programme merit partic- ular consideration here; both have attracted controversy. The researchers attempt to quantify the dimensions of rural poverty, and they discuss some of the cultural confrontations that have arisen between members of the indigenous community and various kinds of 'new rural residents'. Judged according to the conventions employed by other leading social policy researchers (Townsend, 1979), it would seem that about a quarter of the households surveyed in the four locations could be said to be at or below the margins of poverty. That is, they had a household income which was no more than 40 per cent above the qualifying rate for social security benefit. This proportion, which varied somewhat between localities, was pretty similar to the figures found in the equivalent English study, suggesting an underlying condition of rural impoverishment (McLaughlin, 1985). A significant difference in the Welsh case was that, with fewer counter-exam- ples of high-income households, the general standard of living was relatively depressed. Much of this rural poverty is related to the age profile of the population, with substantial numbers of households containing elderly persons who were dependent on benefits and pensions; but it also included younger families and people in work whose incomes barely sufficed to maintain them. The problem of 'employed poverty', reflecting low wage levels and part-time employment, has been noted by others (Midmore et al., 1996). 'Local' people figure strongly among these low- income households, but so also do numbers of hard-up outsiders who have migrated into the area.

Like other evidence of low-wage, low-employment patterns, this confirms the view that restructuring has not got to grips with some of the most basic problems of rural living (Cloke et al., 1997: 73). However, this was not a message designed to appeal to those in the development agencies and the Welsh Office who had commissioned the research. On a smaller scale, perhaps, they faced the same need to hype their rural achievements as exercised them at national level, so that when the research findings began to surface in academic conferences and reports, a row ensued about their validity. The Welsh Office decided not to publish the initial report, and the media then accused officials of suppressing 'devastating' information about the state of rural Wales. In turn, officials resorted to a methodological critique to explain their decision (Cloke et al., 1997: 167), by saying that the research was too qualitative, and too subjective, to bear the weight of inter-pretation put upon it. This attempted rebuttal was ironic in view of the extensive attention the researchers had given to aspects of the cultural universe inhabited by those whose views they had gathered. To facilitate this, they had made much use of those 'unstructured moments' within interviews during which respondents were able to express themselves in their own words. In fact, these qualitative comments did not bear directly on the estimations of household income and living standards. Admittedly, the latter were dependent on a rather narrow database, since not all respon-dents chose to give the relevant information, but they are not out of line with what any informed knowledge of rural labour markets and economies would lead one to expect. For many people, the economics of rural exis-tence continues to involve balancing limited incomes against inflated costs, and it should not have taken the fuel tax revolt of 2000, instigated and led from north Wales, to educate outside opinion about this.

Cloke et al. suggest that the problem lies partly with language. The concept of 'deprivation' has tended to be appropriated by planners and local authorities because it connects to their ability to command and allo-cate a 'reasonable' share of national resources to rural areas. This enables them to indulge in a form of doublethink which both recognizes the problem, as one of under-resourcing, and yet denies its impact upon actual rural people. In other words, spatial conceptions of inequality are substi-tuted for those which are social. By contrast, 'poverty' is a term less acceptable to government because it pinpoints more directly the limitations of the restructuring process, and its unequal effects upon different groups and classes. It also undermines any inclination to suppose that all those residing in rural places are able to participate in the same idyllic state of health, harmony and comfort. Following wider semantic and conceptual changes in this field, it would not be unreasonable to point to the existence of practices of social exclusion in the countryside, which bear heavily on particular social groups and categories – including the unskilled and unqualified young; the elderly (Wenger, 1995); and certain groups identi-fied as 'hippy' travellers and undesirables (Jones, 1993).

The citing of verbatim interview material is more immediately relevant to the analysis of the cultural configurations prevalent in rural Wales. Of course, these are not entirely distinct from more material considerations, since, as Cloke et al. note (1997: 135):

The experience of lack of income can be compounded when new dominant social groups exert their power and economic status so as to deny others the continuing opportunity to belong – socially, culturally and even sometimes politically – to their desired rural lifestyles in their desired rural place.

Impoverishment, deprivation and exclusion then can assume cultural, as well as financial and social forms. While we do not learn all that much from the research about how people actually live, and manage their affairs, in rural Wales, we do glean information about the ways in which they conceptualize their situations. The investigation is premised upon the existence of a *plurality* of lifestyles, implying diversity and some inevitable friction. It is not possible, for example, easily to reconcile the 'deeply rooted community ethic based on like-speaking kith and kin' (Cloke and Davies, 1992: 352) said to be distinctive of rural Wales with the encroachment into the region of groups of people who share none of the essential social characteristics.

Cloke et al.'s readiness to quote from their respondents goes some way to repair the shortage of people's voices which are to be heard within the sociology of rural Wales. Certainly they were remarkably absent from the early works, in which scholars purported to speak instead, with authority, on behalf of others. Now at least some have begun to be listened to. Thus Ashton (1994) uses interview material to rectify the previously 'fleeting' presence of women in the rural studies. She shows just how extensively the wives of Welsh farmers contribute towards both business and community activities. In addition to taking primary responsibility for most or all of the domestic labour around the farm household, they provide numerous services on and off farm, including playing an active part in farm administration and stock handling. Most of this work has hitherto gone unrecognized and undervalued. The combination of a crisis in farming, and the widening of opportunities beyond the farm, provides at least some possibility that the deeply gendered nature of rural work may be renegotiated.

There are more examples of rural voices in *Living in Rural Wales* by Noragh Jones (1993), where we are presented with some extended statements of individual points of view. Part ethnography, part 'imaginative reconstruction' of past and present, the book offers an account of the Rheidol valley, just outside Aberystwyth. This is treated as a microcosm of rural Wales, both in its history of transitions between lead mining, farming, tourism and resettlement, and in the consequential sense of fragmentation and lack of shared background which exists among those who now inhabit it. Throughout the discussion there runs an almost compulsive concern with the complex relationships which have been forged among different sets of locals and incomers. The words of those who are quoted often capture in a vivid way many of the themes which have been considered above. They talk for example about the transformation from a condition where 'there were no strangers in those days' to one where now there are many different groups and individuals, about whom not much is known, so that rumour and innuendo are rife (see also Cloke et al., 1995). In talking, informants display their different, and often inconsistent, perceptions of what rural Wales is about, and how it needs to be protected and/or moved forward, as well as revealing their partial comprehension of the views of others. Some perceive the 'tragicomedy' whereby 'so many brought up here want to get out and so many not brought up here want to come in' (Jones, 1993: 36).

Above all, the book is concerned with portraying the resulting struggles which arise as a form of life which was lived primarily through the Welsh language is pressurized to adapt as English pushes for ever-greater ascendancy. Activities and events which once would have taken place naturally in Welsh are now conducted in English, or in some mixture of the two tongues. On both sides of the language divide, attitudes and standpoints towards this situation vary. There are attempts to create bridges, through which bilingualism can come to be seen as a normal and unproblematic condition in which everyone can participate. There are many incomers who learn Welsh, with varying degrees of success, and even more whose children grow up capable of speaking both languages. But there are also those who will not compromise, for whom rural Wales's identity is wrapped up exclusively with the speaking of Welsh, or who at the opposite extreme see the Welsh language as an unnecessary burden and nuisance. Jones cites examples of newspaper correspondence which put across these, and other, views with great force, and which show how opinion does not split straightforwardly along 'Welsh'/'English' lines. Adaptation, or lack of it, by English residents to what one terms 'the Welsh thing' (Jones, 1993: 59) is complicated, because what is seen to be required is not just adjustment to the language itself, but also to a 'way of life' which surrounds it, which involves residual elements of Nonconformism and parochialism, as well as personal and family connections that are ultimately unachievable by outsiders. Yet there are Welsh and Welsh-speaking people who also find these assumptions and prerequisites equally disputable. The intense battle waged around the language and its future adds a layer of hyper-intensity to the more ordinary issues of trust and acceptance that hold the key to cooperative relationships within small communities everywhere, particularly as they face the need to adapt to new ways. Many of the underlying issues in rural Wales are no different from those played out in other districts, like Cumbria, Cornwall or East Anglia (Hughes et al., 1996); but they always interact with those which are peculiarly the preserve of Wales, chief among which are considerations of language, culture, and nation.

9

Debating the Transformation:
A Welsh Economic Miracle?

As has been noted previously, of all the British regions, Wales was hit most heavily by the recession of the 1980s, losing almost a third of its manufacturing employment in the short period from 1979 to 1983. Among male employees in south Wales manufacturing, job losses reached 32 per cent and female losses were even more severe at 41 per cent; the rest of Wales fared somewhat better, with losses of 19 per cent and 12 per cent respectively. Differences among local economies were even more stark: Barry town saw no less than 80 per cent of its jobs disappear. Apart from the impact upon major industries like steel and metal manufacture, there were particularly heavy losses in textiles and clothing, weighed against some gains in engineering. Unemployment in Wales had peaked at 170,000 in 1986, but by 1990 (even allowing for innumerable statistical redefinitions during the intervening period) the numbers out of work still exceeded the figure for 1980. Wage rates for manual employees had fallen from their previous above-average levels; figures for economic participation were low and the situation in the valleys and in other parts of Wales remained chronic (Thomas, 1991). Against this backcloth, the tale of Welsh recovery seems remarkable: before long it was being hailed by some as an 'exceptional case', capable of setting an example to less resilient regions. Hardened by the experience of adversity, Wales seemed finally to have broken through into enjoyment of the riches of modernity.

The turn-around was slow to occur. Welsh industrial output in 1987 was still 9 per cent below its 1979 level and the recession was judged to have been deeper and the recovery less impressive than in most other parts of Britain (MacKay, 1992). Between 1979 and 1987 male employment had fallen by 134,000 (22 per cent) and full-time female employment by 48,000 (19 per cent); this was balanced somewhat by an increase of 21,000 (14 per cent) in female part-time employment. Relative to UK averages, Wales had fallen back in per capita GDP, personal disposable incomes and consumption expenditures. Rising unemployment, both official and unrecorded, had contributed to falling levels of male economic participation. This depressing picture seemed to offer little cause for hope.

Meanwhile, the decline of its dominant industries and employers had made it more difficult to identify and differentiate the Welsh economy. As with the rest of outer Britain, 'an appreciable proportion of (its) industrial capital lost relevance in a remarkably brief period of time' (MacKay, 1992: 102). The demise of mining in particular left very little of value for subsequent industries (with the possible exception of tourism) except for substantial environmental dereliction that needed to be repaired. The cost in terms of wastage of human capital, accumulated skills, qualifications and experience, was equally severe. Yet in July 1992, for the first time ever, recorded unemployment in Wales fell below the British average. This reduction, which applied to long-term unemployment as well, was hailed as evidence that Wales had made genuine progress in the transition from problem region to one of Britain's more successful and economically powerful areas (Alden, 1996: 155). Labour-force participation rates and growth of real GDP were also converging with British norms. At the same time, however, comparison with other regions in Europe suggested that Wales's relative ranking had not improved significantly during the preceding decade, while the 'prosperity gap' between Wales and most other parts of Britain continued to give cause for concern. Wages were lower than in any other British region, and there were also very marked differences in living standards within Wales. Disposable income per capita for Wales in 1993 was 91 per cent of the UK figure; in South Glamorgan, it came close to the UK average, at 98 per cent; but in neighbouring Mid Glamorgan it was only 81 per cent.

These rather contradictory indications set the tone for much of the analysis of the Welsh economy during the closing years of the twentieth century. Munday (2000) suggests that, while the terminology may have changed, the underlying arguments with regard to its condition remain essentially the same. The issues now being discussed in terms of the consequences of foreign investment, and the choices to be made between its promotion and the encouragement of more endogenous growth, echo earlier debates about the costs and benefits of 'branch plant' development, and the need to embed it more firmly within the local economy. Certainly contributions with titles like 'Wales in transition' (Hill, 2000) and 'A new economic development model for the new Wales' (Cato, 2000) have a daunting familiarity. However, movements have taken place in both theoretical and empirical frames of reference, as well as the actual situation in Wales, which ensure that the debates maintain their vitality, while readings of likely future fortunes continue to be sharply at variance. As ever, there is a need to disentangle myth-making accounts from the reality of contemporary change.

TALKING UP THE REGION

The role played by particular coalitions of local interests in advertising and advocating the merits of their localities as vehicles of growth has long been recognized (Rees and Lambert, 1981; Kearns and Philo, 1993). Molotch (1976) highlighted the importance of local 'boosterism' in his analysis of the city as a 'growth machine', showing how local businesses and politicians could work together in an organized effort to affect the way in which growth was distributed across space. This process of place-marketing has assumed increasing significance in recent years, as the global interdependencies between places have increased, heightening the competition for mobile resources. Since a primary aim has been to entice new economic enterprise, especially footloose high-technology industry, as a means of securing investment, job creation and local economic regeneration, this has tended to mean catering for the demands of business, by allowing capital to play a key role in determining the dominant meanings of place. Sadler (1993: 175) notes how place promotion has involved the 'construction or tailoring of particular images of place, which enmeshed with the dynamics of the global economy and legitimised particular conceptions of what were appropriate state policy responses'. Notions of locality, community and local harmony and togetherness have been mobilized in an intensive manner to convey the exceptional qualities and potential of different locations. Fretter (1993) provides a local Welsh example. In partnership with local borough councils, the WDA, the local training agency and private sector companies, Gwent County Council embarked on a coordinated effort to make the county one of the UK's major growth centres. This involved 'repositioning the Gwent product' (Fretter, 1993: 170) by selling the area as a successful, highly profitable location offering a high quality of life. At that time, Gwent had managed to attract 51 overseas companies, including 15 from the EU, 25 from the USA, and 7 Japanese. Even so, it was said to be suffering still from an 'outdated' image of coal, choirs and rugby.

This local campaign to transform perceptions forms part of a very much larger project to change the meaning of Wales as a place, and more especially as an appropriate site for industrial and business location. Celebration of the economic successes of the 1980s and attempts to airbrush out some of the concurrent failures and limitations have been integral to this endeavour. There has been much talk of renewal, renaissance and revitalization in the 'new' Wales (Cole, 1990; Cooke et al., 1995). Frequent references to Wales as a 'laboratory' for the development of new practices and policies (Mainwaring, 1995: 20; Cooke and Morgan, 1998: 135) add to the impression of exciting and experimental times, with the country moving into a leading position as an innovative pace-setter. Unfortunately, of course, it is remembered less often that most experiments fail. In the world of marketing, including place-marketing, there is always the risk of over-selling and indulging in the sort of hyperbole that ultimately proves to be counter-productive. Some would advise for this reason that a robustly scep-tical stance should be adopted towards the more grandiose claims to the effect that Wales has finally turned the corner.

WALES REVIVED?

Economic development and social transformation in Wales assumed a new significance during the 1980s. There was widespread discussion of the 'new economic miracle' whereby the regeneration of Wales, so long delayed, was finally coming about, despite decidedly unpropitious circumstances. Citing comments from *Regional Economic Prospects*, Thomas (1991) was able to report that by 1989 Wales had seen faster growth than any other northern or peripheral region, and thus appeared to have moved closer economically to the 'south' of Britain. Employment in coal and steel had been reduced to just over 3 per cent of the total workforce, with fewer than 4,000 now engaged in deep-mining coal. On the other hand, jobs in vehicles and motor components had risen to 19,000 (8 per cent of the labour force), outstripping the UK figure of 5 per cent, with further major investments by Ford, Bosch and Toyota yet to come onstream. Whereas throughout the rest of Britain the forces of Thatcherism seemed to be set upon driving the country into deepening unemployment and massive de-industrialization, Wales appeared to be weathering the storm better than could have been expected, by following its own, distinct path and thereby experiencing perhaps the most promising conditions available for experimenting with an alternative model of development (Rees and Morgan, 1991). Against the grain of the prevailing free-market, anti-state ideology, politicians and government offi-cials in Wales were able to maintain, and advertise, a significant degree of state intervention and planning, including initiatives directed at the south Wales valleys, rural and west Wales, and the A55 'Road of Opportunity' in north Wales. Commentators detected a new-found confidence in Wales, befitting its startlingly novel status as an 'economic role model' (Thomas, 1991).

In an assessment with some surprisingly up-beat elements, even the traditional industries of Wales could be discerned to have emerged from their 'scorched-earth' ordeal considerably fitter and leaner (Rees and Morgan, 1991). Both coal and steel now had drastically 'slimmed down' labour forces, improved technologies and increased productivity. While this was not enough to rescue coal from a national UK strategy which focused only upon saving the more profitable coalfields outside Wales, the 'remark-able recovery story' of steel conjured up the image of a phoenix capable of rising from its ashes, with the possibility that it would become a modern, networked operation far better integrated with, and more responsive to, the needs of its customers than in the past. Meanwhile, Welsh employment in electronics grew by 70 per cent between 1978 and 1989 to reach more than 23,000, and there were signs that this sector was now moving beyond the 'persistent stereotype of branch-plant operations and screwdriver jobs' to produce a more rapidly growing professional and managerial workforce. True, such optimistic signals needed to be hedged around with numerous qualifying statements. Even if branch plants were no longer quite so tightly linked to routine production and assembly functions as they had been, in the critically important business and finance sector Wales was still strug-gling to attract anything other than the more mundane 'back room' activities, and there was evidence that many of those following professional and managerial careers saw their stint in Wales as a necessity to be endured before they 'spiralled' onwards, and outwards. No simple story of the replacement of older 'sunset' industries by newer 'sunrise' activity could do justice to the complexity of development in Wales, nor to its emergent patterns of polarization. Nevertheless, there were grounds for seeing Wales as moving beyond its past into the dawn of a new technologically based, socially upgraded future, albeit in ways which continued to be marked by the older history of industrialism.

The thesis that the 'structural legacies' bequeathed by past forms of industrialization in Wales constituted crucial conditions shaping its subse-quent development is elaborated more fully by Morgan and Sayer in their close examination of the British electronics and electrical engineering industries (Morgan and Sayer, 1988). By the 1980s these were at the heart of attempts to use high-technology industry to generate new economic growth and combat regional decline. Indeed, efforts to attract and develop a larger share of electronics became a central, if not dominant, theme of Welsh economic policy. Success in doing so would not only provide a major strand in the diversification of the economy; it would also signal symbol-ically the 'modernization' of Wales through its ability to participate in the most dynamic, technologically advanced, knowledge-based forms of contemporary development. Shiny new steel and glass constructions ousted rusty ironwork as symbols of the contemporary Welsh workplace. The example of Scotland's 'Silicon Glen', where there had been consider-able success in nurturing a viable electronics sector, with significant investment from the United States (Burns and Stalker, 1962; Morgan and Sayer, 1988: 139–42), suggested that Wales should be able to follow suit. But in order to do so, it would have to overcome the restrictions conferred upon it by earlier conditions, including for instance the limited availability of appropriate managerial, technical and business skills and experience; the prevalence of traditional labour practices; and the less tangible elements of its 'militant' reputation, and the impact images of decay and heavy industry had upon potential investors. Morgan and Sayer note how aware employers and managers in the industry were of these attributes of the region, as well as how sensitive they could be to more localized variations within it. Like their key personnel, their preference was for locations outside the coalfield, and away from the older industrial centres; they especially favoured the 'golden triangle' of south-east Wales, an area bounded by Cardiff, Chepstow and Abergavenny.

Developments during the 1980s were marked by a growing gap between the 'core' areas of southern England and the rest of the UK (Lovering, 1991). The economic and social contrasts which developed in 'Thatcher's Britain' are well depicted in spatial terms by Morgan and Sayer's account of differences emerging along the corridor of the M4 motorway. At one end, near to London, there was a vigorous local economy, with a substantial concentration of research and development activity, and a 'healthy' social mix, set amidst a comfortably rural environment. Towns like Reading, Swindon and Bristol were all benefiting from significant growth, and attracting their share of prestigious 'front end' electronics activity, whereas, as we have seen, south Wales remained the closest approximation in Britain to a one-class, 'proletarian' region (Morgan and Sayer, 1988: 143). Indicators for 1985 show unemployment running below 10 per cent in the English counties of Berkshire, Hampshire and Wiltshire, and at 11.4 per cent in Avon, whereas in South Glamorgan it was 14.4 per cent, rising to over 17 per cent in Gwent. Gross weekly earnings for male adults in Gwent averaged £175, compared to £192 in Avon and £212 in Berkshire (Morgan and Sayer, 1988: 146). Examination of the skill profiles for twenty-one electrical engineering firms active in south Wales showed that two-thirds of the jobs in the sector were unskilled, while only 18 per cent required the exercise of technical, professional and managerial abilities. Among electronics companies located in Berkshire, no less than 55 per cent of jobs were in the upper echelons, and only 12 per cent were unskilled (Morgan and Sayer, 1988: 148).

In other words, the high-status, high-income positions that were so important to new middle-class formation in contemporary Britain were not being generated in Wales, but continued to gravitate towards the already relatively prosperous south-east of England. Savage et al. (1992) describe the south-east of England as 'a machine for upward mobility' which promotes large numbers of people from within the region (and abroad) into middle-class positions in management and the professions, before exporting some of them to other regions. Such migration can occur either during the working career, or at retirement. At the time of study, figures relating to the period from 1971 to 1981 suggested that Wales was not among the 'magnet regions' to which these migrants were attracted; they went mainly to East Anglia, the east Midlands and the south-west. Like the rest of the west of Britain, Wales showed a relatively localized pattern of middle-class recruitment, producing its professionals from within, including many who had originated outside the middle class. Migration rates among Welsh managers were modest, with a small overall net loss. In 1981 the proportion of professionals in Wales was near to the national (England and Wales) average, but managers were seriously under-represented among its population, only Scotland having a lower ratio. In common with other parts of Britain with substantial areas of rurality, Wales had a notable over-representation of members of the 'petit bourgeoisie', whose mobility, both social and geographical, was low. The study concluded, however, that, in the light of rising expectations for movement among the middle classes in general, and the dispersal of many of them away from the south-east, then '(r)ather than each region having its own distinct "middle class", the processes of migration tend towards a more homogeneous national middle class' (Savage et al., 1992: 169). This process of diffusion certainly made a significant impact upon Wales from the 1980s onwards. Even so, it has been suggested that middle management in Wales is still marked by a lack of mobility, attributable to the peculiar strength of attachment people have to place; this has particular consequences for women in management positions, since it enhances the impact of gendered expectations about the priority to be given to work as opposed to home and family commitments (Charles et al., 2000).

Throughout their discussion, Morgan and Sayer insist on the theoretical and practical importance of disaggregating such trends, in order to understand properly the processes through which quite specific local effects were being created. They show that there were a number of exceptional cases of firms in Wales capable of promoting highly skilled employment, and providing conditions resembling those of modern office work, rather than old-style manufacturing. Nevertheless the impression remains that Wales was picking up mainly the routine 'back-end' activities within the more established, and therefore less innovative, branches of these industries. Being part of a so-called high-tech industry did not guarantee a share in its most desirable features. There was much talk of the basic 'screwdriver' jobs involved in assembling televisions and videos, rather than the opportunities for gaining expertise and exercising influence associated with activities like software development or research. In comparison with south Wales, a much larger proportion of the electronics workers located in the south-east of England, both male and female, could be said to be 'in a position of strength vis-à-vis their employers on account of their specialist technical and market knowledge; indeed they might be thought of as a new labour aristocracy' (Morgan and Sayer, 1988: 223); and their pay rates adapted accordingly. In Wales by contrast, semi-skilled employees in the newer industries were managing to get only about half the pay earned by the surviving miners and steelworkers.

However, although most firms within the sector consisted of 'headless' plants directed from outside Wales, Morgan and Sayer contend that it was not sufficient to dismiss them merely as passive branch plants. Although lagging in terms of comparisons across the industry as a whole, firms in this sector were still at the leading edge for the region, both technologically, and in terms of labour and management practices. Electronics and electrical engineering companies spearheaded the spread of single-union agreements, no-strike deals, simplified pay structures and more 'flexible' working arrangements which ensured the demise of previous systems of labour control. Driven by the need to create more jobs, the Wales Trades Union Congress (TUC) did what it could to assist in the process. Meanwhile the Welsh Development Agency was busily promoting impressions of Wales which highlighted its rurality and tranquillity, and subverted preconceptions about the Welsh labour force by emphasizing the range of newer industries already present in Wales, and how much their employees differed from the old industrial workforce. The new employers were selecting workers primarily for their 'behavioural' characteristics, such as compliance with an ordered environment of discipline and cooperation, and responsiveness to performance-related pay, and were building upon existing local class and community patterns to achieve this. This meant that they were highly selective with regard to both the places, and the types of persons, they chose to recruit. Established gender divisions within Welsh society made an important contribution here, by providing a ready supply of new and inexperienced female workers who were prepared and able to fill jobs which were deemed unsuitable and demeaning by men whose ideas were still framed by older traditions of work. In south Wales, 58 per cent of the 1981 electronics workforce consisted of female production workers; at the other end of the M4 corridor, there were only half as many (29 per cent).

Morgan and Sayer describe vividly how social innovations within the plants located along the M4 corridor interacted with the characteristics of their localities to create a range of distinctive outcomes (1988: 221). In the more favoured locations, within what was widely perceived as a 'middle-class' social milieu, American companies took the lead among the vanguard firms to foster a climate of responsible autonomy and institutional learning for their employees. They grasped the importance of organizing work around new ideas of labour flexibility, motivation and the extensive use of internal labour markets and job transfers to create career movement and retain loyalty among highly skilled employees. They laid stress on high-level communication skills, both between management and workers and among workers themselves. Accomplishing this depended upon maintaining rapid and sustained economic growth and expansion, but ensured that those working for them were placed onto an advantageous social and economic escalator. The more traditional employers, however, stayed closer to the industrial practices that were familiar to south Wales; their organizations were more bureaucratic, with more firmly etched lines of demarcation between management and workers; and they had lower expectations about employee skill and involvement. Morgan and Sayer note how strongly location decisions within the sector were influenced by considerations of the availability of skills. Preferred location was a prime issue for key workers, who wanted to be part of a prestige environment, where they could experience elite lifestyles. Firms were responsive to these cultural preferences, as well as to more 'objective' factors like access to markets and to major government research and development facilities. Companies within the sector had something like a 'herd instinct' encouraging them to cluster together, but they also gained a range of cross-benefits from proximity to one another. This clustering was happening to such an extent that in the English counties there were signs of anti-growth sentiment developing among those local interests which did not share in the major benefits. In Wales, the problem was quite different: how to lure more of the well-paid and economically dynamic jobs further west.

So far as the social consequences of these labour-market changes were concerned, then, Lovering appears justified in concluding that 'Fordist' and 'Post-Fordist' types of work were spatially, as well as temporally, patterned. He writes that

> It seems reasonable to infer that the worker who is valued for his or her skills, experience and adaptability – the 'post-Fordist' worker – is increasingly concentrated in the south. Conversely, the basis on which workers are required in the north and periphery is more likely to be their competitive low cost. (Lovering, 1991: 25)

Within this pattern, Wales held a somewhat equivocal position. Lovering agrees that in a number of respects, it showed 'affinities' with southern England. Its recovery from the depths of recession was better than other peripheral regions, but still hugely different from the south. By the end of the decade, Wales had made up around half the jobs lost in its opening years; this compared very favourably with Scotland and northern England, yet over the same period southern England had actually *increased* its employment level by some 180 per cent. Furthermore, the aggregate figures for Wales hid the marked, and growing, disparity between its eastern and western parts. Most of the growth in Wales had taken place in the south-east, and in Clwyd in the north. This was true of both new plant openings, and foreign investment, vital elements in economic revitalization. Their respective contributions to the evolving picture became hotly debated. In the case of each, there were important questions about the extent to which economic revival had to be bought at the expense of further loss of autonomy and the risk of long-term insecurity.

DEPENDENCE NEW STYLE? BRANCH PLANTS AND OVERSEAS INVESTMENT

Of the new manufacturing openings in Wales between 1966 and 1984, 43 per cent were 'branch plants' (half with their head offices outside Wales); 44 per cent represented new developments, and 13 per cent were provided by firms transferring in (McNabb and Rhys, 1988). The bulk of new openings were in the counties of Gwent, Mid Glamorgan and Clwyd. Figures for inward investment from the Welsh Affairs Committee of the House of Commons showed that, out of 330 projects between 1983 and 1987, eighty-eight were in Mid Glamorgan, seventy-nine in Gwent and sixty-eight in Clwyd. Together these accounted for 73 per cent of the £898.6m involved. This geographical concentration supports Lovering's vision of a possible future comprising 'the continued marginalization of most of the geographical periphery and northern England, alongside the selective development of some favoured zones within those areas' (Lovering, 1991: 13).

The limited geographical spread of inward investment was one of several criticisms levelled at the reliance placed upon it as a main instrument for economic revival (McNabb and Rhys, 1988; Thomas, 1991). Other objections were that inward investment would increase the dependence of the Welsh economy by exposing it to decisions made elsewhere, within the headquarters of national (UK) and multinational corporations, particularly during times of economic pressure. The attraction of footloose investment could be seen as an 'easy-come, easy-go' option which would not provide the long-run sustainability needed for economic good health. Units which were subordinate within larger organizations lacked discretion and were confined to less rewarding and influential functions; hence Wales experienced the 'under-representation of senior management, skilled administrative and technical staff, and research and development personnel' (McNabb and Rhys, 1988: 196). Branch plants would also be less likely to build links with other firms and organizations within the local economy, since their main connections would be with the 'parent' organization and its network of suppliers and customers, and this would leave the Welsh economy increasingly fragmented and disconnected. Economically, this meant that the local multiplier would be low and opportunities for the generation of further jobs and added value would be lost. Critics also suggested that claims made for the *selective* attraction of branch plants were unjustified; given the dire state of the economy, any chance of gaining work had to be seized, even if the jobs were intrinsically undesirable and designed to take advantage of local labour. The upshot was that Welsh workers would be exploited for their cheapness, and treated as fodder for low-grade and unfulfilling work.

Such claims could be contested. For example, McNabb and Rhys (1988) contend that there was no evidence to support the view that the high incidence of branch plants was to blame for the severity of job losses in Wales. Although closures of branch plants accounted for more than half (57 per cent) of the manufacturing jobs lost between 1966 and 1984, this was because they affected relatively large firms/workforces. Branch plants accounted for 70 per cent of all manufacturing employment, whereas new business start-ups produced only 15 per cent. Allowing for differences in size distribution, branch plants survived as well or better than local and new firms; the record of survival in north-east Wales was particularly good. Strictures about the limited role played by research and development activity seemed more applicable: among the standard British economic regions, the share of employment in research was lowest for Wales, and declining. At the same time, 'local Welsh subsidiaries of foreign companies have been leaders in the introduction of new production technologies and computer based manufacturing systems' (McNabb and Rhys, 1988: 196). A similar mixed verdict is delivered by Thomas (1991: 53): some of the problems have been overstated, or are being tackled, while foreign inward investors were 'not necessarily the main culprits'. Likewise, accepting that economic strategy in Wales had concentrated heavily on the attraction of mobile industrial capital, Morris et al. (1991) note that this had brought some real successes, with firms which offered decent, and well-integrated, jobs. Nevertheless these exceptions were not enough to counteract the conclusion that 'Wales is a low wage peripheral country which has attracted a disproportionate amount of low-paid assembly jobs' (Morris et al., 1991: 189).

WALES FOR SALE? THE ROLE OF FOREIGN INWARD INVESTMENT

The strategic importance of foreign direct investment (FDI) within the developing Welsh economy also attracted great attention, and publicity (Davies and Thomas, 1974; Roberts, 1994), and the arguments surrounding its contribution reiterated many of the themes already considered. Statistics stating that, with only 5 per cent of the UK population, Wales was managing to attract some 20 per cent of foreign investment and a similar share of the resulting jobs were recycled endlessly as prime evidence of a sea change in Welsh fortunes. The figures were greeted as 'positive proof that industrialists saw Wales as a modern economy and a prime location fom which to serve the European market' (A. Williams, 1990: 21). Consequently foreign-owned firms were responsible for a rising proportion of Welsh manufacturing employment, reaching 28 per cent by 1991, or 67,000 employees. The 'inward investment boom' of the 1980s was held to have given Wales an 'increasingly cosmopolitan look' (Roberts, 1994). According to Hill and Munday (1994), in the ten years preceding 1992 Wales benefited from 545 inward investment projects, amounting to 16 per cent of all such projects in the UK. These were estimated to have produced around 37,000 jobs. Between 1993 and 1997 another 179 projects, 14 per cent of the UK total, were located in Wales. While this made a substantial contribution to the revitalization of the Welsh economy, its impact should be kept in proportion: Cooke and Morgan (1998) calculate that the jobs created represented no more than 6 per cent of all Welsh employment.

Initially, as elsewhere in Britain, the way was led by US investment, which continues to be the largest overseas contributor to the Welsh economy; but there was steady diversification as Wales gained more projects from Germany, Canada and from Asian, above all Japanese, investment sources. By 1987 Wales had a significant employment concentration in Japanese-owned companies, eleven of which were providing some 5,000 jobs. Like work in other foreign-owned businesses, these jobs were associated with good rewards and working conditions, and high productivity. The selection of Wales as a platform for Japanese inroads into Europe gained particular prominence. By 1997 there were fifty Japanese firms situated in Wales, a number which is still growing. The reasons behind the wave of Japanese investment in Britain, and more specifically in Wales, were examined in a number of reports (Dunning, 1986; Little, 1986; Munday, 1990). They agree that the primary consideration was the access Japanese companies would gain thereby to British and European markets; locating in Britain rather than elsewhere in Europe had the additional advantage of enabling firms to operate through the English language. The choice of location inside Britain was then subject to very careful review, in which the availability of suitable labour assumed great importance. Thanks to early successes and a highly supportive climate for development, Wales managed to establish itself as a preferred location for Japanese employers. Agencies like the WDA devoted considerable energy to maintaining this position.

Munday notes that initial uncertainties about how well Welsh labour would adapt to the Japanese style of management had been 'mitigated by heavy recruitment of women, among whom traditional labour values and practices are less seriously considered' (1990: 43). According to figures he provides, by April 1989 just over half the workforce in Japanese companies in Wales was female. Further control was exerted over workers' attitudes and dispositions by recruiting the bulk of these employees from among young people and school-leavers. The 'handpicked' nature of Japanese workforces was also secured by other more dubious measures such as preferential recruitment of married women, and direct replacement of older workers by those who were younger and supposedly more energetic (Morgan and Sayer, 1988). Such strategies were underpinned by often questionable assumptions about labour qualities, such as that 'young women are more dexterous and have the aptitude for fine assembly work' (Munday, 1990: 71). Of course, there is an extensive literature showing that perceptions of this sort are by no means unique to Wales, nor to foreign employers (Rees, 1992; Walby, 1997; Charles et al., 2000). By such means, it proved possible to attract labour of the desired quality, at particularly low cost, and to build a significant reputation for 'good' industrial relations. Japanese investment grew thanks to both imitation effects and to expansion and diversification among those companies that had already settled in Wales. The lack of an existing strong Welsh manufacturing base may also have played a significant part in the story, because it meant that there was less prospect of local opposition to foreign development, as happened in other areas, although some early projects in Wales did meet with resistance strong enough to prevent them from proceeding.

A key part in getting the Japanese 'invasion' moving was played by the Development Corporation for Wales (DCW), an early private–public partnership dating back to 1958, which worked hard to persuade Sony to make the first Japanese investment, in Bridgend in 1974. DCW was later absorbed into Wales Investment Location (WINVEST) which in turn became Welsh Development International. Together with key local authorities, these agencies were prominent members of the growth coalition which hailed overseas investment as a preferred route out of Wales's economic malaise. They were able to ensure that Wales could provide the necessary package of financial support, and vacant factory premises, to respond quickly to interest from overseas investors. Infrastructural investments, including improvements to the road network, such as the M4 motorway, A55 Expressway and the Heads of the Valleys road, meant that Wales was able to compete favourably with other 'deprived' regions as an accessible site within which there were sufficient reserves of labour, and enough attractive greenfield development land, to accommodate the exacting demands of companies which were in a position to choose between any number of willing partners. Of course, this meant that such firms had considerable ability to dictate the terms on which they settled in Wales.

Not all the features associated with distinctive Japanese systems of employment were imported into Wales. There was no guarantee of lifetime employment for Welsh workers; their wages were not related to length of service, nor were they rewarded with large productivity bonuses and welfare benefits. On the other hand, notions of team spirit, more egalitarian relationships between staff and production workers, improved consultative processes and strict work regimes were enforced. Above all, the renowned Japanese drive to achieve quality in production was placed at the heart of the operations of the Welsh subsidiaries. Relations with trade unions in Wales were mostly amicable, and the historical reputation for militancy was dispelled as Japanese companies lost hardly any production time through strike actions. The negative aspects of Japanese investment differed little from those displayed by FDI from other sources. Real decision-making power remained outside Wales; the senior directors were invariably Japanese and the major areas of marketing, finance and production engineering were kept firmly under Japanese control. There was limited scope for local talent to rise far up the organizational ranks and it was rare for local managers to exert control over Japanese employees. Harsher critics, such as representatives of the TGWU, levelled accusations that Wales was becoming a 'coolie economy' subjected to 'Samurai management'. Since the Japanese firms in Wales were engaged mainly in producing well-established commodities, such as televisions and video recorders, they were not likely to create many new or technically exciting spin-offs; most of the research and development activity and technical innovation flowed from Japan. While Japanese management devoted major effort to building links with local suppliers, in order to satisfy European directives about the balance of local content, and did much in the process to help them to raise the quality of their own operations, the scale and nature of Welsh manufacturing meant that it was incapable of supplying a high proportion of the inputs needed, including particular key components. These were obtained mostly from elsewhere in the UK. Summarizing the situation, Munday (1990: 137) concludes that 'the existence of a high level of foreign-owned capital in a small region may lead to a truncation of the economy, technology and skills dependence, as well as dependence on outside sources for decision making', with deleterious implications for the economic future. However, economic desperation left Wales with little option but to pursue its policy of jobs at any price, and for a while at least jobs in Japanese firms seemed more secure, and at least as well-rewarded, as anything else which was on offer.

EVALUATING THE OVERSEAS CONTRIBUTION

Wales is still in receipt of more than its proportionate share of foreign direct investment; currently it accounts for something like a third of all industrial investment in Wales, and is concentrated mainly in the manufacturing sector. It is inevitable that such a huge contribution to Wales's economy should become caught up in debate and controversy, with various attempts to evaluate the positive and negative effects (Gripaios, 1998; WAC, 1998; Phelps and MacKinnon 2000; Cato 2000). Two myths of inward investment are prevalent (Day et al., 1998). One is that it has been crucial to the restoration of a healthy industrial base following the collapse of the traditional industries, and is responsible for injecting a new dynamism into Welsh economic life. The other view is more gloomy, and sees Wales in danger of becoming fixed into a demeaning posture as a supplicant for external support, at the price of an economy of low wages and limited opportunities. Both over-simplify, for polemical reasons, and the truth most likely lies somewhere in between.

Almost inevitably, emphasis on FDI as a mainstay of recovery is conducive to a focus on success in winning large mobile projects. Securing one or two big projects can easily outweigh the quantitative gains to be made from a host of smaller investments, or local start-ups. The record is littered with celebrations of spectacular gains, like the Ford engine plant in Bridgend, Toyota on Deeside in north Wales, and most notoriously the Korean electronics firm Lucky Goldstar (LG) in Newport. Mainwaring (1991: 83) rightly comments that investments such as these, which are geared to EU rather than just UK markets, cannot simply be dismissed as 'peripheral' operations; they are major components within global corporate strategies, and for this reason there is ample evidence that they form a relatively stable element within the modern Welsh economy. Nevertheless, with so many economic eggs put into so few baskets, the risks of things going dramatically wrong are equally large, and even the largest and apparently most carefully considered investments are not immune from adverse conditions. The huge project instigated by Lucky Goldstar promised to deliver more than 6,000 direct jobs, and twice as many again indirectly. The public contribution towards this was estimated to be some £248 million, or £40,000 per job. Owing to a downturn in the Korean economy, only a fraction of the anticipated jobs actually materialized. This strengthens the doubts expressed by the Welsh Affairs Committee among others as to the cost-effectiveness of such a grand project (WAC, 1998), and the fear that the opportunity cost of other possibilities foregone was excessive. Nor are all projects so highly desirable: the example Munday cites (2000: 53) of Pembrokeshire's 'success' in competition with Poland and Namibia to secure 150 jobs in a Chinese-owned factory assembling shoes is symptomatic of occupying a pretty humbling position within the world economic order.

Such reliance upon inward investment can be interpreted in different ways. There is an obvious risk that Wales will be trapped into a situation where it will be compelled to maintain its standing as a low-wage economy offering least resistance to foreign domination and exploitation. This is the developmental equivalent of the poverty trap, since any move to escape its confines by improving labour conditions would threaten to frighten off future investment, while risking the loss of part of that which already exists. This is a situation confronted by most of Britain, as a result of policies which have stripped labour of many of its historic defences, while offering greater 'flexibility' than competitor economies, resulting in a workforce which works longer hours, for lower wages, than much of the rest of Europe. As Mainwaring (1991) noted, among others, Wales was extremely vulnerable throughout this period to competition from southern Europe, which, though handicapped by poorer communications and infrastructure, contained vast untapped labour reserves willing to work at very low costs. A decade later, it was noted that Wales's position as a prime low-cost production location within the European Union was now under threat from the countries and regions of the former Eastern Bloc (Jones, 2000), as well as from Third World economies beyond Europe. As part of an enlarged European periphery, there is an obvious danger of Wales being forced to compete downwards in order to stay in the game.

Returning to the issue of FDI a decade after his work on Japanese inward investment, Munday is compelled to ask why such notable and much-advertised successes have had so little overall impact on the economy. He estimates that by 1996 employment in the foreign-owned sector had risen to 75,000 employees, of whom 20,000 worked for Asian companies, out of a total workforce of some 973,000. However, the true extent of foreign ownership of 'Welsh' industries is unknown. A misleading concentration on 'greenfield' development and grant-aided projects has obscured the increasing part played by mergers and takeovers within the overall global organization of production – a recent example with implications for Wales would be the takeover of the Asda supermarket chain by the US company Wal-Mart – which means that, in common with most other parts of the developed world, economic developments in Wales are exposed increasingly to the vicissitudes of the world economy. In this respect, FDI has proved to be a gateway not just to Europeanization, but to globalization, and the ever-retreating prospect of ensuring some form of genuinely Welsh control over the economic changes governing the lives of Welsh people.

Despite these dangers, the advent of FDI did not seem to attract anything like the same degree of scepticism and downright hostility as tended to be associated with the presence of 'English' companies in Wales. Rather, quite apart from its direct effects, Wales was able to bask in the glow cast by association with the most dynamic of industrial nations, and with the allegedly invaluable cultural and organizational innovations they were able to import with them (Day, 1998b). Plants under foreign ownership tended to be relatively large, and the presence of 'gold standard' brand names like Siemens, Bosch, Sony and Brother were highly symbolic of the 'new' Wales. Much was made of the 'mentoring' role which could be adopted by foreign companies, and the possibilities they afforded for technology transfer. With their help, it seemed possible that Wales might somehow 'jump' the development barrier and gain access to the riches of advanced 'high-tech' economies. Whatever the overall balance of gains and threats, it did seem that the experience of foreign, and especially Japanese, investment had done much to improve the image of Wales, while also acting as a good advert for multinational capital. By 1985 the Japanese Ambassador was able to tell the *Western Mail* that the 'Japanese people know the Welsh as an artistic people who love poetry and song and as an industrious people. These values held by the Welsh people seem to strike a chord in Japanese hearts, for they are values shared by us.' There was also applause for the 'rural friendliness' shown by the Welsh towards Japanese staff. The impression of Wales as a place where workers could meet the exacting standards for quality and cooperativeness expected of Japanese employees was a major boost to confidence. The leading Japanese commentator on global economic change, Kenichi Ohmae, goes so far as to include Wales among his list of significant 'region states', defined as natural economic zones which act as powerful engines of development in the modern world because they are primarily oriented to and linked with the global economy, rather than their particular national systems. According to Ohmae (1996: 89), such region states 'welcome foreign investment. They welcome foreign ownership. They welcome foreign products. In fact they welcome whatever will help employ their people productively, improve their quality of life, and give them access to the best and cheapest products from anywhere in the world.'

Indeed, the necessity for this 'welcome invasion' (Davies and Thomas, 1976) by FDI could be argued on several grounds. Without it, the manufacturing base in Wales would have been inadequate to regenerate itself (McNabb and Rhys, 1988). Like the rest of Britain, Wales suffered from the poor availability of risk capital, and excessive demands for short-term returns on investment (Rees and Morgan, 1991), and the indigenous rate of new firm formation has been low. This leads some to join the *Financial Times* in pointing to a disappointing lack of entrepreneurial 'drive' among the Welsh. Others saw the problem as more structural, attributable to the inheritance of over-specialization and large-scale industry, and the consequent absence of a Welsh business class. Gaining a disproportionate share of overseas investment short-circuited many of these problems. For a while flattering comparisons between Wales and other more advanced regions became almost de rigueur (Morgan, 1987; Osmond, 1991). Such comparisons were encouraged when Wales succeeded in gaining partnership status with one of Europe's most economically advanced areas, the German region of Baden-Wurttemberg, and then through that partnership gained admission to the select club of the European 'motor regions'. The politician who helped set up the partnership admitted that his aim had been to 'uplift Welsh aspirations' through rubbing shoulders with those who were better off (Zepf, 1996).

By now, social scientists were eager to take what lessons they could from successful foreign exemplars in order to 'clone' success elsewhere. Increasingly the reference points reached beyond Britain, to regional performance in other European countries, in North America or the Pacific rim. The 'third Italy' of Emilia-Romagna, the Rhone-Alpes in France, Rhineland-Westphalia, and the Basque Country of Spain joined Japan and Silicon Valley as models to be emulated. This outward gaze was necessary because, with the exception of the south-east of England, which was recognized to be a special case, no British region offered an example particularly worth following. A tantalizing glimpse of an exception was provided still by Scotland's Silicon Glen, where serious claims could be advanced that it had managed to secure a 'totally integrated industrial segment' with enough critical mass for self-sustaining growth (Munday, 1990: 129); but even this was subject to considerable debate (Turok, 1993). Otherwise the feeling was widespread that Britain as a whole represented a 'failure' economically, and there was an extensive literature on its inability to compete. For example, Lovering (1991) described the UK as still on the long-term slide from 'workshop of the world' to residual status as a domain of low-skill, low-technology activity, with Wales being dragged down along with the rest, towards the status of a 'periphery within a periphery'.

The downside of overseas investment was that it made Wales even more prone to external control, while the benefits it conferred were often debatable. Roberts (1994: 85) mentions the risks of low skill linkages and weak multiplier effects, despite associated costs such as loss of structural autonomy. She laments the lack of reliable empirical measures of the effects, and the over-resort in their absence to anecdotal impressions. This renders evaluation prey to hype and public relations gloss, which tends to exaggerate the extent to which salvation lay in the hands of overseas companies prepared to make a continuing commitment to Wales. On the basis of one survey of 100 firms in south Wales conducted in 1986, it was concluded that the range of existing policy measures, with its emphasis on securing FDI, was proving totally inadequate to deal with the amount of job displacement occurring as existing companies restructured to cope with the combined pressures of technological change, economic recession and global competition (Morris and Mansfield, 1988). Although often highly publicized, the inward investment projects surveyed had created few jobs, and the skill levels involved in direct production were very low. There was only limited sourcing of materials at local level, and although some demand had been generated for business services, often these were provided by units which were themselves branches of larger national organizations. Meanwhile, expanding and restructured firms in Wales were being pushed towards increased subcontracting, peripheral employment and more 'flexible' technologies. About half the jobs generated in the firms surveyed had gone to women, a welcome boost for female employment, but still inadequate both numerically and in quality to replace what had been lost. The jobs available for take-up by men were insufficient to compensate for male job losses elsewhere.

More positively, it was noted that the bulk of investment into Wales went to units which were sole operations on a UK or even European scale, and therefore far less likely simply to fold in the event of downturn than was often assumed. Hill and Munday (1991) provide further confirmation that jobs arising from inward investment were less precarious than those created by indigenous firms. Collis (1992) concurs that over the period from the 1960s to the 1980s overseas-owned companies shed employment at a rate that was similar to or lower than indigenous firms, while maintaining good investment and productivity records. He attributes the improvement in the share of this investment attracted to Wales to the combination of 'stability and welcome': stability with regard to an existing cluster of overseas investors, attitudes to work and industrial relations, conjoined with a welcoming approach taken by national and local authorities. The drawbacks Wales presented as an investment destination centred on fears of potential skills shortages, and the lack of a 'clear and coherent' image overseas. In a comparison of foreign- and domestic-owned manufacturing firms in Wales, Munday and Peel (1998) found that, during a recession, employment, sales and asset values held up better in the foreign-owned sector.

Phelps and MacKinnon (2000) found a high proportion of overseas plants in Wales carried out at least some sales, marketing or research and development activity; they were not purely manufacturing 'branch' plants. They also spent more on training than the average UK company. Three-quarters of the respondents to their survey had had substantial programmes of reinvestment after their initial establishment, and reported that one of the benefits of repeat investment was an upgrading of skills.

BOOSTERS AND DETRACTORS

Against the background of the prolonged and agonizing dismantling of the former economy, it was natural enough that a certain pride should be taken in the way that Wales had managed to thrust itself to the top of the regional league tables for attracting foreign investment. Furthermore, as we have seen, there are encouraging signs that, amidst the multiplying branch plants and foreign-owned units dotted around the country, some at least are proving capable of playing a more positive role than previously envisaged, as they bed down within Wales (Price et al., 1993). Driven by their own competitive quest for sustainability, these firms have been making increasing demands for 'quality' upon Welsh workers, suppliers, technology, and infrastructure. For instance, the German company Bosch took a lead in training up the skills it required via partnerships struck with local colleges of further education, surprising them into rising above their previous limitations (K. Morgan, 1997a), and other inward investors have put similar pressure on local labour markets and the vocational training system (Rees and Thomas, 1994). This was just the kind of stimulation to local development that the supporters of, and cheerleaders for, FDI had anticipated.

Since it was obvious that there was not an inexhaustible supply of new overseas investment, development agencies within Wales had a parallel need to assist in ensuring that they maximized their share of the growing proportion of repeat and expansion investment from firms which were already based in the country. Hence new efforts were devoted to encouraging cooperation between firms, and to creating links between them, the universities and other 'centres of excellence', so that they could work together on issues of skills formation and technical development. To this end, the Welsh Development Agency has displayed growing sophistication in its strategic initiatives, with programmes such as the formation of 'Team Wales' and efforts to mobilize supplier chains via 'Source Wales' (Morgan, 1997b). Supporters saw within this the potential for promotion of a new kind of 'regional innovation strategy', that 'helps to safeguard existing jobs, embed existing foreign plants, promote more robust linkages between these plants and indigenous firms, and helps to disseminate best practice throughout the regional economy' (Morgan, 1997a: 501). Making aims like this more explicit within regional policy could be regarded as a much overdue response to earlier criticisms of the limitations of 'branch plant' development; but it was also reflective of shifts in the prevailing perspectives and language of regional growth. In theoretical terms, these changes of emphasis could be put into the context of a newly emerging approach within regional studies, summed up as the rise of a 'network' or 'associational' paradigm, which represented a kind of 'third way' between the state and the market (Cooke and Morgan, 1993). Exponents of associationalism emphasize the importance of collaborative and social modes of economic organization. Thus Paul Hirst, an advocate of 'associative democracy', contends that by embedding the market system in 'a social network of co-ordinative and regulatory institutions', it is possible to increase levels of democratic participation, while helping diverse interests to work better together to achieve their substantive goals. A pluralistic system of this type would be able to maximize decentralization and voluntary self-government (Hirst, 1994), achieving both economic and political gains. There is a close affiliation between this view and a number of other positions relating to the need for fostering new kinds of 'flexibility' and for the promotion of social capital as a crucial basis for successful economic performance that had been promulgated during the 1980s and 1990s (Piore and Sabel, 1984; Coleman, 1990; Putnam, 1993). They formed aspects of the turn towards a more institutionalist style of economic analysis which laid stress upon the need to pay greater heed than in the past to the necessary social conditions for economic and political effectiveness. Highly reminiscent of Emile Durkheim's insistence on the importance of the normative underpinnings of instrumental relationships, this encouraged a more sociologically informed conception of regional economies as consisting always of vital social, as well as economic, bonds.

In these terms, regions which flourished were seen to do so because they possessed strong social networks, ties of 'trust' or forms of 'social capital', which, among other benefits, promoted cooperation and mutual learning. Conversely, under-performing regions were held to be handicapped by an impoverished social framework which inhibited collaboration and favoured self-interested competitiveness or rivalry. The significance of social capital was stressed especially by the American sociologist Robert Putnam on the basis of his researches in Italy. He defines this elusive property as comprising 'features of social organization such as trust, norms and networks, that can improve the efficiency of society by facilitating coordinated actions' (Putnam, 1992: 167). To a large extent, he sees the accumulation of social capital as a by-product of other activities occurring within a given social context, especially the ways in which people associate and act together within a range of voluntary bodies and organizations. The presence of dense networks of secondary associations contributes towards the formation of a 'social fabric of trust and cooperation' that enables people to collaborate effectively towards economic and political, as well as social and cultural ends. The way in which regional institutions, such as regional governments and development agencies, operate is held to be greatly influenced by the kind of social context within which they exist, although such institutions are seen as also having the power to shape regional identities and strategies.

While Putnam refers almost exclusively to the Italian experience, it was more or less the same kind of social infrastructure and cultural depth that had been thought to contribute so much towards the impact of Japanese industrial and organizational cultures during the 1980s. It was fashionable to argue that a large part of the rise of Japanese, and other Asian, economies stemmed from the influence of forms of knowledge and cultural values which were not formalized or made explicit, but more implicit within the social organization and conduct of everyday life (Pascale and Athos, 1982). However, there were considerable reservations about the extent to which this kind of culture could be replicated elsewhere, including in Wales (Day, 1998b). Similarly, Putnam's analysis leads him to conclude that it is not feasible to attempt to impose the filaments of social capital from above, since they need to grow organically, over long periods of time. Institutional history moves slowly, and social capital takes years, if not decades to build; there is no quick fix to be achieved. Indeed, a large part of Putnam's discussion is devoted to showing how patterns which were laid down in Italy during the early Middle Ages continue to shape the outcomes of contemporary regional politics. This suggests that regional development may not be particularly amenable, in the short term, to even the most enlightened social engineering. Nevertheless attempts continue to be made to bring it about.

Drawing on these ideas, Kevin Morgan has outlined the concept of a 'learning region' as applicable to Wales (Morgan, 1997a). Such a region would possess a 'robust networking culture' that would enable it to engage in a collective enterprise, working towards an agreed set of long-term objectives. Following Putnam's lead, he depicts regional growth as an interactive process revolving around sets of institutional routines and social conventions which allow various partners to learn from one another, and to innovate together. 'Team Wales', consisting of government, local authorities and economic development agencies, working together with private-sector interests, might be considered to constitute such a partnership (WAC, 1998).

The practical question which arises from the work of Putnam and others relates to the extent to which some of the necessary elements, such as loyalty and team spirit within companies, well-integrated supply chains and a sense of shared goals, can be helped into existence. Morgan argues that there is room for optimism, because such features are not necessarily as 'culturally embedded' as has been assumed (Morgan, 1997a: 494). Within this perspective, a more sanguine view can be taken of branch plants as 'learning' or listening posts that are in touch with local conditions and demands, and able to relay this knowledge back to HQ, which otherwise would not be able to react to changed circumstances so effectively. The secret of strong regional performance rests on building the institutional capacity, linkages and networks which can enable the rapid circulation and sharing of such knowledge and information. There is backing for Morgan's position in Phelps and MacKinnon's finding (2000: 59) of a significant degree of local initiative in reinvestment decisions, and therefore scope for development agencies to play a part in offering support. The question which is posed is whether or not Wales has the capacity and foresight to behave in this way and, more broadly still, whether peripheral regions can become centres of innovation.

Locating Wales alongside some of the accepted 'exemplars' of successful European development – Baden-Wurttemberg, Emilia-Romagna and the Basque Country – Morgan and Cooke have set about examining the nature of 'the associational economy'. Regional achievements are measured against the yardsticks furnished by the network paradigm, in that

> High trust, learning capacity and networking competence are now widely perceived to be associated with relative economic and social success. Each of them is founded upon a high capability in social interaction and communication rather than either individualistic competition or strong state-led economic development programmes. (Cooke and Morgan, 1998: 5)

As observed above, it is important to Cooke and Morgan's adaptation of the idea of social capital that it is conceived of as something which can be created and destroyed over relatively short periods, rather than being deeply entrenched within long-term social developments and firmly sedimented institutions. In these terms, during the past century Wales can be presented as having undergone a process of the destruction and reconstruction of critical forms of social capital. Gradually (and at times quite violently) earlier versions of working-class, occupational and rural communities, with all their elaborate and integrated patterns of social relationships, have been tested to destruction, and replaced with more self-conscious, and to some extent deliberately engineered, networks of social relations. Effectively, one historically constructed version of Wales has been dismantled and is in the process of being replaced by another. A plethora of organizations and agencies in the fields of 'community development', industrial support and economic enterprise have been set up to assist in this process. Cooke and Morgan's contention (1998: 151) is that whereas more formal regional policy has done 'little or nothing to enhance the developmental capacity of the regions it purported to help', or to help raise the learning and innovative capacities of firms receiving regional aid, such 'bottom-up' local and regional initiatives have indeed been at the forefront of regional innovation. Once again, Wales is proposed as a 'regional laboratory' in which these networking experiments can be taken further. Despite its hitherto sorry record of sluggishness and decline, suddenly it seems there are grounds for optimism.

The principal example of Welsh networking activity exhibited by Cooke and Morgan in defence of this view is participation in the European Union's Regional Technology Plan (RTP). Here it is noted that the record of institutional cooperation already established between Welsh agencies was sufficient to persuade the EU to include Wales among the first batch of regions to take part in the project, from 1994 onwards, where it was joined by regions from Holland, France and Germany (Limburg, Lorraine and Saxony). The project's aim was to identify and assist those regions which had the capability of achieving consensus around some long-term objectives, and the plan was designed to encourage bottom-up, integrated and strategic action to build social capital. The fact that Wales was involved so early could be interpreted as a pay-off for the many years of self-publicity surrounding its recovery, as well as a follow-up to its earlier role as an economic partner to the European 'motor regions'. Two years previously south Wales had been nominated as a European technopole, again on the basis of its 'extraordinary' success in attracting a disproportionate share of high-technology FDI jobs between 1984 and 1992 (Huggins, 1997). South Wales was considered to have 'the appropriate regional coherence and identity' to become a truly networked region, and a focus for innovation in the UK.

There is a notable shift in emphasis between earlier perceptions that 'large swathes of the Welsh industrial economy were dominated by foreign-owned branch plants geared towards low-skilled production activities' (Morgan, 1997a, citing Morgan and Sayer, 1988) and the later 'revisionist' view that there is a need now to abandon those 'cruder versions of branch plant syndrome (which) portray these as low pay low skill assembly based operations with no multiplier effects' (Cooke and Morgan, 1998: 147). It does appear that there is some justification for this reappraisal, though much of the evidence remains inconclusive (Phelps and MacKinnon, 2000). However, the conception of a 'network' of relationships which link together a set of formal economic actors and organizations in an artificially constructed partnership is something very different from the organic framework of social relationships which constitutes the kind of regional identity described by Puttnam and other theorists of 'social capital'.

In a series of critical interventions (for example, Lovering, 1996, 1999a, 1999b) John Lovering has sounded a cautionary note about some of the misleading interpretations which have gained currency both within and beyond Wales. He challenges the 'dominant interpretation' that Wales has been transformed from a structurally disadvantaged peripheral economy to one characterized by a new core of modern, world-class, high-technology companies (1999a: 13). In an effort to restore a sense of proportion to some of the wilder claims, he notes that assessments of the strength of recent performance depend greatly on the precise comparisons that are made. Thus, while Wales seems to do rather well on certain measures when judged against averages for the whole of Britain, it is not the only British region in which manufacturing has staged a recovery, nor in which it remains a significant part of the contemporary economy. Placed against the other 'northern' British regions, Wales seems less exceptional in this respect. Even then, more manufacturing activity actually takes place in Greater London than occurs in Wales. The growth in Welsh manufacturing has been from a low starting point, and amounts to very few actual new jobs (possibly no more than a few thousand).

Lovering's point can be developed further. Much of post-war economic analysis and British industrial sociology as well has been excessively preoccupied with the fate of manufacturing industry, which continues to be treated as if it has a privileged position in terms of wealth creation and the provision of 'real' jobs. There are lingering effects here of a certain species of misguided materialism, which sees production as a matter of tangible things, combined with a degree of nostalgia for a time when Britain functioned as the world's workshop. The obsession with manufacturing industry pervades the analyses of the Institute of Welsh Affairs (IWA, 1993, 1996); its report *Wales 2010: Three Years On* contains the remarkable chapter heading 'Praise the Lord we are a manufacturing nation'. Manufacturing industry has also been at the heart of the concerns of the WDA and other development bodies in Wales. Yet the reality is that the de-industrialization of Britain, and Wales, has been part of a much larger and longer process through which the lifeblood of contemporary economies has shifted towards the production of less tangible cultural and social artefacts, located largely within the so-called 'service' sectors. Even the very term 'service' sometimes makes these appear to be no more than secondary activities, ancillary to more 'primary' forms of production. Yet modern Wales, like the rest of Britain, is fundamentally a service economy within which manufacturing plays an important but limited role.

This point connects with a number of important observations made by Lovering, such as his reminder of the continuing strength within Wales of public-sector activity, and thus the extent to which key developments continue to be shaped by state intervention and by various kinds of state subventions. This reiterates a theme from his earlier work on the idea of internal colonialism (Lovering, 1978a), where he also stressed the extent to which transfer payments via the British state flowed into, rather than away from, Wales, thus qualifying any simplistic conclusion that Wales was subject to external 'exploitation'. Of course, those who argue the case for a radical transformation do acknowledge the significance of knowledge-based activities and cultural forces to twenty-first-century Wales; the notion of the 'learning' or 'intelligent' region' makes this evident. They also note the hugely important role played by marketing and the construction of imagery. For example, Morgan admits that quite possibly the only factor which has differentiated Wales from other, equally deserving, marginalized regions has been the level of hype produced by its publicity machine. The promotion of the idea of an economic miracle in Wales itself owed much to the activities of the Welsh Office and the WDA in 'a sophisticated and remarkably successful process of "image management" involving the careful manipulation of the media and the selective promotion of "research" through private consultants' (Rees and Morgan, 1991: 169). In other words, 'success' itself has been as much a cultural product – a matter of image-making – as a hard material reality. Nevertheless the scale of industries like tourism, education, social care and their various service 'products' in contemporary Wales tend to be sidelined by seemingly inexhaustible discussions about the need to raise skill levels and improve quality within the manufacturing sector.

Lovering situates some of these questions within a broader onslaught on what he regards as a critical intellectual deformation that has exercised a sway over recent debates: the 'new regionalism' and its institutionalist bias. This is the current of thought which has seized upon the evidence of growing regional variations and the importance of new kinds of industrial 'flexibility' to assert the potential for local mobilization of resources to trigger endogenous development. He cites for example Storper's judgement that, once economies move beyond mass production, it is the region which provides the fundamental basis of economic and social life (Storper, 1995). From this perspective, the power of certain regions to develop, and to gain advantage over others, is seen to depend upon the way in which local effort is orchestrated through networks and relationships of partnership and trust. With the right kind of coordination, it is suggested, the various elements of regional government and industry can come together in 'systems of innovation' (Brazyk et al., 1998) which generate new and positive forms of economic and social change. Wales was nominated as a critical instance for testing such a theory, on the grounds that it possessed the most fertile conditions in Britain for the expression of such a system at a 'regional' level (Rees and Morgan, 1991: 158). This was seen as making the vital connection between arguments for a more devolved form of governance, and the desire for enhanced economic growth. In both respects, Wales could be empowered. However, Lovering believes much in this argument is unfounded speculation, which encourages a tendency to slip too readily from abstract concepts to supposed realities. There is a particular danger of confusing spatial with institutional parameters. The cloudiness as to whether and in what sense 'Wales' can be said to have gained from economic changes, when there are such sharp discontinuities of conditions between areas and among sections of the Welsh population, reflects this uncertainty. After all,

> the short journey from Cardiff/Newport to the south Wales valleys takes one from heady prosperity and the vision of a future at or near the heart of Europe, to the depths of industrial dereliction. The same experience can be obtained by travelling from Shotton to Bethesda in North Wales. There is now a vivid sense of this type of difference and disjunction within Wales, which is partly spatial, partly social and economic – different parts of Wales are very nearly 'worlds apart'. (Day, Mackay et al., 1998: 172)

Lovering explains the gap between the regionalist discourse, and the more mundane reality, in terms of the ideological pull such ideas exert over intellectuals who are close to new seats of regional power. The way in which Wales has changed, and to some extent matured, as an autonomous entity during the 1980s and 1990s has enabled Welsh issues, including those of the economy, to be addressed with a greater degree of confidence, and an increased seriousness. There have been new opportunities for academics and intellectuals to make a difference, and with the achievement of devolution in the closing years of the century these have continued to expand. There is an obvious role for academics within the emergent regional state which now focuses on the National Assembly. Welsh social scientists have assumed positions as 'critical friends' towards the key agencies and policy-makers, as well as working with them in various capacities as advisers and consultants. There are also numerous personal ties and sympathetic under-standings among those who by origin and experience form part of the same regional-metropolitan elite, and who are located within the expanding Welsh service class. As a leading figure within the WDA once put it, naturally they sing from the same hymn sheet. The concentration within Cardiff of both the major institutions of regional governance and many of the leading academics with an interest in Wales has facilitated an intimate interaction, at times verging on the incestuous. Many other influences have brought contemporary academia closer to the worlds of policy- and decision-making and increased the rewards for contributions to 'practical' knowledge, and this is bound to blunt the critical edge. Lovering notes the absence of much investigation of the institutions and individuals who now play their part in the formulation and execution of economic policies in Wales. This is a salutory reminder that there is an almost total lack of scrutiny of the nature of power relationships within Wales, its patterns of elite formation and of the way in which networks of relations of influence are constructed and managed.

10

Language, Culture and Nation: Wales in the Melting Pot

THE TURN TO CULTURE

Since the 1980s, sociology has taken a notable turn or, conceivably, detour towards stressing the importance of cultural issues. Questions of meaning and significance, of value and interpretation, have been accorded far greater priority than they were given in the past, along with a cluster of related topics, such as social identity and difference, variations in lifestyles, forms of communication and patterns of representation. Their growth in prominence has been linked to the rise of social constructionist perspectives, which emphasize the active processes through which these meanings and significations are created, reproduced and changed by social actors. Among the issues this has helped bring to the fore have been: the formation of ethnic relations, the nature of nationality and national identities, definitions of belonging and the shaping of various types of communities (for examples, see Brah et al., 1999; McCrone, 1998; Cohen, 1985). The turn towards culture was itself prompted in part by a preceding movement which had placed language, and other systems of signs, at the centre of social understanding (Chaney, 1994; Lash and Urry, 1994). These emphases were hardly new to Wales however; indeed, as we have seen, whether explicitly or implicitly, they have been close to the heart of many of the debates taking place within Welsh society, and among Welsh social commentators. In a fundamental sense, it has long been apparent that what we mean by Wales is a cultural matter; it is decided largely by our construction of images, visions and interpretations – or to put it slightly differently, how we choose to understand the 'matter' of Wales. It is entirely appropriate therefore that one of the prime inspirations for the development of cultural studies, Raymond Williams, should himself have been Welsh, and been formed individually and socially in that 'border country' where Wales shades across into something else (Williams, 1958, 1960). He spent much of his life grappling with the questions of identity and belonging which this posed. Now it seems the rest of the world has caught up with Williams and the Welsh in grasping the importance of these critical concerns, and real-izing that few if any can be exempt from their effects.

Their relevance is highlighted in a quite specific way by the changes taking place in the rural districts of Wales, described earlier, and this explains why more recent rural analyses have turned towards the 'qualita-tive' investigation of meanings, attitudes, cultural norms and conventions. As a result of change in the Welsh countryside, 'cultural' struggles of various kinds have become more visible and obdurate, while at the same time the theoretical frameworks being utilized to comprehend them have given greater weight to cultural factors (Cloke and Little, 1997). Since there have been crucial historical and intellectual moments during which a particular version of rural society has been identified not just with rural Wales in its entirety, but with the reality of the whole Welsh social forma-tion (Rees, 1984: 29), any alteration in the circumstances bearing upon its validity has consequences of the most far-reaching kind. The following cry from the heart is just one illustration of this:

> We are being mutilated, dispersed, atomised. You cannot count a single county in the West as a Welsh county any more. Looking at the linguistic map is like looking at a patchwork quilt. A patch of Welsh community here, a patch lost to English, then another little patch of Welshness. (Llywelyn, 1986: 245)

This comment is a response to the processes of population recomposition and social change which have been helping to transform the nature and meaning of rural Wales. One notes within it the smooth but insistent move-ment between references to place (the western counties), to language and national belonging; for this commentator, they all flow seamlessly together. Others might wonder however in what sense a change in language, alone, signifies an end to Welshness as such. Yet this is meant quite literally; the writer is in anguish about the prospect for 'the continuation of our people', because:

> every time a home in *Y Fro Gymraeg* goes to a foreigner we die; every time a young Welshman [*sic*] leaves *Y Fro Gymraeg* we die . . . Our country, Wales, has ceased to be. Only the empty, meaningless name remains, without the substance of society and locality.

Nowhere in the text (which is a translation) is it made explicit that 'Welsh' here must be read as meaning 'Welsh speaking'; but that is the equation which makes the textual transitions work, and for the writer, evidently it goes without saying. The idea that Wales is a rural and Welsh-speaking entity echoes Alwyn Rees's rejection of industrial south Wales as the venue of 'rootless nonentities' (Rees, 1996), and the propositions of Saunders Lewis and others that, since the true essence of Wales and the

Welsh is rural, there should be mass withdrawal from the urban industrial zones. Thus a conception of Wales, as it is imagined, has the most drastic consequences for potential action, encouraging a retreat into what has been termed 'fortress Wales' (Rawkins, 1979). Llywelyn reaches the same conclusions; he proposes a movement, or organization (Adfer), to draw the Welsh people back into a 'complete' Welsh society in the rural west, with the tacit correlate of the elimination from it of all non-Welsh influences. In the context of events occurring in the late twentieth century, it is difficult to exorcise altogether the fear that such propositions evoke of some future version of purification via forms of 'ethnic cleansing' (R. T. Jones, 1986). As with Morgan's depiction of the *gwerin* (1986: 137), the 'people' whose survival is seen at risk here is conceived of as comprising that population 'who had always been in Wales down the ages, through thick and thin, refusing to budge in the ebb and flow of conquests and oppressions'. However, by now we know that this is not the only way in which Wales, and the Welsh, can be constructed. There are other, competing, versions which can be espoused just as fiercely; because Wales, and Welshness, are contested constructs, and they are fought over socially and politically, as well as on the terrain of culture.

In fact, as has been shown above, the population movement which has actually occurred has been the reverse of what Llywelyn intended; Welsh people have continued to move away from the more rural areas, mainly to England, and increasingly within Wales towards the expanding metropolis of Cardiff and South Glamorgan. Their places have been taken by incomers, the vast majority of whom come, unsurprisingly, from more prosperous parts of England, such as the home counties, and border districts like Shrophire, Cheshire and Hereford. Approaching 20 per cent of the total population living in Wales were born outside the country (although in some cases this may mean no more than a few miles from its boundaries, or even simply refer to the location of the nearest maternity hospital). The proportion of those born outside Wales is markedly higher in the rural counties of Ceredigion, Gwynedd and Powys. This makes areas of Wales significantly more cosmopolitan in terms of people's origins than most parts of Britain (Giggs and Pattie, 1992), and the scale of the movement has created major problems of assimilation, particularly with regard to the future of the Welsh language and the cultural institutions supported by it. A pamphlet issued by Cymdeithas yr Iaith, the Welsh Language Society, in 1979 and written by a future Member of Parliament, referred to migration as by far the most important political issue facing Wales, specifically in relation to the survival of Welsh distinctiveness and identity (Griffiths, 1992: 77). Twenty years later heated controversy surrounded statements by a local politician in Gwynedd who said that migrants into his area were a 'drain on the community' (Glyn 2001), and English movement into rural areas was being likened in its effects on Welsh rural society to the disease of foot and mouth.

WALES – THE LINGUISTIC DEFINITION

There are many for whom the identity of Wales is defined above all by its possession of a distinctive language (Osmond, 1988: 121). Indeed for some the language can be seen as 'the only obvious remaining symbol of Welsh difference and identity' (Aitchison and Carter, 1998: 176), which necessarily makes it of paramount importance for the future existence of Wales. However, this language is spoken by less than a fifth of the population, and there are vast tracts of Wales where it is not heard at all. On the other hand, there are substantial areas within which it remains, if sometimes only just, the preferred majority language. Emyr Llywelyn was quite correct in his depiction of the geographical pattern as resembling a patchwork quilt; better still, the range of the language has been likened to a fast drying pond, which leaves behind increasingly separated patches of dampness. The process through which the linguistic boundaries of Welsh-speaking Wales, *Y Fro Gymraeg*, have shrunk, and fragmented, has been described and analysed at regular intervals by Harold Carter and his colleagues (Carter and Williams, 1978; Aitchison and Carter, 1985; Carter and Aitchison, 1986; Aitchison and Carter, 1998, 2000). Over the course of the twentieth century the proportion of the population able to speak Welsh fell from around half to just under a fifth, continuing a decline dating back to the industrial revolution (Davies, 1990; C. H. Williams, 2000b). In 1900 it was still possible for individuals, and even entire communities, to live wholly through the medium of Welsh; 15 per cent of those then living in Wales were recorded as monoglot Welsh-speakers. By the end of the century it was difficult for anyone living anywhere in Wales to block out the incessant bombardment of English, the language of business, commerce and the media as well as most people's vernacular.

On the basis of 1981 census data, Aitchison and Carter were able to identify five main remaining areas of concentration of the language, where approaching 70 per cent of the resident population could speak Welsh. These zones were becoming fragmented through their intersection with the consequences of tourism and migration, including retirement settlement, and an increasing number of communities were being Anglicized. The number of communities meeting a threshold of 80 per cent Welsh-speaking had fallen from 279 to 66 in twenty years (Carter and Aichison, 1986). In a few small, remote communities it was still possible to find rates of 90 per cent or more

Welsh-speaking; these places were all in rural Wales and formed islands set in a sea of encroaching Englishness. Memories of events surrounding the language are long, and the historic legacy is inscribed deeply within the Welsh-language community. For instance, the numbers able to read and write Welsh drop significantly below the numbers of speakers, particularly among the older age groups. This reflects a situation in which Welsh has been the vehicle of everyday speech for local communities, but has had to fight for recognition as the language of education and officialdom. Consequently there are those still alive who grew up when Welsh was a denigrated language, discouraged in the school room and place of work, whereas using English conferred social prestige. Policies adopted towards the language ever since the Acts of Union with England (1536–43) have created a fund of evidence and examples on which to support a historical account of the systematic subordination and oppression of Welsh, and of resistance to it. At the same time, a significant gap also developed between styles of vernacular Welsh, used locally, and the more formal and literary Welsh associated with the educated elite of professionals, teachers and ministers, a gap considerably wider than that which exists between received pronunciation in English, and its regional dialects. Language use in Wales has become closely associated with questions of social status and prestige, and the social uses of power, and these divisions reach into the half million or so speakers of Welsh, as well as separating them from those who are not able to speak the language.

The geographical splits which emerged following the industrial revolution were mirrored by linguistic divisions. English became the dominant language of industrial Wales, and therefore was identified with the forces of modernization and progress (Day and Suggett, 1985; WLB, 2000); Welsh was affiliated more closely with the 'traditionalist' Wales of rurality, religion and an old-fashioned middle class of preachers, teachers and public servants. Notoriously, comments made about the language at the time tended to taint Welsh-speakers with backwardness, even primitiveness and barbarity. Actions in defence of the language were made to seem retrograde, concerned to restore things to a past condition. Attitudes have changed markedly since, and the language is now accorded equal official recognition with English, and forms part of the nationally determined school curriculum for all pupils in state schools in Wales. The Welsh Language Board, set up in 1993 under the Welsh Language Act, is charged with ensuring that all public-sector organizations operate a language scheme stating what measures will be used to implement the equal treatment of the two languages. Large private-sector organizations, such as retailers and utility providers, have also taken steps to recognize the reality of a bilingual environment. Survey evidence suggests that the public is generally quite positively disposed towards the Welsh language and its maintenance (Aitchison and Carter, 1998; WLB, 1999): that three-quarters of the population believe Welsh and English deserve equal status, and 88 per cent feel the Welsh language is something to be proud of bears out the opinion expressed by the Board's first chairman, that 'the Welsh language is the common property of all Welsh people, whether they speak the language or not. It is part of the cultural heritage of all the people of Wales.' However, positive attitudes do not necessarily lead to commensurate action (Gruffudd, 2000).

Although the Welsh language is proportionately strongest in the north and west of the country, the largest absolute numbers of Welsh speakers are to be found in urban centres, such as Cardiff, Swansea and Llanelli, and there have been significant signs of recovery and growth in the use of the language among young urban professionals, who are sending more of their children to Welsh-medium schools, which have a reputation for providing high-quality education (Davies, 1990; Baker, 1985). The ability to speak, read and write Welsh has been increasing among younger age groups, and the demographic picture looks more positive than it has for many years. Indeed, there is a certain social cachet to be associated today with the use of Welsh, and for Carter, this signifies the transformation of the language from its rural and religious domains into a more urban, secular and forward-looking phenomenon, as 'new or renewed bases for language reproduction have replaced the traditional or declining bases' (Aitchison and Carter, 1998) to enable the regeneration of the language. Supporting evidence for this view is provided by local studies conducted in the south Wales valleys, where among working-class as well as middle-class parents there is new enthusiasm for expressions of Welsh identity, and for Welsh-language education (Davies, 1990; Roberts, 1995). According to one regional survey, no less than two-thirds of residents in the valleys said that they would like to be able to speak Welsh; most of those who could speak Welsh had acquired it as learners (Adamson and Jones, 1996). Colin Williams describes this transformation in the base of the language in the following terms (Williams, 2000b: 25):

> Historically, the hearth, the farm, the chapel and community have been the traditional domains which sustained a Welsh-medium network of agencies of language reproduction. With the secularization of society and the breakdown of the relative homogeneity of rural communities, an alternative, urban, formal set of domains have been constructed in the urban industrial environments.

Chief among these new domains is the school, but Welsh-language media also play a key role, particularly television, and in more recent years, as Williams comments, 'for the first time in living memory, major British newspapers are hailing the Welsh film industry, youth scene and most of its associated activities as "energized", "sexy" and "cool"'. Here too, 'Welsh' signifies the use of the Welsh language.

POPULAR PROTEST AND THE LANGUAGE MOVEMENT

This change reflects the outcome of a protracted struggle. While activism on behalf of the language has a long history, it was the twin crises of rural depopulation and the decline of the language in the Welsh 'heartlands' which brought about a political awakening of the Welsh-speaking intelligentsia in the 1960s; they acted as the spearhead for the growing assertiveness of the Welsh-speaking middle class. By then the language was in danger of becoming the property of an elderly, declining population living in the rural areas. It was associated with occupations and social milieux that were in decline. With the language in danger, there was a serious threat to other associated features of what was seen as a distinctive Welsh way of life (Bowie, 1993; Trosset, 1993). The language was the main vehicle of transmission and reproduction of a culture complex, and distinctive sense of being, including a literary and oral heritage of song and poetry, and their celebration in popular local festivals (*eisteddfodau*). It was plausible therefore to equate the disappearance of the language with the effective extermination of a particular version of the Welsh people and their unique cultural inheritance. This was the spectre held out by the writer Saunders Lewis in 1962 in his cathartic radio lecture, 'Tynged yr iaith' (The fate of the language), which inspired a new generation of language activists. The period from the 1970s onwards saw a phase of heightened struggle around the language, driven by a perception that, if nothing was done immediately, it would be too late to reverse the trend. The politicization of language issues in Wales made the future of the Welsh language into the central question of national or 'ethnic' politics for some twenty or thirty years. This occurred against the background of wider currents of social protest and unrest in Britain (and the western world in general) in the late 1960s and 1970s. Looking back on it, it is easy to see in this the characteristic shape of a 'new social movement', with its emphasis on the cultural and symbolic mobilization of a cross-class coalition, headed by professional people, intellectual activists and students (C. H. Williams, 1982).

There was a two-pronged strategy: in party political terms, the Welsh National Party (Plaid Cymru) became closely identified with popular support in 'Welsh Wales' – its major successes occurred where the language was strongest. Meanwhile, headed by the Welsh Language Society (Cymdeithas yr Iaith Gymraeg), activists pursued a campaign of civil disobedience and non-violent direct action which involved street demonstrations, occupation of administrative centres like post offices, action against university officials and staff, and symbolic attacks on media targets, like broadcasting transmitters (C. H. Williams, 1977). It is indicative that the targets of this movement were predominantly cultural – the media, education, and the use of English as the preferred (or, more often, the only) language of administration and the law courts. It led to the movement being labelled as an example of 'cultural nationalism', which to some extent was usurping the role played by Plaid Cymru during its early days (C. H. Williams, 1982b, 2000b). Perhaps the archetypal form of protest adopted by Welsh-language sympathizers at this time was to paint out or remove road signs and place names written in English; that is, symbolically to remove English from the landscape of Wales. The actions were relatively peaceful (indeed, pacifism had been a marked strain in the early nationalist movement in Wales) but involved strong emotions, and an escalating level of confrontation, with increasing numbers of people appearing before the courts, and being sentenced to pay fines or spend time in jail. There was considerable mobilization among highly reputable, and usually law-abiding, people like ministers of religion, university professors, writers and broadcasters, which exerted growing pressure on the normal workings of the political system.

The highly centralized British state was slow to respond to claims being made from Wales. At this time both 'nationalism' in the sense of assertions of separateness and a desire for greater autonomy, and 'difference' in relation to attachment to a minority language and culture, tended to be treated from the centre as trivial or negligible matters, often dismissed as simply reactionary. This was akin to the tendency within social science to relegate such matters to the realm of the 'primordial' (Jenkins, 1997). The British state was strong and unified, and such questions did not interest the vast (English) bulk of the electorate, certainly when compared to the 'bread-and-butter' issues of the economy, employment and welfare which tended to dominate elections. Lack of response fostered the growth of antagonism, and the emergence of a degree of fringe violence: small numbers of extremists were prepared to resort to more drastic action, such as parading in quasi-military uniforms (the Free Wales Army) and blowing up pipelines carrying 'Welsh water' to English cities. They won very limited active public backing. More significant for government was the extent to which the nationalist party was able to consolidate its hold over voters in Welsh-speaking areas, and so pose a growing political and electoral threat, particularly at times when there was a delicate (UK-wide) balance of power. In British terms, the issue has always been whether the nationalists would be strong enough to tip the balance between the mainstream political parties.

During the 1970s and 1980s the central focus of Welsh political life shifted. There was greater involvement with questions to do with the general restructuring of the Welsh economy, and the need for jobs, and for most people these issues bore little connection to language. The emergence of new aspirations among new social levels tended to sideline the struggle over language, making it seem peculiarly the preoccupation of those parts of Welsh society which were excluded from or outside the mainstream processes, and still fighting ancient battles, reminiscent of the glory days of nineteenth-century Liberal Nonconformity (Adamson, 1991a). The language movement seemed to be fixated upon the aims defined by its founders, namely 'the preservation of Welsh cultural and spiritual values primarily through the maintenance of a small-scale, predominantly rural, communitarian lifestyle' (C. H. Williams, 2000b: 20). When the minority agitated for special protection and assistance to keep the Welsh language alive, this was liable to be seen as a diversion from more important matters, a claim for an 'unfair' share of resources, which almost constituted reverse discrimination against the mass of non-Welsh speakers (G. A. Williams, 1985). This prompted various expressions of hostility from within the Welsh population; indeed, the fiercest opposition to the demands of language activists was voiced within Wales itself. In this context, nationalist politicians in Wales made some crucial adjustments to their positions. They paid closer attention to the economic and social claims of the urban population, and began to stress more firmly the view that Wales's problems would be solved only when there was greater devolution of power and control from the centre. In a sense, they adopted a more ordinary sort of politics, and by distancing themselves from questions of language and culture, they began to make greater headway with the majority population in the traditionally Labour-voting parts of Wales. To some extent, 'economic' nationalism could be said to have supplanted cultural nationalism (though not without a considerable internal political struggle within Plaid Cymru). This enabled a broader appeal to be made to a sense of Welshness which was not tied to speaking Welsh, or participating in Welsh-language culture, but which nevertheless confronted the 'British' orientation that had grown up in Wales during the era of industry and empire.

However, the language question did not and could not go away; first, because it continued to be the prime issue for dedicated activists, to whom it represented a focus of demands that were non-negotiable (C. H. Williams, 1982b); and secondly, because, as ever, the way in which Wales was developing threw up new sources of tension and controversy, within which the language question became embroiled. Economic recovery in the 1980s triggered a new wave of migration of English people into the Welsh countryside, attracted by cheap housing and good living conditions. Their presence began to tip the balance in previously Welsh-speaking communities, taking the struggle deep into the 'Welsh heartland' itself (Jones and Williams, 2000; Evas, 2000). The battle was not exclusively about language, but linked ethnicity to control of property and territory (Borland et al., 1992). One result was a campaign against second-home owners and in-migrants which included violence against property, and quite widespread arson (more than a hundred houses in rural areas were burnt down), in the name of a shadowy organization called 'the sons of Glyndŵr' (Meibion Glyndŵr). The campaign extended to attempts to fire-bomb English-owned businesses in Wales and estate agents in Liverpool and Chester who were selling Welsh properties. Although threats were directed at particular individuals, there were no physical assaults on people. At a lower level of intensity, but probably with greater salience for most people, numerous local confrontations arose around housing development, schooling and the use of Welsh in daily life. A myriad of small-scale incidents lent weight to ancient stereotypes of the English as 'colonialist' and domineering in manner, and made this seem simply the latest in a long succession of English incursions against Wales and Welshness.

Given this recent history, let alone the far longer record of English oppressiveness and attempts at times to extirpate the language, the status of the Welsh language and its place in contemporary Wales are unavoidably contentious. Thus, according to Day and Rees (1987: 1),

> The role played by language in the structuring of Welsh society is a crucial one. For many, the Welsh language is a critical marker of ethnic identity; now, as in the past, therefore, its survival and even growth is a necessary condition of a distinctive national existence for Wales. This particular construction of 'Welshness' is not universally shared, of course, and alternatives exist which not only mobilise different cultural resources, but may actually be antipathetic to Welsh-language culture.

The inference is that the Welsh language is as much a divisive force within Wales as it is a badge of distinctiveness; as an essential symbol of Welshness, it is widely endorsed even among those who do not speak the language, and yet at the same time it relegates them to a diminished status. Thus it plays a large part in making Wales into a 'plural' society, adding a particular twist to the 'veritable kaleidoscope within which the key ethnic, linguistic, cultural and social class ingredients combine in contrasting proportions and combinations which change in character, across both time and space' (Giggs and Pattie, 1992: 43). Indeed, as has been seen with regard to the bitter arguments which have raged about the effects of migration on housing, social status, language and the damage done to aspects of the 'indigenous' Welsh culture, the combination of these elements is decidedly volatile. Giggs and Pattie note how examining these issues is fraught with difficulty, since there is only a limited amount of hard evidence to assist with resolving the various debates. When evidence is evaluated, the patterns revealed are complex, and spatially varied, so that it is possible to derive markedly differing conclusions on the basis of particular local examples. Furthermore, even the data themselves can be contaminated by problems to do with the subjective estimation of different linguistic competences. Needless to say, limited factual evidence does little to prevent people from taking up radically contrasting political positions, or advocating drastic policy measures, according to their impressions of the underlying situation.

LANGUAGE PLANNING AND SURVIVAL

The greater part of the social scientific work on the state of the Welsh language has been done from the perspective of geography or sociolinguistics; sociological contributions are few and far between. A brief and critical history of these investigations is provided in Williams and Morris (2000), which notes the prevailing bias towards spatial analysis. The focus on the historic fate of the Welsh 'heartland' as a dwindling base from which the language can be reproduced is said to encourage a preoccupation with the need for a 'region or a set of spaces' within which the language can remain dominant, or at least equal with English, and hence with the question of how a viable Welsh culture can survive without its heartland communities (Williams, 2000b: 24; Evas, 2000). The emphasis becomes about the management of some form of spatial planning. According to Williams and Morris, this lends itself all too readily to absorption within a diffusionist perspective, where a seemingly inexorable external threat will eventually wear down the powers of resistance of the minority-language community. This gives the appearance of a rearguard action being mounted against the inevitable, which in turn fits with what is said to be an underlying evolutionary assumption among sociologists that the minority language is a relic of the past, an aspect of 'tradition' that is bound to be replaced by more modern influences. Undoubtedly there are some accounts according to which efforts devoted to protecting the language are not just doomed, but are taken to represent definite obstructions in the path of necessary progress (Davies, 1997). While this is a view Williams and Morris attribute most firmly to non-Welsh sociologists, it also pervades much of the writing from within the Welsh language, since the current state of affairs is depicted as a sorry decline from a 'golden age' when the language was secure and unchallenged, at least within the stronghold of *Y Fro Gymraeg*. We have seen how this perspective was characteristic of classical Welsh rural sociology. However, to approach language and culture from this direction is to reify it as something fixed and static, rather than recognizing how it has to be continually created and recreated through processes of change. Williams and Morris state that the tendency to reify language, or to regard it as the unique point of departure for analysis, is typical of linguistics and the sociology of language. They argue instead for treating minority language groups in the same terms as any other social groups and, perhaps most especially, in the same way as social class groups. That is, rather than pursuing specialist debates about issues such as language change and language shifts, code-switching and the various 'domains' of language use, they prefer to concentrate upon language as an instrument of social action, but also as a powerful structuring force which contributes towards the formation of social groups and allegiances.

A 'defensive' concern with language reproduction leads to emphasis being laid upon the role of the family, household and, increasingly in contemporary circumstances, the school, in ensuring the maintenance of the linguistic minority. Research suggests growing difficulties in the former sphere, where there are more mixed or linguistically fractured households, and the family is subjected to far greater countervailing pressures from outside, for example through peer groups, the media and popular culture (Harrison et al., 1981; Gruffudd, 1998; Aitchison and Carter, 1998). Reliance on the school, although shown to be highly effective in creating basic linguistic competence, is no guarantee that this will translate into actual language use, after or beyond schooling. Alternative institutional arenas within which the minority language can be deployed, and perhaps developed, include the labour market and the local community. Williams and Morris seek to tie all these together in an argument which traces changes in the situation of the language, and in relationships among language groups, to the processes of economic restructuring. Periods of rapid economic change are seen as responsible for the occurrence of successive waves of migration into Wales, which have decisive consequences both for local communities and for competition within local labour markets.

Work on the 1981 population census statistics for Wales suggested that people born outside the country were significantly over-represented amongst its higher occupational groups (Williams, 1987a). Conversely, Welsh-speakers were found in disproportionate strength among the unskilled and semi-skilled manual categories. The figures as presented are difficult to interpret (Williams and Morris, 2000: 33), since the categories overlap to some degree, and they exclude a substantial third group, those born within Wales who do not speak Welsh. Thus the basis on which the percentages have been calculated is unclear, and in many ways represents an artificial construct. However, comparison of the equivalent 1991 statistics leads Williams and Morris to conclude that Welsh speakers have lost ground within most, if not all, socio-economic categories, and therefore that the cultural division of labour has intensified, due to the penetration of local labour markets by in-migrant, non-Welsh-born individuals. Welsh speakers, who constituted 19 per cent of the working population at that time, were found to be over-represented among professionals, 25 per cent of whom spoke Welsh, as well as among the agricultural workforce, where the proportion speaking Welsh rose to 42 per cent. There is evidence here of the continuing closeness of association between ability to speak Welsh, and the 'traditional' areas of employment in farming and the professions, particularly teaching. The vast majority of Welsh-speaking women professionals are teachers (Jones and Morris, 1997), as indeed are about half the professional men who speak Welsh.

There has been much debate about the significance of these kinds of associations. As noted, Williams and Morris find support for the argument that there is a cultural division of labour, with many of the best occupational positions in Wales going to 'spiralists' recruited by or within agencies and organizations which are based outside its borders. Others however have seen signs that a Welsh-speaking minority enjoys labour-market advantages denied to, and resented by, the bulk of the population (G. A. Williams, 1985: 293). Contrary to immediate appearances, these are not incompatible positions. Using tabulations from the 1981 census, Giggs and Pattie (1992) confirm that English-born individuals are indeed over-represented in high-status occupational positions in north and west Wales, and also among the 'petit bourgeois' or small business sector. On the other hand, Welsh speakers, especially those who are 'literate' in the sense of being able to read and write Welsh, are over-represented in similar positions in the south. In both instances, we are seeing the effect of complicated career paths and experiences of social mobility through spiralism which take individuals into particular elite positions, or relatively highly rewarded jobs. Examples would be positions in the culture industries and in key government and public-sector jobs. From Giggs and Pattie's account, it is not possible to determine whether this amounts to 'internal colonialism' or should be attributed simply to the results of normal social and occupational mobility. Blackaby and Drinkwater (1997) back up the paradoxical picture whereby those who are unable to speak the Welsh language enjoy a slight differential advantage in those areas which are most strongly Welsh-speaking, whereas a Welsh-speaking minority is very well represented in professional and technical jobs in the south-east region of Wales, where around 95 per cent of the population have no ability to speak Welsh. This provides evidence of movement within Wales of highly educated Welsh speakers seeking career progression. For cultural or social reasons, they make their moves towards the larger opportunities available in the Welsh cities. For very similar reasons, others who originate from areas beyond Wales move in to take up vacant occupational places in rural and west Wales. The two sets of movements do not necessarily occur in the same economic sectors; in other words, although there will be some overlap, Welsh and non-Welsh speakers may not be competing directly for the same jobs. In neither instance is there clear evidence of 'discrimination', although at an anecdotal level those who wish to make such claims will be able to find sufficient supporting examples. More generally, Blackaby and Drinkwater find that Welsh speakers are less likely to face unemployment and, in the case of women, more likely to have full-time jobs, than those who do not speak the language.

As all these sources agree, the group which seems indisputably to be least successful in terms of occupational achievement is the non-Welsh-speaking, Welsh-born population, sometimes referred to as 'Anglo-Welsh', which fills the bulk of the remaining blue-collar, 'proletarian' jobs and many of the positions in routine service industries. As Gwyn Williams contended, English-speaking members of the Welsh working class may well experience relative deprivation when they perceive the government subsidizing what they encounter as a middle-class minority of Welsh speakers. As a result, they may feel themselves to be doubly colonized, by both outsiders and privileged insiders; certainly one source of opposition to the transfer of greater political powers into Wales has been a fear that this might advantage Welsh speakers over compatriots who could not speak the language, a fear which opponents of devolution tried to use to their advantage. The tale of how the recognition of the right of one deprived group to support and succour can raise new grievances and a sense of unfairness among those whose entitlements fall just outside those of the group in question is sadly familiar. As a result, there are those whose own sense of Welshness at present contains a strong dash of anti-Welsh-language sentiment. This is a prime example of the way in which language differences can cut across potential similarities of economic position and interest. From a different direction, occupants of middle-class positions within north Wales appear to be oriented differently according to whether or not they can speak Welsh; hence class groups are fractioned by language use (Morris, 1995). Gruffudd (2000: 199) suggests that the condition of Welsh-speaking workers in 'the heartland' and their English-speaking counterparts in the valleys may be equally rooted in experiences of colonialist economic exploitation which have 'robbed people of wealth and livelihood', and some of their language as well. For him, with respect to language, the more important phenomenon is that the emerging awareness of the achievements of a new kind of Welsh-speaking professional class has given the

Welsh language a 'remarkably positive boost', making knowledge of it once again a desirable possession. Williams and Morris argue likewise that the language has gained a prestige and value for certain kinds of social mobility which provides new motivation for non-Welsh speakers to ensure that their children acquire the language (2000: 37). That is, it has become an asset for those who wish to gain access to certain kinds of occupational rewards, in areas of local government, public service and particular professions. More than in the past, those who hold such positions are able to exercise influence from the urban centres, the 'centres of power' in modern Wales (Aitchison and Carter, 1998: 174). The argument put forward by Williams and Morris constitutes virtually a mirror-image of a rival analysis, which sees patterns of labour-market differentiation in Welsh-speaking parts of Wales as heavily influenced by forms of social closure practised on nationalistic grounds (Fevre et al., 1997).

THE LANGUAGE OF THE COMMUNITY

In their analysis of Wales as a plural society, Giggs and Pattie (1992) pay special attention to arguments relating to language and social status, and the claims often put forward that English migrants do not merely dilute the Welshness of the areas into which they move, but attempt to assume dominance over the local population (G. Williams, 1986). That they are arrogant, assertive or 'colonial' in their behaviour is a common theme of many local responses (Cloke et al., 1997). In a considerable over-simplification of the reality, all those who are English-born are sometimes characterized as if they enjoyed significant affluence and social status in comparison to the local population – although this is difficult to reconcile with an alternative conception that 'thousands of English drop-outs and drug-dullened idlers' have found their way into Wales (Morris, 1998: 409). Giggs and Pattie show very well how considerations of class and ethnicity interact to make these matters extraordinarily controversial. Instructively, their own conclusions, though drawn from a careful analysis of data, are not exempt from controversy, when they slip from sober academicism towards polemic. Often it is the choice of vocabulary which gives the game away: thus, their comments on the 'disquieting preoccupation with cultural elitism among some Welsh-speaking Welsh people' and the activities of certain language 'zealots' in 'touting' language qualifications and proficiency as the key to Welsh nationality (1992: 57) brought a response from Aitchison and Carter (1999: 181) who identify such views with more extreme statements advocating the 'euthanasia' of the Welsh language. The words employed give some flavour of the intensity with which the fate of the language tends to be discussed;

just as the resort to terms like 'flood', 'swamping' and references to 'disease' in relation to English migration into Wales are all too familiar from wider debates on immigration to Britain and Europe. On the other hand, for many, it is highly dispiriting that a significant degree of success achieved in defending and securing the future of the Welsh language through educational reform and political campaigning should be jeopardized by the sheer numbers of people now intruding into its space, who are neither prepared to assimilate to it, or often even to acknowledge its existence. In this situation, accusations of exclusivity and even 'racism' are liable to fly in either direction.

The rapidity of the changes taking place at local level have certainly inspired a number of strong expressions of concern. Thus a policy paper issued by Plaid Cymru in 1988 reiterated that migration was a key political issue, constituting a threat to the maintenance of Welsh nationality and to 'the development in progressive directions of our people's sense of national identity' (cited in Griffiths, 1992: 74). It argued accordingly for the introduction of planning controls over the housing market, still greater efforts to improve the economic conditions of the areas most affected so as to retain local population, and the need to make the protection of Welshness a strategic principle of action by Welsh agencies and quangos. Gwynedd County Council likewise sought to extend local authority powers to take account of the impact of developments on language and culture, to limit the creation of new housing, and to restrict the availability of holiday homes. Under Welsh Office guidance, and to varying degrees, local authorities have built potential impact on Welsh-speaking communities into their structure planning process as a 'material consideration' (C. H. Williams, 2000c). One of the more drastic proposals was Ceredigion's plan to restrict new housing in areas where half or more spoke Welsh to those who had lived within 25 miles of the site for at least five years (Aitchison and Carter, 1999). More recently the Welsh Assembly has circulated proposals to curb the further sale and acquisition of former publicly owned housing in rural areas. A number of these measures were incorporated into the policy recommendations produced by a new organization, Cymuned, in its submissions to the National Assembly of Wales in November 2001. Defining Welsh as a living community language, which is under severe threat of extinction as such, the organization aims to safeguard the 'territorial integrity of naturally Welsh-speaking communities' (Cymuned, 2001: 7). To do so it suggests the restriction of housing development according to a definition of local need, priority within the housing market for those who are 'local' (having lived within 10 miles, for ten years or more), and steps to be taken to encourage those who move into the area to learn and use the Welsh language. Recent statements by British government ministers about the need for immigrants and refugees to learn English so as to integrate into the host society are seen as lending weight to this expectation. The Cymuned approach, with its emphasis on sustainable development and holistic planning, exemplifies Colin Williams's observation (2000b: 27) that issues of rural community are being rediscovered and repackaged by the language movement in ecological form, as a matter of the survival of the 'cultural species' and a necessary response to globalization. This is borne out by the statement that the indigenous language is 'part of the fine environmental web that makes every area unique' (Cymuned, 2000: 31). In other words, there is a reassertion of the ultimate significance of the heartland as the basis for survival of the language as a natural living reality, which also resonates with a contemporary politics of 'difference' and of recognition and representation.

Of course, it is not only in rural Wales that these problems have been encountered. Similar developments have occurred in the English Lake District and in Cornwall, areas also under threat from the urban exodus and the leisure explosion; but in Wales the presence of a distinct language, and the differentiation by perceived nationality of those involved adds a crucial further dimension, and makes resolution far more intractable. The pressures exerted by inward migration on land use in the Welsh national park areas has led to various proposals for limiting further housing development. Interestingly, when such suggestions were made in the Pembrokeshire National Park, claims that they were 'racist' were rebutted by the argument that they had nothing to do with the Welsh language. Concepts of language, race and nationality have become deeply intertwined, and a number of incidents and events occurring during recent years have seen these issues re-emerging, and being expressed with some considerable vehemence. Referring to the situation as it stood at the end of the 1970s, a Canadian political sociologist noted how nationalism in Wales had been circumscribed by 'an almost subliminal preoccupation with the Welsh speaking areas and an unspoken assumption that politics were merely the means to the salvation of language and culture' (Rawkins, 1985: 303). This he saw as undermining efforts to build a party machine that would represent the wider Welsh nation, and quite possibly setting unavoidable boundaries to its ability to construct this wider appeal. Thus:

> If the objective of *Plaid Cymru* has been to mobilize the Welsh nation as a political force, its twenty year venture in serious party-building must be termed a failure. Examination of *Plaid Cymru*'s history, along with a perusal of election results, would probably lead the observer to conclude that the party of Welsh nationalism has reached the limits of its potential. (Rawkins, 1985: 297)

The proof of this assertion lay in the defeat of the 1979 devolution referendum, where the inability to win support from non-Welsh-speaking voters had produced a four to one ratio of votes against the proposal to increase decision-making powers within Wales. This result was in line with the confinement of electoral support for nationalist politicians to around 12 per cent of the popular vote in general elections. Despite the best efforts of a 'modernising' faction within the party, who were trying to redirect attention towards issues about economic and social justice (Rawkins, 1979; C. H. Williams, 1982b), support for Plaid Cymru appeared to be trapped within the Welsh-speaking heartlands. Hence, Rawkins contended, the work of forging a 'politically relevant' national identity, that was capable of making a difference to relationships of power, remained to be done; language continued to divide the nation rather than bind it together. It is a view re-iterated by others such as Knowles (1999: 311): 'for Welsh nationalists, the territory that matters has always been the land inhabited by native Welsh speakers, not Wales as a whole, or Wales as an independent political entity.' There have been very significant developments in Welsh politics, and in conceptions of national identity, which make this assertion no longer fully applicable; but the resurgence of language issues at the present time demonstrates that linguistic wounds are very far from healed, and it is evident that, as well as creating deep rifts between sections of the Welsh population, they are still capable of bringing about significant divisions within the nationalist camp as well.

11

Nation, Nationalism and Ethnicity

Sociology has long abandoned any pretence that nations and national identities are fixed and static realities which reflect some underlying genetic or other such essential structure, such as a common language. Rejecting such views positions us on what McCrone refers to as 'the familiar if somewhat boggy terrain' of considering whether or not nations are 'real', or should be treated as items of discourse situated within social and political practice (McCrone, 1998: 4). This is likely to occasion fierce debate, because there are many who have major personal and political investments in advancing a particular type of answer to the question. For a while, it was possible for most sociologists to duck the issue. Following the horrors of the Second World War, nationalism seemed a thoroughly discredited ideology, and in any case the theorists of modernization provided reassurance that it was a retrograde force which would be eliminated by further progress towards global stability and rationality. Even in the early 1980s it was possible to poke fun at the conventional wisdom for treating such 'narrow' nationalists as Basques, Kurds, and the Welsh who rebelled against 'their' nation-state as 'particularly silly and dangerous' (Seers, 1983: 10), victims of some doomed atavistic instinct. Those who took such behaviour seriously, and tried to evaluate it more sympathetically on its own terms, were likely to be marginalized, in the same way as nationalist politics were regarded as a 'fringe', slightly eccentric, activity. All this has changed dramatically; as McCrone notes, the literature on nations and nationalisms has exploded in recent years, as the phenomena themselves have pushed their way ever higher up the cultural and political agenda.

In Wales of course, like other strongholds of minority nations, nationalism and nationality never went away. On the contrary, for at least a couple of centuries there has been a strong current of opinion and political organization devoted to asserting the distinct and separate identity of Wales as a nation, a people and a form of consciousness. The historian Merfyn Jones remarks that this is the foundation on which a distinctive Welsh history rests, in that 'Wales exists because nationalism says that it exists. In this sense Wales becomes a process rather than a place, and thus a fit subject of history'

(1982b: 20). This statement provided the text for an examination of how sociology should approach the question of Welsh nationhood, in which it was argued that national identity should also be viewed as an affiliation which needed to be produced and reproduced, and not just taken for granted (Day and Suggett, 1985: 92). This presumption would oblige sociology to discover how this was done, and to set about deconstructing ideas, myths and definitions of nations and nationality to see how they had been formed and propagated. In fact, once looked at in this way, nationalism appeared to be an exceptionally flexible conceptual field, an 'evolving matrix of definitions and competing constructions' (Day and Suggett, 1985: 97). When applied to the Welsh context, this encouraged such questions as: how many concepts of Wales? and how many ways of being Welsh? In other words, it problematized Welshness.

There are those for whom such questions seemed too 'clever', and excessively analytical. They miss what might be seen as the obvious answer: that Wales does have a history; it has a physical existence, within certain boundaries; it is an administrative entity; and it contains its own properties of 'land, water, livestock, labour power and brains' (Emmett, 1982a: 170). All of these could be regarded as the conditions upon which an unproblematic assertion of the existence of Wales can be made – except that every single one of them is riddled with problems. One does not have to be a devotee of globalization, for example, to see how it hard it is to assert nowadays that the land, livestock, water and even brains located inside Wales somehow belong to it, and it alone; earlier discussion of the role of foreign inward investment in recent economic development makes that woefully apparent. Over time, physical frontiers have changed, administrative arrangements have been overhauled, and the history, far from being settled, has been reworked again and again, and remains in contention. Thus the obviousness of Wales cannot withstand scrutiny. Indeed, Isabel Emmett herself was far too good a sociologist to miss this; in her work on the young men of Blaenau Ffestiniog, for example, she explains how from the 1960s onwards they had 'won, with some panache, the right to be themselves and to be Welsh in a different way from the way of their fathers' (Emmett, 1978: 100). In finding Welsh ways of becoming hippies, mods and bikers, the Blaenau boys had picked up ideas from outside Wales, and adapted and assimilated them to make them into something different; their Welshness was not contained within any predetermined territorial boundaries. Later on, and with much more effect, Welsh rock bands performed the same feat.

In fact, all Emmett's work on Wales is centred on the question of what it is to be Welsh, and how Welshness is performed in everyday practices. In her study of a north Wales village (Emmett, 1964), the answer encompasses such activities as poaching fish and not filling in tax forms, both seen as ways of challenging the perceived dominance of 'ruling England'. Again, we are reminded of Raymond Williams's insistence that the actual Welsh cultural formation has been produced in a prolonged interaction between 'always diverse' native elements and the dominant and alternative effects of an occupying power (Day and Suggett, 1985: 93). It is not a simple, or homogeneous phenomenon (no culture ever is). Emmett (1982b) noted the novel, 'aggressively' Welsh, tone that was struck in the responses of working-class youth in Blaenau Ffestiniog to post-war changes. Others also commented on the new-found assertiveness in Wales and tried to provide explanations for it in terms of wider social shifts. Khleif (1978) suggested that it formed part of a global structural change, linked to the development of new systems of labour associated with post-industrialism, particularly the rise of a well-educated 'knowledge' class. His argument is typical of sociological attempts to explain nationalism, and national identity, by anchoring it in structural conditions which give it a particular and specifiable social location. Such structural accounts of nationalism, and ethnicity, were prevalent during the 1970s and 1980s.

CLASS VERSUS ETHNICITY? THE STRUCTURAL LOCATION OF WELSH NATIONALISM

According to Khleif, post-war university expansion had enabled the provision of new cadres of technical and services personnel, skilled in the handling of information, to fill the growing demand for professional and managerial employment. At the same time, economic growth had brought about the industrialization of previously isolated peripheries. In Wales this combination of modernizing forces had produced a new middle class, highly conscious of their working-class antecedents, and also 'very proud of their Welshness, of their ability to speak Welsh, of their ability to live a full Welsh life' (Khleif, 1978: 108). 'Heavily ethnic' in their attitudes and behaviour, this class could use their Welshness to lever social mobility, and also to regain a sense of community and authenticity in the face of pressures towards an impersonal, bureaucratic, social order. This is the grouping which is captured in Williams and Morris's discussion of social mobility and occupational segmentation. Khleif manages to present its members both as crusaders against the twentieth century, and among its main beneficiaries. Psychologically, they are seen as attaining a degree of wholeness, compared with which the non-Welsh-speaking population remain 'marginal' beings. Recovery of a suppressed ancestral language overcomes the legacy of 'torn consciousness, ambivalence, self-hatred and language hatred, and split or suppressed identity' which bedevils Wales, and which permits one of

Khleif's informants to call a person who cannot speak Welsh 'a Welshman without having much Welshness' (1978: 115).

On this account, the key relationships in play in Welsh society are those between English colonizers, the Welsh colonized, and a 'pro-English', Anglo-Welsh intermediary class; but for Khleif, the main struggle now is between the two categories of the Welsh, who confront issues of language and identity on a daily basis. The English have become interested bystanders, largely waiting upon the outcomes of a decolonization process. Emmett had doubted whether Welsh culture, with its emphasis upon a shared way of life, could survive the growth of a middle class (1964: 140). This was because she had absorbed the conception of a *gwerin* which rose above social distinctions. By contrast, Khleif sees the advent of such a middle class as the basis for cultural resurgence, able to inspire greater self-confidence through leadership and example. Both are attempting the difficult task of bringing together considerations of social structure and cultural change, but doing so while working within different assumptions about the nature of 'Welshness' and its historical reality. There are confusions in Khleif's account that are symptomatic of the difficulty analysts face in getting behind surface appearances and perceptions to do this: for example, his contention that the members of the rising middle class are at one and the same time the children of coal miners and spring from rural homes blurs important distinctions in a quite predictable way, more compatible with the mythology rather than the reality of the way in which this class has been formed.

Khleif's approach has clear affinities with Hechter's model of internal colonialism (Hechter, 1975); like other analyses of the period, both resort to Third World analogies and examples to explain developments in Wales. The growth in Welsh consciousness at the time could be seen as part of a wider upsurge of 'ethnonationalism' among dependent ethnic groups, inspired by the example of anti-colonial liberation struggles to assert their right to self-determination, and freedom from 'alien' rule (Esman, 1977; Tiryakian and Rogowski, 1985). In the steady expansion of the force-field of nationalism, their time to assert themselves seemed to have come (Connor, 1977). Williams (1985) contends that under the pressure of structural change within economy and society, there were those for whom some kind of nationalism had become the only form of expression available. This was a consequence of the splintering of class divisions, and the way in which they had interacted with ethnic factors. Thus the various class relationships which occur across different branches of a modern economy, and between the publicly and privately controlled sectors, result in the subdivision of the main social classes into a number of distinct fractions; these are patterned differently between parts of Wales which are 'core', 'enclave' or marginalized. In all three, there is a tendency for dominant social positions to be occupied by people who are non-Welsh, including the bulk of managerial and skilled jobs in the marginalized, rural areas. Those workers who are part of the core labour force, working in the larger firms and organizations, are more likely to be unionized and to gain from strong labour organization and political support, through which they can force concessions from employers and the state. They are likely to adhere to the Labour Party. The marginalized workforce lacks this power and therefore ends up in the worst rewarded jobs. Overall, classes fragment along ethnic lines, and there is an awareness that ethnic groups are stratified within the general division of labour. Hence for subordinate groups, the adversary 'can only be defined as the capitalist system imported and directed by "foreigners"' (G. Williams, 1985: 332). This makes the 'natural' political outcome appear to be some form of nationalistically tinged socialism.

Though this argument looks very like Hechter's 'cultural division of labour' thesis, Williams is at pains to state that he has no intention of putting forward a culturalist explanation, which he equates with taking a primordial view of ethnicity; for him, culture is a symptom, rather than a cause, of political opposition, which stems from economic processes which generate conflicting social positions. This is a statement which encapsulates much of the theoretical debate during the 1980s. The revival of various sorts of nationalist politics and the evident staying-power of ethnicity as a phenomenon had made it necessary to reconsider some of the one-dimensional predictions made by earlier modernizers. This coincided with a fundamental rethink going on within Marxist social theory in particular, under the influence of European thinkers like Gramsci and Althusser, which was aimed at moving away from reductionist theories of class and economic determinism, to take greater notice of the influence of political and ideological factors. The relationship between different aspects of society – economic, political and cultural – and the need to give due significance to their separate and interlocking dynamics became a prime focus of theoretical effort (Laclau, 1977; Hindess, 1987). This had a very clear bearing on discussions about where Welsh nationalism, as a political ideology and set of interests, fitted into the developing framework of contemporary social relations. Typically, the first-order question was to determine how nationalism corresponded to Welsh class relationships; virtually no attention was given to equivalent issues to do with gender, or other fundamental sociological categories (Day, 1984).

From his perspective of neo-Marxism, influenced by contact with the Latin American *dependistas*, Williams was able to designate the 'marginalized' population as the principal carriers of nationalism. In his words, they consisted potentially of all those threatened with being left out of the integrated sector, those whose economic survival is threatened by the encroachment of 'new' developments. It also includes those faced with inadequate housing and without resources, because they are enclosed within a dependent society which is not in control of its own means of production and mode of development and whose resources flow either towards the 'foreigners' or towards those sectors which are dominated by them. (1985: 333)

This coalition of forces, which includes a variety of different social group-ings, was said to be able to mobilize around its sense of being a dominated, exploited and excluded community. Its main target in this regard might well be the state, since government organizations are seen as failing in their role of counteracting the unfairnesses of the system, acting in reality on behalf of the dominant interests. Hence members of the local bourgeoisie within the marginalized areas, such as small business owners, who find it hard to compete with firms from outside, may choose to align themselves with local interests and local identities, rather than with others who are in the same class, but represent external control. While Williams does not fore-close on the question of who precisely the Welsh and non-Welsh are within this equation, he does note that, where certain occupations require Welsh-language qualifications, this generates a career structure that is 'specifically Welsh' (1985: 329), closed to non-Welsh speakers.

Although Williams's argument does not necessarily have to be under-stood in spatial terms, since elements of marginality and exclusion could be found more or less anywhere within Wales, it does run the risk of confining the support base for nationalism to a disadvantaged minority particularly identified with rural north and west Wales (compare G. Williams, 1980), and with the Welsh language. Furthermore, as he acknowledges, ideologi-cally its stance is prone to a number of difficult contradictions: in its opposition to agencies of the state, that are also viewed as working on behalf of the people, and in its resistance to 'progress' in the form of various kinds of development. Thus a majority of Welsh people could conceivably find themselves ranged on the other side of the divide, along with the 'foreign' enemy. Alternative interpretations address this possibility. Day (1984) suggests that there are a number of distinct strands which come together within ethnic and regional consciousness in Wales, in ways which both enable and handicap the achievement of nationalist aims. Given the development of new differentiations in working-class positions, and the relative expansion of most forms of middle-class employment, there is now a bewildering variety of potential specific local class configurations, and (as we have seen in the example of rural Wales) the very real possibility that different population segments can occupy the same space while living in fundamentally different economic worlds, and displaying quite disparate cultural and political perspectives. This signifies new levels of fluidity within Welsh society, and new possibilities for ideological alignment.

Three particular components are examined which have contributed towards the growth of national consciousness during the twentieth century. First, there is an expanding administrative, professional and clerical work-force which stands to gain from the steady expansion of the machinery of government and administration within Wales. Over time, a significant apparatus of governmental and semi-governmental organizations has been created, which has developed a momentum of its own, as more and more institutions appear to take their place within a network of regional or 'national' bodies (Day, 1980). These provide substantial numbers of jobs and career opportunities for a 'bureaucratic' middle class which can present itself as responsible for, and representative of, the population at large. Much of this growth has occurred in Cardiff. Members of this grouping are characterized as relatively pragmatic supporters of the regionalist consensus which was described by Rees and Lambert (1981). Alongside the professional and instrumental pressures they exert, there exist the demands made by adherents of a more traditional vision of Wales and the Welsh heritage, led by a cultural intelligentsia who have been radicalized by the crisis of the language and the associated aspects of the 'Welsh way of life'. The two factions strike an uneasy partnership, but together can wield an effective fusion of 'expressive cultural nationalism and middle class pres-sure' (Day, 1984: 45) . Finally there are those who feel they are capable of doing a better job of managing Wales than the existing state and state agen-cies, which have been failing consistently to cope with recurrent problems of development and equity. These come closest perhaps to Khleif's 'new' middle class, consisting as they do of well-educated, technocratic and polit-ically adept individuals frustrated by the conviction that things would improve if they were able to wrest control from the established power-holders. At the time of writing, Day instanced the group who had drawn up Plaid Cymru's *Economic Plan for Wales* in the late 1960s, and shown that they could more than match the ranks of Welsh Office officials working on the same task; but the description might fit equally well the nexus of academics, experts and consultants which Lovering (1999a) later identified as proponents of the 'new regionalism'. Having distinguished these diverse factions, an attempt is made to map them onto the territory of Welsh pol-itics, and especially some of the divisions then current within Welsh nationalism. The conclusion reached is that they present a difficult chal-lenge for any attempt to weld them together into a single force, because when explored in depth, the rival positions they represent invoke irrecon-cilable conceptions of how national interests should be defined and national boundaries set; but this is difficult to address openly without casting doubt on the belief that they share a common ethnic and national situation.

The most explicit sociological treatment of the relationship between social classes and nationalist politics in Wales is by Adamson (1991a). So far as more recent developments are concerned, he is interested mainly in the economic and social restructuring that has taken place in industrial/urban south Wales, and its impact on the traditional Welsh working class. As already described, Adamson sees this as having become split, with an upwardly mobile section breaking away as it has been lifted into new types of jobs and situations, including larger numbers of non-manual occupations or forms of 'mental' work. This change in economic structure has disturbed the solidarities and patterns of class consciousness associated with old-style communities and occupations, and weakened the hold of established, and by now rather hidebound, Labourism. Growing elements within the working class are freed from previous constraints to find new, and alternative, political and ideological positions. Prominent among these is nationalism, which is attuned to their sense of Welsh identity, and carries memory traces of earlier radical and egalitarian achievements. It also holds out new solutions to the problems of regional development and political control. Hence it is the 'new working class', together with elements of the urban middle class, which begins to find nationalism an attractive option. As Adamson (1991a: 168) puts it:

> nationalism can be seen as the ideological response of a mobile section of the working class to the failure of labourism to respond to the changing social and political climate of the region. It offered a radicalism and a conception of social justice which was not bound within working-class imagery and culture but was not entirely alien to it.

This explains why from the 1960s onwards the Welsh national party, Plaid Cymru, began to make inroads into the previously massive dominance of the South Wales Labour Party. Initially construed as an ephemeral 'protest vote', Adamson argued that this signalled a more permanent change. Subsequent events, especially the results of the first elections to the National Assembly of Wales, when Labour suffered heavy defeats in a number of its 'core' valley constituencies, would seem to confirm that Plaid Cymru has indeed become the main rival to Labour. Thus, within Wales, it could be said that nationalism has provided a platform from which to challenge Labour's historic hold over working-class supporters. In other comparable industrial centres where there was no such possibility, the British Labour Party has had to grapple with other forms of 'third-party' politics, until eventually reaching some resolution in its transmogrification to 'New Labour', with a programme directed mainly at the middle groups

within British social structure (usually represented somewhat euphemisti-
cally and nationalistically as 'middle England'). Following Adamson, in
Wales the same middle groups can exercise a degree of choice, between
British-oriented Labour and a stronger sense of Welsh identity.

As will be evident by now, the social bases of support for Welsh nationalism can be construed in a variety of ways, which include: the
marginalized population; the 'new' working class; the 'new' middle class;
as well as several more restricted subgroups and fractions. Despite these
differences, which reflect the way in which commentators draw upon
different phases of Welsh politics, and developments in different parts of
Wales, to arrive at their conclusions, there is some underlying agreement
that, as a set of beliefs and political practices, it is not possible to reduce
nationalism to class interests in any simple way. Rather, it appears to offer a
means of drawing different groups together into alliances. Its ability to do
so is aided by the extent to which as an ideological cement it is 'free-
floating' (Adamson, 1991a), 'malleable' (Day, 1984) or exceptionally flexible
(Day and Suggett, 1985). That is, contrary to some efforts to give nationalism a fixed class location, it does not belong inherently to any one
particular class. It is not, for example, an intrinsically 'bourgeois' ideology,
as has often been suggested (Nairn, 1977). This leaves it an open question
how far the boundaries that come to be defined around national groupings
correspond to economic, spatial or cultural differences (Day, 1984: 49). The
fact that the correspondence is imperfect allows much room for the ideological work of constructing ethnic and national identities, which may
serve to simplify and harden boundaries, perhaps by accentuating certain
cultural features and playing down economic similarities which cut across
them. An example would be Williams's anticipation of a political opposition that is 'naturally' conducted 'in the name of the people rather than the
proletariat' (G. Williams, 1985: 333). In other words, the shared economic
positions which would place people together into the working class (or
proletariat) could come to be over-ridden by an appeal to the national or
ethnic differences setting them apart. This would be 'natural' only in the
sense that it is easy to construct such an appeal, perhaps because the gap
between ethnic groupings has grown particularly wide. At the same time, it
is difficult to conceive of ways of stating a nationalist platform that would
be equally attractive to all of the diverse social groups listed above, span-
ning the range from the rising elements of a service class to the excluded
and deprived marginalized classes. As with other forms of 'third way' or
'new' politics, holding such a combination together would be a very tricky
exercise. These problems are not confined to 'practising' nationalists, nor to
politicians: the tensions and strains that exist within and between
competing definitions of Welshness become an everyday problem for Welsh

people to solve; the creation and retention of their distinctive national identity is an intensely practical problem.

FROM NATIONALISM TO NATIONAL IDENTITIES

Adamson attributes universal qualities to nationalism, as a form of political practice that is manifested in many contexts and many forms (1991a: 176). In a similar vein Day and Suggett suggest that it is one of the ever-present ways in which people can become conscious of their social existence as it is transformed over time (1985: 98). However, in neither of these sources is nationalism regarded as a rigid bloc of ideas which neatly corresponds to a given social class, class fraction, or even ethnic collectivity. Instead, the emphasis is on the way in which the many elements which make up nationalism can be deployed situationally, in order to bring together into alliance some particular combination of potentially disparate elements, that otherwise might go off in a variety of directions. The capacity to do so effectively depends upon the fuzziness and uncertainty of national identities, and the room this allows for creative uses of ambiguity. Selective emphases, and an ability to turn a blind eye to certain realities, play an important part in this.

While nationalism, as an ideology, is possibly escapable by some, national identity is far harder to avoid. Often it seems as if the world is inherently subdivided into nations and nation-states, although commentaries show that historically these are a relatively recent invention (Hobsbawm, 1990; Miller, 1995). The same could be said of ethnicity. In a social universe organized along ethnic lines, everyone must have an ethnic position, since membership is conferred by either inclusion or exclusion; if you are not part of an ethnic group, then by definition you become absorbed into its ethnic 'other'. It is only comparatively lately that this has become generally accepted in sociology, where previously there had been an inclination to follow popular usage in regarding ethnicity as something which only minorities possessed, as if the majority constituted an ethnicity-free zone. In Britain, there has been an added difficulty in getting the same sort of recognition for 'local' varieties of ethnicity as has been accorded to more exotic versions. The inclusion of examinations of the nature of Scottishness, or Irish or Welsh identities, alongside those of black or Asian Britishness, has been unusual (Brah et al., 1999), and it is still the ethnic nature of the English which tends to provide the unspoken norm. Recent controversy in relation to the 'ethnic' categories employed in the British Census of Population has highlighted this.

For respondents in Wales, the 2001 census form presented scope to nominate themselves as British, Irish or 'Other White', as well as providing tick boxes for those regarding themselves as Asian, Black, Chinese, Other or Mixed categories, and various subdivisions thereof. There was no designated space for 'Welsh' identifiers, nor indeed for those who regarded themselves as 'English'. In Scotland, the Scottish Parliament ensured the inclusion of a 'Scottish' option. A campaign was mounted for the inclusion of the Welsh as a category, failing which some people said they would refuse to complete the form; several thousand signatures were collected for a petition to Parliament on the matter, and a boycott was organized by the fringe 'Independent Wales' Party. The anger expressed in Wales during this episode was part of a generally heightened sensitivity to matters of ethnic affiliation and identity. In the period surrounding the taking of the census a number of examples of name-calling and ethnic stereotyping occurred, the most notorious of which were the much-publicized comments of a well-known television presenter on a BBC light-entertainment programme, who rehashed an ancient joke to ask what the Welsh were for. This was referred for consideration to the Race Relations Board, as was the case of another broadcaster whose job with a Welsh company was not renewed, allegedly because his voice sounded insufficiently Welsh. Identity questions do appear to have taken on a new urgency.

In common with most sociological approaches to national identity, there has been a tendency to frame questions about what it means to be Welsh within an examination of the nature and politics of nationalism as a more or less explicit ideology. More recently, however, the argument has been developed that it is necessary to separate investigation of national identities from the study of nationalism, in order to gain a better understanding of how the two are related (Thompson et al., 1999; Fevre and Thompson, 1999). On the whole, the major theories of nationalism have not concerned themselves with discovering how individuals make sense of questions of national identity through their social relationships and interactions with others. It is apparent, for example, that many of the English migrants and visitors who come to Wales have never given a moment's thought to the identity of the Welsh, or to those characteristics which might make them in any way different. It is only when they begin to interact with Welsh people that these become matters of real importance. Frequently the immediate responses are banal and ill-considered – such as the belief that Welsh is spoken only in order to exclude (and comment upon) outsiders, or that all Welsh people are besotted with rugby football. These notions can quickly become the stuff of crude stereotyping and hostile social relations. Other, more favourable generalizations can be just as crude – that all Welsh people are musical, emotional, hospitable and so on.

Fortunately, as Noragh Jones (1993) and others have begun to show, it is possible to advance beyond such positions, and there can be considerable depth and subtlety to the ways in which particular individuals then think through the problem of what exactly constitutes the nature of national or ethnic difference. Yet, despite their disagreements about the origins and nature of nationality, the main theoretical approaches to nationalism have tended to take for granted the essential uniformity of the national identity towards which nationalism is directed. In other words, they have assumed that the nation means the same thing for all those involved, and that the various rituals and symbols of nationhood carry identical meanings for everyone who responds to them; nationality then forms the basis of a more-or-less homogeneous collective identity. Of course, this is precisely what nationalism tries to achieve, for instance through the way in which it seeks to construct an agreed history of the nation, or to assert its underlying and essential traits and characteristics. In these terms, 'nationalism as an ideology is concerned with the structuring of the nation as a "people", and as such is oriented towards concealing differences rather than recognizing them' (Thompson et al., 1999: 53). This, however, is the desired outcome of nationalist ideology, rather than its precondition. Nationalists must work to create such a sense of identity, and to minimize divisive variations and contradictions among their followers.

In recent years there have been some particularly graphic examples of the processes through which national identities can be manufactured and polished, for example, among Croats, Chechens and Eritreans. They rely upon the cultivation of beliefs and practices which draw a particular group together, while exaggerating the distance between it and those who are felt not to belong. Prior to such work, there is scope for a multiplicity of operational definitions of national identity. These are the product of negotiations and interactions among individuals and groups, much of whose work is done at a local level, as people utilize their various experiences in local social contexts (Thompson and Day, 1999; McCrone et al., 1998). Attitudes to Welshness and Englishness, and resulting conceptions of identity, may be affected most critically by what happens at the school gates, in the local shop, in the playground, or at work, rather than by arguments conducted at the political level. Consequently the nature of national identity has to be treated as eminently contested and constructed. A number of significant recent contributions have drawn attention to the everyday (Billig, 1995) and flexible (Jenkins, 1995; Calhoun, 1997) nature of nationalism and national identity. This is a lesson which has been taken on board by those interested in the analysis of the formation of Welsh identities. There has been an increasing interest in the many ways of being Welsh which coexist at a given time.

While there are always plenty who are prepared to propose their own particular identity as exceptionally tortured and difficult, it is invidious and unnecessary to try to rate contrasting identities for their relative complexity. Sociological work on identity amply demonstrates that no identity is simple (Jenkins, 1996). More and more it is coming to be recognized that in some senses we are all mongrels and hybrids, whose identities can be interpreted in a variety of ways (Hall, 1996). Still, it is widely accepted that Welsh identity is hard to pin down. Thus Welshness has been described as 'an amorphous and variable collection of cultural and social attributes' (C. H. Williams, 1982b: 186), as a 'graded phenomenon' (Osmond, 1985: p. xix) and as 'especially complex' in nature (Wyn Jones and Trystan, 1999: 73). The history of the language issue alone has created a 'crisis in identity' (Howell and Baber, 1990), as well as an identity in crisis. Furthermore, we have seen how commentators who have examined the various factions and positions within Welsh nationalism have suggested a number of different and competing conceptions of the social underpinnings which lay beneath them, beginning with Rawkins's (1979) distinctions between the economic modernizers, the cultural traditionalists and the militants. During the 1960s and 1970s these groupings engaged in an intense struggle to redefine the 'true' nature of Welshness. This made it clear that even among those who were committed to a nationalist political agenda, a plurality of meanings attached to being Welsh, according to the social and class locations of those involved. It is reasonable to suppose that, as Wales has become a more diverse and fragmented place, so the number of possible varieties of Welshness have increased, and the scope for unifying them together within a single framework of political or ideological assumptions has declined. This is because 'the question of "What is Wales" remains unanswered, and may never be answered, given the dynamic nature of social and cultural change. It certainly indicates that no single concept of Wales is stabilized' (Williams and Morris, 2000: p. xxxii; cf. G. Williams, 1984).

WAYS OF BEING WELSH

The complications of Welshness, and the uneven development of different forms of Welsh identities, have been tackled in a number of ways. At the most general level, broad distinctions have been identified between different orientations towards national labels. Balsom's 'three Wales model' (Balsom, 1985; Balsom et al., 1984) rests on distinctions derived from survey data in which people are asked to designate themselves Welsh, British, English or other. At the time of the 1979 general election it was determined that 57 per cent of those surveyed termed themselves Welsh, and 34 per cent British. When these categories were cross-classified according to ability to speak Welsh, three distinct sociolinguistic groupings emerged, corresponding to different parts of Wales: *Y Fro Gymraeg*, Welsh Wales and British Wales. The latter consisted of the eastern flank of the country together with an outlying area centred on Pembrokeshire. How individuals identified themselves was a good predictor of the structure of their political support: only in British Wales was there significant Conservative support, while Plaid Cymru's stronghold was confined to *Y Fro Gymraeg*. Balsom accepted that the results from such surveys would vary over time; 1979 happened to be rather a low point in Welsh self-confidence, so he contended that his figure for Welsh-identifiers had some solidity. Osmond (1985) also notes that survey results tend to oscillate somewhat, following events and external influences, making identity appear a variable quality. The prospects for an effective assertion of Welsh nationhood were seen to depend upon the 'wide distribution and pervasive character of a sense of Welsh identity' (Balsom, 1985: 13). The failure to specify the nature of the underpinning 'culture' and its causal impact has been said to make this analysis no more than a 'journalistic venture' lacking substance (Williams and Morris, 2000: p. xxix).

Balsom argued that the changes taking place in the valleys area of 'Welsh Wales' were exerting the greatest pressure on the long-term viability of a separate Welsh identity; since Welshness there was not anchored in the language, the increasing loss of economic and social distinctiveness in industrial south Wales was narrowing the likely appeal of nationalism. Balsom's expectation that the proportion of the population regarding themselves as British rather than Welsh was likely to increase has not been borne out by events. In a study of the 1997 devolution vote, Wyn Jones and Trystan (1999) found that 63 per cent of their sample declared themselves to be Welsh, and only 26 per cent British. Surveying opinion in the valleys, Adamson and Jones (1996) recorded as many as 85 per cent calling themselves Welsh, and only 9 per cent British. Roberts (1995) also notes a revitalization of 'Valleys Welshness'. Yet it is also recognized that results such as these can be misleading, since people may not regard Welsh and British as completely exclusive categories. In fact, when Wyn Jones and Trystan asked respondents to place themselves on the Moreno scale, which tries to measure national identity along a continuum, it was found that 68 per cent of those questioned saw themselves as some *combination* of Welsh and British; only 17 per cent said they felt solely Welsh, while another 12 per cent regarded themselves as British, but not Welsh. Respondents who were further towards the 'Welsh end of the spectrum' (Wyn Jones and Trystan, 1999: 74) were found to be more likely to turn out to vote, and more likely to favour the establishment of a Welsh assembly.

A large number of people in Wales thus appear to operate with dual, or overlapping, national identities; to varying degrees they are simultaneously

Welsh and British. In a plural society, there is nothing especially astonishing about this: 'Wales' and 'Britain' form different levels within a hierarchy of identifications which stretch from the local, and parochial, to the continental, and global (Jenkins, 1997: 41). The material from which they are constructed is not packaged into nice tidy bundles, but is messy and ill-defined. This means that people have to concern themselves with drawing boundaries and deciding what it is that they contain. Different identities nest within one another (Herb and Kaplan, 1999; Thompson et al. 1999). So, in different contexts and for different purposes, someone may see themselves as hailing from Pontypridd and the valleys, a south Walian, Welsh, British and European, while another is self-defined as from Anglesey, a Welsh-speaker (*Cymro-Cymraeg*), north Walian, Welsh, European – but not British. To explain these identities, each would have to provide some ostensive definition; for instance, one individual might associate Britishness with the monarchy, a colonial power, and the celebration of Englishness, whereas for the other it signifies a shared history of fighting wars, inventing sports or establishing ideals of mutual welfare. Such definitions are not idly constructed, but develop together, often in contradistinction, through an elaborate history of interaction and exchange. As Jenkins (1997) insists, the 'plurality' of Wales is not new; for thousands of years it has been created by the movements of individuals and groups across territory, by engagement with its neighbours (not just England, but also Ireland, and continental Europe), and by involvement in many streams of tradition and discourse. Consequently Wales is characterized 'internally by diversity and, in its external relations, by its open and much-trampled cultural boundaries' (Jenkins, 1997: 150).

Jenkins cites as one definition of Welshness that proposed by Howell and Baber, namely that Wales is distinguished by 'separate history, instinctive radicalism in religion and politics, contempt for social pretentiousness, personal warmth and exuberance, sociability, love of music and near obsession with rugby' (Howell and Baber, 1990: 354). Jenkins notes that this is a gendered construction; it could also be said to be south Walian in some of its aspects. More to the point, it is a compendium of clichés and half-truths which belong more within the realm of speculation and self-assessment than reasoned truth. Yet this is exactly how most such descriptions and classifications work! Usually they represent the most rough and ready sort of empirical generalization, as noteworthy for what is left out as for what is included. Howell and Baber put up their definition in conscious counterpoint to an alternative version, focused on the Welsh language, which they would see as excluding those 'English-speaking Welshmen' (such as themselves?) who would 'spiritedly and justifiably' assert their own distinctive Welshness. Hence its full significance can be grasped only in conjunction with the meanings attached to this alternative construction.

Distinctions of this kind are not invented merely for the sake of it; they serve a vital social purpose. Jenkins suggests that the various levels in the hierarchy of identity can be distinguished according to the sort of consequences they carry; each of them invokes particular ideas of rights and responsibilities, forms of social recognition and access to economic and social resources (Jenkins, 1997: 41). Each of them lays claim, through processes of inclusion and exclusion, to certain entitlements. Thus there are many Welsh people who feel 'excluded, patronized and devalued' (Jenkins, 1997: 150) by being treated as second-rate citizens because they do not speak Welsh; while, on the other side, there are those who feel just as affronted by those who proclaim themselves to be Welsh without possessing what they believe to be the key qualification. These differences matter, if only because they are used to legitimize demands and decisions said to be made on behalf of Wales and the Welsh. At a wider spatial level, they work in just the same way as the various definitions of community which are deployed more locally to privilege the views and opinions of some local residents over those of others (Day and Murdoch, 1993; Cloke et al., 1997).

WELSHNESS AND 'RACE'

Richard Jenkins refers to the existence of a strand of 'authoritarian and exclusionary' linguistic-nationalist rhetoric in Wales which purports to lay down such rights and responsibilities. We have seen relevant instances, as well as counter-examples of positions which seek to deny their validity. Where disagreements occur, these can become stated in quite ferocious terms, and this can intrude even into the quiet waters of academic discourse. Examining some of the threads which go to make up the various positions within Welsh nationalism, Denney et al. (1991) raise what they term the 'inevitable allegation' that Welsh nationalism, as and when it becomes more 'extreme' in its methods and rhetoric, is also led towards 'racism'. They do not actually provide a specific instance of this allegation being made, although as has been noted before, it would be possible to provide empirical examples of claims of both racism and a desire for 'ethnic cleansing' being made either way across the Welsh linguistic divide. Using illustrations from a number of literary and political sources, Denney et al. deconstruct nationalist positions into a set of ideal types – that is, purified abstractions which are not necessarily to be found empirically in exactly that form, but which help towards the analysis of a complex reality. Among these categorizations there is indeed said to be a position of racial separatism, in which Welshness appears to be traced to a genetic foundation of blood and kinship, which needs to be kept unpolluted by alien influences. This is said to provide the justification for the more violent kinds of resistance offered to potential threats, including legitimations (though not practices) of physical violence. However, it is also seen as a marginal influence within nationalism in Wales.

The other two positions identified are seen as more central. One consists of a sociolinguistic approach, which combines the defence of the Welsh language and associated culture with an attack on the capitalist economic order that is held to be undermining it. This is held to be close to the views of the Welsh Language Society. Finally, there is a position of cultural pluralism, advocated more recently by Plaid Cymru, which works within the democratic process, through parliamentary means, but aims to gain separate institutions for Wales, within a European context. This position shows greater confidence about the capacity of Wales to assimilate and absorb new influences. Each of these positions is held to relate to a particular way of defining the 'imagined community' of Welshness. All three draw on a common stock of ideas about community, smallness, rurality and the importance of the *gwerin*, but the distinctions between them reveal some 'basic differences in the way in which nationalism is conceptualized and acted upon' (Denney et al., 1991: 161). Hence once again Welsh nationalism is shown to be a highly differentiated type of movement. Despite the suspect traces that are revealed, the accusation of racism is found to be not proven.

The methodology employed in this analysis, by developing ideal types, explicitly seeks to tease out distinctions and to create separations where they may not exist in reality. Thus it is entirely likely that elements of all three positions could be found interacting with one another in particular settings and contexts. For example, the much celebrated poetry of R. S. Thomas, which provides one of the quoted sources, is far too complex to be reduced to any single set of meanings, so that any 'racist' element within it, if it is present at all, must coexist in highly complex ways with other aspects, such as Christianity (Wintle, 1996). Similarly, the debates and schisms which have occurred at various points within Plaid Cymru mean that any given statement of its political position has only a provisional quality. More recent problems faced by the party in deciding how to respond to statements about migration originating from within its ranks underline this; there is no single, automatic reflex response which represents the party's standpoint. There is then a problem about the extent to which conclusions about varieties of nationalism can be reached from a limited set of key texts and examples. It was partly on such methodological grounds that Denney et al. came in for severe criticism from Glyn Williams (1994). Writing from the standpoint of discourse theory, as developed especially by French social theorists, Williams argued that the body of material ('corpus') used was inadequate and selective. Furthermore, he sees the authors as having a 'conspiratorial' view of nationalist thought, which enables them to trace its development and meaning back to the motives and intentions of various individuals and agents, whereas discourse theory tries to 'decentre' the subject and provide an internal account of the way in which a particular discourse works – its pattern of coherence – that enables a more objective reading of its meaning. This is said to eliminate the risky business of attributing subjective motivations. In other words, there are quite fundamental differences of theory and method between the critic and the criticized, which represent distinct, and probably irreconcilable, positions within social analysis.

However, there is also a strong vein of polemic running through the attack, which if one was not wholly persuaded by French discourse theory it might be tempting to attribute to the motivations of a conscious 'subject'. The arguments put forward by Denney et al. are said to exemplify an 'aggrieved ethnocentrism', appropriate to 'transient voyeurs' casting their eyes over a country to which they do not belong (Williams, 1994: 87, 95). Their approach is interpreted as an attempt to 'pathologize' minority culture, by attributing to it 'mystical' and mythical properties, and denying it reason. This places it within the 'modernist', evolutionary discourse said to typify most sociology (Williams and Morris, 2000). There are a number of interesting features of the way in which the argument proceeds, which amount to a statement of who can say what about Wales. The work of Hechter, who at the time of writing *Internal Colonialism* had never been to Wales, is accorded an authority denied to a group of academics each of whom had lived in the country. The ability to speak Welsh is said to confer an insight into the cited texts that is denied to those who have not mastered the language – even though all the texts in question were written in English (including those by R. S. Thomas). As the editors of the journal in which the exchange appeared state, there is clearly far more at stake here than a dispute about modes of sociological analysis. In a thoroughly reflexive and 'postmodern' fashion, these contributions made by sociologists (working at the time within the same academic department) form part of the very discourse of Welshness and nationhood which they are investigating. As Williams concludes, this brings into question the extent to which any sociological account can pretend to be able to have the final word about the 'truth' of national identity. However, few now would adhere to the model of an objective social science which is capable of ascertaining such absolute truths.

At the end of his article, Williams emphasizes how very different 'his' conception of Wales is likely to be from that of the three authors to whom he is responding. He also wishes to make space for a conception (probably different again) of Wales which involves 'English language, sport, religion etc.' (1994: 91). Hence it is apparent to him that 'Wales'

> achieves a variety of meanings within discourse, there being no such thing/ place as Wales outside discourse. The meaning of Wales is not only variable, but it is a matter of struggle to locate it in the symbolic where it achieves significance. (Williams, 1994: 101)

Although the term 'racism' is bandied about rather freely in this exchange, few contemporary meanings of Wales and Welshness rely on racial reasoning in any strict sense. That is, they do not attribute the properties of Welshness, in whatever form it is construed, to biological or genetic inheritances. However, in the looser sense in which the term 'racism' tends to be used at present, there are numerous prominent forms and practices of cultural and social exclusion which come close to deserving the epithet. Things are said about the Welsh, and about other ethnic groupings in Wales, especially the English, which if transposed onto different ethnic categories (such as 'Asians' or 'blacks') would immediately be taken as statements of racism. The appropriation of the term 'white settlers' to refer to non-Welsh migrants, a usage borrowed from Scotland, itself makes a direct link to the use of racial categories, while also seeking to align the Welsh, who for the most part are white, with racially oppressed groups who are not. Taking up Jenkins's point (1997: 167) about how nominal identifications can summon up virtualities of various sorts – such as rights and responsibilities – it becomes apparent that there are serious weaknesses in the vocabularies available to people with which they can make, and refute, legitimate claims of this type. Discussions about the impact of migration on local communities lure people into saying things which rely upon generalizations of the same kind as are employed in debates about 'race' – that 'they' (migrants or locals) all do this, or that, in a deterministic way, as if 'they' are clones of one another. Individual variations are lost within the categorical language of distance, and differentiation. As a result, it becomes hard to make points in an acceptable manner, or to engage in rational debate about how the boundaries of 'community' should be defined, and maintained, or adapted and developed, without giving offence. Yet time and again when people are challenged for what they have said, they deny that they are in any way being 'racist'. Rather, they say that their aim is to defend that which is theirs, and to clarify what social expectations attach to 'membership' of a particular community.

Issues of race, ethnicity and consequent social inclusion and exclusion remain extremely delicate and touchy matters in Wales and, as Williams concedes, Denney and his collaborators have shown some bravery in confronting these issues. Interestingly, by contrast to the heat with which these relationships between the Welsh and non-Welsh (English) have been discussed, there has been very limited debate in relation to the position of the 'non-white' ethnic minorities in Wales, those for whom the issue of 'race' and its effects is usually seen as most relevant (C. Williams, 1999a, 1999b). To some extent this reflects the relatively small proportion of ethnic minority individuals living in Wales; with the exceptions of Cardiff (6 per cent) and Newport (3.5 per cent) the proportions of ethnic minority residents at county level range between 0.5 per cent and 1.3 per cent of the population. The overall figure for Wales in 1991 was 1.5 per cent. The fact that the majority of these individuals reside in the main cities of south Wales makes it possible for most to see 'race' as a south Wales issue (C. Williams, 1999a: 274). A sizeable section of this minority population is long-established, and has its roots in the imperial role of Wales, and the part played by its dock industries. Historically, as well as in more recent years, there have been a number of examples of racial violence and hostility occurring across Wales (Evans, 1991), that are at odds with the self-image of Wales as a peculiarly tolerant and hospitable nation. Examining this gap between popular impressions and historical reality, Charlotte Williams traces it to the influence of the ideology of the *gwerin*, and notes the limitations whereby this conception, which is based upon an idea of cultural homogeneity, leads people to cling to an 'imagining of sameness and . . . a view of culture as fixed and static rather than fluid and ever changing' (1999a: 277). She argues that the construction of Welshness with which it is associated, in which the Welsh are seen as naturally sensitive to the sufferings of others as a consequence of their own experiences of cultural oppression, has led to a degree of complacency and collective amnesia, and thence to the silencing of 'race' as a topic for discussion. Yet hard evidence shows that people from ethnic minority backgrounds living in Wales are no less likely to experience inequalities of opportunity and condition than those in other parts of Britain; for instance, unemployment rates among ethnic minority workers are far in excess of those seen among whites. As yet, Williams remains the exception in seeking to broaden the range of discussion in relation to varieties of ethnicity and forms of exclusion and inclusion in Wales.

WELSHNESS AS PRODUCTION AND PERFORMANCE

For the most part the work sociologists and political scientists have done on Welsh nationalism and national identity has been confined to creating typologies or classifications which do not succeed in getting a complete hold on the *processual* nature of identity formation. Taken as a snapshot at a given point in time, survey data of the kind used by Balsom or Wyn Jones are not able to illuminate the ways in which identities are formed or changed, and therefore can generate only a restricted set of possibilities – particularly when, like the census classification, they rely on fixed categories of answers. In contrast to the choice Balsom offers between three, virtually fixed, versions of Welshness, Roberts (1995) finds in his study of social imagery in the valley communities of Blaina and Nantyglo that people are capable of innovating new and unexpected possibilities. In the face of the changing social and economic circumstances of the valleys, and especially the diminishing influence and clarity of class identities, valley people are exploring new kinds of Welsh identity, which are neither 'British', nor the same as what is conventionally understood as Welshness in Welsh-speaking Wales. As they reshape their understandings of Welshness, his respondents are simultaneously redefining their 'imagined' communities. They are well aware of aspects of exclusion and closure in the way in which others, particularly Welsh-speakers, relate to them, but they also perceive common ground and some sort of shared historic background. The result is that identity becomes a source of 'deep sensitivities and confusions'. Roberts advocates the development of 'a more complex model for the interpenetration of social identities . . . which takes more fully into account local situated experience and relationships with other sources of identity' (1995: 82).

The argument that different variants of 'nationalist' or national identification are intimately connected with struggles to gain or maintain control over particular places and their various assets and resources has been expanded upon in a series of publications by Borland, Denney and Fevre. Slightly revising their earlier classification (Denney et al., 1991), they identify at least four different versions of 'community' which are utilized in the politics of cultural contestation in north-west Wales, as ways of responding to, or resisting, the threat of metropolitan/English domination (Borland et al., 1992; Fevre et al., 1999; Borland et al., 2001). Each definition provides a specification of who it is that has the right to speak for the region, and to expect privileged access to its goods, and helps as well to indicate an appropriate strategy for implementing these rights and expectations. Thus the conception of north Wales as an 'open' community to which all can have access implies acceptance of a positive multiculturalism, associated with ideas of 'citizenship' for all those who live within Wales, whereas the 'racially closed' conception of community boundaries more obviously relates to an attempt to maintain closure through various types of exclusion, such as efforts to close off particular kinds of jobs, control housing assets and so on. There are said to be two versions of the 'culturally closed' community in operation, which do not depend upon assertions of 'racial' distinctiveness, but employ religious or secular definitions of appropriate qualifications for membership. An ability to speak Welsh is the lynchpin of the secular form. These contrasting possibilities constitute different ways of 'doing' Welsh nationalism, or of 'being' Welsh, in north Wales. They act as mobilizing concepts, which stimulate people into action whenever there is a perceived threat to one of these versions of community. In these terms, the response to population change and inward migration in north Wales can be seen as mediated through the existing constructs of community and national identity; rather than excessive migration 'stirring up' nationalism, it is nationalism which makes migration, and its effects, seem excessive (Fevre et al., 1999). At the same time, each of the constructions is itself a potential site of conflict and resistance. Their coexistence and interplay demonstrates how 'nation-building which seeks after fixed categorizations is denying its own reality' (Borland et al., 2002). On the contrary, it is suggested, the differing definitions may be of use to a nationalist move-ment, since they can be deployed pragmatically in different contexts, and for different audiences. For this to be successful, however, the inconsisten-cies and contradictions among them would have to be insulated from one another, a very difficult thing to accomplish in everyday political practice.

A more detailed insight into the organization of one particular version of Welshness is provided by an American anthropologist, Carol Trosset, who learned Welsh so as to gain access to the social milieu of those who live within the medium of the language. Trosset's aim was to discover what was fundamental and shared within Welsh culture, and why it was that 'out of all the experiences lived in Wales, only some are popularly deemed to have any ethnic significance' (Trosset, 1993: 54). For those who speak Welsh, she argues, there is a dominant ideology which revolves around the centrality of the language, and a cluster of activities and values which are associated with it. These include participation in *eisteddfodau*, with the peripatetic National Eisteddfod as the crowning event; preferences for Welsh-language over English-language media; and the adherence to certain distinctive styles of behaviour and conduct. This is a world-view which Borland et al. would characterize as culturally closed. For some, it is possible to live almost entirely within an environment dominated by these traits; but even for those who do not, according to Trosset, the ideology is 'hegemonic' since it sets standards for and influences the views of everyone who lives in Wales – all Welsh people either think within this frame of reference, or have to respond to the way in which others use it.

Two aspects of Trosset's analysis of this construction are particularly relevant here. First, she argues that people can be ranked in varying levels of 'Welshness' according to the extent to which they conform with these ideological expectations. Those who show exemplary commitment to the performance of 'ethnically relevant activities' hold positions close to the centre of the conceptual system. For instance, they speak 'good' Welsh, actively contribute to the Welsh media or perform in and/or adjudicate at competitive festivals. Those who do so form a close-knit cultural elite which is able to set the terms on which Welsh ethnicity is defined and allocated. In a social, rather than merely geographical sense, it is they who occupy the Welsh 'heartland'. Secondly, this is not the only distinction which is operating to classify and divide the population of Wales; in fact there are many competing forms of identification, including regional and local loyalties, religious and political affiliations, such that Wales resembles a series of superimposed jigsaw puzzles of boundaries and memberships. The end result is a pattern of social organization which can be described as 'sectarian' (Douglas and Wildavsky, 1982) through which different groups of rival insiders compete with each other to see who exemplifies most purely the qualities of the true insider (Trosset, 1993: 57). Essentially this argument generalizes for all of Wales, or at least for 'Welsh Wales', the model of cross-cutting affiliations put forward by Frankenberg (1957) and others as typical of the small Welsh rural community. Frankenberg of course pointed to the enormous value of finding or creating an external enemy or 'stranger' onto whom these divisions and disagreements could be displaced.

Even amongst Welsh speakers there are many who will find the dominant ideology as described by Trosset alienating and oppressive. This could be true of anyone who is not part of the cultural elite, or whose knowledge and use of Welsh is found wanting, or who is not a 'native-speaker' but who has acquired Welsh as a second language. Hence the statement that it is 'axiomatic' in much of Gwynedd that 'by learning and, of course, by speaking Welsh one becomes a fuller member of the community' (Bowie, 1993: 179) depends upon whose definition of 'community' one abides by. There are many first-language Welsh speakers who have little interest in or enthusiasm for much of what passes as 'Welsh' culture in the dominant version. For them, as well as others, it is true to say that 'the articulation of Welshness is a chronic process inextricably bound up with the ongoing struggles to define place and "belonging"' (Thompson et al., 1999: 60). These contests occur within the limited spatial zone of north-west Wales, inside *Y Fro Gymraeg*. Local experience, and local knowledge, play a crucial part in shaping how it is that individuals imagine themselves as 'belonging', both locally, and to some wider national community of Wales and the Welsh. Conceptions of Welshness, and non-Welshness, are produced in ongoing social interaction (Thompson and Day, 1999) and are deeply embedded in the routine practices of everyday life in Wales.

WALES – A NATION AGAIN?

Explaining the failure of the 1979 referendum campaign, a supporter of the devolution process in Wales expressed his sense of the incongruity and near-irrelevance of arguments conducted in terms of administrative efficiency, control of bureaucracy and reform of government for those for whom the *raison d'être* of devolution as a recognition and expression of nationhood seemed patently obvious (Foulkes et al., 1983: 174). The existence of two such different forms of discourse surrounding the same process could be interpreted as an expression of the eternal contest between sentiment and strategy, or emotion versus reason (Trosset, 1993: 168). On the one hand, the transfer of political powers is viewed as a recognition of something which already exists, and which has a powerful command over people's loyalties and affections – the nationhood of Wales. On the other, it represents a pragmatic measure to improve government, which in due course possibly may lead towards the development of a stronger sense of nationality. Within the latter position, opponents were liable to see concealed the dangers of a 'slippery slope' towards growing separatism. The relative success of the subsequent devolution proposals of 1997 can then be debated in terms of whether or not they make Wales a nation 'again' (Taylor and Thomson, 1999), so implying the recovery of some lost state of affairs. In this debate the emotion/reason dichotomy surfaces in the form of a choice between basing Welsh governance upon 'ethnic' or 'civic' criteria. This is a distinction which has been at the centre of arguments about nations and nationalism for some time (McCrone, 1998; Brubaker, 1996): do nations represent an instrument of territorial jurisdiction, or are they rooted in 'blood' and a community of descent?

The dilemma is well captured by Aitchison and Carter. In the Welsh case, they suggest, 'all others aspects of separateness having been lost', it might be thought that identity can rest only upon language; consequently

> to be Welsh in any meaningful way, a person must speak, or at least under-
> stand, Welsh. Otherwise he or she is no more than someone dwelling in a
> defined area called Wales; and ethnically, no more than a version of provincial
> English. (Aitchison and Carter 2000: 3)

Now it is manifestly not true of the Scots, or the Irish, that without a distinctive language their identities are merely 'variations on a central theme' of Englishness. The view that without the language 'it is difficult to envisage what being Welsh would mean' misses the multiple nature of nationality and national identity, and the way in which they are constructed out of a cluster of attributes and characteristics. The real danger appears to be that an alternative conception of Welshness might undermine the claims of the Welsh-speaking community within Wales to represent the defining essence of Welsh identity and nationhood.

Yet the risks involved in taking an ethnic stance on the government of Wales appeared to be underlined in the 1997 referendum outcome by the poor turnout and low level of support for the creation of a Welsh assembly. While there was strong backing for this among Welsh speakers, and Plaid Cymru voters, there were large sections of the population who either opposed devolution, or seemed to be altogether detached from the process. This latter group included many of those who were migrants to Wales, and who therefore would be unlikely to feel themselves part of an ethnic conception of Welshness (Wyn Jones and Trystan, 1999; Curtice, 1999). Consequently, the result was an extremely narrow majority of only 6,742 votes in favour of devolution, with barely more than half the eligible electorate taking part. This meant that the National Assembly for Wales came into being without a firm bedrock of legitimacy, faced by a major challenge:

> to embody and imbue a sense of national identity which can incorporate all those living in Wales. Given the heterogeneous nature of the Welsh population, this must inevitably be a civic identity based on identification with institutions and place, and the values they represent, rather than ethnic markers such as place of birth or ancestry (Wyn Jones and Trystan, 1999: 90).

In other words, highlighting ethnic qualifications could only serve to accentuate the divisions within Wales; unity had to be built instead around an alternative set of attachments to social relationships and organizational arrangements. The severity of this task was strengthened by comparisons made with Scotland, and the much greater degree of backing given to plans for a Scottish parliament. Part of the explanation lay in differences of perceived national identity. Whereas survey evidence showed that two-thirds of Scots regarded their identities as primarily or exclusively Scottish, the fragmentation of Wales along 'ethnic' lines meant that only 43 per cent of Welsh respondents put their Welshness first – and only 17 per cent entirely disavowed 'Britishness' (Curtice, 1999). People self-identified as 'British' were less favourable to devolution, and especially fearful of a possible break-up of the United Kingdom. Behind these differences, it has been said, there lie deeper contrasts between the two countries in that the institutional basis for Welsh nationhood is weaker, and less coherent (Paterson and Wyn Jones, 1999).

Although both Wales and Scotland can be numbered among the 'stateless nations' (McCrone, 1992), there are significant differences between them. The union of Wales with England predates that between England and Scotland by some 170 years, and English domination over Wales goes back even further, into at least the thirteenth century. After union, Scotland was able to maintain strong elements of independent national existence, espe-cially its own legal and educational systems, which were lacking in Wales. A sense of Scottish nationality is therefore more firmly set onto the founda-tions of distinct social and political organization. In Wales, the sense of difference has owed more to cultural factors, such as the language and reli-gion, but these have been, and are, internally divisive. Even in the more immediate context of the devolution campaign, Scottish public opinion was led more firmly by those who occupied key institutional positions, acting together within the Constitutional Convention founded in 1989. This brought together politicians, leading figures in the churches, and civic and public dignitaries. In Wales, most of the running was made from within the political parties, which (with the exception of the Conservatives, who remained intransigently hostile) were able to achieve only a belated and limited rapprochement around the goal of establishing an assembly with strictly limited powers. Thus, despite the steady build-up of a range of state and quasi-state agencies and national bodies and organizations from the late nineteenth century onwards (Day, 1980), Wales could be said still to lack an autonomous and proactive civil society. What institutional appar-atus there was seemed fragile, and inadequately mobilized. Hence rather than reflecting the existence of a nation, the Assembly's creation appeared more like a project to build and animate one (Paterson and Wyn Jones, 1999; Osmond, 1998b; Morgan 2000). The fact that at the first Assembly elections, an even smaller proportion of the population (46 per cent) turned out to vote confirmed that there was a hill to climb to win public commitment to the institution.

The establishment of the National Assembly has stimulated much discus-sion, and a flurry of research about its impact on Welsh society (Osmond, 1998a; Chaney et al., 2001). In the words of Ralph Fevre, devolution has 'turned Wales into the natural laboratory that some social scientists have always thought it might be' (Fevre, 2001), and there is the sense once again that the country is on the cusp of significant change. The Assembly aspires to forge a much closer relationship with Welsh civil society than existed under the old regime of the Welsh Office and Cabinet representation for Wales at Westminster – a system frequently characterized as distant and colonialist. The watchwords for the new regime are participation, accounta-bility, access and empowerment. The sources of this transformation lie both within Wales – in the discontent with 'quangocracy' and the gulf between popular sentiment and the performance of central government – but also in wider commitments to 'modernization' and 'partnership' on the part of the reconstructed New Labour administration which has been in power in Britain since 1997 (Morgan and Mungham, 2000; Day and Thompson, 2001). In the run-up to the formation of the National Assembly for Wales, these aims became subsumed into a guiding concept of 'inclusiveness', which has been incorporated into the machinery of the new institution (Chaney et al., 2000: 48; Day and Thompson, 1999); uniquely, the Assembly has a duty to promote equal opportunities in all its activity. However, the gap between the rhetoric of greater public participation and the reality thus far of lukewarm enthusiasm and disengagement among a majority of the population is clearly enormous. Quite obviously, the divisions and disjunctures within Welsh society cannot be resolved simply by a stroke of the constitutional pen. As has been widely emphasized, devolution must be understood not as an event, but as a continuing process (Davies, 1999).

The presence of the Assembly creates new opportunities and demands for research. It has brought a new awareness of the continuing gaps in our knowledge of contemporary Wales and how its social organization is structured, not least with respect to the collection of relevant statistical information (C. Williams et al., 1999). It is therefore difficult at present to assess the often contradictory claims made about the lack of civic capacity in Wales, and yet the existence of relatively well-integrated networks of personal contacts: the evidence about the range and depth of existing connections in the various arenas of civil society is decidedly mixed (Day et al., 2000). Preliminary investigations of the Assembly's workings, and its attempts to build bridges out into the wider society, have begun to fill in some major knowledge gaps with respect to the position of various kinds of 'minority' groups, such as people with disabilities and members of minority ethnic groupings, as well as providing information on the more general situation of women, and the voluntary sector (Chaney et al., 2000). This has already revealed the limited extent to which identities founded upon disability, faith, language, sexuality, lifestyle and gender have been researched within Wales. There has also been some critical consideration of the meaning of 'inclusiveness', and the extent to which it represents a socially feasible objective. It has been noted that the term has several possible interpretations (Day and Thompson, 1999; Chaney and Fevre, 2001), and that in the course of the devolution campaign its significance tended to broaden out from rather narrow beginnings, as it seemed capable of gathering support from an increasing range of social and political partners. Plaid Cymru, newly named in English as 'the Party of Wales', took the opportunity to reposition itself by endorsing an inclusive philosophy. Stating that it regarded all Welsh people as equal, irrespective of race, creed, colour or language, its leader said that it was 'a national party, but our nationalism is a civic nationalism' (cited in Chaney and Fevre, 2001). In the first elections to the Assembly in May, 1999 Plaid Cymru obtained almost 31 per cent of the vote, and ran Labour a very close second.

Day and Thompson (1999) suggest that at least four distinct meanings of 'inclusiveness' are to be found circulating within the framework of policy statements and discussions about devolution and its contribution to creating the 'new Wales'. The first is *political* and is concerned with holding together some form of agreement across the widest possible span of organized party political opinion. It is addressed primarily to those who are politically active. Secondly, there is a more *civic* meaning, aimed at extending involvement and participation in the democratic process so as to integrate back into it the large numbers of people who had been alienated and disenchanted by the prevailing democratic deficit and crisis of representation in Wales. This seems to be directed towards the preponderance of people in Wales, the 'middle ground'. The third interpretation is more *social* in the sense of seeking to reincorporate into society those particular groups and categories which had previously been subject to processes of social exclusion and marginalization from the mainstream. Here inclusion is directed mainly at the poor, the long-term unemployed, and the deprived former centres of industry. Finally there is the *pluralistic* meaning, according to which an inclusive process is one in which all the diverse voices, interests, and viewpoints within Wales can be heard, a fully inclusive 'empowerment' of the people as they are actually organized in civil society. These alternative conceptions represent outcomes which are increasingly difficult to accomplish, and the last presents a truly profound challenge (Day et al., 1998). To be able to achieve it would require decision-makers to have available to them the most thorough and systematic grasp of the nature of contemporary Welsh society, the extent of diversity and difference within it, and the relevance to it of issues of 'multiculturalism' and new forms of social and political integration which have barely begun to be tested, let alone applied. Providing this depth of understanding presents the social scientific community in Wales with a worthy and substantial challenge for its future efforts.

Conclusion

It has been said that sociologists enjoy picturing themselves astride some major historical watershed, and that this leads them to conceptualize social change as a succession of clear-cut breaks, rather than grasping it as an uneven combination of leads, lags and continuities (Bradley, 1996: 213). In Wales, as has become clear, there is also a temptation continually to hail the new dawn. Bringing these two tendencies together might be expected to result in a great exaggeration of the novelty of current circumstances. Undoubtedly there are deep continuities running through Welsh society, but nevertheless it is apparent that over recent years Wales has been changed, profoundly and irreversibly. The country continues to go through interesting times, partly as a consequence of powerful long-run trends, and partly as a result of unexpected shocks. Two recent examples of the latter were the announcement by Corus, the struggling Anglo-Dutch steel corporation, that it intended to cut back capacity and shed labour, a large part of it in Wales, and the entirely unpredicted outbreak of foot and mouth disease which directly affected two areas of the Welsh countryside (the Brecon Beacons and Anglesey) and did far wider damage to the rural economy through its repercussions for tourism and recreation. During 2001, large parts of the countryside were practically closed to outsiders, magnifying the existing sense of a siege mentality among some of its residents. These events added to the pressures already felt by communities under stress, but the disproportionate response to both situations bears out Dai Smith's contention that perceptions of the Welsh past tend to be more potent than present realities (Smith, 1999: 33).

As the last remaining bastion of traditional heavy industry in Wales, steel makes a significant contribution to the Welsh economy (Fairbrother and Morgan, 2001). In 2000, 12,000 Welsh steelworkers created over £2bn of output, and contributed around £400 million to GDP (WERU, 2001). As well as providing a source of well-paid, mostly full-time employment, it was estimated that for every Corus job there was another employee somewhere in Wales dependent upon it, since 700 of the 2,000 suppliers to Corus's Welsh operations were based in Wales. This meant that the total Welsh job loss arising from the Corus decision approached 6,000. Even so, the strength of the reaction to the Corus plans suggested to some that 'the public and government in Wales remain almost irrationally attached to the industry, out of all proportion to actual employment' (WERU, 2001: 19). There were immediate offers of support, of a kind usually denied to other pressurized manufacturing industries. Some £66m of regeneration money was to be put into the affected communities, along with schemes to provide retraining and help redundant steelworkers with compensation payments. However, the Welsh Assembly proved powerless to halt the redundancies; instead members of the Welsh Economy Research Unit concluded that 'the Corus episode proved that the sum of government, union and public pressure was wholly inadequate to constrain a company who [*sic*] saw its future best served by actions which were seen locally to bear socially divisive and negative consequences'. Shareholder interests came first.

Inevitably, the impact was localized. The closure of Ebbw Vale, with a loss of over 800 jobs, was potentially ruinous locally, whereas it could be argued that the economy of Newport and the M4 corridor was probably large and diverse enough to withstand the redundancies at Llanwern. At Shotton in north Wales the decision meant the loss of a third of the workforce, some 400 jobs, together with a similar number in the supply chain. Although serious, this was nothing like the devastation wrought by previous cuts, when Shotton alone had lost 6,500 steel jobs in 1980 and it could be claimed that no community in living memory had suffered such a loss in so short a period of time (Jones, 2001). Moreover, since most of the Corus workforce resided within a short travelling distance of the steelworks, the impact would be concentrated in a few wards in the county of Flintshire. Given the problems of matching new opportunities to the skills and experiences of the redundant workers, the classic ingredients were present for structural unemployment, much of which would be disguised as non-participation, as older workers withdrew from the labour market. Meanwhile, however, Flintshire succeeded in securing a new Airbus contract at Broughton, together with new investment by Toyota, involving the expected recruitment of some 700 additional aerospace employees and a further 250 or more skilled jobs in auto-engineering. Competition for such vacancies is intense. At Aerospace it is the practice for new recruits to work for up to two years on non-standard agency contracts before being offered normal company terms of employment. Like the rest of Wales, Flintshire has retreated from a past based on heavy industry and manual employment. In general its newer jobs are cleaner, and many require workers with high levels of technical and communication skills, although some demand few skills at all. The new industries have brought more flexible employment and greater opportunities for women to participate in a labour market from which many were previously excluded. In this context, although the steel cutbacks were a blow, they were far from fatal to the local economy.

Likewise the damage done to farming by foot and mouth, coming on top of BSE and other food scares, and added to the generally precarious state of the industry, was very great indeed. But panic reactions which dissuaded visitors from coming to rural Wales spread the damage much further, and hit the whole range of rural service industries. Hotels, bed and breakfast accommodation and visitor centres virtually shut down for most of a year, and small businesses which relied upon seasonal trade were put into jeopardy, along with agricultural suppliers. Vociferous lobbying by the farmers, making heavy use of traditional images of country living, tended to drown out the voices of these other rural interests, and while there was immediate sympathy and concern for the plight of the farmers, who eventually were well compensated for the loss of their stock, it took far longer for other needs to be recognized, and there was no such ready assistance for them. Meanwhile, there were many rural residents for whom the entire crisis represented little more than a major, but temporary, inconvenience.

The effects of these exceptional and dramatic factors have to be set against the background of the underlying condition of Wales, of which, as we have seen, there is more than one interpretation. On the one hand, there are the versions described by John Lovering as cheery but selective, which see Wales as a triumphant example of economic regeneration and social modernization, which has not only succeeded in overcoming its lowly position within the United Kingdom, but is now at the leading edge even of European and global developments. Its new-found role as a focus for innovation and outward-looking internationalism, with a revivified economy, is matched by a new political settlement that opens up possibilities for greater public participation and democratic renewal. Wales has entered the new millennium in a confident frame of mind, with an overhauled set of institutions.

This optimism has to be pitched against alternative accounts which emphasize the extent to which, notwithstanding major transformation, the fundamentals remain unchanged (Lovering, 1996, 1999; Fevre, 1999). Despite all the economic and industrial upheavals, economic life in Wales undoubtedly still has many negative features. The latest surveys of the state of the Welsh economy remind us that Wales is one of the poorest regions of mainland Britain, competing for the bottom rung of the ladder with the north and north-east of England, and generally doing somewhat less well than Scotland. In fact, recent years have seen Wales slipping back, in terms of GDP, with output per head standing at 82.2 per cent of the UK average in 1997, and in earnings, which have shown a continuous relative decline for more than twenty years (Brooksbank, 2000). Household incomes in Wales remain stubbornly some 10 per cent below the British norm. Wages are particularly poor for Welsh men in non-manual employment. While those with manual jobs do slightly better than average for Great Britain, their earnings have fallen markedly along with the disappearance of the older, more skilled, types of male jobs from the economy. Relatively well-paid and dependable working-class jobs used to be one of Wales's strengths; as the example of steel shows, this is no longer the case. Women in Wales do rather better, and those who are in full-time work manage on average to earn a little more than their equivalents in at least three out of the eleven other British regions, putting their earnings at around 92 per cent of the national figure. Even allowing for a low starting point, this is a modest achievement, and even this calculation omits the substantial proportion of women who work part-time, and whose average hourly earnings are only 70 per cent of those of full-time workers. When part-time workers are added to those in self-employment, and the high numbers of those who are economically inactive owing to long-term sickness and disability, Wales has a significant population stratum of low-paid workers and people dependent on benefit. The latter include many who have calculated that, in view of the opportunities available to them, it is not worth even attempting to enter the labour market.

The structure of employment has undergone many changes, and is considerably more diverse and robust than it used to be. Nevertheless Wales has had a problem in attracting and keeping the right sort of jobs. Too many are low-skilled, demand little of the workforce and provide no prospect of improvement or promotion. There is a lack of opportunities in key growth sectors like research and development, and financial and business services. According to Lovering, even today, more people work casually or part-time on Welsh farms (12,000) than are employed in foreign-owned high-tech industries. The public sector continues to bulk large in the Welsh economy. More than a third of employment is still to be found in public-sector services, including health, education and administration, and these offer comparatively advantageous conditions, especially for women who succeed in gaining access to white-collar jobs within them. Wales therefore stands to lose more than other areas from any further movements towards privatization of employment and provision in these sectors, which will be likely to bring about rationalization and a deterioration in conditions. Where new jobs do appear in the private sector, they tend to be in call centres and warehousing operations, some of which have already shown themselves to be vulnerable to sudden shifts in demand or changes in technology. Yet the choice remains between taking up these restricted options, or making do with nothing at all. While the National Assembly has set ambitious targets for future development (for example, see Betterwales.com), it would appear that current trends are moving them further away from the possibility of realization (Brooksbank, 2000: 252). Having qualified for additional support from European Structural Funds on the grounds of comparative need, there have been loud complaints that Wales has been slow to get moving in making use of it, and that political in-fighting and institutional incapacity has weakened the ability of 'Team Wales' to act together. In this respect, the signal which was given when, for some months, responsibility for economic development in Wales was undertaken as a second job by the Assembly's First Minister was not particularly encouraging.

Whether this reading of the situation seems unduly pessimistic depends upon precisely where you stand within Wales. From an observation point in the Cardiff Bay area, or the newly upgraded City of Newport, there are many of the signs of progress and prosperity. Despite setbacks from time to time, these areas have enjoyed a lengthy boom, and through their growth no doubt have contributed more than their fair share towards an expansion in employment in the Welsh construction industry. They offer the prospect of effective economic revitalization and physical refurbishment, and can compete well with other growth centres in terms of their array of consumer services and 'lifestyle' opportunities. Yet at the same time, they have their own problem areas and estates, where the severity of economic deprivation and social problems can match those found anywhere else in Britain. Within a short distance from these centres of expansion, conditions deteriorate and social circumstances plummet to levels that attract widespread notoriety and condemnation. The extent to which Wales has been subjected to such fragmentation and disintegration has been a central message of the preceding discussion. From the vantage point of the hilltop estates of the valleys, from rural south Pembrokeshire, or north-west Wales, the view is very different. The limited inroads made by positive new developments into such areas has to be offset against the continuing decline of their traditional economic and social bases. Plaid Cymru's Economic Development spokesman had the brute facts of such uneven development in mind when he asked what use new jobs in Cwmbran could be to people who lived in Holyhead or Milford Haven. This was part of a plea for setting more precise regional targets within Wales; but there is nothing to suggest that agencies, even with the help of the new Assembly, have increased their ability to direct employment towards those areas where it is most needed. Consequently young people growing up in such places face especially difficult choices, between staying local and suffering from the limited prospects available there, or moving elsewhere to seek out better chances. If they happen to lack the essential qualifications and learning capacities which can fit them to the demands of the contemporary labour market, then these choices are highly circumscribed. In fact, Wales has an exceptionally high rate of youth unemployment and this includes many young people whose chances of ever establishing themselves in secure and rewarding work are extremely poor. This has given rise to an unfolding research agenda to do with education and training, skill development and the transition to work which shows how many of the present problems do continue to bear the imprint of the past, as individual trajectories are conditioned by the experience of different social settings (Rees et al., 2000).

Like the rest of Britain, Wales has witnessed the dismantling of the old collective identities of class and neighbourhood, with the Corus closures more or less completing the work that was done during the crisis of the coal industry. The traditional communities of the industrial working class, like the village communities of rural Wales, were remarkable social creations, but there is little left of either of them now. They had their origins and were capable of being reproduced, under quite different historical circumstances; almost certainly, we will never see their like again. The conditions of life today are altogether more mobile, more subject to flux. In a social universe consisting increasingly of 'networks, mobilities and fluidities' (Urry, 2000), individuals lead more isolated lives, which means that they are less closely connected to places than in the past and have to cope with much higher levels of uncertainty. Flows of all sorts are hollowing out existing societies, creating problems for regulatory powers at all levels from the local to the regional and national. This situation elicits differing responses. Two frames of reference have become particularly prominent in attempts to come to terms with it: those of 'community' and 'identity'. Bella Dicks has discussed the tension between these in relation to ideas of heritage, and the difficulties of imagining, and imaging, the Welsh communities of the past (Dicks, 2000). Should a singular collective identity be attributed to Wales, or should it be represented instead in terms of a constellation of fragmented and conflicting identities? To take the first route is to risk the dangers of romanticism, and essentialism, over-simplifying and reducing the actual historical diversity, and in the process opting for just one out of a number of equally plausible (and partial) possibilities. On the other hand, any attempt to define heritage inclusively, and to celebrate difference, still has to operate through some assertion of sameness, of what the different versions have in common. The problem of drawing and defining boundaries and divisions cannot be avoided. This dilemma has obvious parallels with attempts to define the Wales of the present, and future.

Within Welsh policy and action, there is a strong strain that is concerned with the maintenance and reassertion of community, and innumerable agencies, organizations and local groups are working actively towards community regeneration and integration. Appeals to community were used to great effect in Wales during the political campaigns of the 1970s and 1980s, and more recently, groups protesting about fuel prices, food imports and supermarket purchasing policies have done so in the name of defending their particular communities. The idea of Wales as a 'community of communities' has been widely endorsed. Programmes like Communities First and People in Communities, primarily directed at the most deprived parts of Wales, applaud and seek to build upon the exemplary work that has been carried out in both rural and urban Wales to harness the strengths of community, so as to overcome local problems and increase the involvement of local people in managing their own affairs. These practical experiments in community-building are aimed most especially at those who are still committed to, or trapped within, their local societies, and they echo the themes of social capital, embeddedness and participation which have been gathering momentum among social scientists. Yet those who work in this field are aware that community is a deeply problematic concept; it can be as divisive as it is unifying, and the strength of social networks can be used to exclude those who are vulnerable and feared, or who are simply different (Day et al., 1998; Coffield, 2000).

Whereas 'community' emphasizes similarity and those things which people hold in common, 'identity' seems to offer a better handle on complexity, variety and difference. There is a growing recognition that the prevalence of more 'flexible', heterogeneous sorts of experiences and relationships demands a more differentiated analysis than in the past: as Bauman puts it, identity sprouts from the graveyard of communities (Bauman, 2001: 151). So, writing about the position of women in Wales, Teresa Rees (1999) alerts us to the significance of the multiple identities which we all possess, and to the way in which a variety of forms of disadvantage and discrimination overlap and interact, cutting across the apparent simplicity of gender categorizations. Similarly, whilst noting how there has been a pervasive lethargy in dealing with minority issues in Wales, which has left members of ethnic minorities with a deep sense of marginalization and a feeling of being only loosely affiliated to dominant definitions of Welshness, Charlotte Williams also warns against treating such minorities as if they were uniform, single-culture groups. She and Paul Chaney welcome the potential which devolution and the creation of the National Assembly gives for reworking conceptions of Welsh identity, and imagining Wales in new and different ways, but also note the very limited range and backgrounds of the personnel who have actually come to fill positions within the Assembly (Williams and Chaney, 2001). They stress the importance of developing multiple modes of social, cultural and economic, as well as political, engagement if Wales in future is to be truly inclusive. These arguments have a direct bearing, for example, on the way in which the new Welsh government sets about mainstreaming its commitment to equality of opportunity. There is no reason to think this can be achieved without meeting opposition – far from it. Recurrently, efforts to expand upon the very many different ways of being Welsh are likely to run up against those who seek to foreclose on identity by assigning it to fixed and immutable forms.

It would be absurd to suppose that these oppositions between openness and closure, exclusiveness and inclusiveness, are in any way specific to Wales. The literature on globalization and postmodernity is replete with references to the way in which the forces bringing about a broadening of social and cultural horizons can lead to efforts to maintain closure. Globalization and localization go hand in hand, and celebrations of diversity are matched by new forms of tribalism and exclusivity as people hunt out the security of old or newly invented forms of identity. As Castells (1997: 66) observes, when the world becomes too large to control, actors often try to shrink it back to their own size and reach. Confirmation for this is readily available from within Wales, and at the present time especially (though not exclusively) from developments in the more rural areas, where identity dilemmas are being played out with particular vigour. For those who speak Welsh, and who value their roots in the Welsh-speaking communities of rural Wales, both the economic and political changes that have taken place have brought about new and expanding opportunities; but pursuing them adds to the pressure for outward movement among local people. An entire generation of able and qualified young people risks being lost to the flesh-pots of Cardiff. Meanwhile the opening up once again of major house-price differentials between the various British regions, with property values soaring in southern England, is generating a new pulse of migration to-wards parts of Wales. Cymdeithas yr Iaith reiterates its warnings that the prevailing economic conditions threaten to undermine Welsh-speaking communities. A new outburst of graffiti enjoins local people to 'hold their ground' (*Dal dy dir*) against the incoming tide, and makes familiar demands for jobs, language and housing (*Gwaith, iaith, tai*). Suggestions are floated that Wales should be partitioned. The tiny Independent Wales Party proposes the introduction of residency rules, to apply to all local authority wards where 40 per cent or more of the local population spoke Welsh in 1991, that would formalize approximately half the country as the heartland terri-tory of *Y Fro Gymraeg*. Even the very suggestion alarms others, who worry about its implications for economic development, enterprise and social order. The ironies of the situation were amply evident during the emergency brought about by the collapse of tourist demand in 2001, when drivers crossing north Wales could see, within a few miles of one another, large illu-minated signs on the A55 Expressway welcoming visitors to Wales, and newly painted slogans across the railway bridge in Blaenau Ffestiniog advising English people to 'go home'.

References

Aaron, J., T. Rees, S. Betts, and M. Vincentelli (1994). *Our Sister's Land: The Changing Identities of Women in Wales,* Cardiff, University of Wales Press.

Adamson, D. (1988). 'The new working class and political change in Wales', *Contemporary Wales* 2, 7–28.

—— (1991a). *Class, Ideology, and the Nation: A Theory of Welsh Nationalism,* Cardiff, University of Wales Press.

—— (1991b). 'Lived experience, social consumption, and political change: Welsh politics into the 1990s', in Day and Rees, 1991: 103–23.

—— (1996). *Living on the Edge: Poverty and Deprivation in Wales,* Llandysul, Gomer.

—— (ed.) (1997). *Social Exclusion and Economic Regeneration,* Pontypridd, University of Glamorgan.

—— (1998). 'Social segregation in a working class community: economic and social change in the South Wales Coalfield', Conference Paper, Leuven, Belgium.

—— (1999). 'Poverty and social exclusion in Wales today', in Dunkerley and Thompson, 1999: 41–55.

—— and S. Jones (1996). *The South Wales Valleys: Continuity and Change,* Pontypridd, University of Glamorgan.

Aitchison, J. and H. Carter (1985). *The Welsh Language: An Interpretative Atlas 1961–81,* Cardiff, University of Wales Press.

—— (1998). 'The regeneration of the Welsh language: an analysis', *Contemporary Wales* 11, 167–199.

—— (2000). *Language, Economy and Society: The Changing Fortunes of the Welsh Language in the Twentieth Century,* Cardiff, University of Wales Press.

——, G. Day, B. Edwards, T. Moyes, and J. Murdoch (1989). *The Upper Ithon Valley: A Social and Economic Survey,* Aberystwyth, Rural Surveys Research Unit.

Albrow, M. (1996). *The Global Age: State and Society beyond Modernity,* Cambridge, Polity.

—— (1999). *Sociology: The Basics,* London, Routledge.

Alden, J. (1996). 'The transfer from a problem to powerful region, the experience of Wales', in Alden and Boland, 1996: 127–57.

—— and P. Boland (1996). *Regional Development Strategies: A European Perspective,* London, Jessica Kingsley.

Allen, V. (1981). *The Militancy of British Miners,* Shipley, The Moor Press.

Altbach, P. G. and G. P. Kelly (eds.) (1978). *Education and Colonialism: Comparative Perspectives,* London, Longman.

Amin, S. (1976). *Unequal Development*, Hassocks, Harvester Press.

Anderson, P. and R. Blackburn (eds.) (1965). *Towards Socialism*, London, Fontana.

Asby, J. and P. Midmore (1996). 'Human capacity building in rural areas: the importance of community development', in Midmore and Hughes, 1996: 105–24.

Ashton, S. (1994). 'The farmer needs a wife: farm women in Wales', in Aaron et al., 1994: 89–106.

Atkinson, J. (1984). 'Manpower strategies for flexible organizations', *Personnel Management* (Aug.), 28–31.

Baber, C. and L. Mainwaring (1988). 'Steel', in George and Mainwaring, 1988: 207–32.

—— and D. Thomas (1980). 'Glamorgan economy', in A. H. John and B. Williams (eds.), *Industrial Glamorgan*, Cardiff, Glamorgan County History Trust: 519–80.

Baker, C. (1985). *Aspects of Bilingualism in Wales*, Clevedon, Multilingual Matters.

Ballard, P. H. and E. Jones (eds.) (1975). *The Valleys Call*, Ferndale, Ron Jones Publications.

Balsom, D. (1985). 'The three-Wales model', in Osmond, 1985a: 1–17.

——, P. J. Madgwick and D. van Mechelem (1984). 'The political consequences of Welsh identity', *Journal of Ethnic and Racial Studies* 7, 160–81.

Barber, C. (1982). *Mysterious Wales*, Newton Abbot, David and Charles.

Bateman, D. and P. Midmore (1996). 'Modelling the impacts of agricultural policy changes in the LFAs of Wales', in Midmore and Hughes, 1996: 13–43.

Batey, P. (ed.). (1978). *Theory and Method in Urban and Regional Analysis*, London, Pion.

Bauman, Z. (2001). *The Individualized Society*, Cambridge, Polity.

Beacham, A. (1964). *Depopulation in Mid Wales*, London, HMSO.

Beddoe, D. (1988). 'Images of Welsh women', in Curtis, 1988: 227–38.

—— (2000). *Out of the Shadows: A History of Women in Twentieth Century Wales*, Cardiff, University of Wales Press.

Bell, C. (1968). *Middle Class Families*, London, Routledge & Kegan Paul.

—— and H. Newby (1971). *Community Studies*, London, Allen & Unwin.

Bell, M. M. (1994). *Childerley*, London, University of Chicago Press.

Betts, S. (ed.) (1996). *Our Daughters' Land: Past and Present*, Cardiff, University of Wales Press.

Beynon, H. (1973). *Working For Ford*, Harmondsworth, Penguin.

—— (ed.) (1985). *Digging Deeper: Issues in the Miners' Strike*, London, Verso.

Billig, M. (1995). *Banal Nationalism*, London, Sage.

Blackaby, D. and S. Drinkwater (1997). 'Welsh-speakers and the labour market', *Contemporary Wales* 9, 158–71.

Blackaby, F. (ed.) (1979). *De-Industrialisation*, London, Heinemann.

Blackwell, T. and J. Seabrook (1985). *A World Still To Win: The Reconstruction of the Post-War Working Class*, London, Faber & Faber.

Blandford, S. (1999). 'Aspects of the live and recorded arts in contemporary Wales', in Dunkerley and Thompson 1999: 111–25.

Blauner, R. (1969). 'Internal colonization and ghetto revolt', *Social Problems* 16(4), 393–408.

Blewitt, J. D. (1983). 'A sociological analysis of labourism with specific reference to Port Talbot', unpublished Ph.D. thesis, University of Wales Aberystwyth.

Bollom, C. (1978). *Attitudes and Second Homes in Rural Wales*, Cardiff, University of Wales Press.

Borland, J., G. Day and K. Z. Sowa (eds.) (2002). *Political Borders and Cross-Border Identities at the Boundaries of Europe*, Rszezow, University of Rszezow Press.

Borland, J., R. Fevre and D. Denney (1992). 'Nationalism and community in north west Wales', *Sociological Review* 40, 49–72.

——, —— and C. Williams (2002). 'Inclusion and exclusion in the politics of nationalism', in Borland, Day and Sowa, 2002: 159–77.

Bowen, E. G. (1959). 'Le Pays de Galles', *Transactions of the Institute of British Geographers* 26, 1–23.

—— (1986). 'The geography of Wales as a background to its history', in Hume and Pryce, 1986: 64–87.

Bowie, F. (1993). 'Wales from within: conflicting interpretations of Welsh identity', in Macdonald, 1993: 167–93.

Boyle, P. and K. Halfacree (eds.) (1998). *Migration into Rural Areas*, Chichester, John Wiley.

Bradley, H. (1996). *Fractured Identities: Changing Patterns of Inequality*, Cambridge, Polity.

Bradley, T. and P. Lowe (eds.) (1984). *Locality and Rurality*, Norwich, Geo Books.

Brah, A., M. Hickman, and M. Mac an Ghaill (1999). *Thinking Identities: Ethnicity, Racism and Culture*, London, Macmillan.

Brazyk, H.-J., P. Cooke and M. Heidenreich (eds.) (1998). *Regional Innovation Systems*, London, UCL Press.

Brennan, T., E. W. Cooney and H. Pollins (1954). *Social Change in South-West Wales*, London, Watts and Co.

Bristow, G. (2000). 'Renewing rural Wales', in Bryan and Jones, 2000: 71–85.

Broady, M. (1973). *Marginal Regions: Essays on Social Planning*, London, Bedford Square Press.

—— (1980). 'Mid Wales: a classic case of rural self-help', *The Planner* (July), 94–6.

Brooksbank, D. (2000). 'The Welsh economy: a statistical profile', *Contemporary Wales* 13, 239–69.

Brown, P. and R. Scase (eds.) (1991). *Poor Work: Disadvantage and the Division of Labour*, Buckingham, Open University Press.

Brown, R. and P. Brannen (1970). 'Social relations and social perspectives among shipbuilding workers', *Sociology* 4.

Brubaker R. (1996). *Nationalism Reframed: Nationhood and National Questions in the New Europe*, Cambridge, Cambridge University Press.

Bryan, J. and C. Jones (2000). *Wales in the Twenty-First Century*, London, Macmillan.

Buchanan, K. (1968). 'The revolt against satellization in Scotland and Wales', *Monthly Review* 19(10), 36–48.

—— (1970). 'Economic growth and cultural liquidation: the case of the Celtic Nations', Celtic League, *Annual*, 7–20.

Bulmer, M. (1975). 'Sociological models of the mining community', *Sociological Review* 23, 61–92.

—— (ed.) (1978). *Mining and Social Change*, London, Croom Helm.

Burns, T. and G. M. Stalker (1962). *The Management of Innovation*, London, Tavistock.

Byron, R. (ed.) (1995). *Economic Futures on the North Atlantic Periphery*, Aldershot, Avebury.

Calhoun, C. (1982). *The Question of Class Struggle*, Oxford, Blackwell.

—— (1997). *Nationalism*, Buckingham, Open University Press.

Campbell, B. (1995). *Goliath: Inside Britain's Dangerous Places*, London, Methuen.

Cardoso, F. H. (1977). 'The Consumption of Dependency Theory in the United States', *Latin American Research Review*, 7–24.

Carney, J. and J. Lewis (1978). 'Accumulation, the Regional Problem and Nationalism', in Batey 1978: 67–81.

Carter, H. (1975). 'The crisis of the Valleys and its challenge', in Ballard and Jones, 1975: 27–38.

—— (1996). 'Life in a Welsh countryside: a retrospect', foreword to Rees, 1996: 1–10.

—— and J. Aitchison (1986). 'Language areas and language change in Wales 1961–81', in Hume and Pryce, 1986: 1–25.

—— and S. Wheatley (1982). *Merthyr Tydfil in 1851: A Study of the Spatial Structure of a Welsh Industrial Town*, Cardiff, University of Wales Press (Board of Celtic Studies).

—— and S. Williams (1978). 'Aggregate studies of language and culture change in Wales', in Williams, 1978: 143–65.

Carter, I. (1974). 'The Highlands of Scotland as an underdeveloped region', in E. De Kadt and G. Williams (eds.), *Sociology and Development*, London: Tavistock, 279–311.

Castells, M. (1996). *The Rise of the Network Society*, Oxford, Blackwell.

—— (1997). *The Power of Identity*, Oxford, Blackwell.

Cato, M. S. (2000). 'A new economic development model for the new Wales', *Contemporary Wales* 13, 68–93.

Champion A. and A. Green (1988). *Local Prosperity and the North–South Divide*, Warwick, Institute of Employment Research, University of Warwick.

—— and C. Watkins (eds.) (1991). *People in the Countryside: Studies of Social Change in Rural Britain*, London, Paul Chapman.

——, A. Green, D. Owen, D. Ellin and M. Coombes (1987). *Changing Places, Britain's Demographic, Economic and Social Complexion*, London, Edward Arnold.

Chaney, D. (1994). *The Cultural Turn*, London, Routledge.

Chaney, P. and R. Fevre (2001). 'Welsh nationalism and the challenge of "inclusive" politics', *Political Opportunities, Social Movements and Democratization* 23, 227–54.

——, T. Hall, and B. Dicks (2000). 'Inclusive governance? The case of "minority" and voluntary sector groups and the National Assembly for Wales', *Contemporary Wales* 13, 203–29.

—— and A. Pithouse (2001). *New Governance – New Democracy?* Cardiff, University of Wales Press.

Charles, N., C. A. Davies, D. Blackaby, P. Murphy, N. O'Leary and P. Ransome (2000). 'It's still there! Maintaining the glass ceiling in Wales', *Contemporary Wales* 13, 116–37.

Chen, S. and T. Wright (eds.) (2000). *The English Question*, London, Fabian Society.

Clavel, P. (1983). *Opposition Planning in Wales and Appalachia*, Cardiff, University of Wales Press.

Cloke, P. (ed.) (1987). *Rural Planning: Policy into Action?* London, Harper & Row.
—— and J. Little (eds.) (1997). *Contested Countryside Cultures*, London, Routledge.
—— and P. Milbourne (1992). 'Deprivation and lifestyles in rural Wales: rurality and the cultural dimension', *Journal of Rural Studies* 8(4), 359–71.
—— and L. Davies (1992). 'Deprivation and lifestyle in rural Wales: towards a cultural dimension', *Journal of Rural Studies* 8(4), 349–58.
——, M. Goodwin and P. Milbourne (1995). '"There's so many strangers in the village now": marginalization and change in 1990s Welsh rural life-styles', *Contemporary Wales* 8, 47–74.
——, —— and —— (1997). *Rural Wales: Community and Marginalization*, Cardiff, University of Wales Press.
——, —— and —— (1998). 'Inside looking out: different experiences of cultural competences in rural lifestyles', in Boyle and Halfacree, 1998: 134–50.
——, M. Phillips, and D. Rankin (1991). 'Middle-class housing choice: channels of entry into Gower, South Wales', in Champion and Watkins, 1991: 38–52.
Coffield, F. (ed.) (2000). *Differing Visions of the Learning Society*, Bristol, The Policy Press.
Cohen, A. P. (ed.) (1982). *Belonging: Identity and Social Organisation in British Rural Cultures*, Manchester, Manchester University Press.
—— (1985). *The Symbolic Construction of Community*, London, Tavistock.
Cole, D. (ed.) (1990). *The New Wales*, Cardiff, University of Wales Press.
Coleman, J. S. (1990). *Foundations of Social Theory*, Cambridge MA, Harvard University Press.
Collis, C. (1992). 'Overseas inward investment in the UK Regions', in Townroe and Martin, 1992: 142–9.
Connor, W. (1977). 'Ethnonationalism in the First World: the present in historical perspective', in Esman, 1977: 19–45.
Cooke P. (1980). 'Capital relation and state dependency: an analysis of urban development policy in Cardiff', in Rees and Rees, 1980: 206–30.
—— (1981a). 'Class relations and uneven development in Wales', in Day et al., 1991: 147–78.
—— (1981b). *Local Class Structure in Wales*, Papers in Planning Research, 31, Cardiff, Department of Town Planning, UWIST.
—— (1983a). *Theories of Planning and Spatial Development*, London, Hutchinson.
—— (1983b). 'The regional division of labour', in Williams, 1983a: 72–87.
—— (1985). 'Class practices as regional markers: a contribution to labour geography', in Gregory and Urry, 1985: 213–41.
—— and K. Morgan (1993). 'The network paradigm', *Environment and Planning D*, 543–64.
—— and —— (1998). *The Associational Economy: Firms, Regions and Innovation*, Oxford, Oxford University Press.
——, A. Price, and K. Morgan (1995). 'Regulating regional economies: Wales and Baden-Wurttemberg in transition', in Rhodes, 1995: 105–35.
Cooper, D. and T. Hopper (eds.) (1988). *Debating Coal Closures*, Cambridge, Cambridge University Press.
Cordell, A. (1959). *Rape of the Fair Country*, London, Victor Gollancz.
Cottrell, A. and R. Roslender (1986). 'Economic class, social class, and political forces', *International Journal of Sociology and Social Policy* 6(3), 13–27.

Coxon, A. (1978). 'Social process and ethnic identity, personal reflections on the Gregynog Papers', in Williams, 1978: 268–71.

Crompton, R. (1993). *Class and Stratification*, Cambridge, Polity.

Cronin, A. J. (1937). *The Citadel*, London, Victor Gollancz.

Cross, M. and G. Payne (1991). *Work and the Enterprise Culture*, London, Falmer Press.

Crow, G. and G. Allen (1994). *Community Life: An Introduction to Local Social Relations*, Hemel Hempstead, Harvester Wheatsheaf.

Curtice, J. (1999). 'Is Scotland a nation and Wales not?', in Taylor and Thomson, 1999: 119–48.

Curtis T. (ed.) (1986). *Wales: The Imagined Nation*, Bridgend, Poetry Wales Press.

Cymuned (2001). *Housing, Work and Language*, Aberystwyth, Cyhoeddiadau Cymuned.

Daunton, M. (1977). *Coal Metropolis: Cardiff 1870–1914*, Leicester, Leicester University Press.

—— (1981). 'Down the pit: work in the Great Northern and South Wales Coalfields, 1870–1914', *Economic History Review* 34, 578–97.

Davies, B. (1976). 'Towards a new synthesis', *Planet* 37/8, 54–9.

Davies, C. (1997). 'Minority language and social division: dead ends, linguistic time bombs and the policies of subversion', in Frost, 1997.

Davies, C. A. (1990). 'Language and national identity', in Jenkins and Edwards, 1990: 35–45.

—— (1998). 'A oes heddwch?', in Hughes-Freeland, 1998: 141–59.

Davies, E. and A. D. Rees (1960). *Welsh Rural Communities*, Cardiff, University of Wales Press.

Davies, G. and I. Thomas (1976). *Overseas Investment in Wales: The Welcome Invasion*, Swansea, Christopher Davies.

Davies J. (1974). 'The end of the great estates and the rise of freehold farming in Wales', *Welsh History Review* 7, 186–221.

Davies, R. (1999). *Devolution: A Process, Not an Event*, Gregynog Papers 2, Cardiff, Institute of Welsh Affairs.

Davies, T. (1978). 'Capital, state and sparse populations: the context for further research', in Newby, 1978: 87–106.

Davis, H. H. (1979). *Beyond Class Images*, London, Croom Helm.

Day, G. (1978). 'Underdeveloped Wales?', *Planet* 45/6, 102–10.

—— (1979). 'The sociology of Wales: issues and prospects', *The Sociological Review* 27(3), 447–74.

—— (1980). 'Wales, the regional problem and development', in Rees and Rees, 1980: 230–51.

—— (1984). 'Development and national consciousness: the Welsh case', in Vermeulen and Boissevain, 1984: 35–49.

—— (1987). 'The reconstruction of Wales and Appalachia: development and regional identity', *Contemporary Wales* 1, 73–89.

—— (1989). 'A million on the move', *Contemporary Wales* 3, 137–60.

—— (1991). 'The regeneration of rural Wales: prospects for the 1990s', in Day and Rees, 1991: 211–31.

—— (1993). *A Skills Profile of South Gwynedd*, Report to the South Gwynedd LEADER Network, Bangor, University of Wales.

Day, G. (1997). 'Poverty and social exclusion in Wales – the rural dimension', in Adamson, 1997: 7–14.

—— (1998a). 'A community of communities? Similarity and difference in Welsh rural community studies', *The Economic and Social Review* 29(3), 233–57.

—— (1998b). 'Working with the grain? Towards sustainable rural and community development', *Journal of Rural Studies* 14(1), 89–105.

—— (1999). 'The rural dimension', in Dunkerley and Thompson, 1999: 75–89.

—— and M. Fitton (1975). 'Religion and social status: *bucheddau* and its implications', *Sociological Review* 23(4), 867–91.

—— and —— (1978). 'Religious organization and community in Mid Wales', in Williams, 1978: 242–52.

—— and M. Hedger (1990). 'Mid Wales: missing the point', *Urban Studies* 27(2), 283–90.

—— and D. Jones (1995). 'Development at what price? Economic and spatial peripherality in north-west Wales', in Byron, 1995: 299–314.

—— and J. Murdoch (1993). 'Locality and community: coming to terms with place', *Sociological Review* 41(1), 82–111.

—— and G. Rees (1987). 'Images of contemporary Wales: researching social and economic change', *Contemporary Wales* 1, 1–6.

—— and —— (1991). *Regions, Nations and European Integration: Remaking the Celtic Periphery*, Cardiff, University of Wales Press.

—— and R. Suggett (1985). 'Conceptions of Wales and Welshness: aspects of nationalism in nineteenth-century Wales', in Rees et al., 1985: 91–115.

—— and D. Thomas (1991). 'Rural needs and strategic response: the case of rural Wales', *Local Economy* 6(1), 35–47.

—— and A. Thompson (1999). 'The Politics of inclusion? A preliminary assessment of the implications of Welsh devolution', paper presented to the Conference on Nationalism, Identity and Minority Rights, University of Bristol.

—— and —— (2001). 'Where next for the new Britain? The third way and the challenge of devolution', *Renewal* 9(1), 6–18.

——, C. Caldwell, K. Jones, D. Robbins and H. Rose (eds.) (1981). *Diversity and Decomposition in the Labour Market*, Aldershot, Gower.

——, D. Dunkerley and A. Thompson (2000). 'Evaluating the "new politics": civil society and the National Assembly for Wales', *Public Policy and Administration* 15(2), 25–38.

——, M. Fitton and M. Minhinnick (1998). 'Finding our voices', in Osmond, 1986b: 290–300.

——, P. Knight and E. Morris (1998). *Where do We Go from Here?*, Cardiff, Wales Council for Voluntary Action.

——, R. Mackay, S. Chakravarty and S. Jones (1998). 'Two myths of inward investment', Memorandum of Evidence to the Welsh Affairs Committee, Fourth Report, London, The Stationery Office, 169–80.

——, G. Rees and J. Murdoch (1989). 'Social change, rural localities, and the state: the restructuring of rural Wales', *Journal of Rural Studies* 5(3), 227–44.

De Vane, R. (1975). *Second Home Ownership: A Case Study*, Cardiff, University of Wales Press.

Denney, D., J. Borland, and R. Fevre (1991). 'The social construction of nation-alism, racism and conflict in Wales, *Contemporary Wales* 4, 149–65.

Dennis, N., F. Henriques and C. Slaughter (1956). *Coal is Our Life*, London, Eyre and Spottiswoode.

Dicks, B. (2000). *Heritage, Place and Community*, Cardiff, University of Wales Press.

Dos Santos, T. (1970). 'The structure of dependence', *American Economic Review* 60(2), 231–6.

Douglas, M. and A. B. Wildavsky (1982). *Risk and Culture*, Berkeley, University of California Press.

Duncan, S. (1989). 'What is locality?', in Peet and Thrift, 1989: 101–19.

Dunford, M. and D. Perrons (1983). *The Arena of Capital*, London, Macmillan.

Dunkerley, D. and A. Thompson (eds.) (1999). *Wales Today*, Cardiff, University of Wales Press.

Dunning, J. H. (1986). *Japanese Participation in British Industry*, London, Croom Helm.

Emmett, I. (1964). *A North Wales Village: A Social Anthropological Study*, London, Routledge & Kegan Paul.

—— (1978). 'Blaenau boys in the mid-1960s', in Williams, 1978: 87–101.

—— (1982a). '*Fe godwn ni eto*: stasis and change in a Welsh industrial town', in Cohen, 1982: 165–202.

—— (1982b). 'Place, community and bilingualism in Blaenau Ffestiniog', in Cohen, 1982: 202–21.

Esman, M. J. (ed.) (1977). *Ethnic Conflict in the Western World*, London, Cornell University Press.

Evans, G. (1974). *Land of My Fathers: Two Thousand Years of Welsh History*, Swansea, John Penry Press.

Evans, N. (1989). 'Two paths to economic development: Wales and the north-east of England', in Hudson P., 1989: 207–27.

Evans, N. (1991). 'Immigrants and minorities in Wales 1840–1990: a comparative perspective', *Llafur*, 4(5): 5–25.

Evans, N. (1998). 'Regional dynamics: north Wales, 1750–1914' in E. Royle (ed.), *Issues of Regional Identity*, Manchester, Manchester University Press: 201–25.

Evas, J. (2000). 'Declining density: a danger for language?', in Williams, 2000: 292–310.

Fairbrother, P. and K. Morgan (2001). *Steel Communities Study: Implications for Employment, Learning and Regeneration*, National Assembly for Wales, Cardiff, ELWa & WDA.

Fevre, R. (1986). 'Contract work in the recession', in Purcell et al., 1986: 18–34.

—— (1989). *Wales is Closed*, Nottingham, Spokesman.

—— (1991). 'Emerging "alternatives" to full-time and permanent employment', in Brown and Scase, 1991: 56–70.

—— (1999). 'The Welsh economy', in Dunkerley and Thompson, 1999: 57–74.

—— (2001). 'Foreword', in Chaney et al., 2001, v–viii.

—— and A. Thompson (eds.) (1999). *National Identity and Social Theory: Perspectives from Wales*, Cardiff, University of Wales Press.

——, D. Denney and J. Borland (1997). 'Class, status and party in the analysis of nationalism: lessons from Max Weber', *Nations and Nationalism* 3(4), 559–77.

Fevre, R., D. Denney and J. Borland (1999). 'Nation, community, and conflict: housing policy and immigration in north Wales', in Fevre and Thompson, 1999: 129–48.

Fleure, H. J. (1926). *Wales and her People*, Wrexham, Hughes & Son.

Forde, C. D. (1934). *Habitat, Economy and Society*, London, Methuen.

Fothergill, S. and Gudgin, G. (1982). *Unequal Growth*, London, Heinemann.

Foulkes, D., J. Barry Jones and R. A. Wilford (eds.) (1983). *The Welsh Veto: The Wales Act and the Referendum*, Cardiff, University of Wales Press.

Francis, H. (1990). 'The valleys', in Jenkins and Edwards, 1990: 109–20.

Francis, H. and D. Smith (1980). *The Fed: A History of the South Wales Miners in the Twentieth Century*, London, Lawrence & Wishart.

Frank, A. G. (1971). *Sociology of Development and Underdevelopment of Sociology*, London, Pluto.

Frankenberg, R. (1957). *Village on the Border*, London, Cohen & West.

—— (1966). *Communities in Britain*, Harmondsworth, Penguin.

Fretter, A. D. (1993). 'Place marketing: a local authority perspective', in Kearns and Philo, 1993: 163–74.

Frost, G. (ed.) (1997). *Loyalty Misplaced*, Reading, University of Reading.

Furtado, C. (1967). *Development and Underdevelopment*, Berkeley, University of California Press.

Gamble, A. (1981). *Britain in Decline*, London, Macmillan.

——, D. Marsh and T. Tant (1999). *Marxism and Social Science*, London, Macmillan.

Gellner, E. (1964). *Thought and Change*, London, Weidenfeld & Nicolson.

—— (1983). *Nations and Nationalism*, Oxford, Blackwell.

George, K. D. and L. Mainwaring (1988). *The Welsh Economy*, Cardiff, University of Wales Press.

Giddens, A. (1984). *The Constitution of Society*, Cambridge, Polity.

—— (1999). *Runaway World: How Globalisation is Reshaping our Lives*, London, Profile Books.

Giggs, J. and C. Pattie (1992). 'Wales as a Plural Society', *Contemporary Wales* 5, 25–63.

Glyn, S. (2001). 'Our way of life is dying . . . that's why I had to speak out', *Daily Post* (19 Jan.).

Goldthorpe, J., D. Lockwood, F. Bechhofer and J. Platt (1969). *The Affluent Worker in the Class Structure*, Cambridge, Cambridge University Press.

Gonzales-Casanova, P. (1965). 'Internal colonialism and national development', *Studies in Comparative International Development* 1(4), 27–37.

Gramsci, A. (1971). *Selections from Prison Notebooks*, London, Lawrence & Wishart.

Grant, G. (1978). 'The provision of social services in rural areas', in Williams, 1978: 61–75.

Gripaios, P. (1998). 'The Welsh economy: an outside perspective', *Contemporary Wales* 10, 32–49.

Gregory, D. and J. Urry (eds) (1985). *Social Relations and Spatial Structures*, London, Macmillan.

Griffiths, D. (1992). 'The political consequences of migration into Wales', *Contemporary Wales* 5, 64–80.

Gruffudd, H. (1998). 'Young people's use of Welsh: the influence of home and community', *Contemporary Wales* 10, 200–18.

Gruffudd, H. (2000). 'Planning for the use of Welsh by young people', in Williams, 2000: 173–207.

Gruffudd P. (1994a). 'Back to the land: historiography, rurality and the nation in interwar Wales', *Transactions of the Institute of British Geographers* NS 19, 61–77.

—— (1994b). 'Tradition, modernity and the countryside: the imaginary geography of rural Wales', *Contemporary Wales* 6, 33–48.

—— (1995). 'Heritage as national identity: histories and prospects of the national pasts', in Herbert, 1995: 49–67.

Guy, C. M. (1995). 'Retail development in Wales: current trends and issues', *Contemporary Wales* 8, 161–82.

Halfacree, K. (1995). 'Talking about rurality: social representations of the rural as expressed by residents of six English parishes', *Journal of Rural Studies* 11(1), 1–20.

Hall, S. (1996). 'Who needs "identity"?', in Hall and du Gay, 1996: 1–17.

—— and P. du Gay (eds.) (1996). *Questions of Cultural Identity*, London, Sage.

Harloe, M. (ed.) (1981). *New Perspectives in Urban Change and Conflict*, London, Heinemann.

Harper, S. (1989). 'The British rural community: an overview of perspectives', *Journal of Rural Studies* 5(2), 161–84.

Harrington, M. (1962). *The Other America: Poverty in the United States*, New York, Collier.

Harris, C. C. (1987). *Redundancy and Recession*, Oxford, Blackwell.

—— (ed.) (1990). *Family, Economy and Community*, Cardiff, University of Wales Press.

—— and R. M. Lee (1988). 'Conceptualising the place of redundant steelworkers in the class structure', in Rose, 1988: 174–82.

Harrison, G., W. Bellin and B. Piette (1981). *Bilingual Mothers in Wales and the Language of Their Children*, Cardiff, University of Wales Press.

Harvey, D. (1982). *The Limits to Capital*, Oxford, Oxford University Press.

—— (1985). 'The geopolitics of capitalism', in Gregory and Urry, 1985: 128–63.

Healey, M. J. and B. W. Ilbery (1985). *The Industrialization of the Countryside*, Norwich, Geo Books.

Hechter, M. (1975). *Internal Colonialism: The Celtic Fringe in British National Development, 1536–1966*, London, Routledge Kegan Paul.

Hedger, M. (1995). 'Wind energy: the debate in Wales', *Contemporary Wales* 7, 117–34.

Herb, G. H. and D. H. Kaplan (eds.) (1999). *Nested Identities: Nationalism, Territory and Scale*, Oxford, Rowman & Littlefield.

Herbert, D. T. (ed.) (1995). *Heritage, Tourism and Society*, London, Pinter.

Herbert, T. and G. E. Jones (eds.) (1995). *Post-War Wales*, Cardiff, University of Wales Press.

Hill, S. (2000). 'Wales in transition', in Bryan and Jones, 2000: 1–9.

—— and M. Munday (1991). 'Foreign direct investment in Wales', *Local Economy* 6(1), 21–34.

—— and —— (1994). *The Regional Distribution of Foreign Manufacturing Investment in the UK*, London, Macmillan.

Hilton, K. J. (ed) (1967). *The Lower Swansea Valley Project*, London, Longmans Green.

Hindess, B. (1987). *Politics and Class Analysis*, Oxford, Blackwell.

—— and P. Hirst (1977). *Mode of Production and Social Formation*, London, Macmillan.

Hirst, P. (1994). *Associative Democracy: New Forms of Economic and Social Governance*, Cambridge, Polity Press.

Hobsbawm, E. (1968). *Industry and Empire*, London, Weidenfeld & Nicolson.

—— (1990). *Nations and Nationalism Since 1780*, Cambridge, Cambridge University Press.

—— (1994). *The Age of Extremes*, London, Michael Joseph.

—— and T. Ranger (1983). *The Invention of Tradition*, Cambridge, Cambridge University Press.

Hobson J. A. (1910). 'The general election: a sociological interpretation', *Sociological Review* 7, 105–17.

Holland, S. (1976a). *Capital Versus the Regions*, London, Macmillan.

—— (1976b). *The Regional Problem*, London, Macmillan.

Holton, D. (1996). 'Has class analysis a future?', in Lee and Turner, 1996: 26–42.

Hopkin, D. and G. S. Kealey (1989). *Class, Community and the Labour Movement: Wales and Canada 1850–1930*, Llafur, Society for the Study of Welsh Labour History.

Howe, J. (1999). 'The selling of rural Wales', *Contemporary Wales* 12, 155–72.

Howell, D. (1977). *Land and People in Nineteenth Century Wales*, London, Routledge & Kegan Paul.

—— (1991). 'The 1984–85 miners' strike in north Wales', *Contemporary Wales* 4, 67–98.

Howell, D. W. and C. Baber (1990). 'Wales', in Thompson, 1990: 281–354.

Howells, K. (1985). 'Stopping out, the birth of a new kind of politics', in Beynon, 1985: 139–47.

Hudson, P. (ed.) (1989). *Regions and Industries: A Perspective on the Industrial Revolution in Britain*, Cambridge, Cambridge University Press.

Hudson, R. and A. Williams (1986). *The United Kingdom*, London, Harper & Row.

Huggins, R. (1997). 'Competitiveness and the global region: the role of networking', in Simmie, 1997: 101–23.

Hughes, G., P. Midmore and A.-M. Sherwood (1996). 'Language, farming and sustainability in Wales', in Midmore and Hughes, 1996: 75–104.

Hughes-Freeland, F. (ed.) (1998). *Rituals, Performance, Media*, London, Routledge.

Hume, I. and W. T. R. Pryce (eds.) (1986). *The Welsh and Their Country*, Llandysul, Gomer.

Humphreys, E. (1983). *The Taliesin Tradition*, London, Black Raven Press.

—— (2000). *The Taliesin Tradition*, Bridgend, Seren.

Humphreys, R. (1995). 'Images of Wales', in Herbert and Jones, 1995: 133–60.

Humphrys, G. (1972). *South Wales*, Newton Abbot, David & Charles.

Hutson, J. (1990). 'Family relationships and farm businesses in south-west Wales', in Harris, 1990: 119–39.

Hymer, S. (1979). *The Multinational Corporation: A Radical Analysis*, Cambridge, Cambridge University Press.

IWA (1988). *Rural Wales: Population Changes and Current Attitudes*, Cardiff, Institute of Welsh Affairs.

—— (1993). *Wales 2010: Creating Our Future*, Cardiff, Institute of Welsh Affairs.

IWA (1996). *Wales 2010: Three Years On*, Cardiff, Institute of Welsh Affairs.

Jackson, B. (1968). *Working Class Community*, London, Routledge & Kegan Paul.

Jenkins, D. (1960). 'Aber-porth: a study of a coastal town in south Cardiganshire', in Davies and Rees, 1960: 1–66.

—— (1971). *The Agricultural Community in South-West Wales at the Turn of the Twentieth Century*, Cardiff, University of Wales.

—— (1980). 'Rural society inside outside', in Smith, 1980: 114–26.

Jenkins, J. G. (ed.) (1969). *Studies in Folk Life: Essays in Honour of Iorwerth Peate*, London, Routledge & Kegan Paul.

—— (1976). *Life and Tradition in Rural Wales*, London, Dent and Sons.

Jenkins, R. (1995). 'Nations and nationalisms: towards more open models', *Nations and Nationalism* 1(3), 369–90.

—— (1996). *Social Identity*, London, Routledge.

—— (1997). *Rethinking Ethnicity: Arguments and Explorations*, London, Sage.

—— and A. Edwards (eds.) (1990). *One Step Forward? South and West Wales Towards the Year 2000*, Llandysul, Gomer.

—— and Hutson S. (1990). 'Gender relations, family relations and long-term youth unemployment', in Harris, 1990: 99–118.

John, A. (1984). 'A miner's struggle? Women's protests in Welsh mining', *Llafur* 4 72–90.

Jones, C. (2000). 'Comparative disadvantage? The industrial structure of Wales', in Bryan and Jones, 2000: 11–23.

Jones, D. (2001). 'The Shotton redundancies: economic change and regeneration on Deeside', Submission to the Welsh Assembly as part of the University of Wales *Steel Communities Study*.

Jones, G. E. (1995). 'Post-war Wales', in Herbert and Jones, 1995: 1–9.

Jones, Glyn (1968). *The Dragon has Two Tongues*, London, Dent (Revised edn, ed. T. Brown, Cardiff, University of Wales Press).

Jones, H. and C. H. Williams (2000). 'The statistical basis for Welsh language planning: data trends, patterns and processes', in Williams, 2000: 48–82.

Jones, I. G. (1981). *Explorations and Explanations: Essays in the Social History of Victorian Wales*, Llandysul, Gomer.

Jones, K. and D. Morris (1997). *Gender and the Welsh Language: A Research Review*, Cardiff, Equal Opportunities Commission.

Jones, L. (1937). *Cwmardy*, London, Lawrence & Wishart.

Jones, N. (1993). *Living in Rural Wales*, Llandysul, Gomer.

Jones, O. (1995). 'Lay discourses of the rural: developments and implications for rural studies', *Journal of Rural Studies* 11(1), 35–50.

Jones, R. M. (1982a). *The North Wales Quarrymen: 1874–1922*, Cardiff, University of Wales Press.

—— (1982b). 'The state of the nation', *Sociology of Wales Newsletter* 5, 14–20.

—— (1989). '"Of men and stones", radicalism and protest in North Wales, 1850–1914', in Hopkin and Kealey, 1989: 101–18.

—— (1999). 'Social change in Wales since 1945', in Dunkerley and Thompson, 1999: 11–24.

Jones, R. T. (1986). 'The shadow of the swastika', in Hume and Pryce, 1986: 234–44.

Kearns, G. and C. Philo (1993). *Selling Places: The City as Cultural Capital, Past and Present*, Oxford, Pergamon.

Keen, R. (1999). *Our Welsh Heritage*, Gregynog Papers 2/3, Cardiff, Institute of Welsh Affairs.

Kenny, M. (1999). 'Marxism and regulation theory', in Gamble et al., 1999: 35–60.

Kerr, C. and A. Siegel (1954). 'The inter-industry propensity to strike: an international comparison', in Kornhauser et al., 1954: 189–212.

——, J. Dunlop, F. Harbison and C. Myers (1960). *Industrialism and Industrial Man*, Cambridge MA, Harvard University Press.

Khleif, B. (1978). 'Ethnic awakening in the first world: the case of Wales', in Williams, 1978: 102–19.

Knowles, A. (1999). 'Migration, nationalism and the construction of Welsh identity', in Herb and Kaplan, 1999: 289–316.

Kornhauser, A., R. Dubin and A. Ross (1954). *Industrial Conflict*, New York, McGraw-Hill.

Laclau, E. (1977). *Politics and Ideology in Marxist Theory*, London, New Left Books.

Lash, S. and J. Urry (1987). *The End of Organized Capitalism*, Cambridge, Polity.

—— (1994). *Economies of Signs and Space*, London, Sage.

Law, D. and R. Howes (1972). *Mid-Wales: An Assessment of the Impact of the Development Commission Factory Programme*, London, HMSO.

Law, D. and N. Perdikis (1977). 'Population stability and the rate of industrial development in mid-Wales', in Sadler and Mackay, 1977.

Lee, D. J. and B. S. Turner (1996). *Conflicts about Class: Debating Inequality in Late Industrialism*, London, Longman.

Leonard, D. (1980). *Gender and Generation: A Study of Courtship and Weddings*, London, Tavistock.

Lewis, G. J. (1979). *Rural Communities: A Social Geography*, London, Longman.

Lewis, H. (1984). 'Industrialization, class and regional consciousness in two peripheral regions: Wales and Appalachia', mimeo.

Lewis H. M, L. Johnson, and D. Askins (eds.) (1978). *Colonialism in Modern America: The Appalachian Case*, Boone, NC, The Appalachian Consortium.

—— and E. E. Knipe (1970). 'The colonialism model: the Appalachian case', in H. M. Lewis et al., 1970: 9–31.

Little, A. D. (Management Consultants) (1986). *The Japanese Experience in Wales*, Cardiff, WINVEST.

Little, J. (1991). 'Women in the rural labour market: a policy evaluation', in Champion and Watkins, 1991: 96–107.

Llewellyn, R. (1939). *How Green was my Valley*, London, Joseph.

Llywelyn, E. (1986). 'What is Adfer?', in Hume and Pryce, 1986: 244–52.

Loach, L. (1985). 'We'll be here right to the end . . . and after: women in the miners' strike', in Beynon, 1985: 169–79.

Lockwood, D. (1966). 'Source of variation in working class images of society', *Sociological Review* 14(3): 249–63.

Lovering, J. (1978a). 'The theory of the internal colony', *Planet* 45/6: 89–96.

—— (1978b). 'The theory of the internal economy and the political economy of Wales', *Review of Radical Political Economics* 10, 55–67.

Lovering, J. (1983a). 'Uneven development in Wales: the changing role of the British state', in G. Williams, 1983: 48–71.

—— (1983b). *Gwynedd – A County in Crisis*, Coleg Harlech Occasional Papers in Welsh Studies 2, Harlech.

—— (1985). 'Defence spending and the regions: the case of Bristol', *Built Environment* 11, 193–206.

—— (1991). 'Southbound again: the peripheralization of Britain', in Day and Rees, 1991: 11–37.

—— (1996). 'New myths of the Welsh economy', *Planet* 116, 6–16.

—— (1999a). 'Celebrating globalization and misreading the Welsh economy: the "new regionalism"', *Contemporary Wales* 11, 12–60.

—— (1999b). 'Theory led by policy, the inadequacies of the "new regionalism": illustrated from the case of Wales', *International Journal of Urban and Regional Research* 23(2): 379–95.

Lowe, P., T. Bradley and S. Wright (eds.) (1986). *Deprivation and Welfare in Rural Areas*, Norwich, Geobooks.

Luke, P. (1976). 'The ideal research site', *Planet* 30, 52–3.

McCrone, D. (1992). *Understanding Scotland: The Sociology of a Stateless Nation*, London, Routledge.

—— (1998). *The Sociology of Nationalism*, London, Routledge.

——, R. Stewart, R. Kiely and F. Bechhofer (1998). 'Who are we? Problematising national identity', *Sociological Review* 46, 629–52.

Macdonald, R. and H. Thomas (1997). *Nationality and Planning in Scotland and Wales*, Cardiff, University of Wales Press.

Macdonald, S. (ed.) (1993). *Inside European Identities: Ethnography in Western Europe*, Oxford, Berg.

Macintyre, S. (1980). *Little Moscows: Communism and Working-Class Militancy in Inter-War Britain*, London, Croom Helm.

MacKay, R. R. (1992). 'Wales', in Townroe and Martin, 1992: 97–107.

McKenna, C. J. and D. R. Thomas (1988). 'Regional policy', in George and Mainwaring, 1988: 263–90.

McLaughlin, B. (1985). *Deprivation in Rural Areas*, Report to the Department of the Environment.

—— (1986). 'The rhetoric and reality of rural deprivation', *Journal of Rural Studies*, 2, 291–307.

McNabb, R. (1980). 'Segmented labour markets, female employment and poverty in Wales', in Rees and Rees, 1980: 156–67.

—— and D. G. Rhys (1988). 'Manufacturing', in George and Mainwaring, 1988: 187–200.

—— and J. Shorey (1988). 'The labour market', in George and Mainwaring, 1988: 111–32.

Mainwaring, L. (1991). 'Wales in the 1990s: external influences on economic development', in Day and Rees, 1991: 73–88.

—— (1995). 'Catching up and falling behind: south-east Asia and Wales', *Contemporary Wales*, 8: 9–28.

Mann, K. (1991). *The Making of an English Underclass*, Oxford, Oxford University Press.

Marr, A. (1999). *The Day Britain Died*, Harmondsworth, Penguin.

Marsden, T. (1998). 'New rural territories: regulating the differentiated rural spaces', *Journal of Rural Studies* 14(1), 107–18.

Marshall, G., D. Rose, H. Newby and C. Vogler (1988). *Social Class in Modern Britain*, London, Hutchinson.

Martin, R. and B. Rowthorn (1986). *The Geography of De-Industrialisation*, London, Macmillan.

Massey, D. (1978). 'Regionalism: some current issues', *Capital and Class* 6, 106–25.

—— (1979). 'In what sense a regional problem?', *Regional Studies* 13, 233–43.

—— (1983). 'The shape of things to come', *Marxism Today* 27, 18–27.

—— (1984). *Spatial Divisions of Labour: Social Structures and the Geography of Production*, London, Macmillan.

—— (1985). 'New directions in space', in Gregory and Urry, 1985: 9–19.

—— and R. Meegan (1982). *The Anatomy of Job Loss: The How, Why and Where of Employment Decline*, London, Methuen.

—— and H. Wainwright (1985). 'Beyond the coalfields, the work of the miners', support groups', in Beynon, 1985: 149–68.

Michael, D. (1983). 'Before Alwyn: the origins of sociology in Wales', in Williams, 1983: 17–34.

Middlemass, K. (1979). *Politics in Industrial Society: The Experience of the British System since 1911*, London, Andre Deutsch.

Midmore, P. (1991). *Input–Output Models and the Agricultural Sector*, Aldershot, Avebury.

—— (1996). 'Making the countryside work: the problems of rural Wales', *Planet* 120, 92–7.

—— and G. Hughes (1996). *Rural Wales: An Economic and Social Perspective*, Aberystwyth, Welsh Institute of Rural Studies.

Milbourne, P. (1996a). 'Hidden from view: poverty and marginalisation in rural Britain', in P. Milbourne, 1996b: 89–116.

—— (ed.) (1996b). *Revealing Rural 'Others'*, London, Cassell.

Miller, D. (1995). *On Nationality*, Oxford, Oxford University Press.

Molotch, H. (1976). 'The city as a growth machine', *American Journal of Sociology*, 82, 309–32.

Monbiot, G. (2000). *The Captive State: The Corporate Takeover of Britain*, London, Macmillan.

Moore, R. (1974). *Pit-Men, Preachers and Politics*, Cambridge, Cambridge University Press.

Morgan, K. (1983). 'Restructuring steel: the crises of labour and locality in Britain', *International Journal of Urban and Regional Research* 7(2), 175–201.

—— (1986). 'Re-industrialisation in peripheral Britain: state policy, the space economy, and industrial innovation', in Martin and Rowthorn, 1986: 322–60.

—— (1987). 'High technology industry and regional development: for Wales, see Greater Boston?', *Contemporary Wales* 1, 39–51.

—— (1997a). 'The learning region: institutions, innovation and regional renewal', *Regional Studies* 31(5), 491–503.

—— (1997b). 'The regional animateur: taking stock of the Welsh development agency', *Regional and Federal Studies* 7, 70–94.

Morgan, K. and G. Mungham (2000). *Redesigning Democracy: The Making of the Welsh Assembly*, Bridgend, Seren.

—— and A. Sayer (1988). *Microcircuits of Capital: 'Sunrise' Industry and Uneven Development*, Cambridge, Polity Press.

Morgan, K. O. (1963). *Wales in British Politics 1868–1922*, Cardiff, University of Wales Press.

—— (1981). *Rebirth of a Nation: Wales 1980–1980*, Oxford, Clarendon Press.

—— (1995). 'Wales since 1945: political society', in Herbert and Jones, 1995: 10–54.

Morgan, P. (1983). 'From a death to a view – the hunt for the Welsh past in the romantic period', in Hobsbawm and Ranger, 1983: 43–100.

—— (1986). 'The *gwerin* of Wales – myth and reality', in Hume and Pryce, 1986: 134–52.

Morgan, R. (2000). *Variable Geometry UK*, Cardiff, Institute of Welsh Affairs.

Morgan, R. H. (1983). 'Population trends in mid Wales: some policy implications', in Williams, 1983a: 88–102.

Morris, D. (1995). 'Language and class fractioning in a peripheral economy', *Journal of Multilingual and Multicultural Development* 16/5, 373–88.

Morris, J. (1995). 'McJobbing a region: industrial restructuring and the widening socio-economic divide in Wales', in R. Turner, 1995.

—— and R. Mansfield R. (1988). 'Economic regeneration in industrial south Wales: an empirical analysis', *Contemporary Wales* 2, 63–82.

—— and B. Wilkinson (1989a). *Divided Wales: Local Prosperity in the 1980s*, Cardiff Business School.

—— and B. Wilkinson (1989b). 'Wales: the growing divides', *Welsh Economic Review* 2(1), 67–73.

—— and —— (1995). 'Poverty and prosperity in Wales: polarization and Los Angelesization', *Contemporary Wales* 8, 29–45.

——, P. Cooke, G. Etxebarria and A. Rodrigues (1991). 'The political economy of regional industrial regeneration: the Welsh and Basque "models"', in Day and Rees, 1991: 177–91.

Morris, Jan (1998). *Wales: Epic Views of a Small Country*, London, Viking (revised from *The Matter of Wales*, 1984).

Morris, L. (1985). 'Renegotiation of the domestic division of labour in the context of male redundancy', in Newby et al., 1985: 221–43.

Munday, M. (1990). *Japanese Manufacturing in Wales*, Cardiff, University of Wales Press/Institute of Welsh Affairs.

—— (2000). 'Foreign direct investment in Wales – lifeline or leash?', in Bryan and Jones, 2000: 37–54.

—— and M. Peel (1998). 'The comparative performance of foreign-owned and domestic manufacturing firms during recession: some descriptive evidence from Wales', *Contemporary Wales* 10, 50–80.

Murdoch, J. (1988). 'State institutions and rural policy in Wales', *Contemporary Wales* 2, 20–45.

—— and Day, G. (1998). 'Middle class mobility, rural communities, and the politics of exclusion', in Boyle and Halfacree, 1998: 186–99.

—— and Marsden, T. (1994). *Reconstituting Rurality*, London, UCL Press.

NAW (2000). *Welsh Index of Multiple Deprivation*, Cardiff, National Assembly For Wales.

Nairn, T. (1977a). 'Culture and politics in Wales', in Nairn, 1977b, 196–215.

—— (1977b). *The Break-Up of Britain*, London, New Left Books.

—— (2000). *After Britain*, London, Granta.

Newby, H. (ed.) (1978). *International Perspectives in Rural Sociology*, Chichester, John Wiley.

—— (1979). *Green and Pleasant Land: Social Change in Rural England*, London, Hutchinson.

—— (1980). 'Trend report: rural sociology', *Current Sociology* 28(1), 3–133.

—— (1986). 'Locality and rurality: the restructuring of rural social relations', *Regional Studies* 20, 209–16.

——, J. Bujra, P. Littlewood, G. Rees, and T. Rees (eds.) (1985). *Restructuring Capital: Recession and Reorganization in Industrial Society*, London, Macmillan.

Nichols, T. and P. Armstrong (1976). *Workers Divided*, London, Fontana.

—— and H. Beynon (1977). *Living with Capitalism*, London, London, Routledge & Kegan Paul.

Nisbet, R. (1966). *The Sociological Tradition*, New York, Basic Books.

Ohmae, K. (1996). *The End of the Nation State: The Rise of the Regional Economies*, London, HarperCollins.

Osmond, J. (ed.) (1985). *The National Question Again*, Llandysul, Gomer.

—— (1988). *The Divided Kingdom*, London, Constable.

—— (1991). 'Wales and Baden-Wurttemberg', *Planet* 86, 62–7.

—— (ed.) (1998a). *The National Assembly Agenda*, Cardiff, Institute of Welsh Affairs.

—— (1998b). *The New Politics in Wales*, London, Charter 88.

Owen, T. M. (1986). 'Community studies in Wales: an overview', in Hume and Pryce, 1986: 91–133.

Page, A. C. (1977). 'State intervention in the inter-war period', *British Journal of Law and Society* 4, 175–203.

Pahl, R. (1965). *Urbs in Rure*, London, Weidenfeld & Nicolson.

—— (1970). *Patterns of Urban Life*, London, Longmans.

Parry-Jones, D. (1952). *Welsh Country Upbringing*, London, Batsford.

Parsons, T. (1966). *Societies*, Englewood Cliffs, Prentice Hall.

Pascale, R. T. and A. G. Athos (1982). *The Art of Japanese Management*, Harmondsworth, Penguin.

Paterson, L. and R. Wyn Jones (1999). 'Does civil society drive constitutional change?', in Taylor and Thomson, 1999: 169–98.

Paxman, J. (1999). *The English: Portrait of a People*, London, Michael Joseph.

Paynter, W. (1972). *My Generation*, London, George Allen & Unwin.

Peate, I. C. (1940). *The Welsh House*, Liverpool, H. Evans.

Peet, R. and N. Thrift (1989). *New Models in Geography*, London, Edward Arnold.

Petro, P. (1998). *Travels in an Old Tongue*, London, Flamingo.

Pettigrew, P. (1987). 'A bias for action: industrial development in mid Wales', in Cloke, 1987: 102–21.

Phelps, N. A. and D. MacKinnon (2000). 'Industrial enclaves or embedded forms of economic activity? Overseas manufacturing investment in Wales', *Contemporary Wales* 13, 46–67.

Philo, C. and Kearns, G. (1993). 'Culture, history, capital: a critical introduction to the selling of places', in Kearns and Philo, 1993: 1–32.

Pickvance, C. (ed.) (1976). *Urban Sociology: Critical Essays*, London, Methuen.

Pilcher, J. (1994). 'Who should do the dishes? Three generations of Welsh women talking about men and housework', in Aaron et al., 1994: 31–47.

Piore, M. J. and C. Sabel (1984). *The Second Industrial Divide: Possibilities for Prosperity*, New York, Basic Books.

Poulantzas, N. (1975). *Classes in Contemporary Capitalism*, London, New Left Books.

Preston, P. W. (1987). *Rethinking Development*, London, Routledge.

Price, A., K. Morgan and P. Cooke (1993). *The Welsh Renaissance: Inward Investment and Innovation*, RIR Report 14, Cardiff, University of Wales.

Priestley, M. M. and M. C. Winrow (1975). *Social and Economic Stress in Wales: A Study of Social Deprivation and Economic Unbalance*, Lampeter, St David's University College.

Pryce, W. T. R. (1986). 'Wales as a culture region', in Hume and Pryce, 1986: 26–63.

Purcell, K., S. Wood, A. Waton and S. Allen (1986). *The Changing Experience of Employment*, London, Macmillan.

Putnam, R. (1993). *Making Democracy Work: Civic Traditions in Modern Italy*, Princeton, Princeton University Press.

Rapport, N. (1993). *Diverse World Views in an English Village*, Edinburgh, Edinburgh University Press.

Rawkins, P. M. (1979). 'An approach to the political sociology of the Welsh nationalist movement', *Political Studies* 27, 440–57.

—— (1983). 'Uneven development and the politics of culture', in Williams, 1983: 214–30.

—— (1985). 'Living in the house of power: Welsh nationalism and the dilemma of antisystem politics', in Tiryakian and Rogowski, 1985: 294–314.

Rees, A. D. (1996). *Life in a Welsh Countryside*, Cardiff, University of Wales Press (original publication 1950).

Rees, D. B. (1975). *Chapels in the Valley*, Wirral, Ffynnon Press.

Rees, Gareth (1980). 'Uneven development, state intervention and the generation of inequality: the case of industrial South Wales', in Rees and Rees, 1980.

—— (1984). 'Rural regions in national and international economies', in Bradley and Lowe, 1984: 27–45.

—— (1985). 'Regional restructuring, class change and political action: preliminary comments on the 1984–85 miners' strike in south Wales', *Environment and Planning D: Society and Space* 3, 389–406.

—— (1997). 'The politics of regional development strategy: the programme for the valleys', in Macdonald and Thomas, 1997: 98–112.

——, S. Gorard and R. Fevre (1999). 'Industrial south Wales: learning society past, present or future?', *Contemporary Wales* 12, 18–36.

——, ——, —— and J. Furlong (2000). 'Participating in the learning society: history, place and biography', in Coffield, 2000: 171–92.

—— and J. Lambert (1981). 'Nationalism as legitimation? Notes towards a political economy of regional development in south Wales', in Harloe, 1981: 122–37.

—— and —— (1985). *Cities in Crisis: The Political Economy of Urban Development in Post-war Britain*, London, Edward Arnold.

Rees, Gareth and K. Morgan (1991). 'Industrial restructuring, innovation systems and the regional state: south Wales in the 1990s', in Day and Rees, 1991: 155–76.

—— and T. Rees (eds.) (1980a). *Poverty and Social Inequality in Wales*, London, Croom Helm.

—— and —— (1980b). 'Poverty at the periphery: the outline of a perspective on Wales', in Rees and Rees, 1980: 17–32.

—— and —— (1983). 'Migration, industrial restructuring and class relations: an analysis of south Wales', in Williams, 1983: 103–19.

—— and M. Thomas (1991). 'From coalminers to entrepreneurs? A case study in the sociology of re-industrialization', in Cross and Payne, 1991: 57–78.

—— and —— (1994). 'Inward investment, labour market adjustment and skills development: recent experience in south Wales', *Local Economy* 9, 48–61.

Rees, Goronwy (1964). 'Have the Welsh a future?', *Encounter* (March), 3–13.

—— (1972). *A Chapter of Accidents*, London, Chatto & Windus.

Rees, T. (1988). 'Changing patterns of women's work in Wales: some myths explored', *Contemporary Wales* 2, 119–30.

—— (1994). 'Women and paid work in Wales', in Aaron et al., 1994: 89–106.

—— (1992). *Women and the Labour Market*, London, Routledge.

—— (1999). *Women and Work: Twenty-five Years of Gender Equality in Wales*, Cardiff, University of Wales Press.

—— and S. Fielder (1991). *Women and Top Jobs in Wales*, Report for HTV Wales, Social Research Unit, Cardiff University.

—— and —— (1992). 'Smashing the dark glass ceiling: women and top jobs in Wales', *Contemporary Wales* 5, 99–114.

Regan, C. and F. Walsh (1976). 'Dependence and underdevelopment: the case of mineral resources and the Irish Republic', *Antipode* 8(3), 46–59.

Rhodes, M. (ed.) (1995). *The Regions in the New Europe*, Manchester, Manchester University Press.

Riley, H. (1978). 'In the Upper Afan Valley', *Planet* 45/46, 97–101.

Robbins, D., C. Caldwell, G. Day, K. Jones and H. Rose (eds) (1981). *Rethinking Social Inequality*, Aldershot, Gower.

Roberts, A. (1994). 'The causes and consequences of inward investment: the Welsh experience', *Contemporary Wales* 6, 73–86.

Roberts, B. (1995). 'Welsh identity in a former mining valley: social images and imagined communities', *Contemporary Wales* 7, 77–93.

Roberts, K. (2001). *Class in Modern Britain*, Basingstoke, Palgrave.

Rose, D. (ed.) (1988). *Social Stratification and Economic Change*, London, Hutchinson.

Rosser, C. and C. C. Harris (1965). *The Family and Social Change*, London, Routledge & Kegan Paul.

Rosser, D. K. (1989). 'The decay of a Welsh-speaking street community: migration and its residual effects', *Contemporary Wales* 3, 119–135.

Runciman, W. G. (1999). *The Social Animal*, London, HarperCollins.

Rutherford, T. (1991). 'Industrial restructuring. Local labour markets and social change: the transformation of south Wales', *Contemporary Wales* 4, 9–44.

Sadler, D. (1993). 'Place marketing, competitive places and the construction of hegemony', in Kearns and Philo, 1993: 175–92.

Sadler, P. G. and G. A. Mackay (eds.) (1977). *The Changing Fortunes of Marginal*

Regions, Aberdeen, Institute for the Study of Sparsely Populated Areas, University of Aberdeen.

Savage, M., J. Barlow, P. Dickens and T. Fielding (1992). *Property, Bureaucracy and Culture: Middle-Class Formation in Contemporary Britain*, London, Routledge.

Scott, W. J., J. Banks, A. H. Halsey and T. Lupton (1956). *Technical Change and Industrial Relations*, Liverpool, Liverpool University Press.

Scourfield, J. and M. Drakeford (1999). 'Boys from nowhere: finding Welsh men and putting them in their place', *Contemporary Wales* 12, 3–17.

Seers, D. (1983). *The Political Economy of Nationalism*, Oxford, Oxford University Press.

Sennett, R. (1998). *The Corrosion of Character*, New York, Norton.

Sewel, J. (1975). *Colliery Closure and Social Change*, Cardiff, University of Wales Press (Board of Celtic Studies).

Shapiro, H. D. (1977). *Appalachia on Our Mind: The Southern Mountains and Mountaineers in the American Consciousness, 1870–1920*, Chapel Hill, University of North Carolina Press.

Short, B. (1992). *The English Rural Community: Image and Analysis*, Cambridge, Cambridge University Press.

Simmie, J. (ed.) (1997). *Innovations, Networks and Learning Regions*, London, Jessica Kingsley.

Smith, A. D. (1991). *National Identity*, Harmondsworth, Penguin.

Smith, D. (ed.) (1980). *A People and a Proletariat: Essays in the History of Wales 1780–1980*, London, Pluto.

—— (1984). *Wales! Wales?* London, George Allen & Unwin.

—— (1999). *Wales: A Question of History*, Bridgend, Seren.

Storper, M. (1995). 'The resurgence of regional economies: ten years later', *European Urban and Regional Studies* 2, 161–221.

Stead, P. (1995). 'Popular culture', in Herbert and Jones, 1995: 107–32.

Symonds, A. (1990). 'Migration, communities and social change', in Jenkins and Edwards, 1990: 21–34.

Taylor, B. and K. Thomson (eds.) (1999). *Scotland and Wales: Nations Again?*, Cardiff, University of Wales Press.

Taylor, J. G. (1979). *From Modernization to Modes of Production: A Critique of the Sociologies of Development and Underdevelopment*, London, Macmillan.

Thomas, B. (1962). 'Wales and the Atlantic Economy', in *The Welsh Economy: Studies in Expansion*, Cardiff, University of Wales Press.

Thomas, D. (1991). 'The Welsh economy: current circumstances and future prospects', in Day and Rees, 1991: 39–59.

—— and Day, G. (1991). 'Rural Wales: problems, policies and prospects', *Welsh Economic Review* 5(1), 37–49.

Thomas, G. (1964). *A Welsh Eye*, London, Hutchinson.

Thomas, I. C. and P. J. Drudy (1987). 'The impact of factory development on growth town employment in mid-Wales', *Urban Studies* 25, 361–78.

Thomas, M. (1991). 'Colliery closure and the miner's experience of redundancy', *Contemporary Wales* 4, 45–66.

Thompson, A. and G. Day (1999). 'Situating Welshness: "local" experience and national identity', in Fevre and Thompson, 1999: 27–47.

—— and —— (2001). 'Standing up for civil society', *Radical Wales* 23–5.

Thompson, A., G. Day and D. Adamson (1999). 'Bringing the "local" back in: the production of Welsh identities', in Brah et al., 1999: 49–67.

Thompson, F. M. L. (ed.) (1990). *The Cambridge Social History of Britain 1750–1950, Vol 1: Regions and Communities*, Cambridge, Cambridge University Press.

Thurston, R and J. Beynon (1995). *Men, Masculinities and Violence: A Leverhulme Trust Study*, Pontypridd, University of Glamorgan.

Tiryakian, E. A. and R. Rogowski (1985). *New Nationalisms of the Developed West: Toward Explanation*, London, Allen & Unwin.

Tönnies, F. (1955). *Community and Association*, London, Routledge & Kegan Paul.

Town, S. (1978). *After the Mines: Changing Employment Opportunities in a South Wales Valley*, Cardiff, University of Wales Press (Board of Celtic Studies).

Townroe, P. and R. Martin (eds.) (1992). *Regional Development in the 1990s: The British Isles in Transition*, London, Jessica Kingsley/Regional Studies Association.

Townsend, A. (1991). 'New forms of employment in rural areas: a national perspective', in Champion and Watkins, 1991: 84–95.

Townsend, P. (1979). *Poverty in the United Kingdom*, Harmondsworth, Penguin.

Trist E. L., G. Higgin, H. Murray, and A. Pollock (1963). *Organizational Choice*, London, Tavistock.

Trosset, C. (1993). *Welshness Performed: Welsh Concepts of Person and Society*, Tucson, University of Arizona Press.

Turner, R. (ed.) (1995). *From the Old to the New? The British Economy in Transition*, London, Routledge.

Turok, I. (1993). 'Inward investment and local linkages: how deeply embedded is "Silicon Glen"?', *Regional Studies* 27, 401–17.

Urry, J. (1981). 'Localities, regions and social class', *International Journal of Urban and Regional Research* 5, 455–74.

—— (1984). 'Capitalist restructuring and recomposition', in Bradley and Lowe, 1984: 45–64.

—— (2000). *Sociology Beyond Societies*, London, Routledge.

Van Den Berghe, P. (1978). 'Education, class, and ethnicity in Southern Peru: revolutionary colonialism', in Altbach and Kelly, 1978.

Vermeulen, H. and J. Boissevain (eds.) (1984). *Ethnic Challenge: The Politics of Ethnicity in Europe*, Gottingen, Edition Herodot.

WAC (1998). *Investment in Industry in Wales*, Cardiff, Welsh Affairs Committee, HMSO.

Waddington, D., M. Wykes and C. Critcher (1991). *Split At the Seams?: Community, Continuity and Change After the 1984–5 Coal Dispute*, Buckingham, Open University.

Walby, S. (1997). *Gender Transformations*, London, Routledge.

Wales Rural Forum (1994). *A Strategy for Rural Wales*, Llandysul, Gomer.

Walker, A. (1992). 'Women and the organisation of the labour force in the Aberystwyth hotel trade', *Contemporary Wales* 5, 131–64.

Walls, D. (1978). 'Internal colony or internal periphery? A critique of current models and an alternative formulation', in Lewis et al., 1978: 319–49.

Wallerstein, I. (1974). *The Modern World System: Capitalist Agriculture and the Origins of the European World Economy in the Sixteenth Century*, New York, Academic Press.

Wass, V. and L. Mainwaring (1989). 'Economic and social consequences of rationalization in the south Wales coal industry', *Contemporary Wales* 3, 161–85.

Weber, E. (1979). *Peasants Into Frenchmen: The Modernisation of Rural France, 1870–1914*, London, Chatto & Windus.

Weller, J. (1978). 'Appalachia's mineral colony', in Lewis et al., 1978: 47–55.

Welsh Office (1967). *Wales: The Way Ahead*, Cmnd 3334, Cardiff, HMSO.

Wenger, G. C. (1978). 'Ethnicity and social organization in north-east Wales', in G. Williams, 1978a: 120–32.

—— (1980). *Mid-Wales: Deprivation or Development*, Cardiff, University of Wales (Board of Celtic Studies).

—— (1982). 'The problem of perspective in development policy', *Sociologia Ruralis* 22, 5–16.

—— (1995). 'Ageing in rural north Wales: twelve years of domiciliary visiting services', *Contemporary Wales* 7, 153–72.

WERU (2001). 'The limits of devolution, the global economy, Corus and regional responses', *Welsh Economic Review* 13(2), 19–20.

Westergaard, J. (1965). 'The withering away of class', in Anderson and Blackburn, 1965: 77–113.

—— and Resler H. (1975). *Class in a Capitalist Society*, London, Heinemann.

Williams, A. (1990). 'From cradle to reincarnation', in Cole, 1990: 12–26.

Williams C. (1999a). '"Race" and racism: what's special about Wales?', in Dunkerley and Thompson, 1999: 269–86.

—— (1999b). 'Passports to Wales? Race, nation and identity', in Fevre and Thompson, 1999: 69–89.

—— and P. Chaney (2001). 'Devolution and identities: the experience of ethnic minorities in Wales', *Soundings* 18, 169–83.

——, G. Day, T. Rees and M. Standing (1999). *Equal Opportunities Study for Inclusion in the European Structural Fund Programme*, Cardiff, National Assembly For Wales.

Williams, C. H. (1977). 'Non-violence and the development of the Welsh language society', *Welsh History Review* 8(4), 426–55.

—— (ed.) (1982a). *National Separatism*, Cardiff, University of Wales Press.

—— (1982b). 'Separatism and the mobilization of Welsh national identity', in Williams, 1982: 145–202.

—— (2000a). 'Community planning through language planning intervention', in Williams, 2000b: 221–46.

—— (ed.) (2000b). *Language Revitalization: Policy and Planning in Wales*, Cardiff, University of Wales Press.

—— (2000c). 'On recognition, resolution and revitalization', in Williams, 2000b: 1–47.

Williams, D. (1950). *A History of Modern Wales*, London, John Murray.

Williams, G. (1977). 'Towards a sociology of Wales', *Planet* 40, 30–7.

—— (ed.) (1978a). *Social and Cultural Change in Contemporary Wales*, London, Routledge.

—— (1978b). 'Social ranking in a Welsh Community', in Williams, 1978a: 253–67.

—— (1980). 'Industrialisation, inequality, and deprivation in rural Wales', in Rees and Rees, 1980: 168–84.

Williams, G. (1981). 'Economic development, social structure, and contemporary nationalism in Wales', *Review* 5(2), 275–310.

—— (ed.) (1983a). *Crisis of Economy and Ideology: Essays on Welsh Society 1840–1980*, Bangor, BSA Sociology of Wales Study Group.

—— (1983b). 'On class and status groups in Welsh rural society', in Williams, 1983: 134–46.

—— (1984). 'What is Wales? The discourse of devolution', *Journal of Ethnic and Racial Studies* 7/1, 138–59.

—— (1985). 'The political economy of contemporary nationalism in Wales', in Tiryakian and Rogowski, 1985: 315–36.

—— (1986). 'Recent trends in the sociology of Wales', in Hume and Pryce, 1986: 176–192.

—— (1987a). 'Bilingualism, class dialect and social reproduction', in Williams, 1987a: 85–98.

—— (1987b). 'The sociology of Welsh', *International Journal of Sociology* 66.

—— (1994). 'Discourses on "nation" and "race": a response to Denney *et al.*', *Contemporary Wales* 6, 87–104.

—— and Morris D. (1995). *Peripheral Economic Structure, Labour Markets and Skills: Report of the TARGED Labour Supply Survey*, Bangor, Research Centre Wales.

—— and —— (2000). *Language Planning and Language Use: Welsh in a Global Age*, Cardiff, University of Wales Press.

Williams, G. A. (1978). *The Merthyr Rising*, London, Croom Helm.

—— (1984). 'Women workers in contemporary Wales', *Welsh History Review* 16, 530–48.

—— (1985). *When was Wales?*, Harmondsworth, Penguin.

Williams, L. J. (1989). 'The rise and decline of the Welsh economy, 1980–1930', in Hopkin and Kealey, 1989: 7–20.

—— (1995). *Was Wales Industrialised?*, Llandysul, Gomer.

Williams, P. (1977). 'The internal colony', *Planet* 37/8, 60–5.

Williams, R. (1958). *Culture and Society*, London, Chatto & Windus.

—— (1960). *Border Country*, London, Chatto & Windus.

—— (1961). *The Long Revolution*, London, Chatto & Windus.

—— (1975). *The Country and the City*, London, Paladin.

—— (1979). *The Fight for Manod*, London, Chatto & Windus.

—— (1981). 'For Britain, see Wales', *Times Higher Eduction Supplement* (15 May).

Williams, T. (1996). 'Pobl Pontcanna chatter away democracy', in 'Where Wales? The Nationhood Debate', *Western Mail* (June).

Williamson, B. (1982). *Class, Culture and Community: A Study of Social Change in Mining*, London, Routledge & Kegan Paul.

Willis, K. G. and C. M. Saunders (1988). 'The impact of a development agency on employment: resurrection discounted?', *Applied Economics* 20, 81–96.

Winckler, V. (1985). 'Tertiarization and feminization at the periphery: the case of Wales', in Newby et al., 1985: 179–220.

Wintle, J. (1996). *Furious Interiors: Wales, R. S. Thomas, and God*, London, HarperCollins.

WLB (1999). *A Strategy for the Welsh Language*, Cardiff, Welsh Language Board.

WLB (2000). 'Language revitalization: the role of the Welsh Language Board', in Williams, 2000: 83–115.

Wright, E. O. (1985). *Classes*, London, Verso.

Wright, S. (1992). 'Image and analysis: new directions in community studies', in Short, 1992: 195–217.

Wyn Jones, R. (1991). 'Policies for the Welsh countryside: Plaid Cymru', *Rural Wales* Summer 41.

—— and D. Trystan (1999). 'The 1997 Welsh Referendum Vote', in Taylor and Thomson, 1999: 65–93.

Young, M. and P. Willmott (1957). *Family and Kinship in East London*, London, Routledge & Kegan Paul.

Zepf, R. (1996). 'Wales and Baden-Wurttemberg – a dangerous liaison?', *Planet* 116 123–6.

Zimmern, A. (1921). *My Impressions of Wales*, London, Mills & Boon.

Zweig, F. (1952). *The British Worker*, Harmondsworth, Penguin.

Index